Russian Homophobia from Stalin to Sochi

Russian Homophobia from Stalin to Sochi

Dan Healey

BLOOMSBURY ACADEMIC
LONDON • NEW YORK • OXFORD • NEW DELHI • SYDNEY

BLOOMSBURY ACADEMIC
Bloomsbury Publishing Plc
50 Bedford Square, London, WC1B 3DP, UK

BLOOMSBURY, BLOOMSBURY ACADEMIC and the Diana logo
are trademarks of Bloomsbury Publishing Plc

First published in Great Britain 2018
Reprinted 2018

Cover design based on a poster design by Sourena Parham
Cover image © Dawn Aik

A catalogue record for this book is available from the British Library.

ISBN: HB: 978-1-3500-0078-0
        PB: 978-1-3500-0077-3
        ePDF: 978-1-3500-0079-7
        eBook: 978-1-3500-0080-3

Library of Congress Cataloging-in-Publication Data
Names: Healey, Dan, author.
Title: Russian homophobia from Stalin to Sochi / Dan Healey.
Description: New York : Bloomsbury Academic, 2017.
Identifiers: LCCN 2017018018 | ISBN 9781350000780 (hardback) |
ISBN 9781350000773 (pbk) | ISBN 9781350000797 (epdf) | ISBN 9781350000803 (epub)
Subjects: LCSH: Homophobia–Soviet Union–History. | Homosexuality–
Soviet Union–History. | BISAC: HISTORY / Europe / Russia & the Former Soviet Union. |
SOCIAL SCIENCE / Gay Studies. | HISTORY / Social History.
Classification: LCC HQ76.45.S65 H43 2017 | DDC 306.76/60947—dc23
LC record available at https://lccn.loc.gov/2017018018.

Typeset by RefineCatch Limited, Bungay, Suffolk.
Printed and bound in Great Britain

To find out more about our authors and books visit www.bloomsbury.com
and sign up for our newsletters.

For Elena

For Them

CONTENTS

LIST OF ILLUSTRATIONS

PREFACE

This book explores modern Russian homophobia, arguing that it originated in the 1930s in the law and policing practices set in train by the Soviet dictator, Joseph Stalin. Some historical background about the treatment of homosexuality and gender dissent in Russia before and after Stalin's homophobic turn is offered in this preface, setting the context for the essays that follow. Russia's heritage before the 1917 Revolutions, the country's relationship to "Europe" and to the force of modern nationalism, its religious heritage, and the tempestuous politics of its twentieth century, all shaped the ways that the country viewed queer sexuality and genders. These features of Russian and Soviet history and the critical landmarks in the country's treatment of sexual and gender dissent are discussed here.

Gender relations are a field of power, and historians have tied modern gender politics to the rise of the European nation-state.[1] Before the revolutions of 1917, Imperial Russia was a land empire rather than a nation in the Western European sense. The formation of a national community for ethnic Russians, a coherent collective identity, was an incomplete process in nineteenth and twentieth centuries, overshadowed by the larger "burdens" of empire, and their translation, after 1917, in the Communists' internationalist ideology.[2] The "modern," European model of the nation-state dominated by a single ethno-linguistic group was never fully realizable in a multi-national, multi-confessional empire where Russians were predominant but mixed with a diverse collection of Eurasian peoples, many of them retaining their own "national" customs and character.[3] Hence Russian gender politics reflected the conditional, fluid, and diverse sense of Russia's "national community," and as well the problems of a land empire that were distinctive when compared with the overseas empires of its European competitors.

Empire across the Eurasian landmass structured social life and gender relations – and often led to significant imbalances between the sexes. The early Muscovite realm, and then the post-1700 Imperial state were both built on a set of homosocial institutions. The Russian Orthodox Church and its monasteries served as outposts of old Rus on the sparsely settled peripheries; and state's various armies and later, navies, as well as its chancelleries and courtly life all embodied single-sex organization. The heart of the state itself was largely segregated by sex until eighteenth-century Europeanization.[4] It was in the context of a Europeanizing empire that the first legal orders for the mixing of the sexes, and the first prohibitions against male same-sex relations, arose.[5] Emperor Peter the Great's Military Articles (1716) banned "sodomy" in the army and navy.[6] Nicholas I, an authoritarian seeking to stiffen masculine character in his state apparatus, formally extended the ban to civilian men in 1835 – his anti-sodomy law remained in place until 1917.[7] The conquest of Siberia, an "internal colony," between the sixteenth and the eighteenth centuries was another predominantly all-male affair, although indigenous peoples suffered as Russian prospectors, fur-traders, and Cossacks raided their villages and stole their daughters – and sometimes their sons. "Family-lessness" was particularly acute where supply lines were so exceptionally long and outposts so remote.[8] Ironically, under the law passed by Nicholas I, Siberia became a place of exile for male homosexual offenders in the nineteenth century. Nevertheless, enforcement of the law was strikingly lax, and few "sodomites" suffered exile, which was replaced with prison sentences in 1900. The same problems of gender imbalance persisted into the twentieth century and were at their most extreme in the 1930s–50s in the Soviet Gulag camps on the far northern and eastern edges of the country (described in Chapter 1).

In common with the Europeans they would seek to become, Russians drew upon languages of sinfulness, crime, and pathology to construct homophobic views. The predominant state religion in the Russian Empire was Orthodoxy, inherited from Byzantium and displaying a marked negativity toward all sexuality as "sinful," even sex within marriage (a distinction from Western Christianity that sanctified marital intercourse).[9] Nevertheless, in a vast and poor country the Church could scarcely enforce its sexual norms. Pre-1700 Muscovy penitential books and sermons condemned "sodomitical sin," and punishment for sodomy was probably only sporadic, even in monasteries. Penitential books also condemned male lust for boys and youths, effeminizing clothing and makeup for men, and cross-dressing; such prohibitions suggest a popular, age-structured and gendered, erotics between men that remains poorly documented.[10] Penitentials also condemned female same-sex mutual masturbation in less vivid and extensive terms, hinting that women's same-sex acts were less feared. We have little or no research on how Russian Orthodoxy's views on queer sex and gender evolved – if they did – in the eighteenth and nineteenth centuries. The anti-sodomy law of Nicholas I characteristically required Russian Orthodox offenders to seek penance from a priest, cementing a link between religious and secular morality, and illustrating this tsar's mobilization of the Church to enforce social norms after the shock of the 1812 Napoleonic invasion of Russia.[11] By the end of this period a modernizing process was underway in the Church touching on its theology, moral philosophy, and on popular worship; that process seems to have encouraged some enlightened clergy to look to modern medical sexology as a partner in shaping heterosexual morality.[12] We do not know what Orthodox clerics in the decade before 1917 had to say about homosexuality, but we can imagine it remained a "sin" for the majority of Church leaders, with perhaps a handful of educated clerics aware of medical designations of homosexuality as a "disease." Despite excellent scholarship on the history of sexuality in Imperial Russia, we have very little understanding about the late Imperial Russian Orthodox Church's thinking about homosexuality: this would be a history worth writing.[13]

Whatever the tendencies evolving at the end of the Imperial era in Russian Orthodox thinking about same-sex relations, the persecution of the Church and other religious confessions in the Bolshevik Revolution of October 1917, and the Russian Civil War (1918–1921) launched a lethal cultural war between socialists and religion. That onslaught against the Church in Russia relented during the Second World War but did not come to an end until Soviet power disintegrated in the late 1980s. The Soviet Communist repression of the Church made impossible the changes that, in Western Europe, eventually "modernized" the Christian churches' thinking about sexuality inside and beyond marriage. The Western churches' post-1945 encouragement of heterosexual intercourse within marriage, and their increasing acceptance of the secular language of psychiatry and psychology to describe sexual deviation, was not felt in the Soviet Union.[14] There, persecution and secret-police infiltration of the Russian Orthodox hierarchy discouraged theological innovation, and obstructed constructive dialogue with Soviet society. Russia's Orthodox Church had to wait until the 1990s to resume reflection on the modern world and its ills – a process still in development.[15] The Church's recent embrace of the Kremlin's political homophobia may signal a reconsideration of the millennium-long tradition of mistrust of *all* sexuality, in place of a celebration of heterosexuality that reproduces the living body of the Church, and the Russian "nation" that the Church's body is believed to mimic.

Thus, from 1917, Vladimir Lenin's Communists used gender politics as a political battering ram to disrupt the authority of the Russian Orthodox Church, arguably the new Soviet regime's most dangerous opponent. If family life and sexuality had been largely regulated by religious authority before 1917, they were now aggressively desacralized in what is regarded as a "sexual revolution," arguably, the first of three such revolutions in twentieth-century Russian history. Western European socialist ideas of the end of patriarchal male domination, of "free love," and life governed by science, born in the socialist parties of urban Germany and France, and extensively discussed by nineteenth-century Russian radicals, were seized by Russian Marxists; they were imposed on the population of Soviet Russia, 80 percent of which consisted of subsistence peasants suspicious of city life. Almost immediately, in 1917 and 1918, marriage was secularized, divorce radically liberalized, and women's legal status in the family and public life equalized with that of men. Propaganda aimed at women sought to draw them into education, paid work, and politics; such campaigning attacked patriarchal power over wives and daughters.[16] Bolshevik secular and scientific values also led to the legalization of abortion (1920) and the decriminalization of sodomy (in the Soviet Russian republic's criminal code of 1922). The Communist leadership did not discuss publicly or even behind the scenes, in the archival records so far uncovered, exactly why they removed the tsarist crime of "sodomy" from the statute books. However, Lenin's Bolsheviks believed their revolution was an overturning of class and economic hierarchies; they thought of their "sexual revolution" as an important, but secondary, consequence of class revolution, scarcely worth commenting on. The "minimum program" of European socialism, including its critique of patriarchy as a bulwark for capitalist property, was merely a starting point for triumphant Soviet Bolsheviks. Communists shared a utopian confidence that class politics and scientific expertise would answer all questions that arose in the sexual sphere. It remains difficult to piece together what the new regime's attitude toward same-sex relations was; medical and legal experts debated its social significance and there was a fundamental incoherence in Communist approaches, showing "enlightened" tendencies and some, less so. I discuss these variations under the early Bolshevik regime in Chapter 7.

In the same chapter I analyze the Soviet return to a ban on "sodomy" in 1933–34. It was a Stalinist measure, proposed by the security police and backed with relish by Stalin and his Politburo. Stalin personally edited the new penal article. This was the moment when the Soviet state adopted a modern anti-homosexual politics, the birth of modern Russian political homophobia. The context was a profound social and economic crisis, caused by the Stalin ruling group's policies of forced collectivization of agriculture and forced-pace Five-Year Plan industrialization. From the start of these anti-capitalist policies in 1929, life in the cities deteriorated radically as millions flooded into towns to evade collectivization and work in new construction and industrial projects. Housing, food, and basic necessities were all in perilously short supply, criminality was rampant, and the regime and its police interpreted virtually all forms of social disorder and deviance as political resistance to the emerging "socialist" project. A "passport" (internal identity document) system was introduced in 1932 to control and monitor city dwellers. These and other modern policing techniques were brought to bear on social marginals, including female prostitutes and male homosexuals. With the new anti-sodomy law, surveillance of male homosexual activity and networks became a routine part of security and regular police work. Intriguingly, police did not view lesbians as a security threat to the same degree. Nevertheless, as I have discussed elsewhere, they were prosecuted under various laws if political or behavioral non-conformity drew attention to their sexuality.[17]

It appears that enforcement of the law against sodomy ebbed and flowed as the police reacted to a succession of campaigns directed from the Politburo against various "enemies" of the state. In the period from the Great Terror (1937–38) to the death of Stalin (1953) the accessible archival record (again, discussed in Chapter 7) is almost silent about the number of arrests and the ways in which male homosexuals were handled by the police and penal system. It is particularly difficult to say how the law was enforced during the Second World War: invasion, enormous population movements and staggering food shortages made simple survival the priority for millions. War losses on an epic scale opened up a huge gender imbalance in favor of women in the Soviet population which remained a concern for Party policymakers and socialist planners long after victory in 1945.

In the capitalist West, the onset of the Cold War in the late 1940s and early 1950s unleashed a renewed police and political scrutiny of male homosexuals as security risks. Whether similar concerns were raised by Soviet security forces after 1945 remains unknown. With the death of Stalin in 1953, and the reform of ideology and reduction of political terror, a period of liberalization, the "Thaw," opened. Soviet jurists reviewed Stalin's laws to annul or reform them; in 1958, the anti-sodomy law was renewed. Soviet experts also showed a renewed interest in psychiatric treatment for lesbianism. Both of these trends are discussed in Chapter 1.

Nevertheless, a new sense of a right to privacy was felt by the Soviet people after Stalin's death, and this included some gay men (Chapters 2 and 3) and lesbians (Chapter 4). The 1960s–80s saw a "second" Soviet "sexual revolution" that was not launched in laws and decrees from above, as the "first" one had been in 1917, but exploded in social change and lifestyles. The majority of Soviet citizens now lived in cities, and had more private housing than previously; heterosexual activity before marriage was on the increase; marriage was crumbling as a life-long institution and divorce rising sharply; the family was shrinking and appeared in need of fresh measures of support.[18] Political "stagnation" blocked public debate and no decisive policymaking gave shape to this spontaneous "sexual revolution" from below of the late Soviet era.

During the same years, significant change in the lives of Soviet homosexual men and women emerged; some of these changes are explored in Chapter 4. More research remains to be done on this period of dynamism under the ice of "stagnation," including more research on the hostility that increasingly visible lesbian and gay people experienced in Soviet society. Interviews with older gay men and lesbians have revealed that popular incomprehension of, and contempt for, sexual non-conformity pervaded the Soviet family and workplace. Francesca Stella shows that Soviet lesbians of this generation endured less widespread persecution from Soviet psychiatric therapists than previously thought, but "more subtle, 'everyday' mechanisms of surveillance, stigmatisation and shaming" in family, workplace and public settings.[19] Similar work with men who had relationships with men in late-Soviet society, by Arthur Clech, demonstrates that they faced an array of pressures including both psychiatric "cures" and, more frequently, social hostility and violence.[20] Both Stella and Clech point to an important fact about recent Soviet experience of "homosexuality": many, perhaps, most, of their informants have had a "bisexual" life career, with early (heterosexual) marriage and divorce figuring as part of their sexual biographies. In the Introduction, I address the problem of untangling questions of sexual identity in late-Soviet and post-Soviet homosexualities.

It should be emphasized that in the late 1980s on the eve of the break-up of the Soviet Union, Russian queer men and women were not mere victims of widespread homophobia. More and more they were aware of the impact of gay liberation, lesbian feminism, and AIDS/HIV activism in the West (see Chapter 4). They sought ways to translate these liberating ideas to the Soviet context. The democratization of the late 1980s (Soviet leader Mikhail Gorbachev's "glasnost") triggered discussion, conferences, festivals, and ultimately face-to-face exchanges and collaboration with Western LGBT and feminist activists. Communist rule and the Soviet Union ended in 1991, and post-Soviet democratization led very rapidly to the repeal of Stalin's anti-sodomy law, in May 1993.

After the collapse of the Soviet Union in 1991, activism and visibility seemed to offer new realms of freedom in the context of Russia's third "sexual revolution" of the twentieth century, this time, a revolution in public speech about sex (for one example, see Chapter 5). At the same time the economic and political instability of the 1990s shook popular faith in democracy, with the exploitative and shocking sexualization of the public sphere becoming a focus of anger for some.[21] Conservative nationalists began to seek ways to put the genie of "sexual revolution" back into the bottle with calls for a return to "traditional sexual relations" (Chapter 6) and a silencing of the LGBT "sexual minority." This is the historical background to the contemporary emergence of political homophobia that I examine in this book.

*   *   *

This book was completed at the end of 2016 when the presidency of Donald Trump in the USA still seemed unlikely, and before the reports of systematic arrests, detention, torture, and murders of gay men in Chechnya were published by Moscow's *Novaya Gazeta* in April 2017. The Trump presidency has transformed Putin-style populism from a marginal disorder in the politics of our time to its central problem. The Russians speak of "political technologies" when they refer to the techniques of governance: Trump has adopted the full arsenal of populist technologies, and even extended them, from his fabrication of "alternative truth" via Twitter, to his flagrant courting of sexist misogynists, and "dog-whistle" hailing of neo-Nazi sympathizers. He has harnessed deep-seated dissatisfaction with the economics of globalization and transformed that into a populist contempt for liberal values and Muslims as "outsiders." Anti-LGBT politics are currently on the fringe of President Trump's attention span but they remain a likely focus for future campaigning. The USA may well see a resurgence of political homophobia at home, as readers contemplate the story set out in this book.

The brutal violence perpetrated by the authorities in Chechnya under its Putin-protégé, republican strongman Ramzan Kadyrov, came to light in April 2017. Dozens of men were rounded up by security forces under Kadyrov's control and imprisoned in a special secret facility. They were tortured with electric shocks and beaten in an attempt to get them to release names of their gay contacts. By some accounts, at least three men were killed in custody and others were released into the "care" of their relatives, who were ordered to kill them to save the family honor. Others fled the republic with the help of LGBT activists in Moscow and St. Petersburg. Kadyrov announced that he wanted to rid the republic of gay men in time for Ramadan. His strategy of aligning Chechen "traditional Islamic values," using violent political homophobia, with Putin's "traditional family values" campaign is a characteristically grotesque example of his exaggerated devotion to his patron in the Kremlin. The international outcry at the reports has, after a long and sullen delay, led to a show of interest from the President, following concerns raised by German Chancellor Angela Merkel in May 2017, and Putin has ordered the central government's prosecutor general and the interior minister to investigate. Whatever the outcome, the curators of "political technologies" in Russia and the West seem set to continue to play the populist card of political homophobia cynically when the need for a distraction arises.

Oxford, May 7, 2017

ACKNOWLEDGMENTS
AND PERMISSIONS

I could fill another book with the stories of how people have inspired and helped me with this unexpected project. Sadly, the people who most deserve to be named – Russian LGBT activists – are most endangered if I do. So, first and foremost, I collectively salute the individuals who serve now, and did serve in the past, Russia's rich and varied lesbian, gay, bisexual, and transgender organizations. More than once you have taken my breath away with your boldness, courage, and relentless optimism. The same goes for activists who shared their stories with me in Belarus and Georgia. The two people I shall thank openly are Elena Gusiatinskaya, a much-loved friend and guide to whom this book is dedicated; and the late Igor Kon, who was generous with his observations about his country and its fantasies and phobias.

If I listed all the scholarly debts I piled up in the evolution of this book, we would have yet another manuscript. I would have to mention an embarrassingly large number of audiences from Vancouver to Perm, Tver, and Tallinn, who heard versions of these chapters and gave me tremendous feedback; and also the organizers of these gatherings who so generously invited me. So please forgive me if I limit myself to a few individuals who helped by sharing their archival finds, or pre-publication versions of their scholarship, or who gave their time to read versions of these chapters: Ira Roldugina, Ben Noble, Ineta Lipša, Arthur Clech, Helen Lenskyj, David Brandenberger, Chris Waters, Elizabeth Wood, Paul Chaisty, and my student, Edward Beswick, M.Sc., whose thesis on Russian political homophobia was an inspiration. George Chauncey and Laura Doan pushed me to think harder about queer theory, identities, and homophobia. Monica Whitlock shared her extensive research on Vadim Kozin with me, and generously offered her advice. Bernice Donoghue accompanied me to Kozin's apartment museum in 2009: we shall always have Magadan. Lynne Viola and Susan Gross Solomon gave me critical readings of my outline for this book. Any flaws in the result are mine alone.

I have been privileged to work in universities that can justly take collective credit for supporting this research: Swansea University, Reading University, and, since 2013, Oxford University. Elements of the material about the Gulag were derived from a Wellcome Trust-sponsored project ("Medicine in the Gulag Archipelago," grant no. 085948). Rhodri Mogford and his team at Bloomsbury supported the project enthusiastically: many thanks. Gay's The Word Bookshop (London) and Glad Day Bookstore (Toronto) were critical sources of inspiration. I am a child of Toronto's gay liberation explosion of the 1970s, and without the ideas I first encountered in *The Body Politic*, its long-running magazine for sexual liberation, this book would not exist: my heartfelt thanks to the Pink Triangle Collective that gave *TBP* to the world, and especially to collective members Ed Jackson, Gerald Hannon, Tim McCaskell, and Jim Bartley, all of whom provoked me in various ways. Brian Pronger cannot escape mention in this context too. Finally, I don't care if it's not particularly "radical" or "queer" to shout about one's marriage, but let me thank my husband, Mark Cornwall, who took me to Zagreb where I wrote large chunks of this book: happy days.

Oxford and Southampton, January 2017

*   *   *

The following chapters, slightly modified for this book, originally appeared in other publications, and I am grateful for permission to reproduce them.

Chapter 2 was first published as the article "Comrades, Queers, and 'Oddballs': Sodomy, Masculinity, and Gendered Violence in Leningrad Province of the 1950s," by Dan Healey, in *Journal of the History of Sexuality* volume 21, issue 3, pp. 496–522. Copyright © 2012 by the University of Texas Press. All rights reserved.

Chapter 4 was first published as the chapter "From Stalinist Pariahs to Subjects of 'Managed Democracy': Queers in Moscow 1945 to the Present," by Dan Healey, in Matt Cook and Jennifer V. Evans (eds), *Queer Cities, Queer Cultures: Europe since 1945* (London: Bloomsbury Academic, 2014).

Chapter 5 was first published as the article "Active, Passive, and Russian: The National Idea in Gay Men's Pornography," by Dan Healey, in *The Russian Review*, Volume 69, Issue 2, pp. 210–30.

NOTE ON THE TEXT

I have used familiar spellings for well-known Russian names in the body of the text, so Peter Tchaikovsky, and Boris Yeltsin, rather than Piotr Chaikovskii, and Boris El'tsin, for example. I have eliminated the indication of soft signs with the apostrophe in names too: Kazan, not Kazan'. In the footnotes, when citing Russian sources, I use the modified Library of Congress transliteration system. Translations are my own, except where indicated.

LIST OF ABBREVIATIONS

APRF	*Arkhiv Presidenta Rossiiskoi Federatsii*, Archive of the President of the Russian Federation
AU FSB RF po SPb	*Arkhiv Upravleniia Federal'noi Sluzhby Bezopasnosti Rossiiskoi Federatsii po Sankt-Peterburg*, Archive of the Directorate of the Federal Security Service of the Russian Federation, St. Petersburg branch
FSB	*Federal'naia Sluzhba Bezopasnosti*, Federal Security Service (secret police since 1991)
GAMO	*Gosudarstvennyi arkhiv Magadanskoi Oblasti*, State Archive of Magadan Province
GARF	*Gosudarstvennyi arkhiv Rossiiskoi Federatsii*, State Archive of the Russian Federation
GUM	*Gosudarstvennyi Universalnyi Magazin*, State Department Store
KGB	*Komitet Gosudarstvennoi Bezopasnosti*, Committee of State Security (secret police, 1954–91)
LOGAV	*Leningradskoi Oblastnoi Gosudarstvennyi Arkhiv v g. Vyborge*, State Archive of Leningrad Province in the City of Vyborg
MVD	*Ministerstvo vnutrennykh del*, Ministry of Internal Affairs
NKVD	*Narodnyi komisariat vnytrennykh del*, People's Commissariat of Internal Affairs (secret police, 1934–41)
OGPU	*Ob"edinennoe gosudarstvennoe politicheskoe upravlenie*, Unified State Political Administration (secret police, 1923–34)
ROC	Russian Orthodox Church
RSFSR	Russian Soviet Federated Socialist Republic
TsGA SPb	*Tsentral'nyi Gosudarstvennyi Arkhiv g. Sankt-Peterburga*, Central State Archive of the City of St. Petersburg

UR	United Russia Party
USSR	Union of Soviet Socialist Republics, the Soviet Union

Archival citations are accompanied by the following abbreviations:

f.	*fond*, fond
op.	*opis'*, inventory
l., ll.	*list, listy*; page(s)
ob.	*oborot*; obverse

Introduction:

2013 – Russia's Year of Political Homophobia

Tragedy in Volgograd

Late on the night of May 9, 2013 Victory Day holiday, in the central Russian city of Volgograd, a twenty-three-year-old electrician, Vladislav Tornovoi, met a pair of friends not far from his home. One was Alexander Burkov, twenty-two, a neighbor and classmate on Tornovoi's electrical engineering course. The other was a friend of Burkov's, Anton Smolin, twenty-seven, a graduate of the same course, only recently out of prison, for theft. They bought beer and sat down to drink in a kids' playground in the courtyard of the apartment block where Burkov and Tornovoi lived.

What happened next is difficult to establish. Tornovoi did not come home and at 2 a.m. on 10 May, his grandmother phoned Burkov to find him; Burkov, heavily drunk, told her that her grandson was sleeping. Five hours later Tornovoi's body was discovered in the courtyard. He was dead. His head had been crushed with a paving stone; his genitalia were mutilated; a beer bottle had been shoved into his anus. His attackers had dragged his body into a cardboard box and attempted to burn it.

The police quickly arrested Smolin and Burkov as the principal suspects; blood matching Tornovoi's was found on their clothing. Almost immediately, Smolin's supposed motive for the attack was revealed by a police investigator speaking to the media: while drinking with his courtyard buddies, Tornovoi had admitted he was gay, and Smolin claimed their outrage at his "non-traditional orientation" set off the attack. "When things got out of hand, they decided not to stop," the investigator said.[1]

The anti-gay hatred that apparently spurred Vladislav Tornovoi's murder ignited national and global attention. The reason was plain: Russia was then in the throes of a national conversation about the status of its lesbian, gay, bisexual, and transgender (LGBT) citizens. The talking-point of this debate was a bill given first reading in the Duma, lower house of Russia's parliament, in January 2013, which would ban "propaganda for homosexualism, lesbianism, bisexuality, transgender" among minors.[2] The conversation was far from civil: it was marked by homophobic hate speech, threats of abuse, and actual kidnappings of and violence against men thought to be gay. Against the backdrop of these brutal assaults on fellow citizens, the numerous firings of gay and lesbian teachers, media personalities, and others who dared to speak in favor of LGBT rights went almost unreported.[3]

It is impossible to know whether the poisonously homophobic atmosphere generated in the media and social networks prodded Smolin to claim a defense of "homosexual panic." The murderer was already apparently well versed in the ideologies of hatred and conspirology: his Facebook page listed his favorite book as Adolf Hitler's *Mein Kampf*, his favorite movies as "skinhead [flicks], the American X-Files, and anything to do with Nazis"; his favorite pastimes included not just "home" and "starting a family" but "cleansing Rus of black-assed shit."[4] Undoubtedly, Smolin's recent prison stint was marked by the insecurity about masculinity that finds its expression in homophobic insults, sexual threats, and male rape. Friends of Tornovoi, who denied the victim had been anything but a "normal guy," were quick to argue just that. If homosexuality had been the trigger for this crime, they said, it was because Tornovoi had probably made a drunken joke about Smolin's sexual experience behind bars, a homophobic insult to the ex-con's male honor. The murderer's claim of outrage at Tornovoi's supposed homosexuality was in their view a ruse to get sympathy from judges and win respect and fear from his future cellmates. The charges of murder with aggravating circumstances (the use of extraordinary violence and committed by a group) and the investigation in court silenced all hint of the homophobic "factor" in the crime. After a long trial held behind closed doors, in June 2014, Volgograd judges gave both Smolin and Burkov long sentences. The judges ignored Smolin's plea of "homosexual panic" and also ignored any consideration of a "hate crime" in their sentence.[5]

Vladislav Tornovoi's murder, whatever the facts of the case, encapsulated many fears and responses to homosexuality that convulsed Russian society in 2013. The ruling United Russia Party (UR) had been stoking anxiety about LGBT rights and lifestyles from the launch of Vladimir Putin's campaign to return to the presidency in late 2011, culminating in his election in May 2012. The campaign of political homophobia sought to revitalize Putin's popularity before the election; but in the election's aftermath the campaign intensified, aiming to remasculinize the presidency after the limp incumbency of his tandem partner in the presidency Dmitry Medvedev, and mark out Russian distinctiveness in its gender, family, and demographic politics. Putin's political homophobia campaign was launched for domestic consumption, but soon acquired an international component. Before turning to look at the evolution of the Kremlin's 2013 homophobia project, we need to consider the nature of "homophobia" in historical perspective.

Homophobia in politics and history

The word "homophobia" originated in the USA, after the 1969 Stonewall Riot and the explosion of gay liberation in New York City.[6] As an idea, it crystallized in the early 1970s as U.S. gay activists and psychologists attempted to explain the psychological and social origins of hostility to homosexuality. Later Western activism and academic scholarship looked at ideas of "homophobia" through the lenses of lesbian and gay studies, feminism, and queer theory. Between the 1970s and 1990s, new terms were proposed to refine the concept. Theorists spoke of "lesbophobia" (arguing that "homophobia" erased women); they proposed terms like "heterosexism," "heterocentrism," and "heteronormativity" to focus attention on the dominance of heterosexual prejudice, privilege, and norm-setting.[7] The theoretical debate continues.

The concept of "homophobia" gained currency in the West and later, beyond it. Over the decades after Stonewall, "homophobia" was widely used in Western journalism, politics, and everyday speech. By the 1990s, at the dawn of the digital era, it had diffused rapidly as a descriptor of anti-LGBT prejudice around the globe.[8] Global diffusion has not been unproblematic. Finger-pointing at neighboring countries' "homophobia," and chauvinistic boasting about eradicating it at home, have come under attack as "homonationalism," a form of chest-thumping self-congratulation that is less concerned with extending LGBT rights and much more to do with stoking international rivalries.[9] Post-colonial entanglements also cloud how accusations of "homophobia" are read between former metropole and colony, with the British Commonwealth supplying some of the most acute examples in Africa and elsewhere.[10] In the twenty-first century, rapid and transnational diffusion of "homophobia" as a political concept has obscured some of the historical and intellectual baggage that it acquired as it evolved in the West. That historical baggage "haunts" the use of the word beyond Western contexts and contributes to misunderstanding in transnational dialogues about anti-LGBT policies.

The imprint of European fascism, and specifically German Nazism, is a key component that haunts Western assumptions about homophobia. The work of Dagmar Herzog has demonstrated how Nazi ideologists deployed aggressively homophobic language and policies; she has also argued forcefully for the powerful impact of memory of the Nazi past in the shaping of post-1945 European sexualities, including liberalizing attitudes towards homosexual rights.[11] In West Germany and elsewhere, political arguments about the lingering legacies of fascism underpinned the 1960s repeal of laws making male homosexuality a crime. The liberalization of European sexual regulation accelerated in the 1980s under the influence of interpretations of international human rights law that foregrounded rights to a private life protected from state intrusion.[12] Moreover, LGBT campaigning effectively mobilized memory of the Nazi experience in Europe to win the argument for sexual rights. A politics of commemoration of gay and lesbian suffering served to popularize sympathy for contemporary rights struggles. Gay and lesbian activists in the West invoked the Holocaust as a *homosexual* catastrophe in historical writing, in campaigns and demonstrations, and in "outward" directed polemics with mainstream media and wider society.[13] Activists appropriated the pink triangle, the symbol assigned to male homosexuals in Nazi concentration camps, and wore it as a link between contemporary homophobia (including AIDS-related prejudice), and the murderous violence directed at queer men and women under fascism. In 1985, German President Richard von Weizsaecker, speaking in the Bundestag, acknowledged the homosexual victims of Nazism for the first time. The commemoration of homosexual victims of fascist violence gained official approval and became more commonplace in the late 1980s and 1990s in museums and concentration camp memorials in Europe, and at the Holocaust Memorial Museum, established in Washington, D.C.[14] History teaching acknowledged fascism's political homophobia alongside its racial and ethnic hatreds. A form of prejudice that scarcely had a name before 1969, in the Western imagination "homophobia" has become a marker of the authoritarian mindset, tied to political machismo and violence, and after its apogee under the Nazi regime, associated with genocide.

    The burden of historical memory that haunts Western notions of "homophobia," calls for sensitivity when applying the word to places beyond the West. We are obliged to criticize homophobia where we discern it, but we must do so reflectively, remembering that homophobic violence at home took decades to recognize. We must also consider the entanglements of homonationalist rivalries and post-colonial relationships. Such care was seldom taken when Western journalism and social media attacked Russia's policies in 2013–14. Accusations of homophobia cast at Russia proceeded from a cluster of contradictory and "memoryless" assumptions about Russia's place in Europe and the world. We cannot decide if Russia is a part of Europe, or a distinctive "civilization" of its own, and the battles over that ambiguity cloud our reactions.[15] In our amnesia, we also struggle with the idea that a country so much "like us" might take as long as we did (or longer) to wrestle with ubiquitous social and political homophobia. Masha Gessen was surely right to point out in 2013 that we were particularly disturbed by Russian homophobia not only because "Russians are white" and their homophobes could be stylish and fluent, but also because Russia in 2013 presented "the spectacle of history shifting abruptly into reverse."[16] In the USA and Europe, we have come to expect an unbroken curve of progress in the construction of full LGBT citizenship. Yet, as Weimar Germany's history shows, LGBT "progress" is not automatic but can be arrested when political tectonic plates shift.

Moreover, the memoryless accusations of "homophobia" betray an expectation that "we" know best how to get to a better place. At the risk of stating the obvious, there is no single correct path to a "post-homophobic" society and polity, and there is no common starting point in an equally "homophobic dark age." The rights debates about LGBT people in the new accession states of the European Union over the past decade demonstrate that the path to tolerance is not found on a technocrat's roadmap alone, but is built on a subtle blend of cultural, social, and political contestation.[17] What is more, the ultimate design of "full LGBT citizenship" in the European Union is not found in any charter or policy document; it is instead evolving patchwork-style, as Europe's different societies with their different religious, cultural, and historical characters explore what tolerance might look like at home.[18]

Political scientists have begun to analyze the uses of "homophobia" as a political tool. In the process, they have developed conceptually sophisticated frames for understanding contemporary outbursts of hostility to the threat of the sex or gender dissident.[19] Historians have been less engaged with studying homophobia in the past; at least, they have not produced similarly comparative and analytical studies.[20] Students of political homophobia have largely been motivated by the rise of vigorous anti-LGBT movements in Africa and Asia, but also by the continuing activities of well-organized homophobic political forces in Europe and North America. Comparative and transnational perspectives allow us to see when and how state actors and elites "choose" to build a "homophobic project" and what transnational "influence peddling" offers local leaders in terms of ideas and funding. The political trigger for most modern political homophobia campaigns is an economic or national security crisis threatening state stability. Such "homophobic projects" presume a backdrop of genuine or "imitation" democratic politics with elections and other forms of popular mobilization. At stake is usually a contest over national identity construction, in which the nation is said to be under threat from an external, often Western (and previously colonial), ideology of gender and sexual difference. Local "traditions" of kinship, marriage, and gender relations are recast as timeless patterns, often presented as under stress from neoliberal globalization, digital technologies, and social change. Elites deploying a project of political homophobia offer the "solution" of a stronger national community, forged around "traditional" and explicitly anti-LGBT values, frequently, backed by religious teaching. They raise the specter of a dangerous LGBT minority said to be in the grips of Western or colonial influence. Ironically, of course, the nationalism they celebrate is a European invention; so is the panoply of anti-homosexual measures they propose; and local religious institutions are often supported and encouraged in their homophobia by U.S. and European evangelical churches. The payoff for homophobe-politicians is political legitimation, electorates distracted from intractable economic and social problems, and stronger allies among churches and other civil society institutions. Virtually all these features apply to Russia's "year of homophobia," 2013, described later in this Introduction.

This book is an attempt to trace the roots of this recent homophobia from a historian's perspective. It is not an exhaustive study of homophobia in Russia's past; instead, I offer a series of essays, "case histories" that reveal something of the character of modern Russian anti-LGBT attitudes and their origins in the country's troubled twentieth century. In this Introduction, I set out the context for Russia's "year of political homophobia" and chart the evolution of its centerpiece, the country's federal law that bans "gay propaganda" and its impact. I then consider President Putin's views on LGBT citizenship and his promotion of Russia's "traditional values" as the world's attention turned toward his country as host of the Sochi 2014 Winter Olympics. The last section of this introduction offers an overview of the questions this book discusses, and introduces the essays that follow, grouped into three sections: histories of homophobic persecution after 1945, the challenge of LGBT visibility in late twentieth-century Russian society, and the obstacles to writing and commemorating Russia's queer past. The introduction concludes with conceptual remarks on the terminology of LGBT/queer existence, and its applicability to Russia. Through its case histories, this book will reveal some of the origins of homophobia in modern Russia; and it will illustrate the dilemmas facing Russia's LGBT community in its attempts to write itself into the national story and claim full citizenship. A historical understanding of Russia's persecution of its "sexual minorities" will also enable allies and scholars to appreciate the scale of the cultural battle that Russia's lesbian, gay, bisexual, and transgender people face today.

Toward a project of political homophobia

Russia's fresh politics of homophobia arose against a specific economic and political backdrop. The economic crisis of 2008–9 cut the country's booming growth rates of the early 2000s – the source of Putin's popularity – from a peak of 8.5 percent in 2007 to a *contraction* of 7.8 percent in 2009. Growth stumbled after that, faltering in 2013, the year of the "gay propaganda" debate, at just 1.3 percent.[21] The campaign of political homophobia seemed calculated to distract public anger about declining living standards and rising prices. Sections of the public were also coming out to street demonstrations against the Putin political "system" of manipulated elections ("imitation democracy" in one influential diagnosis), state-controlled mass media that gave the opposition no airtime, and the corrupt administration provided by Putin's party, United Russia (UR).[22] In 2011, UR's electoral base in the regions was weakening significantly; this was evident even before the December 2011 parliamentary elections triggered the wave of anti-corruption protest. At an infamous Moscow wrestling match in November 2011, Putin's appearance, which reminded spectators of his intended resumption of the presidency, was met with stunning derision from a mostly male audience of presumed bedrock supporters.[23] A re-launch of the Putin "system" was necessary to bring these core voters back to the paramount leader in time for his election to a third term as President in May 2012, and nationalism and religion were mobilized to the task. A surge in xenophobic, anti-Muslim, and pro-Christian campaigning on TV media, to co-opt Russian ethnic nationalist sentiments, was orchestrated by public intellectuals with Kremlin backing in 2012–13.[24] At the same time, Putin accelerated an existing process of "re-clericalization" of the state: bringing the Russian Orthodox Church (ROC) closer to government and directly involving it in shaping social policy, providing social services, and projecting Russia's voice abroad. This assertion of "moral sovereignty" is part of a wider domestic and international political narrative developed by the Kremlin, UR, and the ROC condemning feminism and LGBT politics as "extremist" and foreign, while promoting heterosexual, "traditional family values" as true to Russian nationhood. The degree to which the ROC influences such discussions within Russia's ruling elite is disputed by scholars; the Church's ties with U.S. conservative Christians offer an ironic vector of influence in an otherwise cooling relationship between Washington and Moscow. Nevertheless, it is clear that in its anti-feminist and homophobic turn, the Kremlin has drawn heavily on rhetoric about protecting religious values.[25]

Conservative-nationalists in post-Soviet Russia have been developing anti-LGBT political ideas and proposing laws to give them force since the end of the 1990s. They were prompted by religious and secular revulsion with post-communist Russia's "sexual revolution" of the 1990s, when sex exploded on screen and in print after decades of Soviet silence. Eager to enact sweeping reform quickly before Communist rule might return, in a 1993 omnibus bill, then-president Boris Yeltsin had repealed Stalin's law against male homosexuality. However in the wake of decriminalization, novels and films of the 1990s used homosexual themes not to celebrate the liberation of a previously repressed sexuality, but to mark characters and scenarios as taboo, strange, or non-Russian. Many spectators and the politicians who listened to them preferred to believe that visible homosexuality was a foreign import, not Russian in origin. These politicians sought to recriminalize gay male sex.[26] In a farcical parliamentary debate in 2002, the Duma considered restoring the Stalin law, and also debated the banning of lesbianism and even fines for masturbation. The initiatives, discussed in Chapter 6, failed dismally.

From this debacle, Russia's conservative-nationalist politicians realized that the return to Stalinist criminal penalties for homosexual acts was impossible. In his first term, President Putin was evidently not ready to abandon Russia's commitment to European human rights norms, and while there was little public affection for the idea of non-heterosexual lifestyles, there was no appetite for repression. Conservatives found they had to refine their anti-LGBT story. They turned to the problem of the visibility of gay, lesbian, and gender-non-conforming identities in the public sphere, and continued working on their political language, particularly at the level of local government. From 2006, the mayor of Moscow year-on-year refused applications from lawyer and activist Nikolai Alekseev for a Gay Pride march in the capital, condemning the idea as "satanic," and mobilizing local Orthodox and Muslim leaders to join in the vilification of queer visibility.[27] Ultimately, pride marches met with mixed fortunes across the country, usually attracting many more anti-gay nationalist, right-wing skinhead, and religious counterdemonstrators than pride marchers, and often ending in violence against the small numbers of LGBT citizens claiming their rights to speech and assembly.

Many in Russia thought that battles over pride marches pitted "extreme" positions against each other in an unsophisticated shouting match with limited political value. "Pride" on the streets of Moscow seemed to matter more to the Western international media than to domestic queer activists and wider society. Most of Russia's LGBT activists apparently opposed the pride parades as unsuited to Russia's narrowing and increasingly nationalist political conditions. The parades were needlessly provocative in a society that still required basic education about sex and gender diversity. Such attitudes were based on hard-won experience. A "first" generation of post-Soviet Russian gay and lesbian activists had largely adopted public and "international" (or "European") tactics in the uncontrolled democracy of the 1990s, with street demonstrations, public LGBT festivals, media conferences, and close financial and intellectual ties with European and U.S. activists and non-governmental organizations (NGOs), and the International Lesbian & Gay Association (ILGA).[28] Yet the 1993 repeal of Stalin's anti-sodomy law had come about as a result of wholesale packages of reform pushed through parliament by Yeltsin's anti-Communist reformers, not because of activist efforts. The "first" generation of LGBT activists, despite some impressive community-building and intellectual activity, had little to show for their efforts by the 1998 financial crisis. That crisis hit gay male publishing ventures and deterred queer activism; many lesbian and gay activists emigrated or abandoned "politics." The crisis also marks a convenient turning point between activist generations with the end of the pre-internet era. From 1999, a turn in Russian politics to incoming President Putin's tougher political rhetoric eventually embraced "managed" or "sovereign" democracy in his second term of office (2004–8); the "first generation" of lesbian and gay activists gave way to a new cohort in new conditions.

The "second," early twenty-first-century generation of activists was the product of the expanding the middle class; they were beneficiaries of the rise of digital media and virtual social networks. Gender and sexual dissidents could come together virtually without the need for the printing press, post office boxes, and bricks and mortar shops, bars, and saunas (although these businesses flourished in the new affluence of Moscow and a few other large cities). This second generation was more committed to low-key community support and carefully targeted public interventions. They focused on "inward-facing" activity aimed at helping LGBT fellow-citizens, while their "outward-facing" initiatives were not aimed scattergun at the full spectrum of mainstream Russia, but were targeted to build alliances with human-rights and oppositional political movements that still understood little about LGBT issues.[29] By the end of the first decade of the 2000s, a strategy of grassroots community building and the slow education of likely allies were yielding a richer network of local organizations and perhaps an incipient awareness in some parts of Russian society of the problems of LGBT existence.

These activities were extremely limited, and arguably less overtly public thanks to digital technologies. Nevertheless, the fear of queer visibility continued to agitate conservative nationalist politicians. The lack of a vocal, visible and ubiquitous Russian LGBT movement did not deter political homophobes seeking to extend their anti-LGBT narratives. As David Murray has pointed out for the case of Barbados, the threat of "spectral sexuality" can be an effective fear-producing bogeyman even in conservative societies where LGBT activism scarcely exists.[30] Moreover, the increasing ubiquity of the internet makes relatively exotic information accessible to far larger audiences than in the pre-digital age. All governments have paid greater attention to the problems of regulating information access, especially attempting to reproduce and preserve "age-appropriate" child-protection restrictions that prevailed with print, radio, and television. Among the devices to which Russia's conservative politicians turned was the idea of banning "gay propaganda" among minors or schoolchildren. Similar measures originated most notoriously in Margaret Thatcher's Britain in 1988 (where "Section 28" of the Local Government Act was not repealed in England until 2003), and many were adopted and are still in effect at local and state level in the USA.[31]

Russian versions of the ban on "gay propaganda" law originated from drafts amending the Criminal Code presented to the Duma between 2003 and 2009 by Deputy Aleksandr Chuev, a campaigner for Christian morality in the Duma's religious affairs committee. He has also targeted abortion and pornography.[32] Having examined Chuev's proposals, government and Duma committees conclusively rejected them in 2009 as contradicting criminal law and human rights conventions. The Chuev law would have criminalized public forms of "propaganda for the homosexual way of life or homosexual orientation," and punished perpetrators of the proposed crime with a ban on working in schools, youth services, the army, and prisons. Chuev's unsuccessful law lacked any distinction between children and adults as targets of "propaganda," and ultimately it foundered on his apparent determination to criminalize adult speech about something that was not in itself a criminal activity.

Russia's regions served as test-beds for variations on the anti-propaganda law, offering conservatives opportunities to craft the language and messages of political homophobia. In 2006, Riazan Province passed an ordinance banning "propaganda for homosexualism among minors." Irina Fedotova and Nikolai Baev, arrested on March 30, 2009 for carrying signs near schools and a children's library saying "Homosexuality is normal" and

"I am proud of my homosexuality – ask me about it," were convicted under this law.[33] Their appeal to the Constitutional Court of the Russian Federation in January 2010 yielded a significant setback for the LGBT community. The court said their constitutional rights had not been infringed by the Riazan authorities, and its positive analysis of the local "gay propaganda" ordinance embedded in Russian jurisprudence the tendentious concepts of "traditional [versus] non-traditional marital relations," terminology which had already circulated in media and popular sexological discourse for some twenty years.[34]

In 2011 and especially in 2012, provincial and regional assemblies around Russia began adopting local versions of the "gay propaganda" law.[35] Did a direct connection exist between the Riazan ordinance and later ones which suddenly blossomed across the country during and after the 2011–12 election cycle? Did Putin's Kremlin coordinate this burst of political homophobia across the country – was it a "homophobic project" in the calculated, political sense that Barry Adam proposes?[36] It is impossible to say with any certainty, given that no comparative research on the regional "gay propaganda" laws exists, and since the Kremlin's decision-making processes have become exceedingly opaque in recent years. President Putin later claimed his government was responding to a genuine public clamor in enacting the national "gay propaganda" ban. Indeed, from available sources a varied picture of local initiative and party coordination driving the local laws emerges, and the geographic and demographic spread of the regional ordinances against "gay propaganda" suggests a resonance with *la Russie profonde*. The texts of these laws varied slightly (some banning propaganda just for "homosexualism"; others mentioned bisexualism, transgender, and a few tendentiously added pedophilia). Local discussion and styles of adoption varied considerably. In first-adopting Arkhangelsk, in September 2011, local authorities organized a broad consultation of representatives of religious confessions, civil-society organizations, and scientific experts; members of the region's only small LGBT community group boycotted the meeting.[37] United Russia and other parties close to the Kremlin backed the measures in Novosibirsk, Magadan, and St. Petersburg. Youth leaders in local legislatures (Arkhangelsk), governments (Magadan), and universities (Arkhangelsk again) expressed support for the laws, and youth leaders may have been key in inter-regional promotion of the law.[38] Elsewhere the law simply appeared on legislative agendas and was adopted unanimously (Bashkortostan).

Some opponents of the "gay propaganda" bans emerged where debate appeared to be less controlled. Legal advisors to local authorities in Samara and Moscow City expressed reservations based on technicalities, similar to those raised by the federal parliament over Chuev's law. Among local politicians, the handful of liberal Yabloko Party deputies in the St. Petersburg legislature opposed the law most consistently and vociferously. Yet St. Petersburg also furnished the national stage with some of its most articulate and aggressive political homophobes. Valentina Matvienko, a Putin ally from the northern capital, declared in November 2011, soon after assuming the post of Chair of the Federal Assembly (parliament's upper house), that a law analogous to the local ban on "gay propaganda" then under debate in her hometown should be passed for all of Russia.[39] Vitaly Milonov, a deputy in the city's legislature, acquired international notoriety, and considerable Russian praise, for the blunt ferocity and crudeness of his anti-gay campaigning.[40]

From Siberia to Moscow – a federal "gay propaganda" ban

The regional debates apparently showed the Kremlin that a national ban on "gay propaganda" would be understood and supported by politicians and the broad public, and that a national debate on LGBT issues could injure Russia's democratic opposition by challenging its patriotism and political virility. The political advantages of launching such a homophobic campaign by the end of 2012 were clear. Late 2011 and the first half of 2012 had been a period of unprecedented rockiness for the presidential system, as urban voters protested corruption and vote-rigging. Re-elected president in May 2012, Putin responded with selective repression to divide and quell the protest movement. One thrust of this repression targeted a Moscow feminist punk band, Pussy Riot, whose guerrilla performances of political protest songs became YouTube hits. Their February 21, 2012 action in the Cathedral of Christ the Savior, singing "Mother of God, Chase Putin Away," was interrupted by church security officials. In March, three of the singer-activists were arrested and charged with "hooliganism motivated by religious hatred." All were denied bail and in their August 2012 trial they received sentences of two years; two of the Pussy Riot feminists served fourteen months in prison colonies before release in a pre-Olympics amnesty in December 2013.[41] The Pussy Riot affair of 2012 dramatized key themes that pre-figured the political homophobia campaign of 2013. It presented a "spectral" threat – feminist "gender" ideology, which has had limited popular purchase in modern Russia – as an existential one for the country's survival. Feminist "gender" thinking challenged "traditional values" and the sanctity of the Russian Orthodox Church. It suggested that feminism was foreign to Russia, "extremist," and inspired by Western forces that desired an unstable and weak Russia. It stirred a loud, negative reaction in the Western media that took on an anti-Russian tinge. It concentrated fire on a corner of the opposition movement that was challenging for Russia's democrats to defend in the court of public opinion. The government's harsh treatment of the Pussy Riot feminists appeared to defend the dignity of the ROC, defend Russia against hostile forces ranged against it, and threw an unflattering light on yesterday's heroes, the democratic opposition movement associated with the protests of 2011–12. (British Prime Minister Thatcher had used Section 28 to damage her opponents in the Labour Party.)[42] These messages could be driven home with a fresh campaign to keep the "gender" issue in the public eye. No queer punk protest in a cathedral was needed to launch the next round in the Putinist argument for "traditional values." A political "project" already existed, tested in the regions and ready to download for the national stage: the specter of "gay propaganda" threatening Russia's children.

The call for the law originated from Siberia in a request to the Duma. In March 2012, the legislature of Novosibirsk Province asked the federal parliament for a national ban on "propaganda for homosexualism" among minors. The Novosibirsk appeal was sponsored by a physician and UR politician, Sergei Dorofeev, and a former construction worker, Aleksei Kondrashkin, also a UR member. (It is unusual for such petitions from the regions to succeed: a clue that this was a Kremlin project.)[43] In the Duma, spearheading the promotion of the law fell to Elena Mizulina (of the Kremlin-loyal "A Just Russia" Party); Mizulina was the Chair of parliament's Committee on the Family, Women and Children. Dorofeev and Mizulina introduced a federal draft "propaganda" law and on January 25, 2013, the Duma approved it on first reading by 388 votes to one, with one abstention.[44] In contrast to Chuev's original proposal, this one did not add "propaganda for homosexualism" to the Criminal Code, but to the milder Code of Administrative Offences and other legislation on child protection. It was in that sense a less blunt, more refined, legal instrument. The early draft law listed specific forms of sexual and gender orientation to be banned from uncontrolled promotion: "homosexualism, lesbianism, bisexualism, transgender." Mizulina conducted continued discussions behind closed doors on the law through the spring. By the third reading (June 11), the final version of the bill dropped this list of orientations, replacing it with the catch-all category of "non-traditional sexual relations." By adopting the ambiguous "non-traditional sexual relations" in place of a list of orientations, lawmakers shifted the focus from individual identities to sexual acts which had previously been defined in Supreme Court judgments as "non-traditional." This was done, presumably, to evade charges that the law discriminated against particular classes of people. The change, and its timing, may indicate that the storm over the Tornovoi murder compelled Mizulina to shed the unambiguously discriminatory list of orientations.[45] She had angrily rejected suggestions her law was generating anti-gay violence.[46] The concept of "traditional sexual relations," incubated in legal decisions and the media, was conclusively embedded in Russian law and in the popular consciousness. The epithets "traditional/non-traditional" assert that the range of sexual activity under consideration is novel, alien, and by implication not indigenously Russian, but from abroad. The new legal concept of "traditional sex" enshrines an old myth of Russia's sexual innocence in national law.[47]

Elena Mizulina's unsubtle promotion of the notion of "traditional" sex and family relations came to the fore during the national conversation about the rights and status of LGBT Russians that the "propaganda" law kicked off. When introducing the draft law in parliament she blamed "gay propaganda" for a rise in "pedophiles" attacking boy children.[48] Similarly, Mizulina frequently linked homosexuality, bisexuality, lesbianism, and transgender identity to pedophilia in her media interviews about the law. When liberal politicians and commentators dared to criticize the proposed law, she dismissed them as working for "the pedophilia lobby," most egregiously when former Deputy Prime Minister Alfred Kokh observed that Mizulina's son, a lawyer, worked for a Belgian law firm with pro-LGBT clients and policies.[49] The single-minded Duma member for Omsk had long claimed the "pedophile lobby" was behind obstacles to her previous child-protection projects.[50] She insistently argued the law was not "homophobic" but was targeted at promoting "traditional family values." In 2013 she authored a parliamentary white paper (in Russian known as a "concept") with a twelve-year plan for Russia's family policy.[51] The "concept" sets out policies aimed at strengthening the "traditional Russian family," defined as exclusively heterosexual, and based on the values of religious confessions "which are an inalienable part of the historical legacy of the peoples of Russia." It proposed that "propaganda for family happiness and traditional family values" should be a state priority.[52] The "concept" sparked a series of calls from politicians across the country for a return to Stalin-style population management strategies, including banning abortion, raising the cost of a divorce sharply, and the conscription of reproductively inactive singletons.[53] Mizulina's hostile public statements about "untraditional" sexual orientation and gender identity piloted a political and social language that large swathes of the Russian commentariat adopted once second and third readings were concluded on June 11, 2013, with 436 deputies approving the measure against one abstention.[54] President Putin quickly signed her bill into law, and it came into force on June 30, 2013.

Banning "gay propaganda" and making propaganda for "traditional sex"

The impact of the president's signature on this law was swiftly felt. In contrast to Thatcher's Section 28, which was never actually used against any "offender" promoting "homosexuality as a pretended family relationship," the Russian "gay propaganda" law was put to immediate use against visitors to Russia and citizens of the country. Three weeks after the enactment of the ban, police investigated Dutch LGBT activists at a Youth Rights Camp in Murmansk; four citizens of the Netherlands were charged under the law and deported, with a three-year ban on returning to Russia. The "first arrests of foreign activists" were widely reported and gave the impression that the law was meant to hit outsiders bringing alien values to the nation.[55] Authorities across the country have investigated, charged, and convicted Russian LGBT campaigners, website and book publishers, journalists, teachers, and other citizens for "violations" of the "gay propaganda" ban.[56] In October 2013, UR politician Vasily Milonov raised complaints with prosecutors over a website aimed at helping gay teenagers, "*Deti-404*" (Children-404). A long legal battle ensued in two jurisdictions, and while the site's originator Elena Klimova has been convicted and fined, her fight has not yet ended.[57] Russia's embarrassing Minister of Culture, Vladimir Medinsky, denied that the nation's most famous composer, Peter Ilyich Tchaikovsky, was homosexual, claiming there was no evidence to prove it, in a September 2013 debate over a planned film biography. (There are stacks of torridly homoerotic letters in the Tchaikovsky archives, as Alexander Poznansky has demonstrated.) The biopic was to be subsidized with funds from Medinsky's ministry.[58] In October that year, the Heraldry Council of the President of Russia commissioned an expert from the Hermitage to examine the rainbow-banded flag of the Autonomous Jewish Province in Russia's Far East to certify that it did not fall foul of the "gay propaganda" ban.[59] The orgy of symbolic homophobic witch-hunting sought ever sillier targets: in November 2014, a memorial to Apple founder Steve Jobs was dismantled after the CEO of the U.S. company came out as a gay man; more recently, a bus shelter in a small town was attacked by local conservatives for its colorful design as "too gay" and in violation of the propaganda law.[60] Russians have been taught how to recognize "gay propaganda" in an astounding array of inanimate objects.

Violence against gay men and lesbians surged in the wake of the passage of this law. Vigilante groups around the country were already operating under the brands "Occupy Pedophilia" and "Occupy Gerontophilia." More cases of their activity were reported from the summer of 2013. They lured male victims with fake online chat, then kidnapped, beat, and tortured their targets once the victim appeared in person for a rendezvous.[61] These groups made little secret of their activities and the authorities turned a blind eye as Western media reports clearly identified perpetrators and documented their stomach-churning crimes.[62] Reports of violence against LGBT people in the Russian media leapt to unprecedented numbers in 2013, although the actual numbers of documented victims of hate crimes remained small (twenty-five individuals, including Tornovoi, by one independent count).[63] The low numbers are first and foremost because no law prohibits hate crimes against LGBT citizens; information-gathering through media searches obviously does not capture many unreported incidents. Also affecting these numbers was the fear of victims to report violence against them based on their "non-traditional" sexuality; an increasingly fearful LGBT citizenry hiding to protect itself; and the state-controlled media's reluctance to report such crimes sympathetically.[64]

Expressions of contempt for LGBT individuals and their human rights were not confined to vigilante thugs and attention-seeking politicians. The Russian Orthodox Church's leader, an alleged ex-KGB officer and a connoisseur of $30,000 Breguet wristwatches, Patriarch of Moscow Kirill I, took the debate on LGBT citizenship to the question of equal marriage and the supposed demographic threat to the survival of the nation that it poses. Three weeks after the "gay propaganda" ban became law, he denounced Western recognition of same-sex unions as "approving sin and codifying it into law in order to justify it." At a ceremony in a recently restored chapel on Red Square, of same-sex marriage he said, "This is a very dangerous apocalyptic symptom, and we must do everything in our powers to ensure that sin is never sanctioned in Russia by state law, because that would mean that the nation has embarked on a path of self-destruction."[65] None of these views was new; the ROC had declared itself against same-sex marriage and civil unions among other human rights for LGBT citizens years earlier.[66] What was significant was the timing and the mode of entry into the national conversation, raising new "spectral" threats: no advocate of equal marriage could be seen anywhere on the Russian political horizon in the summer of 2013.

Quite the opposite. In August, on TV channel *Rossiia-1*'s popular public affairs program *Vesti* (News), one of the country's leading media executives, Dmitry Kiselev, called for even more visceral restrictions on LGBT citizens. He zeroed in on the issue of sperm, blood, and organ donation. "I think that just imposing fines on gays for propaganda among teenagers is not enough. They should be banned from donating blood or sperm. And if they have an automobile accident, their hearts should be buried in the ground or burned as unsuitable for the continuation of life."[67] The language was inflammatory, designed to evoke a visceral reaction in a studio audience, which applauded heartily at these words. Later that year, Putin made Kiselev chief of Russia's international news agency in a restructuring that saw the relatively balanced news provider RIA-Novosti shuttered and its place taken by the tendentiously Kremlin-loyal RT (formerly Russia Today).[68]

President Putin's personal pronouncements about LGBT rights during 2013 merit attention, especially in the run-up to the Sochi Winter Olympics of February 2014. The president's limited statements about the question carried particular weight in an information environment tightly restricting access to the paramount leader, and apparently designed to project an aura of confident, paternalistic authority. Putin adopted an avuncular but firm tone, asserting that Russia was a tolerant nation, but simultaneously a country determined to regulate morality according to its specific "traditions." The president's statements thus conveyed to foreign audiences the key messages to the West and potential international partners about Russia's independence in conservative politics and its resurgence as a "sovereign" power.

In April 2013, as the debate over Russia's "gay propaganda" law roiled at home and abroad, President Putin made an official visit to the Netherlands as part of what would turn out to be a rocky year of celebrations marking four centuries of diplomatic ties between the two countries.[69] In Amsterdam, he encountered a large demonstration against Russia's political homophobia. During a media conference with Dutch Prime Minister Mark Rutte, journalists quizzed Putin about Russia's treatment of LGBT citizens' rights. Putin's responses began with assertions of tolerance:

> So that this is all clear and understood, in the Russian Federation the rights of sexual minorities are not being trampled upon. These people are the very same as all the rest, they enjoy full rights and freedoms. As President of the Russian Federation I consider it my duty to defend their interests and rights, and I suggest that like other citizens of Russia they have no other President but me.
>
> In this regard I want to say that they make their way in their careers, their careers prosper, they are awarded state prizes, orders and medals, honorific titles and honorable citations if they deserve them. That is the practice in our political life; I am certain that it will remain that way.[70]

It is worth pointing out that no leader of Russia in its entire history has ever made such an explicitly positive public statement about the rights of LGBT citizens. ("Enlightened" leaders who decriminalized male homosexuality in the twentieth century – Vladimir Lenin in 1922, Boris Yeltsin in 1993 – were silent about their reasons for doing so. "Liberals" who relaxed Stalinist dictatorship, such as Nikita Khrushchev, were actively homophobic, or in the case of Mikhail Gorbachev, overwhelmed by the tide of events.)[71] In the same interview, Putin chided the Dutch for tolerating "an organization that propagandizes for pedophilia" and a national political party that wants women out of politics; but he also said that talking about such differences was the essence of diplomacy.[72]

In subsequent media encounters, Putin developed an increasingly assertive tone, pushing back against Western criticism more insistently. In the "was Tchaikovsky gay?" debate of September 2013, he repeated his assertions of tolerance, noting that the country had long rid itself of the criminal sanction against homosexuality and that his door was open to meet with members of the LGBT community, to work with them, and to reward them for service.[73] Putin's invocation of toleration for the homosexual genius relied on a popular myth of Russian big-heartedness that finds room for eccentricity if not diversity. The same theme had been often invoked by conservatives as they refined their anti-LGBT rhetoric over the previous two decades.[74]

Less than two weeks later, President Putin returned to the same rhetoric of paternalism and Russian assertion of difference. At the annual Valdai conference bringing foreign academics and business partners together with Russia's leaders, he spoke about the challenges to Russia's identity in the twenty-first century. Here he argued for Russia's independence from the pathway taken by "Euro-Atlantic countries [which] are actually rejecting their roots, including the Christian values that constitute the basis for Western civilization." As evidence of this supposed rejection, he cited recognition of same-sex marriages and adoption, "political parties whose aim is to promote pedophilia," and the erasure of Christian holidays from national calendars. "And people are aggressively trying to export this model all over the world."[75] Challenged to elucidate his stance by Prof. Gerhard Mangott of Innsbruck University, the President reiterated Russian acceptance of the legality of same-sex relations while erroneously pointing out that some U.S. states supposedly still punish homosexuality. He also argued that Russia chose different solutions to its demographic challenges than those – including increased migration, same-sex marriage, and adoption – chosen by the West.[76]

Vladimir Putin further emphasized the international dimensions of Russia's stance limiting LGBT rights in his December 2013 Presidential Address to the Federal Assembly, an annual political "state of the Federation" speech. Here he commented on the country's distinctive upholding of "tradition" in the face of "abstract, speculative ideas, contrary to the will of the majority, which does not accept the changes occurring or the proposed revision of values." Putin went on to assert that Russia was "defending traditional values. . . the values of traditional families" in a world where the alternative was a descent into barbarism. Russia would stand for "the spiritual and moral basis of civilization" against the forces of globalization that crushed local identities and cultures.[77] Tellingly, this striking passage defining Russia's gender conservatism appeared in the section of his speech devoted to Moscow's international image and its foreign relations strategy, especially with allies and trading partners in the Middle East and Africa. A domestic homophobic project was acquiring an international dimension.

Sochi, the Olympic "industry," and Russia's global image

The approaching Sochi Winter Olympics provided a flashpoint that Kremlin strategists had perhaps scarcely anticipated, when they gave the green light to Mizulina's "gay propaganda" ban in early 2013. From the summer of 2013, calls to Western governments to boycott the Sochi games began to come from LGBT leaders in the USA and UK, including Harvey Fierstein and Stephen Fry, who both recalled the world's indulgence of Nazi Germany's 1936 Berlin Olympics as a form of appeasement of fascism. "There is a price for tolerating intolerance," wrote Fierstein, pointing to the world war and Holocaust that followed soon after Berlin 1936.[78] Historically, national boycotts have only rarely blunted the prestige of host nations (e.g. the U.S.-led boycott of the Moscow 1980 games and the reciprocal Soviet rejection of the Los Angeles 1984 Olympics). Since the rise of new social media, the Olympic "industry" has had to respond to popular pressure in the form of online petitions, campaigns targeting commercial sponsors, and mobilization of real-world protests.[79] National Olympic teams argued successfully against refusing to participate at Sochi, relying on the notion of the supposed "apolitical" nature of sport. Yet many Western governments were sympathetic to the issue and spoke about their concerns for LGBT rights in Russia.

Meanwhile, the chance for gestures of solidarity with LGBT Russians that the Olympics offered began to loom larger, as a controversy over two Swedish athletes' rainbow-painted fingernails demonstrated in August 2013 at the World Athletics Championships in Moscow.[80] The same games saw widespread Western misreading on social media of a celebratory kiss between two Russian women competitors as a "podium protest" against LGBT oppression.[81] Russian prevarication about the degree of latitude to be shown to LGBT athletes and visitors in Sochi, including insistence from Vitaly Mutko, Minister of Sport, Tourism and Youth that the "gay propaganda" law would be scrupulously enforced, drew international concern and further calls for podium and "silent" protests. In the wake of Mutko's comments, Putin had to intervene in November 2013, defending the "gay propaganda" law, but warning citizens not to "create a torrent of hatred toward anyone in society, including people of non-traditional sexual orientation."[82] (We now know that the Nazis agreed, under U.S. Olympic Committee pressure, to suspend aspects of anti-Semitic and homophobic persecution during the Berlin 1936 Games.)[83] An ugly homophobic incident while the country was under close international scrutiny might mar a project so closely associated with the president's personal prestige; the rising tide of homophobia generated by the government's own activities was just one of a cluster of challenges to the staging of a successful games.[84]

But Putin was not about to give ground to Western arguments about human rights. In January 2014, during a carefully staged pre-Games interview with Russian and foreign journalists, Putin reiterated his familiar script, although it was subtly altered with falsehoods that were unlikely to be challenged.[85] He pointed out that Russia was a tolerant nation that does not criminalize homosexuality, in contrast to over seventy countries that do (and he repeated the misinformation about U.S. states' penalties for sodomy). The law merely forbade forms of "propaganda," not persons of a particular sexual orientation as such. There was no threat of arrest to spectators and participants coming to the Sochi Games. He defended the Russian Orthodox Church's right to call for re-criminalization of homosexuality, claiming that the ROC, the Vatican, and Islam were of one mind on this issue, and pointing out that the state and church are constitutionally separate in Russia. Putin went on the attack, linking homosexuality to pedophilia, in a duplicitous but obviously deliberate misremembering of the title of the controversial law which he gave as "On the banning of propaganda for pedophilia and homosexualism."[86] Nowhere in the law does the word "pedophilia" appear; Putin was borrowing Elena Mizulina's slur, tagging child abuse and homosexuality, albeit in a more subtle fashion. (No journalist noticed the president's deception.) Putin claimed, again falsely, that other countries, "including European ones," are considering "legalizing pedophilia" but that "the Russian people have their own cultural code, their own traditions."

And he rehearsed the demographic arguments for promoting "traditional family values" in order to restore Russia's birth rate and avoid undesirable Western-style immigration and same-sex family recognition to bolster flagging populations.

Russia's year of political homophobia began with Mizulina's introduction of the "gay propaganda" law in the Duma with justifications that pedophilia was somehow tied to adult homosexuality. It ended with the country's president misleading domestic and world audiences about the state of the law in the USA and Europe, mocking these societies as incapable of defending Western "civilization," and using lies about the "spectral" threat of pedophilia to justify the persecution of a peaceful and harmless segment of Russia's population. Naturally, the "year of political homophobia" did not mark the end of anti-LGBT politics and popular sentiment in Russia. (In fact, during the Sochi Games, the government put new restrictions on adoption of Russian children to countries permitting same-sex marriage.)[87] The gathering storm in Ukraine that coincided with the Sochi Olympics nevertheless shifted the world's attention firmly toward the escalating geopolitical crisis. Yet questions about the nature of the homophobic turn in Russia and its origins remain.

Russian homophobia from Stalin to Sochi

This book is not intended to trace a unified history of homophobia in Russia. Instead, it is my attempt to ask provocative questions and suggest where some answers might be found. Our knowledge about queer Russia is very limited by comparison to what we know about other countries. An enormous range of research still needs to be done. My questions are for the general reader who is puzzled by the current state of sexual politics in the Russian Federation, and for the next generation of scholars of queer Russia, "Western" and Russian, or from other post-Soviet republics, whose curiosity will take them beyond my interests in the chapters that follow.

The questions I discuss in this book relate to the nature of homophobia and what we understand by "homophobia in Russia." What do we Westerners mean by "homophobia"? Can our "homegrown" thinking about homophobia be easily transplanted to the Russian case? What is knowable right now, given the state of research, about the origins of modern hostility to LGBT lives and love in Russia? What are the obstacles to finding out more? How should we read Russian queer archives? How did gay and lesbian experience in the late Soviet, "socialist" world differ from Western, capitalist, queer life? How did Russians respond to a visible lesbian and gay movement after the collapse of Communism in 1991, and after decades of queer "invisibility"? What role does historical memory play in the construction of LGBT citizenship, and what are the barriers facing queer Russians to recovering and reconstituting "their" past? The three parts of this book focus attention on these themes in the history and the contemporary politics of Russian homophobia.

My use of terms for identities and sexual/gender practices requires some comment. I have used "LGBT" and "queer" interchangeably as shorthand for the broad spectrum of practices and identities that deviate from normative heterosexuality. "Homophobia" is an uncomfortable umbrella term for fear of the queer subject: the term tends to obscure more specific forms of "Othering," whether it is hatred of lesbians, trans people, or more complexly queer sexual and gender dissidents. (In the Russian language, "LGBT" – *LGBT* – and "homophobia" – *gomofobiia* – have been widely adopted by friends and foes of queers.) The focus of this book is principally on gay men, and men who had sex with men, with some chapters referring as well to lesbians and women's same-sex relations. This focus reflects the concentration of my interest on state and expert persecution of queer subjects; it also partly reflects the relative weight of available source material. Nevertheless, there is new and important work on Russian lesbian lives emerging, and I rely upon it throughout the book. There is little material specifically addressing the "B" and "T" – bisexual and transgender – of LGBT in these essays. The reasons for this gap are conceptual and also reflect a lack of scholarship.

So far, queer theorists have said little to conceptualize "bisexuality" in Russian lives and love. Most historians and scholars of literature and culture, myself included, have leapt straight to "gay" or "lesbian" as labels for the same-sex relations they observe in Russia's past and present. It is undeniable that this reflex distorts realities: many of the "homosexual" lives discussed by scholars of Russia also present a "heterosexual" element. Before the 1917 Revolution, Sophia Parnok, one of Russia's greatest "lesbian" poets, was married to a man for two years, going on to have far longer relationships with women later in life.[88] In the same way, heterosexual marriage in Soviet times was a rite of passage for many of the "homosexual" men and women discussed in this book. In a world where LGBT ways of living were made invisible, many if not most queerly loving or feeling people intuited their desires through the prism of heterosexuality: it was the only script of love available. Chapter 2 shows that men who had sex together in 1950s Leningrad Province did so while conducting simultaneous straight relationships; and they often used these relationships with women not only to conceal same-sex loves, but also to facilitate them. They used "quiet accommodationism" – the willingness of "straight" bystanders to look the other way when queer affairs happened in their midst – to tap male privilege, and exploit women as shields from suspicion, and also as "bait" for other men. Were these men "bisexual" in the contemporary Western meaning? Perhaps: but historical thinking looks beyond simple similarities to ask how lives in the past unsettle those assumptions.

In her sensitive work on Soviet and post-Soviet lesbian lives, Francesca Stella has shown how for many lesbians, same-sex love figured in a life-course that routinely included heterosexual episodes. In other words, the women she interviewed had both "straight" and "lesbian" careers, sometimes simultaneously.[89] Should they be re-labeled "bisexuals"? A few accept that term, but many "now" consider themselves homosexually oriented, albeit in a hostile social situation. Their experience, and that of male "bisexuals" in one major Ukrainian survey, has little room for "bisexuality" as a liberating "portal" between monosexualities (heterosexuality or homosexuality), conceived by Western bi-theorists.[90] Stella's subjects act and think strategically with their identities, putting more value "on managing one's identity appropriately across different social contexts, which is associated with rules of propriety and risk-assessment, rather than on being 'out'."[91] For Stella, this necessitates a rethinking of the "closet" in the Western sense of a burden of inauthenticity and oppression for same-sex loving people; the closet, in the lives of her subjects, becomes a place of safety and possibility. The everyday hostility to homosexual relations compels these Russian "lesbians" to navigate between poles of an outwardly heterosexual public life and a "lesbian" private or semi-private sphere. The scope for unfettered, liberating, post-homophobic "bisexuality" in the lives discussed by Stella is strikingly absent. Examples such as these suggest that conceptualizing "bisexuality" in Russia past and present requires more research, and simplistic labeling that draws upon contemporary Western models would be misleading. For these reasons, I have generally avoided speaking of a familiar "bisexuality" in the lives of the individuals discussed here – but like Stella, I have pointed out when straight and gay life courses have coincided in the same biography.

Identifying "transgender" lives in the Russian past is another project fraught with complexities and contradictions. From the beginning, as a researcher of Russian queer history, I have sought to point out the challenges for historians in finding transgender subjects in history. In modern Russia (and beyond), doctors and police often labeled "trans-" personalities as "homosexual," and "trans-" fates were determined by attitudes toward homosexuality, and toward gender as part of a "natural order."[92] In this book, I mention some forms of gender-crossing and the ways that Soviet citizens understood it: in Stalin's Gulag (Chapter 1), and in everyday speech in 1950s provincial and metropolitan life (Chapters 2, 3, and 4). Whether these examples and others should be claimed for a Russian transgender history is a question for queer theorists and future researchers. Research on the transgender subject in Russia is still emerging, with most work discussing contemporary questions of psychology and language.[93] This book probes the wider social and cultural frame of homophobic attitudes within which transgender lives were lived; more concentrated thinking on the trans subject in the history of Russia is undoubtedly needed.

*　　*　　*

This book is divided into three parts, and while each essay can be read separately, they are in roughly chronological order. *Part I: Homophobia in*

Russia after 1945 examines three sites of homophobic violence, both physical and psychological, and some responses from same-sex loving men. Research to chart the history of experiences of homophobia in Soviet Russia after Stalin's enactment of his law against male homosexuality has hardly started. These essays shine a light on social worlds where male homosexuality coexisted with the heterosexual majority in an uneasy, and sometimes violently hostile, relationship. Chapter 1 deals with the Gulag, Stalin's forced-labor camp system, through which millions passed over its quarter-century history from 1930, as a "homogenic" site of sexual violence, queer visibility, and fateful labeling. Both male and female queer relations are examined. After 1953, with the reform of the Gulag and de-Stalinization more generally, Soviet "enlightened bureaucrats" worried about the challenge of releasing Gulag inmates into "free" society, and the problem of stabilizing the sex/gender order. In Chapter 2, I present a microhistory of the worlds of same-sex loving men in 1950s semi-rural Russia, illuminating the popular mistrust of homosexuality, but also the degree to which commonplace attitudes accommodated the gender and sexual outcast. Violence was used by homophobes seeking to keep the "homosexual" at bay, but tragically, misogynist violence could also be used by "homosexuals" themselves in their search for self-realization. The final chapter of this section examines a rare artifact in Russia's queer archives – the journal of a victim of Stalin's anti-sodomy law. Soviet popular singer Vadim Kozin's 1955–6 diary reveals the impact of the homophobia surrounding him, and presents a remarkable window on how a "Soviet man" constructed a sense of himself as a homosexual subject. Taken together, these essays argue that the Stalinist anti-sodomy law of 1933–4 launched the modernization of the Soviet homosexual, stigmatizing queer men as political outcasts, and as psychologically "pathological" types.

Part II: Queer Visibility and "Traditional Sexual Relations" looks at the rise of a visible LGBT world in late Soviet and later post-communist Russian society. Chapter 4 charts the history of the gay and lesbian community of Moscow, capital of the Soviet Union and a magnet for queer Soviet citizens because of its expanding opportunities underneath the surface of drab conformity and a rigid ideological carapace. This overview shows how European socialist-world lesbian and gay experience had a distinctive chronology and character quite different from the post-war rise of queer communities in capitalist Western Europe. Chapter 5 analyzes an archive of post-communist Russian gay male erotica, and looks at the opportunities gay men seized in the 1990s to express desire explicitly and publicly, effectively for the first time in Russian history, in the midst of a post-Soviet "sexual revolution." Russian gay men's tastes harnessed national themes and settings, fashioning a distinctive pornographic style in a globalizing culture. This erotica wrestled with both internalized homophobia and society's hostility to queers. In Chapter 6, we examine some landmark responses to increasing LGBT visibility at the turn of the twenty-first century. In President Putin's first term, conservative politicians, alarmed by the "sexual revolution" of the 1990s, debated its impact, including the increased visibility of LGBT Russians. A farcical 2002 debate on the re-criminalization of male homosexuality failed in that aim, but ultimately generated new political rhetoric about the national sexual character. The debate ignored problems with Russian masculinity, and blamed the discontents of the "sexual revolution" on women, male homosexuals, and youth. In this language, as politicians turned to "enlightened" experts for advice, Russian sex was reinvented as innocently "traditional," heterosexual – and patriarchal. This section argues that LGBT freedom and visibility in Russia's late twentieth century were the hard-won gains of countless personal and political struggles, against internalized homophobia, and fears of sexual difference expressed by family and society. The queer voices that emerged in the late Soviet period were not foreign imports, but "Made in the USSR," the product of the creativity and imagination of Soviet LGBT people. Visibility and freedom engendered a backlash, however, as political and "expert" opportunists tried to reinvent Russian "traditional sexual relations" with a new ideology of heteronormativity and political homophobia.

Part III: Writing and Remembering Russia's Queer Past investigates the problems of a "memoryless" LGBT movement in a cultural and political environment that resists the recognition of its history. My argument here is that without adequate historical research and creative and thoughtful memory work, the future of Russia's LGBT citizens will be weakened. The troubling obstacles to documenting Stalinist and late-Soviet persecution of gay men are explored in Chapter 7. The inaccessibility of archival records and their mis-reading by homophobic historians are not merely technical problems for the historical discipline. These irritants have implications for the Russian LGBT movement's mobilization of its own community, and for the effectiveness of its "outward-facing" conversations with allies in Russia's democratic opposition. Chapter 8 turns to examine amnesia in biography as written in Russia today. Life histories of queer men composed by apparent "heterosexuals" in an unsympathetic culture of sex-denying biographical writing stifle LGBT memory. Chapter 9 returns to singer and Gulag prisoner Vadim Kozin, to consider the divergent ways that LGBT memory works in the West and in Russia. Kozin's commemoration in Russia is strikingly different from that of "gay icons" in Europe. The geopolitics of LGBT rights and queer memory are not straightforward, but betray our assumptions about "history" and "progress" embedded in our cultures and our thinking. When it comes to Russia, we need to examine those assumptions more critically. Building queer cultures and reconstructing a queer past will follow unique paths in the countries of the former Soviet Union, but I am hopeful that the region's diversity and its peoples' creativity will spark new opportunities for queer visibility and freedom.

PART I

Homophobia in Russia after 1945

The three chapters of Part I shine a light on some of the roots of mid-twentieth-century Soviet Russia's official and popular homophobia. The post-war years in Soviet Russia were a time of exhaustion and reconstruction. They were also years of heightened social turbulence – and gender disruptions played their part. Wartime losses created a palpable gender imbalance in society, only fractionally redressed by the release of mostly male Gulag prisoners after Stalin's death in 1953. The social disruption caused by Gulag returnees had a sexual aspect: same-sex assaults and relationships had been highly visible in Stalin's labor camps, and authorities worried about how to protect Soviet heterosexuality, apparently in crisis. (We know far less about same-sex relations in the huge Soviet military.) In the aftermath of war, the Soviet regime disingenuously encouraged fleeting, casual heterosexual relations by offering state support for single mothers for the first time, as one means of replenishing the population. After Stalin's death in 1953, new policies turned to concentrate on the "homosexual" Other, giving fresh impetus to official and popular homophobia.

The liberalization of the post-Stalin "Thaw" era of the 1950s–60s was paradoxically a time of sharpening homophobia. Modernization meant a renewal and updating, in legal, medical, and criminological guise, of hostility toward queer sexualities. New forms of surveillance, less politicized than in Stalin's time, but more technocratic, brought larger numbers of queer men and some women under the state's gaze.

In wider society, where information about all sexualities was extremely scarce thanks to censorship and totalitarian controls over books, libraries, and the press, ignorance and indifference meant some queers could exploit ignorance and relative invisibility to carve out spaces of freedom. They were helped by a strong and growing popular sense of entitlement to a private life that was less intrusively policed by the state and its agents. "Visible" queers, whether "outed" by their reputations or by their own gender performance, suffered moral condemnation and vituperation. Yet even these most obvious of queer men could retreat to an interior world – as in the case of the singer and diarist Vadim Kozin – and imagine a life without homophobia.

1

Forging Gulag Sexualities:

Penal Homosexuality and the Reform of the Gulag after Stalin

In May 2013, in the days after the Vladislav Tornovoi murder, the victim's classmates struggled to make sense of the "homophobic" motive apparently explaining the young electrician's death. They remembered Tornovoi as a "normal guy" who fell hopelessly in love with girls and went to extravagant lengths to declare his feelings. Some speculated that the ex-convict Anton Smolin killed him for making a joke about Smolin's supposed "homosexual experience" behind bars.[1] All sides took it for granted that "homosexual experience" and prison went together in these popular explanations.[2] The trope of prison homosexuality is common enough in Russia to serve as a scenario for provocations; in 2009 a prisoner, apparently set up by the jail's authorities, assaulted the convicted oligarch Mikhail Khodorkovsky, accusing him of making sexual advances. A court case against Khodorkovsky collapsed, but not before adding homosexuality to the long list of his supposed sins.[3] Despite the widespread assumptions about homosex and confinement, very little is known about same-sex relations inside Russia's contemporary prison system – or its penal facilities in the past. The Stalin-era Gulag camps, established in 1930 and dismantled in the 1950s, laid the foundations for modern Russia's prison system. The history of homosexuality in Soviet and Russian places of confinement must consider the social world of Stalin's Gulag and the place of homosexuality in that world. Given the fact that at least 11.8 million people passed through the Gulag's labor camps and colonies between 1930 and 1953, a history of Soviet and Russian homophobia can only be told once Gulag homosexuality is better understood.[4]

While Russian prison writing and scholarship about the Gulag say relatively little about sex in Soviet places of confinement, there is some description of *heterosexual* relations in various important landmarks of this literature. This discussion has typically been indirect, relegating sexuality to an adjunct of brief accounts focused on "women and children" in Soviet confinement.[5] Since the "archival revolution" in histories of the Soviet Union, using the Soviet state's official documentation made available after 1991, some respected Russian studies of the Gulag avoid the subject or treat it in a voyeuristic and misogynist fashion.[6] This work, produced in the past quarter-century, still avoids analysis of sexuality from perspectives informed by feminism, queer theory, or history of sexualities studies. Despite the changes in regimes and academic toolkits, our historiographical practices, derived from Western Cold-War "sovietology" and the prudery of late-Soviet ideology, remain resistant to thinking critically and historically about the organization of sex and gender as social systems. A welcome departure is found in the work of Wilson Bell. He has trawled the official documentation available for the camps of Western Siberia and compared it with what is known from memoir literature and previous descriptive histories.[7] His is the most serious scholarly attempt to use the official archives of the Gulag administration to analyze the Gulag's heterosexual life, but other archive-based scholars have also begun to discuss the issue.[8] From Bell's reading of local official records, it becomes clear that Gulag directors and commandants considered sexual activity disruptive to the labor-camp regime and economy, and they took decisions to minimize that disruption. Yet "the regime was remarkably ambivalent about sexual relations in the camp system" and this attitude reflected the widespread confusion felt by authorities dealing with sex and reproduction in free Soviet society.[9] Bell also points to the value of comparative perspectives. The gender- and queer-informed analysis of the Nazi concentration camps' gender and sexual order, as studied by Jane Caplan and Anna Hájková, offers productive and sensitive ways of analyzing power relations and prisoner autonomy in this realm.[10]

If heterosexuality has only just emerged from the shadows in Gulag studies, there has been little sustained and systematic work on same-sex relations in the Soviet camps. Vladimir Kozlovskii's 1986 lexicon of Soviet Russia's homosexual subculture, based on clandestine historical research in the USSR, and 1970s interviews with Soviet gay men, includes a substantial glossary of queer prison terminology and valuable commentary.[11] For female prisoner relations, the work of Olga Zhuk, also partly interview-based, has provided an important if problematic perspective.[12] I sketched a survey of sources on Russian and Soviet prison and Gulag homosexuality available to me in the late 1990s in my first book on Russian homosexuality.[13] Adi Kuntsman's recent articles on the memory of the Gulag queer in contemporary Russophone cultures argue that survivor-memoirists viewed Gulag homosexuality with near-universal "disgust," an emotion that contributes to homophobia in Russian-speaking communities in the present.[14] These diverse perspectives have helped to illuminate the place of homosexuality in the Soviet Gulag.

This chapter explores this question using new sources and approaches. From the archival revolution in the study of the Gulag, it is possible to examine what the authorities said and did with regard to homosexuality. Explicit references to homosexuality in the official archives of the Gulag are extremely rare. A significant taboo on overt discussion of same-sex relations appeared to operate during Stalin's rule, in most documents produced about the Gulag (and other Soviet institutions); this taboo is explored further in Chapter 7. Nevertheless, it is possible to read the official archives "against the grain" with a queer eye on issues such as the regulation of heterosexual sex and the wider motives of commandants and bureaucrats regarding the populations they governed.[15] Memoir and interview sources are also vital to explain the varied dimensions of same-sex relations in the camps, since they can reveal motives and illuminate questions of gender, violence, and consent in sexual interaction. In this chapter I use lesser-known or unpublished memoirs, and my own interviews of Gulag survivors and workers, overtly referring to homosexuality in confinement.[16] These texts are from "observers" of same-sex relations, not those who engaged in them. As Hájková has noted in her study of sexual barter in the Theresienstadt Ghetto, there are no first-person narratives from women who engaged in "shameful" behavior such as exchanges of sexual favors for food, accommodation, or security.[17] It is equally the case that we have virtually no sources documenting the voices of the "Gulag queer" – only sidelong glances at the homosexual as seen by others in society. (This absence of voices – and one important partial exception to it – is discussed in Chapter 3.) Furthermore, the memoir sources mention same-sex relations explicitly for various reasons, and they too must be read with a critical eye to discern motive and interpret the social and political context that allowed Gulag survivors to speak about a previously "shameful" topic.[18]

In this chapter, I first sketch the sexual order of the Gulag including the official worldview that shaped sexual morality in the camps, and then discuss how same-sex relations between men and between women fit into this worldview. The place of same-sex relations in what Bell calls the negotiation of power within the camp society is explored. The next section looks at the reform of the Gulag. Doctors and commandants began discussing homosexuality overtly in their behind-closed-doors conferences and official correspondence, once Stalin died in March 1953; reformists talking about the Gulag queer reveal their understandings of homosexuality, and the troubling threats it posed to heterosexuality, in the 1950s–60s, when the penal system of was partially modernized. I conclude with a brief discussion of the changes in prisoners' attitudes toward homosexuality: those of the "criminals" and those of the rehabilitated political prisoner "returnees" criticizing the Gulag and Stalinism in the 1960s–80s. Through these various lenses we can see an important source of Soviet attitudes towards male and female homosexuality, and the evolution of state homophobia after Stalin's death.

The sexual order of the Gulag

Stalin's Gulag was primarily a place of punishment. However, it was also an economic empire reliant on forced labor. In this secondary, but highly significant, purpose, it was closely tied to the early Five-Year Plans (the first of which was launched in 1929), both in objectives and in organization. The Gulag's "economic model" depended on presumed virtually "cost-free" labor requiring the barest of infrastructure. Prisoners dug canals and mines, built railways, and felled trees, all while colonizing remote "virgin" territories of the Soviet Union, for the socialist project. The "colonial" side of the Gulag as a project was decidedly a lower priority than either punishment or short-term financial profit, and indeed it was largely set aside during the Great Terror of 1937–8, and the Second World War as well. Yet penal colonization was the logical consequence of long-term policies that usually fixed released prisoners to their region of detention, creating mixed penal and free urban settlements like Vorkuta, Magadan, Ukhta, and Norilsk, "company towns" that live on to this day.[19]

This economic model suggests the principal cause for the Gulag administration's hostile view of sexuality in its domain. Heterosexual relations in the camps were generally seen as troublesome, despite a degree of ambivalence, by Gulag managers. Cost controls from the Gulag's economic model must have been a key driver of the rationale to suppress heterosexual sex. Planners assumed that prisoner labor was a very cheap input, with low maintenance costs, and that it was more mobile than civilian populations. Pregnancy and childbirth incurred "maintenance costs." In the mature Gulag, the camp's Sanitary Department (as its health service was called) had to provide antenatal and maternity rations, and care of infants, usually until they were dispatched to orphanages or, less often, relatives of the mother, at the age of two. These children were officially "free" citizens entitled to at least nominal welfare provision. Abortion, officially banned from 1936 to 1955, was in theory illegal even for female prisoners, although such was the pressure of the camps' economic model that "abortion clinics" operated sporadically behind barbed wire even while the abortion ban was in place. At any given moment from the late 1930s, there were tens of thousands of women prisoners held in various stages of maternity regimes, burdening manager-commandants with additional costs.[20] Women prisoners' productivity and mobility were thus reduced, and so Gulag production managers believed that preventing heterosexual relations and pregnancy made economic sense.

The Gulag's gender-imbalanced demography made sexual desire a disruptive force, and difficult to suppress. The prisoner population was overwhelmingly male, and even in the Second World War there was always a significant predominance of men. The population was also dominated by younger and potentially more sexually active men between eighteen and forty years old, significantly younger than the Soviet population at large.[21] Naturally, undernourishment, malnutrition, and outright starvation diminished sexual appetite and reportedly robbed many female prisoners of their physical sex characteristics. Nevertheless, it appears that there were sufficient numbers of well-fed guards and "free" staff, plus privileged prisoners earning or getting better rations, to produce a stratified labor-camp society in which some men competed, often violently, for the limited number of women seen as "available." In this order, sexual activity was sufficiently prevalent to require the establishment and maintenance of maternity wards, nurseries, and "venereal disease" isolation camps.[22]

These material, economic, and demographic considerations go some way to explain the severity of moral policing in the Gulag, and its application to prisoners and to those free persons (guards, commandants, local residents) who entered into relations with them. Bell, and many memoirists, note the widespread surveillance via informers and guards to prevent liaisons between the sexes; the harsh penalties including spells in the punishment cells and extended sentences for conducting sexual and romantic relations (so-called *sozhitel'stvo* or "cohabitation"); the spatial organization of the camps to prevent mixing of the sexes; and the formal division of the camps from 1947 to 1948 into discrete men's and women's zones, with fewer opportunities for easy traffic between the sexes. The inhumanity of the maternity and especially the nursing regime might also be interpreted as an aspect of this moral policing: the entire birth-and-nursing cycle was treated with disdain despite the improved rations and reduced labor quotas. The care provided for new born infants was often grossly negligent and death rates were high.[23] Any offspring surviving the Gulag maternity system were removed from their mothers, who might never see them again.

Economics alone does not explain fully why Gulag administrators conceived of this severe moral system. From the time of the 1917 Revolution, Soviet ideologues and fellow-travelling experts had long been determined to control sexuality as an aspect of personal life with social consequences. The full range of sexual regulation and norms in "free" Stalinist society scarcely allowed for the free enjoyment of romantic love, especially if it interfered with productive labor.[24] If marital relations and heteronormative family life were more loudly celebrated in Stalinist ideology from the mid-1930s, these "benefits" were for the toiling worker, not for inmates of the Gulag, which was a zone of distinct lack of privilege.[25] Related to this principle of zones of privilege and penalty was the discourse of the redemption (*perekovka*, reforging) of the Gulag prisoner. The Gulag regime's deprivation of access to a family life, and the prospect of returning one day to one's family, through control over correspondence and visiting rights, was conceived as a spur to hard work and self-discipline.

Heterosexual family ties were woven into the fabric of incentives dangled before prisoners to motivate their "correction."[26] In the early Gulag, some remote camp complexes such as the Dalstroi mining trust in the Kolyma River basin operated "colonist" programs for the settlement of released prisoners, who could bring their wives and children to the region and establish households.[27] Eduard Berzin, the first secret police commandant of Dalstroi, was alert to the problems of "family-lessness" (*bessemeinost'*) in his "colony," like legions of governors of Siberia in centuries past.[28] Before Berzin's 1938 arrest and execution in the Terror, he envisioned various measures to correct "family-lessness" in his domain. However, Stalin rebuffed Berzin's proposals; and in 1939, the dictator recorded his intention that Kolyma remained cut off from the "mainland" and a place of special detention.[29] This intervention did much to seal Kolyma's fate as a particularly "family-less" Gulag outpost. If, throughout the Gulag's diverse and scattered territories, released prisoners were (in theory) usually permitted to enter into heterosexual and family relations with free local residents, the opportunities for doing so were slim in predominantly male settlements. Ex-prisoners were administrative exiles from the "mainland" of the USSR, effectively "forced" colonists in the region of their camps – which grew into towns with diverse populations in the 1940s and 1950s. Nevertheless, gender imbalance and "family-lessness" was a fixed feature of the Gulag "company town" well into the 1960s.[30]

Ancestors of the "Gulag queer"

In this context, what was the official and unofficial attitude toward same-sex sexuality in the camps? How did homosexuality figure in the Soviet prison world? Early Soviet Russian legislation had decriminalized male homosexuality in 1922, as part of a broader "sexual revolution" that overhauled old regime regulation. However, Bolshevik suspicion of pleasure for its own sake, and determination to mobilize private life, dictated that Soviet homosexuals had little chance to advocate the kind of social emancipation seen in Weimar Germany.[31] In 1933–4, in a process described in Chapter 7, Stalin and the secret police recriminalized male homosexuality (*muzhelozhstvo*, i.e. "sodomy"; lesbianism was never considered a threat). Both social order and national security concerns motivated this change, which was greeted enthusiastically by members of the Politburo.[32] The numbers arrested under the new law were significant, but we do not know their full extent because the relevant archives remain inaccessible, and other problems (examined in Chapter 7) stand in the way of a clear counting of these victims of Stalinist homophobia.

Even if we could put a number on the men convicted under the anti-homosexual law, that statistic would not tell us much about the prevalence of same-sex relations in the overwhelmingly male Gulag. The "Gulag queer" was not only, or perhaps even mainly, a victim of the anti-homosexual law of 1934. Homosexual sex, of course, existed in Russian and Soviet places of confinement centuries before the Gulag was officially established in 1930. The expanding Gulag of the 1930s, with its huge cohorts of recidivist criminals and an inherited infrastructure of earlier penal institutions, also inherited the multifarious criminal subculture of Tsarist prisons, labor colonies, and exile. That subculture was marked by a structured hierarchy around violent and consensual homosexual relations; the evolution over centuries of the subculture's homosexual features is uncharted. The novelist

Fedor Dostoevsky alluded to the existence of male prostitution, and homosexual desire, among his fellow inmates in Omsk, in his prison autobiography *Memoirs of the House of the Dead*, published in 1861–2.[33] Various experts and memoirists diffidently noted male prostitution and coercive relations between men in late-nineteenth-century exile on Sakhalin, a place of particular degradation that attracted growing national and international public concern in the late Imperial era.[34]

An authoritative Soviet criminologist, Mikhail N. Gernet, sketched the dimensions of sexual life in Russian prison as he found it in the early twentieth century, acknowledging that male and female homosexuality were widely visible behind bars.[35] He found prison to be homogenic: some criminals brought same-sex habits to jail, but most were corrupted "here, *in prison itself*," Gernet emphasized. Relations between men resembled both "marriage" and "prostitution" with newcomers encountering seduction and "promises of protection" on the one hand and "intimidation and plain assault ... under the eyes of the entire prison cell" on the other. "Passive pederasts" – the receptive partners in male intercourse – developed what Gernet found to be a particularly feminine psychology and conducted themselves like female street prostitutes in dress, manners, and speech. (Another criminologist found in his survey that the "passive pederast types" were usually younger than the adult "actives" who used them. Age- and gender-structured homosexual relations are examined in Chapter 2.)[36] A colloquial language to describe "unnatural intercourse" circulated in conversation, graffiti, and inscriptions in prison library books. Intellectual "political" prisoners surveyed by Gernet flatly refused to discuss sex in prison, perhaps an indication of how traumatized they were by what they experienced behind bars, and also a mark of their conformity to the prudish conventions of their class. What were the effects on so-called "criminals" of this subculture? Experts said little, except to hint that self-harm was frequently encountered among young prisoners (suffering from "serious neurasthenia, hysteria, hystero-epilepsy, and traumatic neuroses") and venereal diseases were widespread. They remained silent about homosexual assaults as a cause, but clearly they figured among the hazards of prison life.[37]

Lesbian relations also evolved in the Gulag from a prison subculture already visible in tsarist and early Soviet women's prisons. The sexual life of these prisons mirrored in its gendered roles and romantic language the social patterns of the world of women-loving women in free society.[38] In the 1920s, Gernet briefly noted the homosexuality between women prisoners prevailed in confinement thanks to the "unnatural" single-sex regime of the prison. Citing an interview with one party in a relationship between a pair of prisoners in a Moscow jail, he described their courtship:

According to our correspondent, these women [the butch partners] "have all the tricks of men: their gait, their hairstyles, they smoke and wear men's Russian shirts [*rubashki-kosovorotki*] secured with a belt." The courtship began with notes swearing to a mad eternal love, and begging her not to give herself to anyone else. In the notes she said "she would kiss her little mouth and eyes, and wanted to kiss her everywhere."[39]

The object of these notes told the criminologist,

I thought she was nice, she came to me when I was alone, but I was afraid to say hello: she was very direct with me in a mad and powerful way. She grabbed me on the bed and began to kiss my breasts, legs, hands, so unexpectedly that I was lost for words.

During the 1920s, many Soviet criminologists and psychiatrists wrote up case histories of women criminals whose lesbian loves were extraordinary aspects of their "deviant" psychology.[40]

The evolution of the prison subculture of same-sex relations in tsarist and then Soviet Russia is very difficult to trace: continuity and change in wider prisoner subculture is little discussed in our historiographies of the camps; instead, fragmented reminiscences by intelligentsia prisoners present a limited and "timeless" anthropology of Gulag homosexuality.[41] Observers of various prison systems have traditionally viewed incarcerated homosexuality as an eternal and "natural" phenomenon that can have no history. More sophisticated work on this aspect of prison studies reveals the importance of change over time, whether understood in the shifting prison systems themselves, in wider societal conceptions of sexualities, or in the changing nature of the prisoner demographic.[42] There is, in other words, a history to prison homosexualities.

The Gulag's adoption in the 1930s of an industrial-scale, continent-spanning economic-penal model was one of those major shifts that transformed penal homosexual practices. This expansion, in its economic and regulatory practices, amplified the "homogenic" effects of imprisonment. In theory, queer relations did not disrupt the Gulag economic model as drastically as heterosexual relations did. They did not lead to pregnancy, and they quelled sexual impulses without resulting in increased support costs. As we shall see, the authorities ignored or even indulged queer relations in many camps. Queer relations appeared to preserve order and in some cases even improve labor productivity. One caveat must be noted: sexually transmitted infections (STIs) were spread by queer contacts and they were undoubtedly harder to eradicate than heterosexually induced infections, not only because of the unreliability of available treatments in the USSR in the mid-twentieth century. The unspeakability of queerly induced infections made them difficult to prevent, trace, and treat. The habit of confining prisoners with STIs to special compounds took them off the labor balance and contributed to the camps' economic burdens.[43] It is nevertheless worth sketching the broad outlines of what is known about the Gulag queer, even if our picture is "flattened" by an apparent timelessness.

Queer in Stalin's Gulag

The most visible queers in the camps were those viewed as "criminals," both male and female, who paraded their relations whenever the authorities were sufficiently indulgent of "socially friendly" prisoners. The "socially friendly" were inmates from the working class, usually so-called "common criminals" – thieves, robbers, rapists, murderers. In Soviet penal ideology, the "socially friendly" were presumed to be sympathetic to Soviet values and amenable to reforging. This ideology distinguished them from the "socially alien," so-called "politicals" whom the authorities deemed to be hostile to the regime. The "socially friendly" population's freedom to parade even an "undesirable" behavior like homosexuality was at least in part licensed by the general indulgence of "criminals" as retrievable human capital.

Observers of male homosexuality in the camps sometimes noted its ubiquity; sex between men was "more frequent than lesbianism among women" in the view of Efrosiniia Kersnovskaia, a keen observer of life in the huge and remote Norilsk camp complex in the 1940s.[44] The paramedic Aleksandr Yashenkov commented that even before the 1948 separation of the sexes in Vorkuta (another remote northern complex), "there was plenty of sexual perversion in our men's camp, but after the women left homosexualism began to flourish even more."[45] Romanian doctor Aleksandr Tsetsulesku confirmed the prevalence of male homosexual relations in Vorkuta in 1951–2, explaining that the camp he was confined to had only men; he knew of homosexual rapes resulting in injuries he treated, as well as the resort to bestiality by some male prisoners.[46]

Male homosexual relations were not only ubiquitous but highly visible, and registered in a rich code of symbols: nicknames, subcultural terms, and visual signs. These languages resembled those current in the worlds of male and female prostitution in "free" urban Russia of the late Imperial and early Soviet decades; they also owed something to the gendered wordplay of the male homosexual subculture.[47] In a 1959 sketch about Gulag sexuality, Varlam Shalamov said that most male criminals were "pederasts" (he meant the "active" partners in same-sex acts) who sought sex with a class of men who openly took women's names:

> Speaking about women in the criminal world, it's impossible to ignore an entire army of those "Zoikas," "Mankas," and "Dashkas" and other beings of the male sex christened with women's names. It is noteworthy that the bearers of these female names answered to them in the most normal fashion, seeing nothing shameful or insulting in them.[48]

They probably also used feminine grammatical forms of speech.[49] Kersnovskaia too said that "any pretty young man" was in danger of "becoming a prostitute unable to turn anyone away under pain of death," but she imagined that these men were only ever victims of violence and coerced into the role.[50] Another

Gulag survivor recalled that such relations might be consensual and cherished. Yuri Fidelgolts quoted a criminal's petition to the authorities in Vanino Port transit camp in 1950: "And finally in recognition of my cooperation I ask that you permit my wife [*zhena*], the lad Zinka (that is my pet name for him) to remain with me. His surname is Evstratov. Without him I will grow thin and pale."[51] The language of degradation, widely used in the criminal subculture, had many labels for partners in same-sex acts: "*pederast*" and its innumerable derivatives ("*pidar*," "*pedik*"); "*petukh*," meaning "cockerel" and denoting the "passive" partner in male intercourse; "*kobel*" ("male dog," for the aggressive butch woman), and "*kovyrialka*," the "passive" partners of butch lesbians.[52]

The criminal subculture subdued and terrorized the numerically smaller proportion of inmates who were "political" and therefore "socially alien" offenders, and guards encouraged this hegemony of the "socially friendly" prisoners. Although evidence is scarce, it seems likely that teenaged boys, and the more slightly built men among the "politicals," were routinely threatened with rape and sexual humiliation by "criminal" inmates; there was doubtless a class-enmity, a remnant of the anti-hierarchical violence of revolution, in this menace.[53] The April 1930 Shanin Commission that inspected the Solovki Camp of Special Designation (the original Gulag camp on which all later ones were modeled) noted that teenaged boy prisoners were poorly supervised and that adult abuse of them "as passive pederasts flourishes."[54] Yuri Chirkov, a fourteen-year-old middle-class schoolboy arrested in 1935 as a plotter against Stalin, survived the Solovki camps of the 1930s in part thanks to adult "politicals" who protected him from likely sexual humiliation at the hands of criminal inmates.[55] Janusz Bardach devotes the signature episode of his Gulag memoir to the horrific spectacle, in 1941 or 1942, of a young male prisoner's rape in a Kolyma camp bathhouse: "For the first time I realized how vulnerable I was – only twenty-two, alone, and still too weak [from starvation] to resist an assault."[56] Official inspectors reported rape and sexual abuse of younger male prisoners extremely rarely, and cautiously. An inspector's 1939 report of a camp in the Krasnoiarsk region noted that "homosexuality is widespread among juveniles" and seven of these were being prosecuted for "sexual coercion, rape of prisoners . . ."[57] A 1948 prosecutor's summary of "unsatisfactory conditions" across the Gulag camp system, written for the Soviet Union's top prosecutor, hinted at widespread homosexual abuses ("sexual depravity with minors and youth"). He emphasized that such disorder was rife in camps in every region of the USSR.[58]

A culture of women's homosexuality developed in Stalin-era labor camps that was more prolific, and more variable, than in earlier tsarist and Soviet prisons. The Gulag was "homogenic" for women, perhaps even more than for male prisoners. Isaak Filshtinsky, a prisoner from 1949 to 1955 in Kargopol's timber camps, expressed this view in an unusually sympathetic portrait of lesbians with whom he worked. "Naturally, there were some

among them [the "camp lesbians"] who brought their sexual pathology
with them from freedom, but for the majority it was the camp that became
a school of same-sex love for them, something they became accustomed to
under the guidance of experienced adepts."[59] If Gulag memoirists are to be
trusted, same-sex relations among the "criminal" women were not always as
violent as those of the criminal men. Nevertheless, women's relations were
usually gendered, with a dominant, older, and "masculinized" partner
("*kobel*" or "butch" in prison slang) allied with a submissive "feminine"
partner ("*kovyrialka*" or femme), usually younger.[60] As in pre-Gulag prisons,
the butch characteristically wore cropped hair and manly garb; tattooing
seems to have become more prevalent among women criminals in the
1930s–40s.[61] The femme projected a more conventional appearance with
long hair, kerchiefs, and skirts. Violence was not totally excluded: some
memoirists recall younger women being sexually assaulted and thereby
"claimed" by tougher older women. In a vivid chapter on Gulag sexual life,
Konstantin Gursky, a prisoner in the Ukhta camp network in the 1930s–40s,
described tough "authoritative" criminal lesbians, violent and swaggering,
who exploited "young girls who suffered from disastrous love-affairs in
freedom, or unrequited love, or who simply hadn't had the good fortune to
receive their first kiss from a beloved boyfriend." The butch "husbands"
kept a sharp eye out for male suitors attracted to the younger femmes, and
such men were attacked with knives and fists.[62] Maria Kono, a young
university lecturer arrested in Kishinev in 1948, arrived in prison and "an
unheard-of, terrifying, monstrous life began": her cellmates were "from
every layer of criminal society" and their swearing and prison songs baffled
and appalled her. One cellmate, a young prostitute, "felt sympathy and pity
for me, expressing it in indecent caresses." Kono "tried by every means
possible to escape from the prostitute's intimate attentions," clambering up
to the top bunk to put some distance between herself and this figure of
disgust. To Kono's relief, her young suitor was soon removed from the cell,
and she escaped a sexual assault.[63] Another educated woman, arrested in
Leningrad in 1938, and subjected to lesbian advances from a cellmate,
declared a hunger strike until she was moved to a different cell.[64]

Authorities in the camps apparently indulged the solidarity of butch–
femme couples frequently enough. Butches refused to be separated from
their "wives" in the ordinary course of prisoner re-deployments between
camps; these pairs raised havoc when transport was mooted.[65] Some
memoirists who observed lesbian relations in the camps noted their social
organization extended beyond the butch–femme couple to whole "family
barracks" or work brigades of lesbians together.[66] In the 1940s, in the
timber-felling and agricultural subdivisions of Elgen (in Kolyma), women
reportedly shared "family barracks" in butch–femme pairs: the butch went
out to work and the femme stayed behind cleaning, preparing meals that
they brought to their working partners. Attempts by one commandant to
break up the pairs by shaving the heads of the butches were met with loud

defiance.[67] At Kargopol in the early 1950s, Filshtinsky described working with an all-female brigade of prisoners in a sawmill. Their brigade-leader allocated the heaviest work to the "butches" and the lighter work to their "wives," and the work "went just as well as if they were men."[68] The authorities appear to have tolerated these queer collectivities because they kept order and assured a stable level of productivity. They also potentially prevented pregnancies and saved costs associated with maternity.

Class determined the experience of the Gulag queer as forcefully as did gender. Criminals – both hardened recidivists and ordinary worker/peasant offenders – accounted for the majority of Gulag inmates, although the ratio between "political" and "criminal" remains difficult to define and shifted constantly. Perceptions of "political" versus "criminal" status seem to have mattered as much to the everyday existence of the prisoner than any official designation.[69] If queer relations among perceived criminals were flagrant and apparently ubiquitous, there were also homosexually inclined men and women among the educated intelligentsia and technical specialists condemned to the Gulag, mostly "political" offenders. Yet, as Kuntsman has explained, the reluctance to speak openly about sexuality in Russia's educated classes means that we know considerably less about their experience of queer relations in prison.[70]

Indications are that Stalin's anti-sodomy law hit city-dwelling educated men comparatively hard.[71] Leonid Timofeevich Titov, a pediatrician at Solovki in the 1930s (and one of the adolescent Yuri Chirkov's protectors), was reportedly arrested for homosexual offenses while already a prisoner; along with "a whole company of others," he received an additional five-year sentence, according to a prisoner-nurse interviewed in Moscow in 1991.[72] This nurse said she was "dumbfounded" that a doctor could be accused of such activity. The sardonic chronicler of the Gulag's sex life Konstantin Gursky observed that "for some reason," many intellectuals were to be found among the camps' homosexuals – "actors, artists, poets ..." He knew of a violinist and a bookkeeper, caught *in flagrante* in a barracks closet in 1935 in the remote Vaigach camp.[73] A freely hired doctor in another camp remembered how one of her paramedics, a "political," was thrown into the punishment cell for compelling a younger man to have sex with him, in the early 1940s. He had been a college lecturer, someone with an "intelligent appearance ... [c]lever, educated." She could not believe he was guilty until "the complaint [against him] proved to be correct."[74] Educated male prisoners who were not convicts under Stalin's anti-homosexual law had the opportunity, and good reason, to conceal homosexual appetites. They risked losing not only the respect of fellow "politicals," but the opportunity to work in a "soft job" in administration or support roles that their education might confer in the Gulag.

Intelligentsia women also hid their same-sex affairs. Since lesbianism was not illegal, there was no danger of criminal prosecution; but the same loss of class status loomed. Same-sex relations among educated women inmates were "of course hidden, veiled, ambivalent," and some engaged in lesbian affairs managed to conceal their intelligentsia origins from other educated prisoners.[75] Other educated women failed to hide their "fall" into lesbian relationships, and in the eyes of observers they lost their class status, becoming marked as "criminals." Aleksandr Zelenyi, a convict and paramedic in the Elgen region of Kolyma, observed:

And how strange it was that among the *kovyrialki* (femmes) there were people who did not belong to the criminal world. Some were *previously* girls of the intelligentsia. They tried to deny the truth by any means possible and hide it – but it was still true. I will not reveal their surnames.[76]

Zelenyi's discretion about their identities seems eloquent here. Evsei Lvov, a jurist who spent fifteen years in the Kolyma camps from 1938, on political charges, thought "[t]here were many women of the intelligentsia" among the lesbians he observed. He personally knew one former student of a higher education institute in Moscow "who never once wore a skirt in the entire eight years of her imprisonment"; thus he described her habitus as a "butch" Gulag lesbian "despite" her intelligentsia background.[77]

If the social frameworks for criminal queer relations in the Gulag revolved around pre-existing unwritten codes of the criminal subculture, the social setting that framed at least some intelligentsia queer life in the camps was probably the camp theater and the cultural-education department (KVCh). New scholarly work on Gulag theaters and cultural activities is emerging, but none discusses the queer dimensions of these institutions. Yet cultural facilities served as refuges for homosexuals in "free" Soviet society, and arguably, once they were deported to the Gulag, educated homosexuals probably sought to avoid hard general labor and use their talents in the theaters, orchestras, choruses, editorial offices, art studios, and classrooms of the penal world. A 1940 central Gulag decree explicitly banned sex offenders, including those with sodomy convictions, from working in the KVCh; this rule betrays a perception that homosexuals gravitated toward this specialized department of the camps.[78] And it was honored in the breach: popular singer Vadim Kozin, imprisoned in 1945 on sodomy charges (discussed in Chapter 3), served most of his sentence at the Magadan Musical-Dramatic Theater, one of the largest such theaters found behind barbed wire, where prisoners and "free" artists worked side by side. Elsewhere, the KVCh evolved into remarkably extensive networks of facilities presenting opera, operetta, popular and classical music concerts, ballet, choral recitals, films, and dramatic repertoire, publishing newspapers, designing posters, and running libraries; there was employment for a correspondingly wide range of artists, writers, and support and technical staff.[79] (See Figure 1.1.) The probable tendency of queers to seek refuge in the cultural-education department held advantages for camp authorities, by exploiting their talents, and concentrating potentially difficult inmates under the watchful eye of administrators, censors, and informants.

FIGURE 1.1 *Stalin Oblast Corrective Labor Colony prisoner show, 1948.*

Reformist projects and the Gulag queer

After Stalin's death, his successors used reformism to contest the leadership and also to cope with dangerous tensions threatening Communist Party rule. The Gulag as economic empire of the secret police was dismantled during the 1950s. Camps and colonies surrounded by barbed wire became towns run by civilian administrations, with mines, factories, and timber tracts reassigned to their respective economic ministries. Former penal settlements joined a normalized structure of government and administration. This transformation was another major shift in the nature of Soviet society and its penal complex that would have an impact on same-sex relations inside prison camps, and beyond. Of course, after a war in which the Soviet Union had lost 26 million citizens, demographic anxiety already stalked all official deliberations touching on sexuality and gender relations; Stalin's death brought into the open concerns about healthy heterosexuality that lay just beneath the surface in the last years of his life.

Over 2.5 million prisoners were directly affected by the re-fashioning of labor camps into normal towns. Reformers were not confident that the release of prisoners, more than three-quarters of them men, would result in an unproblematic flourishing of heterosexual relations. Indeed, the diagnosis of Gulag medical workers and camp directors in their secret conferences during the years of transition was bleak. The gender imbalance in the Gulag regions was unhealthy, leading to a crisis of heterosexuality, and measures needed to be taken to restore and bolster "normal" sexuality. During the 1950s, Party and state authorities juggled the impulse to release Gulag inmates with the potential, and increasingly actual, problems of absorbing them back into ordinary society. The evidence suggests that they barely managed these competing tasks. The emerging scholarship on the fate of the Gulag returnees reveals that Soviet citizens were often fearful and hostile toward former prisoners, and bureaucrats denied returnees access to work, housing, and other welfare benefits.[80] "Honest" returnees with no genuine criminal past were driven to desperation and not infrequently engaged in disorderly conduct and even anti-government outbursts; criminal recidivists went on a spree of theft, robbery, and rape, and "respectable" citizens complained of the threat to their property and lives. A particular concern was the influence of the Gulag criminal subculture on Soviet youth: tattoos, songs, leaflets, and verse rapidly spread a "cult of criminality" among teenagers and young adults. By the second half of the 1950s, the security police were fighting to rein in waves of hooliganism that they re-classified as "anti-Soviet agitation."

While new research on Gulag returnees says little about sexuality, we can infer that the peculiar and troubling sexual culture of the Gulag must have formed a significant focus of official and popular anxiety about the Gulag returnees. To keep the reform project on track, penal and police officials took certain decisions about the penal sexual culture and its queer elements in particular. We lack access to archives of the highest-level police discussions, but from the choices made, we can posit a determination to shore up heterosexual norms. These decisions took place within a wider context of official reforms touching on gender relations, family policy, and sexuality in a de-Stalinizing socialist society.[81] We do have access to the Gulag system's archives, and there we can read about the anxieties of penal-camp commandants, bureaucrats, and doctors as they contemplated the release of the Gulag queer into free society.

Their concern had several dimensions that add up to a critique of the Stalinist Gulag's de-facto indulgence of queer relations: its homogenic effect. Foremost in their speeches in these closed conferences was the threat of the spread of syphilis and other STIs within places of confinement, and thence to wider society as the camps became normal settlements. STIs in the camps arose "almost exclusively as a result of sodomy," which must be more actively suppressed, as the Gulag's medical director argued in March 1959.[82] In another report he observed, "It's understood that this work should be conducted by regime-operative departments and the surveillance service. But doctors do not have the moral right to stand to one side in the fight against venereal disease."[83] The Gulag medical chief called for the prosecution of prisoner "pederasts" with camp-wide publicity about the reason for their punishment "for engaging in pederasty, [because this] will have a particularly sobering effect, inasmuch as these perversions are not popular even among the criminal-bandit element."[84] Still others called for "educational [vospitatel'nye] measures" to combat homosexuality and thus the spread of syphilis in the camps, although "it must be admitted that it is extremely difficult to subject these prisoners to explanations and public discussions."[85] It appears that reforming doctors and political educators did attempt to conduct lectures and small-group "conversations" with prisoners about the harm caused by "sexual perversions" between men and between women. The Gulag Medical Department's work plan for the first quarter of 1956 included a study "of the reasons for the prevalence of sexual perversions among prisoners and the measures necessary to combat them," and a central medical inspector of the penal system continued to gather material on "sexual perversions" in 1957–8.[86] At least one general survey about lesbian relations in Gulag camps, a poll of the views of commandants, was conducted as a result (it is discussed below). The extraordinary impact of Stalin's death was a loosening of tongues and a classic Foucauldian incitement to discourse about queerness. Reformers argued that this "vice" had once been indulged, and would now be suppressed with new knowledge and overt discussion and shaming tactics to suppress homosexual activity.

Another concern was the role of sodomy in the persistent criminal subculture in the camps. This theme appeared relatively late in reformers' discussions, in 1958–9, and is probably related to the Soviet government's hardening stance against "professional" criminality and "parasitism."[87] Nevertheless, the content of these discussions revealed long-standing concerns, later to be confirmed in survivor-memoir accounts.[88] Conflicts between male prisoners arising from homosexual assaults, abuse, and relationships figured among the problems of keeping order. Some committed murder because of "being forced into sodomy."[89] Forfeits in prisoner card games were pinpointed by camp commandants as the underlying basis for many male homosexual assaults.[90] Police leaders and doctors implied that while Stalin lived, the security services inside the camps had slackened their attitude toward male "sexual perversion" and, implicitly, allowed it to flourish. Some camp medics complained that authorities in their camps still failed to punish male homosexuality with criminal sanctions when it was revealed by doctors.[91]

Khrushchev's government decided that the threat of male homosexuality would be handled by police methods, in the camps and in wider Soviet society. At a 1959 Moscow conference of penal camp directors, Colonel Kashintsev of the Ministry of Internal Affairs prison service observed that a recent secret directive had reaffirmed Stalin's anti-sodomy law, and the new directive was yielding the desired results:

If in 1957 the struggle against sodomy in camps and colonies was not accorded the necessary significance, and those guilty of this [crime] were only punished, in the majority of cases, as a discipline offense, now in

1958, especially after the publication of a special directive [*ukazanie*] of the RSFSR Ministry of Internal Affairs on the struggle with this type of crime, a considerable number of prisoners have been brought to responsibility for sodomy, i.e. 79 percent more than in 1957.[92]

The history of Soviet and later Russian homophobia of the subsequent six decades begins with this inelegant and tantalizing sentence. It is rare evidence that Khrushchev's reformers deliberately discussed Stalin's law against male homosexuality, and chose to keep it. (The archives of the Ministry of Internal Affairs are still not declassified for these years, and we had no knowledge of such a directive until this remark was recently spotted.)[93] The decision to retain the sodomy ban ran counter to the otherwise overwhelming trend of these years, when thousands of Stalin's legislative acts were reviewed by commissions of lawyers, police, and party authorities, and rescinded or relaxed.[94] Reformists deliberately decided to retain the penalty, and viewed the renewal of its enforcement – with many more convictions coming after the secret directive – as a necessary accompaniment to reform. In the new, 1960 RSFSR Criminal Code, voluntary sodomy was punished in article 121 with up to five years' imprisonment. The result was that from 1961 to 1981, 14,695 men were convicted of sodomy offences in the Russian Republic alone, and 22,163 in the Soviet Union as a whole.[95]

Reformists dealt with the Gulag queer in a gendered fashion. Administrators of women's camps found the whole question of same-sex relations among women prisoners disturbing, but as there was no law against lesbian sex, their "solutions" to this "problem" were varied and hesitant. Instead of seeing lesbian solidarity behind barbed wire as valuable, they began to identify its dangers. Reforming doctors and administrators complained about the disruption that jealousy and "scandalous scenes" predicated on "lesbian love" created in their institutions for women, and some suggested that lesbians be isolated in special medical camps.[96] Medical studies of the camp lesbian "for internal use only" were conducted. Some saw the wider implications of releasing "lesbians" into free society: they would "destroy families and corrupt young people."[97] Others proposed that the government should introduce a law banning sex between women.[98]

Ultimately, de-Stalinizing reformers did not heed such calls to criminalize the lesbian, but chose to treat her using psychiatry instead.[99] The authorities' patriarchal view, inherited from the Stalin era, continued to regard the lesbian as a moral problem that was easily "cured" through male intervention of one kind or another. Now deemed a psycho-neurological pathology, such women were prone to hysterics and neuroses, and needed isolation and special medical treatment. In the Gulag archives, there is a sizeable correspondence about the problems of penal camp lesbianism, an autobiography of a woman's experience of same-sex relations in the camps, and a study of the question conducted by the psychiatrist V. S. Krasusky in Rybinsk in the mid-1950s and published "for internal use" only in 1958.[100]

Krasusky's investigation of prisoner lesbianism was based on his own observations in Sheksninskoe labor camp (Vologda Province) plus a countrywide survey of places of confinement conducted by the Gulag's Medical Department. The survey revealed that administrators reported extremely varied proportions of the population of women prisoners in their camps and colonies engaging in lesbian relations: from 5.3 percent in Karaganda corrective-labor camp to 18 percent in Siblag; particular subdivisions of these camps, with high recidivist criminal populations, were said to report as many as 60–80 percent engagement in same-sex affairs. Krasuskii cited fears among administrators that "perverted forms of same-sex cohabitation [were escaping] beyond the bounds of places of detention" and they threatened to destroy prisoners' families. He prescribed a cocktail of solutions: stricter measures to ban women from wearing men's clothes in camps; the isolation of recidivist criminal "butches" ("the so-called *kobly*") in special camps away from innocent first-timers; more conjugal visits (which reformers had already relaunched in 1954); doctors' conversations with "femmes" to explain the "amorality" and health risks of lesbian relations; the use of comrades' courts and other mutual surveillance mechanisms to deter same-sex cohabitation, and various forms of homophobic propaganda in camp newspapers, posters, and radio to mock and shame cohabiting women.[101] It is difficult to know how far these ideas were taken up, but an anonymous reader's positive and critical comments annotate the archival draft of this report. At least one other large-scale study of prisoner-lesbianism was conducted by civilian psychiatrists, starting in this era but not completed until 1965.[102] These papers point to official anxiety about the penal lesbian in the de-Stalinization era, and the search for mechanisms of control and cure. The continued lack of legislation against lesbianism, the concealed medical treatment of lesbians, and psychiatrists' belief that at least "passive" lesbians (the "feminine" partners) were curable subjects all point to a determination to return as many of these subjects firmly to heterosexuality and, if possible, maternity.

De-Stalinizing reform required discussion behind closed doors of previously ignored or suppressed problems before they became socially unmanageable. The transition from a penal economic model to civilian normalization uncovered "perversions" and "scandals" that official reformers felt compelled to speak about for the first time. One of those problems inherited from the Stalin era was homosexuality, perceived as having been fostered in the homogenic Gulag. To restore "normal" heterosexuality, the Gulag queer had to be contained, and the fight against Gulag-generated "sodomy" and "lesbian love" had to be taken to wider society. New knowledge was created by specialists about this problem; and experiments in speaking about homosexuality took place in the camps, piloting a new official language of homophobia. Continued secrecy in the archives and a likely failure to record lectures against same-sex "amorality" obstruct our knowledge about the penal regime's new "homophobic speech." We commonly associate Nikita Khrushchev's de-Stalinization with a liberalizing, "humane" spirit, but for same-sex-desiring Soviet citizens, the spirit of de-Stalinization was marked by modernizing attempts to eradicate their desire using the law, medicine, and expert interventions. The official homophobia of the Stalin era was updated for a more technocratic political order.

Late-Soviet prisoners, Gulag survivors, and the Gulag queer

Was the Gulag eventually transformed into a "normal" Soviet prison system? Geographically it was scaled back considerably, its population greatly reduced, and reformers experimented with variations on the penal regime. The reforms of the 1950s seesawed between optimism about rehabilitating the ordinary criminal, and a much harsher prognosis for "professional" or recidivist offenders. Conditions eased compared to the deliberate negligence of the worst Stalin-era camps, and some more "humane" reforms improved prisoner nutrition, cultural opportunities, and medical services. What remained the same was the system of collective detention in barracks organized in "colonies," with its implications for prisoner socialization, rather than individual isolation in prison cells.[103] To this mix of continuity and change, the existing prisoners' subculture responded with changes of its own. Prisoners appear to have persecuted queer inmates more aggressively in the wake of the more overt anti-homosexual policies of the penal and police authorities. The late Soviet decades appear to have hardened the homophobia in prisoner subcultures, especially among male convicts.

A homophobic shift in tattooing culture in Soviet prisons may have taken root at this time, probably a response to the official persecution of the queer inside and outside prison. Prisoners in Russia may have created a more explicit tattoo-language around homosexual behavior after 1953; reform of the Gulag and the associated explicit targeting of the prison queer as a problem to be resolved seem to have amplified such imagery. In the late Imperial and early Soviet period, prisoner tattooing evolved rapidly and was little understood by wardens and commandants.[104] Criminals inked their bodies more widely during the 1930s and 1940s in the burgeoning Gulag, but experts disagree whether these tattoos were just personal expressions of character and criminal trades, or a full-blown "secret symbolism" designed to mark status in the criminal world.[105] Criminals, however, differentiated themselves more aggressively after 1945 (resulting in "wars" between castes of criminals). More explicit symbolism evolved as post-Stalin reformers bore down on the most hardened "recidivist" criminal caste, the "thieves in law," during the Khrushchev era. Reportedly during and after the 1950s, "shaming and forcible" tattooing of men deemed "degraded" (*opushchennye*) became commonplace.[106] The "degraded" were men known as passive partners in anal intercourse, as fellators of other men, and as convicts under the renewed anti-homosexual laws. Losing at cards, and having no other stake to offer except one's sexual services, had been a route to similar forms of humiliation since the early twentieth century at least. Now an overt branding of the "degraded" queer seems to have emerged.[107]

Shaming tattoos for those convicted under the anti-sodomy law included crudely drawn anuses with slogans exposing the victim's criminal code article (no. 154a before 1960, and no. 121 thereafter).[108] (See Figure 1.2.) Those "made" into "passive homosexuals" in prison might simply have the word "*pederast*" or "*petukh*" branded on their foreheads.[109] Another image was forcibly inked on the back of such men: a naked woman entwined with a snake or phallus, an apple in her outstretched hand, presumably intended to arouse the "active" partner by flattering his heterosexual credentials. The tattoo's incitement to desire and its provocative placement on the body hint at an erotic psychology shared by male prisoners that de-stigmatized the "active" partner.[110]

The evolution of Soviet female prisoners' tattoos has been largely ignored by historians. From the three-volume compendium of tattoo designs collected by prison guard and artist Danzig Baldaev, there are fewer specifically queer tattoos worn by female prisoners. (Generalizations from the Baldaev collection must be made cautiously since their cataloging, provenance, and analysis are erratic; many tattoos are undated.) One recurrent motif from the 1960s is a single eye, surrounded by barbed wire or in combination with other symbols: the butch partner's jealous surveillance of her femme "wife" was implied.[111] The

FIGURE 1.2 Men's "shaming tattoo," displaying sodomy criminal code article 154a, Krasnoyarsk Camps, 1956. Back of prisoner.

butch also appeared wearing a crown, or wielding a phallus.[112] An apparently rare tattoo from Leningrad in 1967 (Figure 1.3) displays a lily, symbolizing the femme, surrounded by the butch's all-seeing eye and a pair of lips, denoting sensuality. In acronym it bears the legend, "I swear to love you only."[113] How these tattoos were read by prisoners, and indeed how "free" Soviet citizens understood them when tattooed ex-convicts displayed them in the public baths or on the beach, remains unknown. Not obviously "shaming" tattoos, they were marks of allegiance and even declarations of love. These images of queerness would have been extremely rare explicit references to homosexuality in "free" society in the late Soviet period – undoubtedly, many ex-convicts probably sought to conceal them or have them covered with new designs.

Public understandings of homosexuality in the late-Soviet period were in part determined by "political" returnees from the Gulag, not by these "criminals." De-Stalinizing reforms ran into the sand after Khrushchev was forcibly retired and replaced by the consummate gradualist Leonid Brezhnev,

FIGURE 1.3 *Woman's femme tattoo, with lily denoting "passive lesbian" and the all-seeing eye of her butch partner. Women's corrective-labor camp near Leningrad, 1967. Right shoulder.*

in October 1964. Brezhnev's neo-Stalinist instincts soon became apparent, and an unofficial popular movement for reform, the "dissidents," emerged in response. The dissident movement was an extremely broad one, with many strands of interests, although it had little feminist and almost no gay strands of activism.[114] The social and literary circles that formed in the 1960s around Gulag returnees, from among the "politicals," constituted one of its most powerful moral centers. As witnesses to the experience of Stalinist terror and repression, the testimonies of Alexander Solzhenitsyn, Evgeniia Ginzburg, Varlam Shalamov, and many other survivors of the Gulag achieved canonical status in Russian literature. The views expressed by prominent and even obscure labor camp survivors about the Gulag queer thus carried a significant moral weight.[115]

As Adi Kuntsman argues, survivors' memoirs propagated a searing homophobia in the service of Russia's moral renewal.[116] The survivor's homophobia was a mirror image of the homophobia expressed by official reformers of the 1950s, but intensified in its horror when describing queer sexuality. In the survivor's memoir, disgust hovers over recollections of the Gulag queer, and the author-survivor always presents herself or himself as a heterosexual representative of the martyred intelligentsia. Gulag survivor accounts work strenuously to put distance between the narrator as heterosexual intelligentsia victim-witness, and the Gulag queer who is typically from the criminal classes, bestial in appetites, perversely inverted in gender performance, and demonic in his or her behavior. Here is how Evgeniia Ginzburg described the lowest circle of hell into which she descended as a Gulag inmate:

> We had arrived. Izvestkovaya. The punishment center to end all punishment centers. The isle of the damned.
> And here they were, the beings whose names were uttered, even in criminal circles, with superstitious dread . . . take the repulsive, goggle-eyed little toad, Zoika the Lesbian. This one was accompanied by three other lesbians of hermaphrodite aspect, with short hair, husky voices, and men's names – Edik, Sasha, and a third one . . . [I recognized some of them who had] been brought along to the compound for antisyphilitic treatment, and I had given them injections . . .
> These humanoids lived a life of fantasy in which there was no distinction between night and day. Most of them never went out to work at all; they simply lay around all the time in their bunks. Those who did put in an appearance out of doors did so merely in order to light a campfire, crouch around it, and bawl out ribald songs . . . An enormous iron barrel glowed red hot. These fiends were constantly boiling something or other on top of it, cavorting around the stove virtually naked.[117]

In Ginzburg's testimony, queer desire was tightly linked to Stalinist oppression. The Gulag's homogenic effects were not analyzed sociologically or ethnographically. The Gulag queer was not a human being whose fate as a returnee from the camps merited consideration; instead, she or he became diabolical symbols of camp life, tokens of the evil of the forced-labor system. The sheer visibility of the queer in the Gulag was proof of the Stalinist (or Communist) system's profound perversion: the Gulag queer turned nature on its head, and the most aggressive and shameless among them brutalized otherwise "normal" innocents. In addition, the queers' lack of shame violated the Russian intelligentsia's moral sensibility that placed a premium on modesty and allusion rather than flaunting of sexuality. Kuntsman also emphasizes the obvious class dimensions of this homophobia: ". . . although the memoirs were not the only source of the criminalization of same-sex relations in the public imagination, they are one of the main grounds for the persistent connection between same-sex relations, low classness, criminality, and monstrosity."[118]

Another source of the survivors' moral stance against the Gulag queer, one overlooked in relation to this homophobia, is the religious belief of many memoirists. Some, like Ginzburg, had been "true believers" in Communism and during the course of their ordeal lost their faith in Marx and turned to God. Not all memoirists were as explicit as Ginzburg in depicting their spiritual journey. Scholars of Gulag memoir literature have noted the influence of spirituality on the most powerful of these texts: for numerous survivors, imprisonment was a "test of faith," and religion a source of fortitude and dignity. Others chose to write of their ethical dilemmas and decisions in secular terms.[119] No scholarship on the links between religious belief and attitudes towards sexuality in Gulag memoir literature exists as yet. It remains difficult to say how far religion influenced the moral outlook of the Gulag survivor remembering sexuality behind barbed wire. Nevertheless it is an influence that has to be considered, and religious morality probably contributed to the imagery of demonization and bestiality employed by some memoirists when speaking of the queer in the Gulag.

Queer visibility and erasure after Stalin's Gulag

The homophobia of late-Soviet society was the product of several specific historical legacies, and the Stalin-era Gulag's "homogenic" culture and post-Stalin responses to it were a significant legacy that clearly influenced the wider Soviet gender order. (By analogy, we can posit that the military was another site of even more hidden "homogenic" forces, about which there has been almost no research.)[120] Stalin's vast expansion of the old Russian penal system greatly extended the sites of single-sex or extreme gender-imbalanced settlement across the Soviet Union. New forms of administration and control instrumentalized heterosexual family ties in the Gulag's scheme of incentives and punishments: heteronormative values underpinned the regime's official rhetoric of "reforging" the Gulag prisoner. Compliant prisoners might be permitted to re-establish contact with their families or establish a new family upon release. Yet the system was mainly destructive of "normal" family ties; many found it psychologically and practically impossible to restore lost relationships after Gulag life and its deprivations.[121]

The nature of same-sex relations behind barbed wire was often brutal, reinforcing hierarchies of gender, age, and the all-important Soviet ideological distinction between the "socially friendly" and the "socially alien." The visibility of queer sex and gender in the Gulag was something new, compared to the culture of the old Russian penal world: Dostoevsky had to cloud his exposure of this painful issue in euphemism, and Gernet struggled to find prisoner-respondents who would talk about queer relations behind bars. In contrast, by the 1950s, in a reforming political environment, Gulag officials, doctors, prisoners, and "political" returnees spoke about the Gulag queer as an all-too-visible feature of penal life. Expert anxiety to suppress and reject this queer visibility paradoxically relied on an "incitement to discourse": discussion of the "problem" of same-sex relations in conferences of doctors and officials, conversations and lectures with prisoners, and shaming articles in prison-camp newspapers. Popular responses spread these overt discourses beyond the control of Soviet officials and experts, in the humiliating tattoos invented and inked on "degraded" prisoners by their fellow inmates; and in the terrifying myth of the Gulag queer propounded in the memoir-literature of the "political" returnees.

Both official and popular attitudes towards homosexuality hardened as a result of the reform of the Gulag and wider reforms of Soviet society under de-Stalinization. Officials saw "family-lessness" and queer visibility as symptoms of defective Stalinism and the renewal and modernization of the means of repression of homosexuality was a necessary feature of de-Stalinization. Although official Soviet morality seldom made mention of homosexuality as a problem in public discourse, clearly homosexuality would be associated with personal and even pathological disorder. The anxiety about homosexual transmission of sexually transmitted diseases would become central to strategies for policing male homosexuality in the 1960s across the Soviet Union (discussed in Chapter 7). Popular hostility followed class and educational lines: with tattooing and probable linguistic innovations, criminal subcultures evolved new ways to stigmatize the queer inmate and mark queer identities, while the intelligentsia "dissident" used the Gulag queer as the ultimate marker of Stalinist degradation. In the experience of hundreds of thousands if not millions of Soviet lives, both those of prisoners and jailers, the penal system of Joseph Stalin and its offspring incubated modern homophobic attitudes even as reformers sought to suppress queer visibility in everyday life. The impact of these attitudes is still felt today, where knowledge of prison-queer visibility continues to shape masculine identities.[122]

2

Comrades, Queers, and "Oddballs":

Sodomy, Masculinity, and Gendered Violence in Leningrad Province in the 1950s

On a wintry November night in 1955, twenty-year-old Russian Red Army private Mikhail Yermolaev met a group of his comrades in the village of Rakhia near Leningrad. They were looking for a good time and found it in Barrack No. 18, a women's dormitory, where a party with vodka was in full swing. Mikhail drank his fill. He began to feel unwell. When his comrades decided to leave the party – perhaps in search of more vodka – they left Mikhail in the care of Aleksei (Alyosha) Kiselev, thirty-seven years of age, who took the soldier home to his room in the village bathhouse, where he lived and worked as a stoker. Kiselev played some music on his treasured gramophone; he told the younger man to undress and lie down. After first throwing up in the toilet, Mikhail went to bed. Later he told the police:

> I woke up and heard Alyosha say, "Get on top of me." At that very moment my belt was undone, my trousers and underpants were down, and my penis was exposed. Then he pulled me toward him and said, "Give it to me, give it to me in the ass." I got on top of him, for Alyosha was on his stomach with his back to me, but I was revolted so I didn't use him, even though my penis was erect. I went back to sleep. . . . After a little while Alyosha came to me again, first turning me over on my stomach. He got on top of me and tried to use me in the ass, but he didn't manage it because I wouldn't let him. He was only wearing his underpants, and I could feel his erection. He didn't say anything. I just turned away and went back to sleep.[1]

At two o'clock in the morning, Mikhail woke up, dressed, and left Kiselev to meet his comrades and catch a train back to his base. Before he left, he gave his host his surname and address. When he got to the station, one of his army buddies asked him, "Well, how did you sleep? They say he's a man and a woman." "Yes, of course – he's a queer [*pidarast*]," Mikhail replied, and no more was said between the men, who went back to their barracks on the late-night train.

What went on between the young soldier and the bathhouse stoker that night? What was Aleksei Kiselev hoping for when he offered Mikhail a bed to sleep off the drink, and why did the soldier accept his offer? What did these soldiers understand by the word "queer" in this time and place? And what did the women of Barrack No. 18 represent for them? Nothing systematic has been written about same-sex relations between men in rural Russia, and to begin to answer the questions that incidents like these pose, we need to consider the social and historical context more broadly.

The era after 1945 in Soviet history is attracting fresh attention. Interest focuses on society's aspirations for a better life after the devastation of war and under the relentless demands of late Stalinism. Recent work often emphasizes the complexity and instability of the last years of Stalin's rule and the ambiguities of de-Stalinization, suggesting that 1945 was a significant temporal landmark in Soviet history.[2] Studies of family policies show the leadership's determination, sustained across the period, to find innovative ways to steer gender relations to solve the demographic crisis and to satisfy political objectives.[3] A significant emerging area of inquiry is the question of how public and private spheres were reconstructed in the postwar years in a "negotiation" between rulers and ruled.[4]

With some important exceptions, the history of Russian sexualities for this period remains relatively unexplored, and yet the acts of individuals in pursuit of a sexual life and the meanings ascribed to their actions can tell historians a great deal about gender relations, public–private boundaries, and the politics of everyday life.[5] Existing accounts of Russian homosexual history in the 1950s describe a primarily urban gay subculture, with Moscow the focus in one detailed excavation.[6] It appears that homosexual self-awareness and experience were confined to a fortunate few in Soviet Russia's largest and most sophisticated cities. Infamous public toilets, cafés, and bathhouses – and the streets between them – formed a surreptitious queer public space where men could meet and then begin the hunt for a corner of privacy in which to realize their desires. Elite students and members of the cultural intelligentsia figure prominently in narratives of those who managed to live queerly in this time and place.[7]

Men also felt queer desire outside of the big cities of Soviet Russia, however, and their experience can be analyzed with an eye to the models developed to study rural queer lives in other contexts. Historical work on such relations in twentieth-century American states, like John Howard's study of Mississippi and Peter Boag's of Oregon, has shown how men used the rural environment to pursue and express same-sex desire.[8] Their work, perhaps unconsciously infused with American optimism, emphasizes the affirmative and the positive in the stories of rural queer men's lives. The subaltern queer world of "wolves" and "lambs" or "jockers" and "punks" (in Boag's description of itinerant worker sexuality on the U.S. northwest coast), for all its toughness, is presented as a site of tenderness and affection too. Homophobia and violence are chiefly external to the subjects of these histories: attacks on same-sex-desiring people come from moral reformers, police, medical experts, and "straight" toughs. Even in Jens Rydström's comparatively mordant study of homosexuality in rural Sweden, male same-sex sexuality is depicted with little reference to violence or brutality, except as imposed upon male homosexuals by a moralizing and medicalizing state and its agents.[9]

My stories come from a different historical context, where the patterns of male sexuality and male violence are comparable to but distinct from the American and Swedish cases. In the two criminal investigations from Leningrad Province examined here, some of the men who had sex together also inflicted violence and brutality upon women and effeminized men. Often they used that violence to facilitate and hide their same-sex sexuality, in one case killing a queer man. It is problematic to interpret these cases as evidence of a positive subaltern queer world, and indeed some observers challenge the simple notion that violence is always external to the same-sex desiring person.[10] In reading these cases, I try to probe the character of queer violence and look for other contexts to explain it. The chief frame of reference I propose is gender, specifically, the dilemmas of masculinity confronting men of the post-1945 generation. The cases raise many questions about these dilemmas. How did men adapt to postwar Soviet conditions in the provinces? What prospects – for jobs, housing, leisure, and sex – faced the demobilized Red Army soldier? How was a young man's private life divided from his public life: in what ways were relations between the sexes changed and changing? How did homosocial bonds affect relations between the sexes? What meanings did homosexual acts carry for these men, and how did they fit in a postwar popular conception of masculinity?

Using two unusual police investigation files from the archives of the province (*oblast*) of Leningrad, the rural district surrounding present-day St. Petersburg in northwestern Russia, it is possible to pose answers to these questions. These cases arose from extreme crimes – rape and murder; therefore, claims to representativeness of the situations they describe must be cautiously advanced. Such criminal violence was nevertheless on the increase in Soviet society in the postwar years, and the unusual element in these cases was evidently the homosexual motive accompanying these crimes.[11] Perhaps for this reason, police investigations into these cases dug deep. In particular, officials interviewed many dozens of witnesses and perpetrators, so the crime files constitute a meaningful body of texts about daily life. Naturally, these are statements to police under an extremely authoritarian, even "totalitarian," regime and might be dismissed as of dubious truthfulness if we presume that state terror and social atomization made people fearful and tight-lipped when dealing with authorities. However, contemporary scholars of Russia see a more complex reality in the relationship between state and society, and I read these case files using their insights and against the backdrop of new interpretations of Soviet social history.[12]

The first case involves eight men accused and convicted of sodomy and rape in 1951. The second, involving the Alyosha Kiselev described in the opening of this chapter, is a murder investigation of the late 1950s that opens a window into a queer life in an unlikely setting. After presenting the facts of each case, I discuss the local context, and then the gendered world revealed in these files, with the dilemmas for men and the responses they shaped, including their relationships with women and their retreat into homosocial spheres. Finally, I explore the meanings that men gave to their sexuality, same and opposite sex, from the evidence of these admittedly extreme and isolated cases. I argue that these men exploited their relationships with women and effeminate men in their attempts to produce homosexual space and homosexual spheres of action. Gender privilege and sometimes even the violent exploitation of women helped these men to build spaces that enabled same-sex sexuality and emotional relationships between men.

Case 1: Rape and sodomy in Nevdubstroi, 1946–51[13]

In January 1951, in the settlement of Nevdubstroi, about thirty kilometers east of Leningrad, a thirty-three-year-old woman, Lidia Babenko, complained to the police about her thirty-nine-year-old unregistered husband, Pavel Grishin. They had lived in his room in a barracks for two years, but soon after she moved in with him, she realized that he had sex with men. Grishin often invited men back to their room for drinking parties or to sleep off the effects of drink, and he then committed sodomy or fellatio with them. Still worse, she said, Grishin forced her to have intercourse with some of these visitors, beating her and restraining her while visitors raped her. In her statements to the police, she named seven men and gave details of several others as Grishin's consenting sexual partners. She also described five incidents when she was raped by some of these visitors with her husband's collusion.

Grishin was immediately arrested, and within a week seven other men were in custody too. The investigation continued until early June, during which time these men were held in Leningrad Prison No. 1 and examined by expert psychiatrists and physicians. Police collected witness statements, and Grishin's snapshot collection (fifty-two images in all) was seized and studied. Prosecutors prepared a lengthy indictment in early June: Grishin was accused of sodomy and being an accessory to rape. Five others, between the ages of nineteen and forty-five, were charged with sodomy, and two men, thirty-two and forty-one years old, were charged with rape. The penalty for consensual sodomy was up to five years' imprisonment; for rape it was between ten and twenty years' deprivation of liberty.[14] Over four days in July 1951, in open sessions in Leningrad Provincial Court, the case was tried, and all these men were convicted. Grishin was sentenced to twenty years in a labor camp with five years' deprivation of rights, the two rapists received fifteen years each, and the five men convicted of simple sodomy got three years each. On appeal, these sentences were upheld by the Supreme Court of the Russian Republic.

Case 2: Sodomy and murder in Rakhia, 1955–9[15]

In Rakhia village, thirty kilometers northeast of Leningrad, on December 14, 1955, the thirty-seven-year-old bachelor Aleksei Kiselev was found dead, hanging in the communal bathhouse where he worked and lived. There were no signs of forced entry to his tiny room, no marks on the body, and no evidence of foul play; apparently, Kiselev had committed suicide. The police reached this verdict and closed their investigation. They noted but did not judge as suspicious the fact that Kiselev's beloved gramophone was missing. Kiselev was known to carry the instrument around the village, visiting and playing music. Since he often made random calls and appeared to some to have "some peculiarities" of personality, it was thought the gramophone had been mislaid.

Three years later, the gramophone turned up – it had been stolen. Police raided a petty thief, twenty-seven-year-old David Morozov, and found the gramophone with a cache of stolen goods. The gramophone was quickly identified by the women who had sold it to Kiselev. Morozov admitted murdering Kiselev and stealing his record player. He claimed that he had been enraged by Kiselev's homosexual advances, killed him, and then hanged him with his soldier's belt, intending to disguise the crime as a suicide.

Kiselev met Morozov the afternoon before his death at the railway station in Rakhia. The two men had known each other for about a year; they met at a party in the room of a young cleaner, Olga, who lived in Barrack No. 18, the dormitory for single women. The barrack had a reputation as a place where soldiers congregated to socialize with young women. After visiting the girls there, Kiselev invited Morozov back to his room in the bathhouse, and Morozov agreed. In Kiselev's small room, there were flowers on the windowsill and the gramophone was on a tiny table. They listened to some music, stepped out to get some food and drink, and returned to the room, where Kiselev fried up some potatoes as music played on the gramophone and Morozov smoked. Eventually, Kiselev asked Morozov to stay the night; the younger man took off his boots and shirt and lay down on the bed. He told police that it was at this point that Kiselev turned off the light and then began to embrace him and touch his penis. Kiselev's persistent sexual suggestions continued through the night, and Morozov said that, exasperated, he finally beat and strangled Kiselev with his belt. He hanged the body and left the room at five o'clock in the morning, taking the gramophone with him.

In March 1959, judges in Leningrad sentenced Morozov to fifteen years for murder, theft, and sodomy. They pointedly rejected Morozov's version of the "homosexual panic" defense, but noted instead that "a personal relationship associated with the commission of sodomy" had existed for some time between the two men, substantiated by medical expertise, and there was therefore "nothing unexpected or perturbing" in Kiselev's sexual approaches.[16]

Rural "settlements of an urban type"

Both of these cases arose in rural villages, yet these were not remote peasant hamlets but what Soviet planners liked to call "settlements of an urban type." They were part of the quasi-industrial hinterland servicing Leningrad. The inhabitants were not collective farmers but wage-earners in local industries and enterprises.[17] Nevdubstroi, founded in 1929 around a new hydroelectric generating station, added to this pivotal enterprise a construction-materials factory following the war. Demobilized soldiers formed a significant part of the workforce. The Stalin-era *Bol'shaia sovetskaia entsiklopediia* (Great Soviet Encyclopedia) notes that Nevdubstroi had a secondary school and the hydro station had its own House of Culture.[18] In the older settlement of Rakhia, the key local employer was a peat-extraction trust; the encyclopedia boasts of the village's public baths, library, club, and school.[19] Close to Rakhia were several military bases where young men were housed and trained for their compulsory service in the Red Army, including nearby Vaganovo, where Morozov was stationed. Many soldiers found jobs upon demobilization in the local peat works. Both settlements had played their part in the drama of the 1941–3 Siege of Leningrad; Rakhia's and Vaganovo's mobile field hospitals served the Lake Ladoga "road of life," and near Nevdubstroi Soviet tanks first penetrated the Nazi encirclement.[20] After the war, the economic activity of both villages contributed to Leningrad's reconstruction.

Post-1945 reconstruction in the Soviet Union was not merely economic but also demographic. The country lost twenty-six million citizens in the war, and, as Mie Nakachi shows, losses in the most marriageable age groups were staggering. After 1945, the average rural male:female sex ratio in the reproductive-age cohort (eighteen to forty-nine years of age) was 28:100.[21] The resulting gender imbalance was stark; as late as 1959, 55 percent of the Soviet population was female. Nakachi argues that the 1944 Soviet decree on families transformed sexual behavior by deliberately encouraging nonconjugal, casual heterosexual liaisons leading to pregnancy and childbirth. State child support was extended to unmarried mothers, and bachelor fathers were relieved of the duty to support their offspring as one means of boosting the depleted population. By 1954, the tenth year of this decree's operation and the last year of Stalin's abortion ban, 8.7 million "fatherless" children had been born.[22]

Some features of this demographic situation can be read in our cases. Setting the casual sexual activity aside momentarily, it is striking that for this era, both Nevdubstroi and Rakhia were unusually well supplied with able-bodied young men. There were also plenty of single women in both settlements, where a large number of young and often migrant workers of both sexes lived, mostly in communal, workplace-owned accommodation: dormitories and barracks rather than flats or houses. After demobilization in 1945, Grishin returned to Nevdubstroi and lived in a dormitory allocated to the construction factory; by 1949 his workplace had given him a room in a "barracks town" (barachnyi gorodok).[23] Similarly, in Rakhia, in 1955, the murder victim himself lived in a tiny room in the bathhouse where he worked, while many of the key witnesses lived in the "women's barrack."[24]

Masculinity, sodomy, and gender relations

In John Howard's study of post-1945 rural Mississippi and in Peter Boag's history of early twentieth-century Oregon, the patterns of male homosociability and the social attitudes that facilitated homosexual encounters were important factors distinguishing urban from rural queer existence. For Howard, men who liked sex together were "resourceful sexual beings" who circulated in a rural landscape and carved out opportunities in unlikely settings: the family home, the local church hall, the automobile, the swimming hole.[25] Boag's Oregon was a hive of itinerant male laborers servicing resource and construction enterprises. These homosocial settings, seasonal work camps, and "hobo jungles" on the edge of cities created sites for sexual relations: as Boag writes, "the men found that the hinterland itself was a sexual space."[26] This was the setting for age-stratified pairings between a mature "jocker" or "wolf" who mentored and protected a younger "punk." The youth performed menial and domestic tasks while learning the ropes at tougher work in logging camps. While observers believed they adopted fixed sexual postures (jocker as inserter and punk as receptor), evidence shows that many punks penetrated their partners and later became jockers with their own punks.[27] Rural Sweden in the early to mid-twentieth century was also a place where casual laborers and farmhands found homosocial workspaces that could be sexualized.[28] Here too, the age-stratified relationship between a mature man and youths or younger men was widely observed. Both Boag and Rydström found for their respective societies that effeminate behavior in queer men and the gender-ordered sexual relations that were reputed to accompany it (masculine insertor, feminine receptor) were more typical of urban same-sex-desiring men. Both observe that effeminacy was relatively rare in the countryside, even among more urbanized migrant workers. Rydström argues that this effeminacy was too indiscreet for the tenuous social networks of queers to tolerate in the rural setting; small-town networks disapproved of and suppressed it.[29]

For historians of early twentieth-century rural queer men, "quiet accommodationism" assisted in the creation of a space for unnamed sexual experience. Denial and deliberate ignorance of same-sex sexuality was a key building block for this space; people acted according to a "regime of silence" to evade acknowledgment of homosexuality, whether that of neighbors or indeed within the self.[30] The realities of rural life could disguise queer tastes from the casual onlooker: physically demanding labor and male homosociability, including mentorship of young men, were relatively ubiquitous. Perhaps in these historical contexts, rural realities tended to naturalize queer tastes for those who experienced them as part of ordinary masculinity. This was possible until the arrival of an urban discourse of "homosexuality" as a medical and sociological category. It is difficult to say whether rural circumstances like these evoked homosexual desire or whether those who felt homosexual desire sought them out.[31]

At the same time, the distinctiveness of the rural queer world should not be overstated. Even before 1914, Boag's itinerant workers were frequent visitors to Portland and other cities between job contracts, and many were familiar with urban patterns of male–male relations, including the existence of the effeminate "fairy" who paraded his gender transgression in louche bars and queer haunts. Rydström too sees a quickening of traffic between rural and urban queer men in mid-twentieth-century Sweden, with the impact of modern communications bringing urban tastes and ideas to the hinterland by midcentury. In both contexts, urban expert use of scientific concepts of "homosexuality" was also proliferating in legal and social work.[32] In other words, in modernizing societies the city and countryside were not separate spheres, but worlds where urban patterns of experience and thought collided with and often challenged or overlapped with rural patterns. In Leningrad Province in the 1950s, sodomy cases from "settlements of an urban type" offer examples of the blend and overlap of "urban" and "rural" forms of queer sexual behavior.

Like any other persons, resourceful queer men circulating through a hinterland that they perceived as a sexualized environment were also capable of ambiguous or morally repugnant acts. The indulgence of male privilege with "quiet accommodationism" could also facilitate the exploitation of youths, of effeminized men, and of women. Grishin's repeated offering of his wife, Babenko, to male friends for sex was an abusive ploy with only two plausible motives: either he was prostituting his wife, or he used her as bait to attract men into sexual scenarios with himself. (Prosecutors found no evidence of prostitution, although defense advocates suggested it un-successfully in appeals to the Supreme Court.) Morozov's murder of the overtly effeminized Kiselev was perhaps an act of self-loathing, of internalized homophobia, to use anachronistic language, and the failure to detect it for three years was a sign that quiet accommodationism could facilitate violent homophobia and misogyny.

The violence of these cases suggests that a feminist as well as a queer language of gender relations and masculine power is required to analyze them satisfactorily. Life between the sexes in post–1945 Soviet Russia was a dynamic and troubled negotiation, as men and women sought to find work and housing and establish a private family life. At the same time, the militarization of this corner of Russia created homosocial space that concentrated men together and permitted a high degree of mobility and circulation through these communities. Military service was a common masculine experience, and demobilization was a longed-for release, but it was also a stage bringing new anxieties. Life between men was nevertheless an arena where differences of age, class, war service, and experience with women were as significant as commonalities. Men's sexuality, including sex with other men, occurred within these contexts and had disturbing features. To understand men's same-sex affairs in this setting, we must examine how these same men ordered their affairs with women.

Between men and women

Pavel Grishin's relationship with his common-law wife, Lidia Babenko, began in 1949, apparently, after his workplace had allocated him a room in Nevdubstroi's barracks town. Babenko was an invalid, blind in one eye and poorly sighted in the other.[33] From the sources, it is difficult to fathom why Grishin started this relationship, since he told psychiatrists that from childhood he had been strongly attracted only to men; but a psychiatric report indicates that he did have sex with Babenko, although he seldom achieved satisfaction with her unless other men were present.[34] Neither husband nor wife was a person with prospects, and they had few assets beyond Grishin's room. Babenko, a peasant from Tula province, had never been married, was childless, and had some schooling but no job. Grishin, an orphan, lived with foster parents, had not finished primary school, and worked as a cleaner through the war for the army; he became a factory caretaker (*dvornik*) after demobilization. Their conjugal life began conventionally enough, with Babenko preparing meals and even bringing them to Grishin at his workplace – it was during one such delivery, not long after they began cohabiting, that she discovered her husband engaged in sex with another man.[35] Perhaps Grishin settled down with Babenko for the convenience of having a homemaker and to make an attempt to suppress what he called in his trial "my illness" – his attraction to men.[36] Babenko depended heavily on Grishin, lacking any alternative income and place to live, and in any case, scarce marriageable men had their pick of younger and more able-bodied women. Her "quiet accommodation" of Grishin's taste for men appears to have been a tragic compromise born of desperate circumstances.

About a year after they began life together, Grishin started to bring men to their room, suggesting that these men have sex with his wife; from the psychiatric reports it seems he did this to initiate scenarios leading to homosexual sex. In the summer of 1950, Grishin's "bait and switch" tactic worked with two men with whom Babenko first refused to have sex. After one such refusal, a well-paid worker with a criminal record, Aleksander Kononov, thirty-nine years of age, a demobilized soldier said to be happily married with children, committed sodomy and fellatio with Grishin. Dmitry Gusev, a nineteen-year-old bachelor, likewise engaged in sodomy with Grishin after Babenko turned him down. With two other men that same summer, Grishin used force to overcome his wife's denial of consent to sex, assisting them to rape her on two occasions. One of these men, Viktor Belousov, was a demobilized semi-invalid, married and employed as a stove fitter, and the other, Vladimir Biryukov, was an unmarried metalworker, well paid, with a previous prison stretch for quitting a job without permission during the war. Biryukov had also let Grishin attempt sodomy and commit fellatio repeatedly on him. In all of these incidents, Babenko served as a means of exchange between men. In the cases when her refusal was respected, the fact of Grishin's offer of his wife was a pretext, a fig leaf of "normal" sexuality that allowed these men to engage in same-sex sex as an ostensible "substitute." Their supposed interest in Babenko gave them a measure of sexual conformity. In the cases when she was raped, Grishin apparently hoped to profit by persuading the rapists to indulge his desire, and with certain men like Biryukov, he achieved this result.[37] In the scenarios Grishin fashioned in collaboration with these men, sex with a woman could be accompanied with considerable physical and psychological violence, but when sex happened between men, consent was carefully constructed. In testimony recorded in the stilted language of the police, a married work comrade, twenty-six-year-old Nikita Pashchenko, described the process of forging consent to homosexual sex: "In a conversation with Grishin he told me that he satisfied sexual desire by means of sucking the penis, and he began trying to incline me to this; at first I would not allow it, but later he started to convince me, and I agreed and allowed him to do it. That was on the steamboat in the stoke-hold."[38] Later, Grishin invited Pashchenko to his room, and he had apparently consensual intercourse with Babenko (according to his testimony; Babenko did not name Pashchenko as one of the rapists). Grishin was unable to persuade Pashchenko to have oral sex again. The case file says little about the nature of the negotiations between men who opted to have sex with each other, except for one striking commonality: they often used the prospect of sex with a woman as a pretext to broach the possibility of homosexual sex.

Men who had sex together in the 1955 Rakhia murder case similarly used relations with women to conceal nonconforming sexuality. David Morozov served in the Red Army from 1952 until his demobilization on September 29, 1955, barely ten weeks before Kiselev's murder. The twenty-two-year-old soldier first met thirty-six-year-old Aleksei Kiselev in the winter of 1954–5 while still in uniform. A sergeant took Morozov to Rakhia to visit Barrack No 18, the women's dormitory. The girls of Barrack No. 18 had a reputation in Rakhia; it was well known that soldiers called on them, and perhaps some supplemented their meager incomes with exchanges of small presents – "treating" – for sex.[39] They were young women like twenty-one-year-old Olga Gurova, a cleaner for the peat-cutting trust, who told police how Kiselev often dropped by with his gramophone "to sit for a while, talk a bit, and play the gramophone. Nobody invited him; he just dropped in on his own." Morozov recalled that he first met Kiselev at a party in Olga's room; Kiselev noticed Morozov and said, "Introduce me to that red-haired fellow." They shook hands, and Kiselev said, "Let's become friends." Kiselev said he had a sister and that Morozov should come to Rakhia again to visit him in his bathhouse room.[40]

Morozov did not go to the bathhouse on that occasion. He told police, "Later I heard from our soldiers and from the girls in Barrack No. 18 that [Kiselev] didn't really have a sister and that he did not love women but was friendly only with soldiers and supposedly entered into a sexual connection with them." Such warnings could also provide useful queer intelligence. Morozov claimed to police interrogators that in the ten months between this meeting and his demobilization, he saw Kiselev five times in Rakhia at the women's barracks, but he always refused his invitations to visit him at the bathhouse. The judges at Morozov's trial clearly found it incredible that the two would not have met during this time to "engage in sodomy," and Morozov's own admission in court that he had received a letter from the older man while he was still in the army gave them some reason to think so.[41] Kiselev apparently admitted Morozov freely to his room; there was no evidence of a struggle there or on Kiselev's body. A rectal examination supposedly confirmed Morozov's long career as a passive sodomite.[42] Circumstantial evidence hinted at a more intimate connection between murderer and victim. Kiselev's bathhouse room offered an ideal location for him to entertain visitors discreetly after hours. Statements to police from soldiers, colleagues, and neighbors indicated that he was notorious for having sex with men in uniform. Finally, it was difficult to understand why, after having supposedly refused repeatedly to visit Kiselev, Morozov would suddenly accept Kiselev's invitation on December 13, 1955 and agree to stay the night with him when he was relatively sober and lived less than a mile away. Even more curious was the fact that Morozov had only just married a woman ten years his senior on October 31, 1955; he had gone from a soldiers' barracks to live in his wife's house within four weeks of demobilization. On the night of the murder, he had a new bride to go home to. Morozov embraced married life for reasons we cannot know; but in 1950s Russia, the eagerness of many single and widowed women to find an able-bodied husband and perhaps Morozov's anxiety about finding a place to live upon release from the army and determination to conceal his same-sex inclinations were among the motives for the alliance.[43]

Here men who were engaged in homosexual relations again instrumentalized ties with women to find and attract male partners and to mask their sexual nonconformity. Barrack No. 18 was not only a notorious place where local soldiers gathered for parties with young women. Kiselev also enjoyed meeting these men in uniform, some of whom responded to his attentions; the girls apparently judged Kiselev as sexually nonthreatening and even intriguing for his adventures with men. Kiselev made himself indispensable to the barracks girls with his gramophone, one of only a handful owned privately in the whole village. His presence at these parties allowed him to court partners to invite back to his room. The barracks girls paid attention to these games: in court, Morozov said that "the girls told me that Kiselev was attracted to me because I'm a redhead."[44] During the initial suicide inquiry in 1955, Mikhail Yermolaev, the twenty-year-old soldier mentioned at the start of this chapter, testified that he met the "queer" (*pidarast*) Kiselev while visiting the "girls" in Rakhia with a group of soldiers from his base.[45] Despite his harsh language, Yermolaev's statement to police lacks any self-justifying or fear of taint by association: he even admitted that he was sexually aroused during Kiselev's seduction and that later he gave Kiselev his address, suggesting this liaison might continue.

In Morozov's statement to the police, he said that Kiselev invented a nonexistent "sister" to lure him to pay a visit to his room at the bathhouse. Whether or not Kiselev actually used this ploy is difficult to establish; what is clear is that as a pretext, the prospect of meeting a young woman was an intelligible motive for further contact between the two men. Finally, Morozov's sudden marriage so soon after demobilization, seen in conjunction with his liaison with and eventual murder of Kiselev, suggests a concerted internal struggle against persistent same-sex desire. The newly demobbed soldier needed not just a woman to house him and care for him, but a fig leaf of masculine respectability to deflect attention from that shameful desire, which, if the medical expertise is to be believed, was for men to penetrate him.[46]

Between men in private

Men's homosocial relations worked to exclude women, to build solidarities between men, and in some cases to facilitate homosexual contacts. Homosociability took various forms: in these cases, all-male drinking-parties (*popoiki*), workplace fraternization, mentoring, and comradeship all figure significantly as primarily private sites where male bonds were made.

Alcohol consumption had long been part of the rituals of friendship, status construction, and courtship between men in Russia.[47] Drinking together relaxed men's routine emotional reserve, created intimacy between them, and cloaked sallies into homosexual territory. Despite the efforts of the Soviet state to reduce men's alcohol consumption, these cases show that drinking was a fixed ritual of masculine culture, one that authorities felt they could do little to alter by intervening directly in the private spaces that men created. Psychiatrists assessing eight defendants in the 1951 Grishin case quizzed each man about his drinking habits. Significant consumption "on payday" (s poluchki) was a common practice: some men admitted to consuming between a third- and a half-liter of vodka on the day they got paid, and one senses that they might have been underreporting their consumption. Nineteen-year-old Ivan Lopukhin said he "definitely drank on payday and on other occasions and more often 300 grams and sometimes even more"; he reported that he drank with company and when alone. Anton Baskov, thirty-eight years old and married, had been drinking since the age of eighteen and got through as much as a liter of vodka a day alone and in company. Payday drinking was part of worker life. Grishin said to psychiatrists that he "[did] not abuse alcohol," but they noted that his liver was enlarged and his general health was poor. This evidence seemed to confirm the consequences of the drinking parties he organized in his barracks room.

In this case, the rituals of drinking together were sufficiently significant to commemorate in snapshots taken and offered as presents "for remembrance, as a keepsake" (na pamiat'). Police removed at least three such photographs from Grishin's collection (see Figure 2.1). One showed a party of five men seated around a small table set with some black bread, in a cramped room, with one young man raising one shot-glass to another, held by a figure whose back is to the camera. It was inscribed on the reverse: "To my friend Pavel from Vanya, a keepsake. Remember how we met. A photograph of April 5. Mikheev, Iv[an] Vas[ilevich]." Perhaps Grishin is himself in this photograph, but there is no other image of him in the case file with which to compare it. Snapshots like these fixed a moment of masculine solidarity in the personal histories of these men and signified deeper intimacies for some men in the frame.[48] Police too recognized the power of drink to create dangerous masculine intimacy. In 1959, during the investigation into Kiselev's murder, a police photographer reconstructed the day Morozov killed Kiselev in 1955 (see Figure 2.2). The murderer was posed pointing to the canteen where he and Kiselev bought vodka and snacks; after drinking some there, they returned with a half-liter of vodka to Kiselev's room in the bathhouse to drink privately.

Friendship, work comradeship, and mentoring younger men and youths were another arena for homosocial bonds that could shade into homosexual relations. Grishin's large collection of photographs hints at a wide acquaintance with men; most of the photos lack inscriptions and cannot be characterized beyond the banal observation that most of these men were under thirty and

FIGURE 2.1 *Snapshot of a drinking party, from Pavel Grishin's collection of photographs. Grishin case file.*

FIGURE 2.2 *"Morozov points out the cafeteria that he visited with Kiselev," police photograph. Morozov case file.*

generally of pleasant appearance. Some with inscriptions hint at significant ties between Grishin and youths of a mentoring or friendly character. An image of two young men sitting in an affectionate proximity bears the dedication: "Nevdubstroi. For remembrance to Pavel Viktorovich Grishin from Zorin Kolya M. 4.XI.48." Another portrait of a clear-faced young man is inscribed: "26.VI.48. For remembrance to Pavel Viktorovich Grishin from your friend Fyodor. A keepsake of working days at Dubrovka." Dubrovka was a neighboring village, and evidently Fyodor and Grishin shared a work assignment there. Another photo, of a trio of schoolboys, was inscribed in a sentimental vein: "For remembrance to Pavel Viktorovich from Sasha, 17 years old. Remember me. Nevdubstroi." Sasha had crossed out an earlier, 1949 dedication of this same snapshot to his mother in order to give Grishin this image; he also gave another portrait of himself in his winter coat, with his "Sasha" written in a schoolboy hand on the margin.

The desire on the part of many men to be remembered, audible in these inscriptions, forms one side, possibly an entirely positive one, of the story of same-sex relations between working men and Grishin. These tokens of memory also remind us that homosexual relations between these men were desired and consensual. Another photo from the collection projects the ideal of male friendship, but also reminds us of the sinister sexual histories that friendship masks (see Figure 2.3). Two men in civilian outfits and workers' flat caps are turned to smile at each other; on the left is Sergei Denisov, named as having had oral sex with Grishin in January 1951. The other is thirty-two-year-old Vladimir Biryukov, who twice raped Babenko and also had consensual relations with her husband. The friendship of Denisov (charges against him were dropped because he only engaged in fellatio) and Biryukov (sentenced to fifteen years for rape) looks "normal" despite the careful tearing of the snapshot in two and the policeman's scrawl noting the names of each likeness.[49]

FIGURE 2.3 *Snapshot of Sergei Denisov and Vladimir Biryukov, with names inscribed by a police investigator. Grishin case file.*

Meanings for men's same-sex relations

Given the character of official documents, the voices of same-sex desiring subjects are distorted; access to an authentic key to the meanings for homosexuality held by these men and those who observed them is not easily gained. Yet some plausible notions can be proposed based on these documents and the historical context in which they were produced. Homosexual relations in these cases had emotional and gendered dimensions that charged them with significance for our understanding of sexuality and of the private and the public in post-1945 Soviet Russia.

Witness and suspect statements taken by Soviet police were reported in an official language that obscures how men in these cases actually explained and described their sexual encounters with other men. In legal discourse, these encounters were often reduced to physiological acts of a "mutual" character. I have argued elsewhere that to consign Soviet male homosexuality to the mere sex act is to adopt the "policeman's lens" for what are in fact complex phenomena with emotional and social dimensions.[50] Recall the stilted phrase used by the court in sentencing Morozov in 1959: "a personal relationship associated with the commission of sodomy." Behind the awkward language lay an unspeakable emotional dimension to men's homosexual encounters, a personal psychological realm that was censored out of all public discourse during the Soviet era, and that remains difficult to explore in post-Soviet Russian culture to this day.[51]

In the 1951 Nevdubstroi case, without idealizing Grishin or the men who raped his wife, Babenko, it is possible to propose that beneath the homosexual acts bluntly described were emotional ties that mattered to these men. These ties were built on existing comradeship and strengthened by the "conspiratorial" process of forging consent to gay sex. Friendship or masculine honor constrained these men from raping each other; here was an important gendered distinction when contrasted with their violent abuse of Babenko.[52] Anton Baskov had known Grishin since 1940 and had been having voluntary sexual relations with him since 1946. In court, Baskov described Grishin as "a great dancer, a merry fellow who would sing and play and dance in any gathering."[53] Ivan Lopukhin repeatedly had oral sex with Grishin over two years and finally consented to sodomy with him in 1951, suggesting a progression to deeper intimacy between the nineteen-year-old and the older man. Grishin's photographs demonstrate that whatever we might think of the object to whom they were addressed, he was capable of inspiring strong feelings in young men. Similarly, if we accept that Morozov's liaison with Kiselev in Rakhia in 1954–5 was more than a one-night stand, we see again the traces of an emotional tie between a younger and an older man, in this case between a soldier in the tricky liminal state of demobilization and an older man with resources and comforts to offer. The age- and status-related distinctions between friends could charge these relationships with erotic power. As David Halperin argues, the pattern of erotically charged differences of age, stage, and gender performance between men is an age-old continuity in homosexual history.[54]

How conventionally gendered were these homosexual relations? Did they mimic heterosexual roles and conform to a stereotype of masculine, insertive, "active" partner, coupled with an effeminized receptive, "passive" partner? In early twentieth-century urban Russia, such stereotypes circulated in the homosexual underground and in the expert world that observed it, distinguishing between the usually older man said to enjoy being penetrated and perceived as effeminate (in Russian, the *tetka*, or "auntie," analogous to the French *tante* or German *Tante*) and younger "pederasts for money" who were their supposed masculine "active" and sexually "normal" counterparts. Such stereotypes persisted in the Soviet underground well into the 1930s and 1940s, albeit in concealed form. The various stereotypes of Russia's urban homosexual subculture seem outwardly similar to George Chauncey's wolves, punks, and fairies for early twentieth-century New York, the city cousins of Boag's jockers and punks in the Oregon hinterland.[55]

Of the protagonists in the first case, only Grishin's psychiatric assessment (commissioned and conducted in the city of Leningrad) pointed to an effeminate character: he was described as "mannered," he flinched from the doctor's tiny reflex hammer, he gesticulated and cried out affectedly, he carried himself submissively, and he was incapable of standing up to criticism. Grishin walked projecting his buttocks, and he "eagerly and nakedly" described his desire for men and the ways in which he realized it. From the age of eight he was particularly devoted to fellatio, but he also had anal intercourse in both active and passive forms.[56] No such characterizations tarnished the psychiatric assessments of the various workers and soldiers found to have had sex with Grishin. It appears that experts sought to cast him alone as the effeminate homosexual, to distinguish him from the men with whom he had sex. Grishin's war service as a cleaner in the army, normally "women's work," probably also contributed to official perceptions of effeminacy surrounding him. How he performed his gender in private with men is harder to discern. In contrast to several witness statements about Aleksei Kiselev's effeminacy, bystanders said little about any unmanly mannerisms in Grishin. This silence may have been more than mere quiet accommodationism. Perhaps witnesses were reluctant to describe such nonconformism in the earlier case, conducted before Stalin's death during a period of heightened but selective terror campaigns. Ultimately, urban experts emphasized unmanly characteristics in their forensic assessment, and this set Grishin apart from the other defendants as a source of contamination.

In the later case, murder victim Aleksei Kiselev's openly nonconforming, effeminate personality emerges as a striking feature of his character, something that achieved the status of an open secret around Rakhia village. In the relaxed post-Stalin atmosphere, it likely seemed easier to admit one had tolerated "odd" behavior in a comrade. The day after his death, police questioned twenty-three-year-old Nikolai Voronin, a metalworker who had known Kiselev for five years. The young man told police: "For some time now Kiselev would come to my place of residence completely without any purpose, when he would sit down, have a laugh, and then go off. In conversation Kiselev constantly referred to himself as a woman. Thus sometimes, instead of saying *ya poshel* or *ya pogulial* ['I went' or 'I went out,' masculine gender], he said *ya poshla, ya poguliala* [feminine gender]. I was aware that Kiselev loved soldiers, and he often spent time with them."[57]

Kiselev's use of feminine grammatical inflections to speak about himself was a flagrant violation of masculine norms. Such queeny outrageousness had been part of Russian gay speech since the end of the nineteenth century, when the male homosexual subculture that exploited the rich gender inflections of the Russian language flourished in St. Petersburg and Moscow. These linguistic arabesques did not disappear under Lenin and Stalin, but terror against homosexuals in the 1930s – after Stalin's criminalization of sodomy in 1934 – did suppress flagrant effeminacy.[58] (It survived into the post-Stalin Soviet era, as shown in Chapters 3 and 4.) Kiselev was known to make frequent forays into Leningrad; he was probably in contact with that underground subculture of gendered, "active-passive" homosexuality. What is extraordinary was his failure to confine this feminizing language to a circle of initiates. It is difficult to know how widely he used it; a laundress Loginova, who lived under the same roof in the bathhouse with him for two years and knew him well, denied "any strange activies by Kiselev," and implicit in this response to police questions was an awareness of his unorthodox reputation.[59]

Loginova's statement mentioned a different kind of gender anxiety, Kiselev's, that was peculiar to the bathhouse work environment: "While I was working in the bath I noticed that Kiselev never washed in the bath when the bath was serving men [that is, during men's hours], and I know that he never even washed with the other male bathhouse employees but always tried to wash alone."[60] Fearing exposure before those by whom one is sexually aroused was not an unusual anxiety found in psychiatric case histories of homosexuality.[61] This shyness too was a kind of gender transgression, a reluctance to participate in the insouciant display of one's body among comrades for whom no desire was meant to exist. Kiselev in his feminized persona evidently found the male gaze too arousing and therefore disturbing to bear.

That Kiselev's squeamishness about being naked around men could be noticed and described says something about its queerness, about its violation of unwritten norms of gender and the public–private border in Russian bathhouse culture. Officials began segregating bathhouses by sex from the seventeenth century. Sexual impropriety was meant to be avoided by preventing men and women from mixing. Some baths built permanently separated men's and women's spaces; others, like Rakhia's communal bath, operated to a schedule of men's and women's hours. The effect was to produce a homosocial environment and one that before 1917 was also often a homosexual one (on the men's side at least). Yet in all respectable discourse, precisely because of the increasingly well-enforced sex segregation of modern facilities, Soviet bathhouses were presented as a desexualized, health-giving, and, increasingly, public realm.[62] Kiselev's discomfort in the washing chamber and the steam room was a token of illicit desire that contradicted these cultural norms by sexualizing a space that was supposed to be public and asexual.

The meanings ascribed to homosexuality by nonparticipants also offer some insights into quiet accommodationism in this time and place. The degree to which sex between men could be tolerated in rural Soviet life illustrates a boundary between the public and the private. The strenuous denials of knowledge that witnesses repeated in the Kiselev investigation, while simultaneously admitting that Kiselev was not like other men, display a tension over knowledge designated as "public" and things viewed as private, personal affairs. Witnesses generally turned a blind eye to Kiselev's peculiarities, sometimes burying them in euphemisms and jokes. One neighbor called him "kind of an oddball" (*kakoi-to chudakovatyi*).[63] Voronin the young metalworker was exceptionally frank; he was "aware that Kiselev loved soldiers" and constantly used feminine grammatical forms, yet Voronin made no comment on these extraordinary facts. The witness Mikhailova observed that "Aleksei himself sometimes said that he'd had a lieutenant over to stay, and then he would laugh, and I never knew if he was serious or not."[64] Bystrova, a stoker who arrived first at the bathhouse on the morning the body was found, admitted that Kiselev told her that "he found some soldiers very beautiful," but "why he said this I do not know." She admitted she knew that some of the soldiers who visited the girls at Barrack No. 18 also visited Kiselev, "but I myself know nothing about it. I don't know who he was friends with or who came to visit him." She ended her long witness statement with the words, "I repeat that I know nothing about Kiselev's friends."[65] Olga the barracks girl denied all knowledge of Kiselev's friends and said she barely knew Kiselev at all.[66] The laundress Loginova was even more adamant in denial. Kiselev "did not like any conversations about women. . . . He was always under my eye, and I never saw a single woman come and visit him, and he never visited anyone nor had close relations with anyone." No one in the bathhouse, she said, was a close friend of his, and she repeated that she knew nothing of his friends or visitors. "I cannot even imagine," she declared, "why Kiselev committed suicide."[67] Only Kiselev's boss, the manager of the bathhouse, a woman named Irina Vaganova, found it impossible to avoid passing some comment on his way of life, for she was the only Communist Party member who was interviewed about him. "Kiselev . . . was a very nervous person. Kiselev made friends with soldiers. I even criticized him for this, for the fact that he invited them to come and stay with him," she reassured police – and then swiftly changed the subject.[68]

Such phrases echo with confused embarrassment before police investigators: these witnesses were caught in a double bind. How could they have ignored, or tolerated, such an "oddball" in their midst? Yet the embarrassment is accompanied by a determination to mark out realms of knowledge and unknowing that constituted boundaries between public reputation on the one hand, and private life (friendship, intimate relationships, motives for love or suicide) on the other.[69] In the postwar era, popular notions of domestic privacy and accepted official intrusion were in flux, and these Russians' quiet accommodationism of men's same-sex relations was only one aspect of a wider negotiation over the private realm in Soviet society.[70]

Gender, silence, and queer (in-)visibility in 1950s Russia

Russia after 1945 was a society marked by war, as Juliane Fürst reminds us.[71] These cases bear the scars of that experience and suggest ways in which gender relations between men and women and between men radically shifted after 1945. Between the sexes, the 1944 family law changes that yielded casual and disorderly heterosexual affairs and the demographic sex-ratio imbalance grossly tilted the postwar scales in favor of men. The aftershocks of total war also generated rising criminal violence, including a significant increase in reported rapes. Women faced bleak and perilous prospects on a diminished sex and marriage market, and some, like Lidia Babenko, might have felt that they had little choice but to endure a violent and loveless partnership.

Despite their advantages, men's lives were also fraught with war-related anxieties. The 1951 Grishin file records the war service of four out of six eligible defendants, and none had a "good war." Grishin was invalided and did "unmanly" work as an army cleaner; two more, Kononov and Belousov, were seriously wounded in combat; and the last, Kuzmin, had lost his wife and children in the Siege of Leningrad. The war damaged their bodies, minds, and families. Transition to postwar life was evidently stressful. Moreover, for younger men like Gusev and Lopukhin, the two nineteen-year-olds convicted of sodomy with Grishin, conscription loomed. In the later Kiselev case, the Cold War threat of new conflict still structured men's anxieties. In the 1950s, when renewed war seemed imminent, the transitions between army and civilian life (in both directions) by cohorts of young men doing compulsory military service were stressful rites of passage.[72] The Red Army pressed its claims on the young, healthy, postwar man, and, as Rebecca Kay has demonstrated for a later period, military service was likely an unwanted hiatus before earning a living sufficient to set up a household.[73] Yet even for the most economically successful men in these cases, dissatisfaction with the male condition found its expression in a flight from officially approved forms of recreation. Rakhia's club and library and Nevdubstroi's house of culture, touted by the *Bol'shaia sovetskaia entsiklopediia*, figure nowhere in these cases. Instead, these men constructed private spaces for illicit pleasures and sexual activity. Grishin transformed his barracks room into a "den of vice"; it was a place of vodka-fueled and often violent escape. The masculine antiutopia of the payday drinking bout was a means of asserting control over a bleakly regimented world. Even if, as in the Rakhia case, the drinking parties in the women's barrack were mixed-sex affairs, it was still a private space in which men held most of the best cards, and the young women who played hostess occupied a subordinate and distinctly disreputable role.

Disorderly heterosexual relations, based on overwhelming male privilege, marked the sexual culture of these villages. Grishin's use of his wife as "bait" for male companionship and his neighbors living behind a plywood partition who made little complaint at what they heard suggest that sexual probity counted for little. Similarly, in Rakhia a little later in the 1950s, the barracks women frequently entertained soldiers even if they flatly denied having soldier-visitors to police. No case was raised against these young women, whose activities might have been judged, in a more ideologically charged era, as "systematic prostitution" meriting re-education if not harsh punishment.[74] The relaxation of heterosexual relations implicitly encouraged in the 1944 decree was realized in a crude microcosm here. Soldiers and officers admitted visiting the women's barrack without particular embarrassment (an officer introduced Morozov to the girls), and their activities were indulged by the village.

If silent indulgence, disorder, and sometimes violence structured hetero-sexual sex life, as illustrated in these rural cases, it should come as little surprise that disorder and violence accompanied homosexual liaisons there too. Quiet accommodationism facilitated exploitation and misogynist violence, as Babenko and Kiselev found to their cost. The commonplace notion of gay men's "shared cultural history," that violence is something done to us by straight men, requires reconsideration by historians as well as by those who study contemporary antigay violence.[75] In many societies, there is plenty of cultural and historical evidence suggesting that violence structured and structures desire between men.[76] By insistently denying same-sex affairs and desires, observers partitioned them off, constructing a sexuality in the shadows of what reluctant onlookers and furtive participants were willing to say. If in these cases a "regime of silence" operated at the popular level in these villages, urban investigators such as forensic psychiatrists were nevertheless determined to expose the dangerous, unmanly, "passive" homosexual and distinguish him from the others who engaged less systematically and more "actively" in same-sex sexual acts. They brought an urban medical discourse to bear on such subjects to make a concealed sexuality legible in modern terms.

Whatever the violence and misogyny that apparently surrounded them, the sexual and emotional ties between many of these men were ardently desired and realized though elaborate rituals of consent. Their same-sex affairs displayed overlapping features of both the rural (age-structured, mentoring) and urban (gender-structured, active-passive) patterns of sexual practice noted in other societies. In Grishin's world some (but by no means all) relations between men were rooted in workplace friendships and in the mentoring of young conscripts. At the same time, Grishin's effeminacy may have structured some of his sexual relations with more mature men. In Kiselev's case, this overtly effeminate village queer apparently frequented Leningrad's urban homosexual subculture. Yet, at the same time, if the statements of his bedmates and the experts who examined them are true, he could be more sexually "active" than any simple reading of his femininity implies. A Russian man who could publicly utter *ya poshla* in 1955 was a complex amalgam of active and passive, of courage and abasement.

3

The Diary of Soviet Singer Vadim Kozin:

Reading Queer Subjectivity in 1950s Russia

Vadim Aleskeevich Kozin (1905–94) shot to Soviet stardom as a singer of apolitical "gypsy romance" songs during the height of Stalin's Terror and then the Second World War. Between 1937 and 1943 he released at least 68 separate phonograph recordings of his work, including no less than three versions of his biggest hit, *Druzhba* ("Friendship").[1] He was a pop star who generated legends: one of the most notorious claims that he entertained the leaders of the Allies when Stalin hosted the Teheran Conference in 1943. Winston Churchill himself was supposed to have asked Stalin to let Kozin sing for him. Yet within a year the singer was imprisoned in the Gulag camps of Magadan in Kolyma, in the Far East, for his homosexuality and supposed anti-Soviet sentiments. Released in 1950, he struggled to rebuild his career while forced to remain a Magadan resident, topping the bill on tours of Siberia with the Magadan Musical-Dramatic Theater in 1955–6. His diary recording eighteen months "on tour" during these years offers a tantalizing glimpse of the everyday life of a Siberian superstar with a queer eye for the Soviet guy. At the same time, the diary raises questions for the historian of the Gulag queer, for its provenance is problematic and its editing, somewhat troubling.[2] In Russia today, the conventional commemoration of Kozin usually erases the memory of his homosexuality. (I discuss these concerns in Chapters 8 and 9.) Despite such worries, Kozin's writing still offers a unique voice in Soviet diaries: the thoughts of a man who suffered under Stalin's anti-sodomy law, and who lived and worked among people who *knew* about his queerness. For all the uncounted tens of thousands of victims of this law, we have virtually no other personal documents registering the voice of the "Gulag queer," or telling us how these victims recovered, if they could, from the damage to their lives.

To begin, I set out the details of the life of an unlikely Soviet superstar Vadim Kozin, and describe the historical backdrop against which he lived his unconventional life. I then examine his diary of this short period, and comment first of all on the special nature of queer diaries as a sub-species of the diary genre; and of "private" personal writing – "intimate archives" in one useful formulation – in the Soviet case more generally. Comparison helps us to see the resemblance of many features that Vadim Kozin's diary shares with an earlier example of the Russian queer diary – the much longer and more scholarly journal of St. Petersburg poet, novelist and vocalist Mikhail Alekseevich Kuzmin (1872–1936), which he kept from 1905 to the 1930s; and with other modern "gay" diaries.[3] Vadim Kozin's 1955–6 diary is a remarkably rich document, one that addresses "the queer dilemmas of the self" that have long confronted Russia's same-sex desiring people: how to reconcile queer desire with being Russian and Soviet, how to situate queerness in the culture of Tolstoy, Lenin, and Stalin, and how to live beautifully and morally in an ugly and immoral world.

In the past twenty-five years, as more examples of personal journals from the turbulent Soviet era have come to light, historians and scholars of literature have begun a fruitful conversation about the peculiar nature of the Soviet diary. I have benefited in my thinking about Kozin's diary from work by Russian literary specialists like Irina Paperno and Boris Wolfson, and historians of Russia like Jochen Hellbeck and Anna Krylova. Some of the most useful guidance I have found about how to read Kozin's diary has come not from a Russianist, but from the historian of queer Victorian and Edwardian England, Matt Cook, whose work on the diary of George Ives is inspiring. With Paperno and Wolfson, I accept that diaries are capacious and malleable as a form of writing, are quotidian in their production, are focused on the intimate sphere, and very much reflect the literary conventions of their time.[4] From Hellbeck, I take that the diary is not just a lone *literary* exercise, but a social and even a public one – one in which the diarist works on his "self" as a persona in history, trying on different masks or modeling different poses, in response to experience in the world.[5] Krylova similarly cautions us to think carefully about the diarist as shaped by environment and unlikely to be as stable and coherent as the "liberal subject" we might hope to find; queer critics like Laura Doan have also pointed out that our projections of LGBT present-day values on past lives distort our grasp of unfamiliar sexualities in history.[6] All this dictates a caution when reading Kozin's journal for a "heroic" queer voice: we must be prepared to find more than one voice, and more than one fixed sense of sexuality and self. Finally, inspired by Cook, I look for what could be called the "queer signature" in Kozin's diary, the features of silence, coding, concealment, and identification that mark queer diaries as tools for processing existence in a homophobic world, and as vehicles for imagining a world beyond homophobia.[7]

The life and loves of Vadim Kozin

Vadim Kozin was born in St. Petersburg in 1905, into middle-class family; his father was a merchant and his mother was a singer from a dynasty of "gypsy" performers.[8] "Gypsy" singers and choirs were hugely popular in the cafés and restaurants of pre-revolutionary St. Petersburg. The "gypsy romance" song genre – celebrating love and tragedy in vivid clichés of starry nights, campfires and fiery dark eyes – were one of Russia's first modern popular music styles. Phonograph records of "gypsy romances" reached a mass audience and created the Russian Empire's first modern singer-stars, such as the "incomparable" Anastasia Vialtseva (a favorite target of the homage of pre-revolutionary drag-artistes, by the way).[9] As a little tyke, Kozin tottered on a chair to put one of Vialtseva's recordings on the gramophone, and then began trying to out-sing her – early evidence perhaps of his queer ear, or at very least, proof of his canny sense of how to weave a story in Soviet Magadan to link his talents to those of the last generation of pre-revolutionary Petersburg artistes.[10]

The 1917 Revolutions brought the nationalization of the family property; young Kozin finished school early and his intellectual formation was a blend of family musical training and self-instruction in the arts; as a youth, he even took odd jobs in the city's dockyards. An attempt to enter a naval training school in 1923 ended in expulsion over his "non-proletarian" origins. Kozin never admitted to any early sexual contact with sailors, but Petersburg (from 1924, Leningrad) had a long tradition of same-sex cruising and sexual liaisons in this milieu.[11] Kozin's diary shows he was alert to the charms of sailors in port towns while on tour in 1955–6. In the 1920s, as his voice changed into a striking tenor, he found work singing and performing wherever he could in the cafés of Leningrad under Lenin's mixed economy. By the mid–1920s, he was learning stagecraft by playing the piano to accompany films in cinemas. He began singing in intermission performances and his talent was spotted by a composer of "gypsy romances," Boris Prozorovsky, who also recognized the young man's ambiguous sexuality, and ultimately would initiate him into sexual activity with men.

The young singer was perhaps equally attracted to women and men, but he would later claim that bad experiences with women led him to feel more comfortable with men. In a 1959 police interrogation about his sexual practices, Kozin said that his first experience was as a youth with a woman of thirty-five, a Russian teacher who seduced him and then threatened him with scandal over claims of pregnancy. He felt revulsion as a result.[12] Not long after he had his first male–male experiences with Prozorovsky. Later in the 1930s, he shared a billet with a male acrobat close to his own age, reportedly a satisfying sexual education. As his career advanced, and both women and men offered themselves to him, Kozin may have wavered between both sexes. To the police in 1959, he explained his sexual drive "as passive with male youths only in my imagination, but physically in reality

I liked to be close to them and just masturbate, or sometimes even just sit close to them and talk to the young man I was attracted to, and when he left and I was alone I would think about him and masturbate. . . . I had the same feeling for women, but then I would be gripped by panic." Aware that proximity with women could end in sexual intimacy, he was filled with "shame and dread" of failure, and that terror had "atrophied my will and mind" regarding relations with women.[13] This detailed "confession," obtained in 1959 after arrest for a second sex offense with a male police decoy is difficult to accept as an absolutely truthful account of his sexual career. Its emphasis on ambivalent desire that might have been directed toward women in better circumstances, and its insistence on sex acts between men not extending to anal intercourse but limited to masturbation or even just cuddling, are excuses often encountered in the testimony of Soviet men caught up by the anti-sodomy law.[14] Yet at the same time the relatively rich sexual and psychological detail suggests Kozin the artiste was at least drawing on some combination of fact and fancy in composing a defensive narrative for his interrogators.[15]

Kozin's musical career blossomed in the 1930s; he toured the Soviet Union with Leningrad's light entertainment companies, and built a repertoire based on the "gypsy" formula and on folklore tunes. The mid–1930s were a confused time for Soviet musical ideologists, who deplored "gypsy romance-ism" for its associations with Old Russia and its taverns and dives; their criticism was part of a larger ambivalence about sexualized popular music, especially American jazz and the "bourgeois" fox-trot. Yet concert and theater managers found audiences could not get enough of this music.[16] Soviet jazz and light music became "socialist" and "realist" thanks to re-branding. Stalin helped the ideologists when he decided that the masses, tirelessly building a bastion of socialism, deserved light music, festivals, and entertainment (as he memorably put it in 1935: "Life has become better, comrades. Life has become gayer!"). Meanwhile, of course, life was becoming anything but gayer in reality, with famine having stalked the countryside in 1932–3, miserable living conditions for millions in the cities, and the use of extra-legal arrests, and deportations to the expanding Gulag. Stalin's 1934 law making male homosexuality a crime justified surveillance and arrests of men for same-sex relations. Kozin's rising popularity probably protected him, for a time, from arrest for his queer sexual proclivities, which blossomed along with his career as he toured the country with Leningrad promoters in the first half of the 1930s.

Vadim Kozin left his native city in 1936, never to return, moving to the Soviet capital Moscow and to critical acclaim as a tenor with a charming stage personality. The public, perhaps disenchanted with an endless diet of high propaganda marches and skittishly nervous about the gathering Great Terror, responded warmly to Kozin's apolitical romantic repertoire, delivered with a sincerity that seemed to reveal his innermost feelings. He was also one of a dwindling pool of talented male voices on the Soviet stage, as political repression and fear reduced the competition. As a singer of songs written for him like "Friendship" and increasingly, as a composer in his own right of ballads like "Autumn," Kozin rode the crest of a wave to Soviet superstardom.

In the late 1930s and early 1940s, the singer lived recklessly, earning a reputation among concert and theatrical bureaucrats for diva-style high-handedness that seemed hardly commensurate with the sacred calling of a Soviet artiste.[17] He declared "war on the microphone," refusing to sing when concert managers tried to cut deals with the state radio broadcaster to transmit his performances live.[18] In the provincial railway junction of Cheliabinsk, Kozin kept concert-goers waiting forty minutes until a mike was removed from the stage, and the region's radio audience was disappointed to find the evening's Kozin broadcast cancelled. He was cut-throat in haggling with theater managers, once demanding a 14,000-ruble fee from Odessa officials during the intermission of a concert performance he threatened to curtail then and there. He presented the state concert authorities with 600-ruble taxi bills while the rest of his entourage took the bus. But through it all, he shrewdly kept his concert audiences on side; as the trade magazine *Soviet Music* remarked in 1940, Vadim Kozin was "the idol of hysterical young ladies and the terror of concert organizations."

Kozin's fame and wealth enabled him to lead an indulgent lifestyle, living in Moscow's Metropole Hotel, then as now a VIP address, and he indulged his sexual appetites as well. Kozin apparently thought nothing of spending 200 rubles on a fine dinner in the Metropole's heavily bugged and secret-police infested dining room for one of his many male companions, who reportedly changed with rapid regularity. The secret police observed, but did not touch, the singer. During the Second World War he performed hundreds of concerts for servicemen at the front and in hospitals, sang for factory workers in the rear, and made rare wartime recordings. To this day a legend, not confirmed in any records, persists among Kozin fans that he performed at the Teheran Conference in late 1943. Churchill was said to have asked Stalin to let Kozin sing at the British Prime Minister's birthday reception.[19] To soar this high was always dangerous in Soviet official life – and for fans, the legend seems to compensate for, and explain, his subsequent disgrace.

The reality of Kozin's fall was probably less glamorous and more typical of the regime's techniques of "talent management." According to Kozin himself, in 1944 Stalin's secret police chief Lavrenty Beria summoned the singer to discuss his repertoire: why was he not singing songs in praise of The Leader? Was he not fully behind the Soviet war effort? Kozin claimed he was a "lyrical singer" and could not alter his repertoire; supposedly his bold refusal to pander to the Stalin cult was the trigger for his downfall.[20] Whatever the truth, the secret police arrested him in May 1944 and in February 1945 he was sentenced to eight years' imprisonment on a combination of charges: propaganda against Soviet power in wartime, sex offenses with minors, and sodomy.[21] He was deported from Moscow and sent to Magadan, gateway to the Kolyma River basin, a huge gold-mining fiefdom of the secret police-run "Dalstroi" Trust. It was the most dreaded of Stalin's Gulag camp complexes: polar temperatures, isolated from the rest of Russia (the so-called "mainland") and with a fearsome death-rate: of some 900,000 prisoners sent there between 1932 and 1956, official records say that almost 128,000 died.[22]

In the capital of Dalstroi the disgraced singer found, like many great stars of Soviet arts and sport who entered the Gulag, that there could be soft landings for those of exceptional talent, and under the patronage of Magadan Camp commandant Aleksandra Gridasova (wife the Dalstroi chief General Ivan Nikishov), Kozin was immediately allowed to perform on the stage of Magadan's Musical-Dramatic Theater. According to one account he was taken straight from a transport ship to the theater and told to sing on the spot. Another legend suggests a darker debut. A closed concert for well-lubricated police workers was held, with General Nikishov in attendance. The program director saved Vadim Kozin's appearance for the opening of the second act. When the curtains parted a sensation erupted: Kozin was standing against a grand piano, surrounded by a sea of artificial flowers. The boozed up crowd began to applaud him but Nikishov stopped the proceedings and berated the audience, and then the singer. "Who are you shouting 'hoorah' for? That pederast?! . . . You – off the stage, take him straight to the punishment cell!" His wife managed to rescue Kozin by admitting him to a prisoner-hospital for a month.[23] It was a public humiliation that must have scarred the singer deeply, even though in fact he continued to perform in the theater's mixed troupe of prisoner and free artistes. In 1950, he obtained early release, and worked as a "free employee" in the camp's cultural facilities as an artist and librarian, cementing a prodigious appetite for reading and book-collection that would last the rest of his life. Soon after Stalin's death in March 1953, with the policy of "de-Stalinization," he became an "artist of the highest category" in the Theater's company. In 1955, he embarked, along with the Magadan company, on the first of a series of grueling concert tours round the region, and it is from this initial period of personal and public optimism that Kozin's diaries date. Kozin's star billing on a nine-month tour of European Russia in 1958 earned the Magadan Theater nearly one million rubles in profit. Kozin seemed poised to stage a triumphant national comeback, if he could only secure full rehabilitation, and with it, the right to move more freely.

A comeback was not to be. Kozin was arrested again for homosexual offenses in October 1959. The Stalin-era law against male homosexuality was not repealed as part of the new leader Nikita Khrushchev's policy of de-Stalinization. In fact, in 1958 the interior ministry issued secret orders, discussed in Chapter 1, to "renew the struggle against sodomy." In October 1959, in Khabarovsk on the last leg of a national tour, Kozin met a young man who turned out to be a police informer. (The "youth" – his age is unknown – already had two counts of sodomy against him dating from

1952 and 1958; he was under duress to entrap the singer.) Kozin invited the young man to his room twice and on the second visit, the singer was arrested, and charged again with sodomy (article 154a).[24] His diary was confiscated, not to be returned to him until 1991. The new affair damaged his reputation irreparably. Kozin served just a few months in prison, but he took this second humiliation as a signal to abandon hope of a comeback or return to Moscow. He lived in Magadan until his death in 1994, and his late career fell under a significant constraint; he was only allowed to give local concerts, and there was a ban on mentioning him in the national press. During the 1960s, in an apparent bid to restore his credentials, he wrote a series of songs dedicated to Magadan under the general title "I Love This Land." Magadan city officials prize these songs today as they boast of the singer's apartment-museum, and a public monument to Kozin, in the heart of the former Gulag capital.

During this phase of quasi-disgrace in the 1960s–80s, two people entered Kozin's life who would be instrumental in engineering a revival of national interest in the singer as the Soviet Union crumbled. They made distinctive contributions to the basis for his contemporary commemoration. A young Magadan journalist, the resolutely, one might say anxiously, heterosexual Boris Savchenko met the singer in Magadan's public library in the 1960s; during the course of two decades of interviews with Kozin, he assembled

FIGURE 3.1 *The Kozin Museum in Magadan.*

biographical material on the almost-forgotten star, publishing his first article on Kozin under Soviet censorship in 1982, and his first full-length biography in 1993. It was Savchenko who helped Kozin to retrieve his diary from the Magadan KGB archive in 1991, and Savchenko took possession of the diary upon Kozin's death in 1994. (The fate of Kozin's diaries, and Savchenko's editing of them, is discussed in Chapter 8.) The other figure was Dina Klimova, a pensioner and fan, who moved to Magadan in the mid–1980s, and who is said to have found Kozin, then a shadow of his former self huddled in a cat- and book-filled one-room flat, and restored his dignity and personal hygiene, in time for the fresh wave of attention he was about to receive, from all over the Russian Federation. The formidable Klimova persuaded the Magadan city council to open the apartment-museum devoted to the city's most famous son, in 1993, and she ran it for some years until her death.[25]

The Kozin diary: chronicling "a life incorrectly lived"

The Kozin diary is a unique document in the archives of the Stalinist experience. Despite the fact that thousands of men were persecuted under the 1934 anti-sodomy law, and millions of men and women passed through the Gulag and witnessed or experienced homosexual relations, we have access to no other documents written *by queers* who entered, or were made, by Stalin's Gulag.[26] As noted in Chapter 1, the post-Stalin flood of memoirs and ego documents produced by Gulag survivors present their authors as impeccably heterosexual. Shamed by searing popular and official homophobia, queers did not share their experience in the Gulag-survivor literary outpouring. Instead, this body of work treated the queer inmate as a horrific symptom of Stalinist oppression, an Other to the martyred intellectual prisoner and generations of intelligentsia readers. The lack of queer voices in Gulag survivor literature, and the Othering of the queer in these memoirs contribute to the homophobic politics of historical memory in Russia today (discussed in Chapter 9). As the diary of a recently released homosexual prisoner, Kozin's journal therefore offers an almost unique opportunity to hear from the object of homophobic disgust. Thanks to Boris Savchenko's biographies and the assiduous spadework of Kozin fans, Kozin's queer diary is endowed with an unusually rich penumbra of documentary materials supplying perspectives on his life. This journal is an essential landmark for queer Russians and historians alike.

Why would Kozin keep a diary in these years?[27] Kozin was officially released from imprisonment in 1950, and continued working in the Magadan Musical-Dramatic Theater. The death of Stalin in March 1953 heralded an era of cautious relaxation. It seems likely that Kozin's designation, soon after the dictator's death, as an "artist of the highest category" emboldened the singer to hope that his life was at last emerging from the shadows. Before 1914, the English homosexual rights advocate George Ives kept a cautiously discreet diary, veiling references to his and other's sexuality, especially fearing that the diary could be used by the authorities as evidence to prosecute him for his homosexuality. Yet during and after the First World War, Ives began to write a fuller and franker account of himself in his diary. Matt Cook says that in this phase of his diary Ives presents "a shifting sense of self and possibility, which in turn reflected a changing cultural climate."[28] Something similar holds true for Kozin in post-Stalin Russia. In a climate when the public-private divide was being renegotiated between the state and the people, it became easier for Kozin to write frankly in his diary, and for him to use it to reflect on the injustice he endured. "Whoever reads these pages," he wrote in September 1956, "should not think that these are the lines of a schizophrenic ... Some lines are the minutes and hours of inexpressible misery and suffering, remorse for a life incorrectly lived. If I had departed even just a little from my truthfulness, and was even just a temporary hypocrite, my life would have been totally different. But I want to be myself. Let he who obtains these notes be an honest man, and someday somehow speak up in my defense, when after my death they throw stones at me."[29] Like Ives who experienced the cultural shift of wartime England, Kozin still faced the danger of prosecution for his homosexuality, but the Soviet political climate had relaxed sufficiently for him to use the diary to fashion justifications for his "life incorrectly lived."

What kind of "self" did Vadim Kozin fashion in his journal? There are complex and multiple voices in the diary: Kozin claims to be a political and sexual conservative, suspicious of and even opposed to de-Stalinization, prudish about allusions to sexuality in songs on the radio and films in the cinema; he is fiercely acquisitive, laying siege to the shops in every town he arrives in on tour and giving a breathless account of what he finds, buys and ships home to Magadan – including a piano from Kamchatka! – and he is a tart gossip, carving up his theatrical colleagues with merciless descriptions of their bad performances and off-stage affairs. Denied the higher education he might have obtained if a proletarian revolution had not intervened, in sharply opinionated detours he displays his considerable knowledge of Soviet and international culture and literature. Time spent in the libraries of the Gulag and "free" Magadan, and later in book shops as well, yielded a stubborn, if provincial, self-conception as a cultivated Petersburger marooned on the other side of the Eurasian continent. That self-image of the sophisticate stranded on the edge of civilization was wreathed with an acute sense of shame about his homosexuality. Kozin devotes fascinating passages to his exploration of the queer "dilemmas of the self," the problems of queer existence that dogged his everyday life as an infamous "pederast." His bitter reflections on the heterosexual hypocrisy of his promiscuous colleagues permeate the diary and constitute an oppressive backdrop. Contrasting with this humiliation, Kozin's musings on the nature of homosexuality and on the homosexual life lived in dignity offer an alternative moral vision. Kozin imagines friendship as a noble bond between men even as he castigates the promiscuity of other gay men in the theatrical troupe. At the same time, his own homosexual appetites are inescapable, and the nomadic existence of a touring artiste offers plenty of scope for Kozin to fall in love promiscuously.

"When will this sanctimonious hypocrisy . . . cease and desist?"

On a day off in June 1955, resting in Sovetskaya Gavan, Kozin complains in his diary about how his homosexuality is viewed by the rest of the touring group:

> The weather is getting on my nerves . . . And the same has to be said for the low level of culture of our artistes. I'm constantly trying to understand why. The point of all their conversations, in the end, leads to bawdiness, double-entendres, coarse jokes. Not just the men, but the women too enjoy this "subject." Despite what they consider to be "my profound moral downfall" it would never enter my head to say such things in company; me, a man of 50, I honestly get quite nauseated listening to their conversations. And these people – the men and the women – believe they are not violating any norms of public morality. To hell with such morality and ethics! It's real, sanctimonious, hypocrisy, of the type that leads to the decline and degeneration of the personality. No, I've got to keep myself apart from them, have fewer points of contact with them.[30]

A month later, two ballet dancers, the Pimenovs, husband and wife, come in for similarly bitter commentary: "throwing aside all decency, they dance like rubbish on stage. And they and their cronies have the right to accuse and condemn me for all kinds of moral deviations. Well I'm a hundred times purer and more crystalline than all of them combined! That is how I feel and I am not pretending or being hypocritical. The bastards, the hypocrites."[31] Kozin's anguish at the coarseness and moralizing of his fellow artistes is a constant theme in the diary. He recounts the sardonic story of his piano accompanist, Boris Terner, who sneaks "a local prostitute, i.e., I beg your pardon, a *pianist*" into his train compartment, and cannot repress his fury at this behavior. "And this philistine (in my opinion) takes every opportunity to refer to me as morally degraded. When will this sanctimonious hypocrisy, this – no let me add – this mass piety, this mass depravity, concealed behind loud phrases about morality, modesty, chastity in daily life, the sacredness of marriage and family, cease and desist? It's all lies, I am purer and more sincere than any of these scoundrels."[32]

In his diary, Kozin rejects the assessment of his character from the homophobic world around him and insists on his crystalline moral purity. The daily diet of heterosexual hypocrisy is not merely a personal or occupational hazard, but is tied, in Kozin's text and perhaps his subconscious, to political oppression too. Another episode of heterosexual promiscuity that he notes in the company he describes as having been covered up "behind the fiction that these are good family men waving Party membership cards."[33] The Communist Party is hypocritical, but it is also incapable of understanding the damage it has done. In Vladivostok in early February 1956, Kozin notes that everyone in the touring group is surprised by his indifference to his soon to be announced rehabilitation.[34] For Kozin, it would only be a partial rehabilitation – the annulment of his baseless conviction for anti-Soviet propaganda; there would be no pardon for his 1945 conviction under Stalin's anti-sodomy law. "I see this as a more sophisticated form of punishment . . . I don't want a pardon, I want an apology for the crimes committed by [Stalin's secret police chief Lavrenty] Beria. I am just one of the millions of his victims."

A month later, in the town of Spassk, Kozin relates a disturbing dream, and this revives memories of political oppression:

I saw Misha Ershov in a dream, I met him in some remote town . . . He told me, with a miserable look on his face, that in Moscow a purge of "the undesirable element" had started, and that he turned out to be one of that "element." What a strange dream! That I should think about, remember Ershov just now after so long.[35]

In the months after the Oscar Wilde trial, George Ives repeatedly dreamt of himself taking Wilde's place in the dock.[36] Here, Kozin records a similar dream of a past purge. Putting this terse allusion to purges of the "undesirable element" down on paper was ostensibly an innocent description of a dream – but it also bore the weight of a sense of injustice that was almost unspeakable. At no point in Kozin's diary does he express a desire for what we might call public homosexual emancipation; Kozin's thirst for justice is not a political project, but a personal one pursued in the pages of his diary. And yet his understanding that he cannot fully participate in the rehabilitation of the "millions of victims" of Beria (if not Stalin) is clear in these entries. The Soviet government's secret 1958 re-affirmation of Stalin's anti-sodomy law was to come two years later. Kozin would never know of this measure until, apparently, the campaign it launched was used against him in 1959 – but his experience of incomplete rehabilitation by the state was poisoned by the homophobic mistrust of his colleagues in the theater company. In his diary, Kozin remains part of an "undesirable element" constructed not just by his heterosexual colleagues but by the Party and state as well. The diary becomes a place to search for the words for his resentment and defiance.

It is also a site for reflection on the nature of homosexuality. Kozin does not speak explicitly in terms of "homosexuality" or "love" between men;

just as George Ives in Oscar Wilde's England felt it prudent to avoid overt references to such love, and just as the Leningrad poet Mikhail Kuzmin's later diary entries also mentioned same-sex affairs in veiled language, Vadim Kozin in the 1950s was forced to avoid incriminating himself by using careful language and often concealing the names of men he fell in love with. Perhaps the pragmatics of writing a queer diary in a homophobic legal environment dictated that Kozin barely referred to homosexuality as a single, coherent concept. It is also possible that Kozin genuinely thought of his same-sex attraction and that of others in disjointed, unconnected terms; he would later present his sex life to police in the 1959 interrogation in just such ambivalent and fragmented language, admittedly, under duress not in the privacy of a diary. In other words – "homosexuality" as we understand it may not have been a coherent concept for him. In these pages it could be a characteristic of "an undesirable element," an unnamable "it," a "joke and mistake of nature," something he "sympathized" with in a comrade, or just a warm feeling of pleasure he got meeting a good-looking young man. In September 1955 in Magnitogorsk, three lads from Moscow called on the singer at his hotel room, hoping to photograph him; Kozin recalled that "one of them I really fancied a lot. I have this feeling that they will come and see me tomorrow. I'm sure of it, and my feeling is never mistaken. I really fancied the two Volodyas, in fact even more than fancied."[37]

As these coded formulas suggest, Kozin saw homosexuality in more than one light – as sometimes a curse and sometimes an ennobling spark. Like Ives, and indeed like Peter Tchaikovsky in his own diary in the 1880s, overtly gender troubling attributes in other queers inspired disdain, pity, and anger in Kozin.[38] In August 1955 in the military factory town of Svirsk, the singer was approached by a desperate figure:

Backstage a young man addressed me, Kuvshinov Fedor Grigorevich – a member of the amateur drama group of the Bokhansky district house of culture. He says he won third place in a Russian song contest in Irkutsk. He looks about 29, speaks with a womanish voice, his language is a bit mentally immature, or more truthfully, half-masculine and half-feminine. He walked up to me and naively asked me in a childish voice, "Can I join your brigade of artistes?" "What do you know how to do?" "I can sing Russian songs, but my luck is bad, there was a lucky fellow, he got hired by Cheremovsky Theater, he gets 350 rubles there. If only that would happen to me, how happy I'd be . . ."

I closed my eyes and listened to this peasant-woman's voice and intonation . . . What could I say to this 30-year-old unmarried man who didn't understand his situation and wanted to escape from his misery into the world of art? This innocent stepchild of nature, guilty of nothing whatsoever. He was afraid of *it*, but he had to adhere to one or the other sex, and here, in this godforsaken hole, he became what I saw before me. A man lacking in culture is twice as unfortunate in this situation. He suffers from persecution, mockery, and he resembles a hen that crows like a cockerel. Surely she [sic] is not to blame? Some experts pronounce ex cathedra that all these problems can be solved by working up a decent sweat! Moronic, self-satisfied chatterers, for whom the sufferings of such unfortunates are alien and incomprehensible, they are in an appalling situation, persecuted and punished, and for what? For a joke and mistake of nature. It drives me to distraction, this moronic slogan: labor is the most radical medicine! The idiots! I'd like to see these fat chatterers with their "scientific theories" be forced to work up a decent sweat and then see whether they're in any fit state to make it on top of a dame! . . .[39]

Here Kozin's sympathy and discomfort mingle in a volatile mix, finally lashing out at the typical panaceas for gender disorders offered by Soviet medicine and law. Homosexuality was an inborn trait, a joke that nature played on an unfortunate minority of people.

He was also capable of seeing the other side of the argument about abnormality. A year later, inspired to reflect on the nature of genius after reading the nineteenth-century diary of the tsarist censor of great Russian poets A. V. Nikitenko (himself of humble peasant origins), Kozin argued that homosexuality was the salt that spurred great artists to excel:

However strange it may seem, this almost unnatural combination of genius with a multiplicity of vices and faults that offend all the norms of morality and behavior invented by people themselves, has existed, exists, and will exist for all time. Such is human nature. Deviations from the norm are the lot of highly gifted people. Genius always comes hand in hand with abnormality. Abnormality always expresses itself in very diverse ways in every talented and gifted person. . . . Tchaikovsky's perversion [izvrashchennost'], persecuted by the law, did not however prevent him from creating musical works of genius, filled with the kind of emotional content of which Rimsky-Korsakov was incapable; for he was less abnormal. And Gogol? Leonardo da Vinci? Chopin? What can one say? . . .[40]

Earlier in the diary, Kozin had compared Rimsky-Korsakov's pedantic character to the genius of Tchaikovsky: "So what if Tchaikovsky violated hypocritical morality, but he was a good, kind-hearted, sympathetic man. The people loved him, his operas and ballets are loved more to this day than the operatic works of Rimsky-Korsakov. There's no getting past it. You can't fool the people, the wise Russian people!"[41] Kozin was not the first queer Russian to hold up the example of Tchaikovsky as a homosexual whose extraordinary creativity redeemed his sexual proclivities; this was a widely circulating argument among homosexuals before and after 1917.[42] It is difficult not to think that the singer, with his penchant for self-dramatization, identified with the great Russian composer, suggesting that his own talent was inextricably linked to his sexual deviance.

Kozin's ideal of homosexual love as expressed in his diary mirrored the dramatic sentimentality of the songs he sang every night on stage. In one of the diary's most indiscreet passages, Kozin alludes to the lyrics of "Friendship" in an ecstatic digression on his passion for a green-eyed man whose name he refuses to divulge on paper. "I'm out of my mind because of a man," he wrote, between concerts in Yuzhno-Sakhalinsk, continuing,

> How I would love, for even just a moment, to look into the depths of those eyes. Why did they cross my path? Again those green eyes. As though I had him with me in my arms. Why did it happen like this? . . . He took the place of everything. Who this man is, no one will ever find out. But I fell in love, like a schoolboy, like a love-struck girl. . . . How many years have passed, and now I see his fateful green eyes again, almost thirty years. Again a tempest shatters my heart, like the start of spring, with the lilacs in blossom, and you are standing before a lush bouquet of marvelous white lilacs that have just begun to open, inhaling their scent and fearing to touch their fragrant, marvelous, white young petals. Oh to kneel before that bouquet and touch it with my lips, to kiss its blossoms tirelessly, to drink the nectar, as it was thirty years ago. I will only let one man read these insane lines. Our life is ordered in a completely different way, and it is impossible to live the way one wishes to. Although in the life I would like to lead, there is nothing of the supernatural. There is good, genuine friendship [*druzhba*], and complete trust in each other, forged with a feeling of such power that it overwhelms even passion and love. Tenderness and friendship stronger than passion and love. A firm handshake after the display of a drop of tenderness and friendship, and life becomes something else entirely. I am in floods of tears as I write these lines, for surely my dream will never come to pass and I will never touch the bouquet of youth and strength? If only life could be different, what a cult of personality he would garner. The man with the green eyes.[43]

Kozin otherwise speaks sparingly of his green-eyed lover, whom he met while on tour, and who followed him from Kamchatka to Sakhalin. "A wonderful person, I am convinced of this . . . I was not mistaken about him. It was right that my diary was silent about him."[44]

In his reflections on this man, and on homosexual love, Kozin relies upon the innocent ideal of "ordinary" Russian masculine friendship that his hit song proclaimed. The Russian version of male friendship and bonding was, throughout the twentieth century, several degrees warmer than anything we are familiar with in the Anglo-American world, more Mediterranean than mid-Atlantic, and more open to physical intimacy. Perhaps, since the 1990s, the visibility of an "out" LGBT community in Russia has inspired a degree of anxiety about "innocent" tenderness and affection between men. More research is needed on masculinity and friendship in Russian culture. We do know that the militarization that accompanied the 1917 Revolution and the Second World War nurtured Russian male bonding's intensity and warmth.[45]

The other, inescapable, reading of this passage from Kozin's diary is the erotic element of his ideal friendship – the bouquet of youth and strength he yearns to kneel before and kiss and the nectar he yearns to taste "as it was thirty years ago" are "insane lines" veering off the path of discretion into forbidden territory. More formally educated homosexual diarists, like George Ives and Mikhail Kuzmin, seldom strayed into such thickets and veiled their erotic fascinations in accounts of innocent encounters or the language of classical Hellenism. Kozin's cultural capital did not run to nostalgia for classical Athens (a common sentiment in modern European male homosexual mentalities), but to the emotion-charged romance of pre-revolutionary St. Petersburg's cafés-chantants instead. His conviction of the purity of his own erotic impulses can be read implicitly, too, in the many passages condemning the promiscuity of gay colleagues in the touring group. One such figure, the tall and handsome singer Mikhail Ivanovich Kabalov, is the perpetual object of Kozin's diatribes for the indiscretion of his liaisons, principally with sailors. (Kabalov, a Moscow operetta performer in the 1930s, may have been convicted under the anti-sodomy law, and he was notorious in Magadan's theater troupe for his homosexuality.)[46] Kozin's sexual envy, and perhaps his memory of his own Petersburg-born attraction to men of the sea, fizzes in his constant remarks about the "young, goodlooking" sailors Kabalov magics into his hotel room or conjures up within hours of arriving in some port town. The self Kozin cultivated in his diary is an amalgam of popular sentimentality and the cultural underworlds (of café and stage life, of gay life) in St. Petersburg-Leningrad, and Moscow, that remained firmly fixed in his outlook. Over the course of half a lifetime he cultivated a modern, European sense of queer self on the remotest edge of the Eurasian continent.

Queer visibility and the dilemmas of the self

Queer visibility, and the dilemmas that this exposure creates, are a critical feature of Vadim Kozin's diary. Everyone around the singer knew about his queer sexual past and present; he could not escape into a closet, without abandoning his career (and even then, his fame was too great). The notoriety of his sexual tastes, the widespread circulation of this knowledge, and the fixing of a deviant sexuality in his criminal conviction all generated crude homophobic reactions in his colleagues. They responded to the certainty and unavoidability of knowledge about his queerness with mistrust and hypocritical moralizing. As I have shown in Chapter 2, in the Soviet 1950s queers could live "below the radar," "in the closet," and exploit society's "quiet accommodationism": when knowledge of queerness was deniable, bystanders might look the other way rather than recognize the obvious queer in their midst. In Vadim Kozin's case, however, the unspeakable had long since been spoken, the genie was out of the bottle, and could not be put back. His exposure was total, the stigma, inescapable. In this sense, living as visibly queer related Kozin to those Gulag prisoners stigmatized with "shaming tattoos" that alerted others to their queer status (discussed in Chapter 1). The singer's queer visibility yielded a particular "dilemma of the self," that of the queer individual exposed in a hostile community. In Russia's queer archives we have very few documents of the experience of such queer visibility, and none, except this one, from a survivor of Stalin's anti-sodomy law and punishment in the Gulag. It thus constitutes a key document in the history of modern Russian homophobia.

Kozin's diary, like that of George Ives, enabled the Soviet singer to understand the dilemma of visibility and at the same time to articulate and dignify his experience. The diary, like Ives's, was a "paper closet" – a place to escape the world's mockery. But it was also a place to confide secrets, such as the secret of the green-eyed lover, to defy the scrutiny of hostile panopticism, and to argue that there was consolation, hope, and even exhilaration in his "life incorrectly lived." Matt Cook refers to George Ives's diary as a place in which "holding back material and rendering it secret served him [Ives] in securing a sense of homosexual selfhood."[47] The same can be said of Kozin's secretive and yet indiscreet passages about his green-eyed lover, and his desires expressed in the diary more generally. Self-construction in diary writing did not have to be explicitly articulated to be consoling, constructive and ennobling.

It would be fascinating to know what Kozin thought of his diary, when Savchenko retrieved these portions of it from the archive of the local KGB in 1991. The biographer merely states that Kozin wanted it published posthumously, citing the September 1956 passage addressed to "whoever reads these pages" quoted earlier in this chapter.[48] Unlike George Ives, who decades later left a commentary on his early twentieth-century diary, the aged Kozin in the last three years of his life was unable or unwilling to annotate his diary or comment upon it. The diary's frankness, and the stigma associated with queer visibility, clearly remained a source of shame and frustration: President Boris Yeltsin would only decriminalize male homosexuality in April 1993, just a few months before Kozin's death. Despite the intercession of the legendary Soviet *chanson* singer Yosif Kobzon, Yeltsin's administration denied Kozin the honor of the title Merited Artist of the Russian Federation. (Cultural officials cited his convictions for homosexuality; on the refusal of this recognition see Chapter 7.) Vadim Kozin died in 1994 celebrated as an artiste, but still mistrusted for being "like that"; no doubt he felt that his diary could not be published except posthumously, and by his chosen biographer, Savchenko.

The power of this diary lies in the way that Kozin's dilemmas mirror and anticipate the dilemmas facing Russia's LGBT citizens in the twenty-first century. Just as Vadim Kozin found refuge in the privacy of his diary, contemporary queers are confined to private spaces and denied full rights to affirming public speech. Just as Kozin feared and despised the public humiliation meted out by state and society in the 1950s, Russia's queers today continue to live in fear of "everyday homophobia" – and many get asylum in Western countries based on the ferocity of the homophobia they suffer. Just as Kozin dreamt of a love that was liberating, and the euphoria of the genuine freedom to love, Russian queers today try to imagine how it might be possible to live freely, be themselves, and still be Russian citizens. Today they do this – in the teeth of grotesque official homophobia – with the help of digital media and a flood of examples of how to resolve the dilemmas of the queer self from around the globe. The extraordinary thing about Vadim Kozin's achievement is that he imagined a world beyond homophobia in shabby notebooks, in the wastes of Siberia, and the gloom of endless Soviet hotel rooms, in a world where there was no visible queer movement. His diary deserves our attention.

PART II

Queer Visibility and "Traditional Sexual Relations"

In Part II, three chapters examine aspects of the rise of queer visibility in modern Soviet and post-Soviet Russia, and official and popular reactions to it. The Soviet people enjoyed a relatively prosperous time in the 1960s and 1970s, becoming more urban and consumerist as well as more educated, thanks to more balanced economic planning and deliberate policies aimed at expanding cities, improving housing, and spreading mass education. Moscow was the shop-window for this "modern" version of socialism, the vaunted capital of the Communist world, a city where planners had freer rein to invest and sometimes even experiment. The brightest and best migrated here to take advantage of the full range of modernity's opportunities – including hundreds of thousands of queer Soviet citizens from all of the USSR's republics. This was the moment of a second Soviet "sexual revolution" (the first followed the 1917 Revolutions). Driven by housing and lifestyle improvements, a revolution in the way people lived, if not in terms of what they were able to say in public, took off for heterosexuals and queers. In the late-Soviet era, Moscow, the largest of the Soviet Union's burgeoning cities, became a crucible of new opportunity for LGBT people. Despite continued authoritarian policing and censorship, gay male cruising sites flourished in the center of the capital and a lively awareness of the multiple meanings of queer life began to emerge from an increasingly diverse, educated, and free-thinking queer population.

All this ferment was challenged in the 1980s by a sense of crisis in the Soviet system, perhaps most notable in the abysmally long war in Afghanistan, accompanied by economic slowdown and ideological malaise. When the Communist Party chose Mikhail S. Gorbachev as its leader in 1985, renewal would include the relaxation and later virtual abandonment of information controls, followed by radical democratization. The stage was set for greatly increased lesbian and gay visibility in the late 1980s and into the post-Soviet 1990s. At first, curiosity and tolerance seemed to greet these unfamiliar social groups. A new, "third," sexual revolution of the 1990s, one characterized by explicit media discussions of sex, and by openness to transnational influence, ensued. Russia, emerging from the Soviet Union in 1991, was enchanted and disgusted as it binged on talking about sex.

The change to a post-Soviet, uncensored, and capitalist, society in the 1990s stimulated queer creativity and organizing. Even before the decriminalization of male homosexuality in 1993 emboldened many, an explosion of queer voices in print media occurred. However much Western LGBT activism and global gay commercialism attempted in those years to "help" post-Soviet queers, Russian LGBT voices were in fact "Made in the USSR": they emerged locally, they were uniquely inflected by the experience of Soviet socialism, and they were not simply derivatives of foreign imports. The lesbian and gay print media of the first post-Communist decade constitutes a unique "archive of freedom," proof that Russian queers had plenty to say that was original. They were nobody's proxies or puppets. Even gay men's erotica and pornography demonstrated a keen national consciousness and Russian pornographers labored assiduously to knit the queer experience into familiar national narratives.

Revolution usually invokes counterrevolution, and the "sexual revolution" of the 1990s would be no exception. The wrenching economic transition to capitalism, the extremes of uncensored media excess (for some compounded by the threatening rise of the internet), and a search for a new national ideology in Russian Orthodoxy to replace discredited Communism all eventually drove a "backlash" against free-for-all democracy. The yearning for order and prosperity fueled President Vladimir Putin's arrival in power at the dawn of the twenty-first century, with an agenda that included the "remasculinization" of Russia. The new president's macho public image and political swagger would be part of a legitimation strategy focused on restoring Russia's declining population, wealth, and power in the world. Plenty of conservative nationalists responded with enthusiasm to this agenda, and the sexual revolution of the 1990s was a target for their concern. An early 2000s political debate about sexual regulation was accompanied by a carnivalesque Duma debate about the status of Russian homosexuals, part of an orchestrated "moral panic." This first attempt to articulate "traditional sex" and "traditional values" failed to curb what limited rights LGBT Russians had gained in the 1990s, but the campaign showed conservatives that a more sophisticated language was needed to promote a counterrevolution in sexual culture. Queer visibility became the prime target that conservatives sought to attack with an agenda focused on "traditional sexual relations." These chapters help to illustrate how modernization, queer visibility, and conservative backlash laid the groundwork for the "gay propaganda" debate of 2013.

4

From Stalinist Pariahs to Subjects of "Managed Democracy":

Queers in Moscow, 1945 to the Present

Moscow was the capital of a victorious Soviet Union in 1945, and in this era of rapid reconstruction and political complexities, "queerness" would eventually come under special scrutiny. Wartime contact with "decadent" Europe threatened to contaminate Soviet "natural" sexuality at a moment when population losses aroused anxiety. Even more provocatively, after the death of Soviet dictator Joseph Stalin in March 1953, the dismantling of the Gulag forced labor camps threatened to infect society with perversions "hot-housed" in places of confinement. Law and medicine were mobilized to contain queer sexualities, while "liberals" and "conservatives" in the Communist Party would disagree over the need for official sex education. Until the collapse of Communist rule, and of the Soviet Union as multi-national empire in 1991, political stalemate arrested the "sex question."[1] At the same time, economic and social evolution transformed the experience of queer sexualities, prefiguring the exuberant and anxious approaches to queerness prevalent in Moscow in the early twenty-first century.

The evolution of "queer" Moscow after 1945 cannot be gauged by the familiar landmarks of Western LGBT history. Under an authoritarian police state there was no legal independent social activism or non-governmental organizing and hence no Russian "homophile" movement linked to any interwar queer communities. Such solidarities, existing in big cities among circles of friends and lovers, had been disrupted by Stalinist anti-homosexual purges during the 1930s.[2] The Soviet state guarded its monopoly on press, radio, and television jealously and operated exceptionally prudish censorship until the late 1980s. Muscovites did not publish their own queer journals until 1990. The year 1968 was not a "revolutionary" moment in Soviet history, but a year of reaction when the USSR led Warsaw Pact armies to crush the Prague Spring. The year's events stimulated unofficial "dissident" activism inside the Soviet Union, virtually none of which was gay-identified. Police surveillance and persecution of dissidence intensified. There would be no Moscow Stonewall, nor could a Soviet community of self-identified "gay" people proclaim itself in the 1960s–70s with demonstrations and pride marches. Feminism was shunned by the political "dissidents" and found little purchase in an underground intellectual milieu that, for complex historical and ideological reasons, rejected gender as a category of analysis. There was little "second wave" feminism inside Russia and no "lesbian separatism." The 1980s HIV/AIDS threat would be perceived and conceived of distinctively by the Soviet medical establishment and media. Moscow in 1989 had a very different history of understanding and living out "queerness" than that of Europe's western capitals.

The fundamental distinction during the period was the Cold War division of Europe into capitalist and socialist states, into the NATO and Warsaw Pact blocs. The Cold War left its marks on queer Moscow. The USSR led a restive bloc of allies, the socialist "people's democracies" of East Germany, Poland, Czechoslovakia, Hungary, Romania, and Bulgaria. Despite "sovietization," these countries had diverging histories of regulating queer sexualities, at considerable variance from Russian traditions and Soviet practice. Finally, the primary adversary in the Cold War was the USA, and after Stonewall, Soviet ideologues and gay Russians were compelled to confront the "Americanization of the homosexual" as a challenge from the opposing ideological camp.[3]

Less provocative but perhaps more pregnant with possibility was the evolution of queer citizenship in the European Union during the 1980s, especially as the last Soviet leader, Mikhail Gorbachev, in office from 1985 to 1991, often spoke of greater engagement with "our common European home." The "political postponement" of queer freedom until the 1990s (felt across the socialist societies of Central and Eastern Europe, as well as the nations of the Soviet Union) triggered a sudden and promiscuous downloading of queer ideas in Russian cultural life. At the same time, capitalist transformation brought an explosion of consumerism, including queer cultures, with trends usually set in Moscow, Russia's wealthiest metropolis. The significance of queer freedom in political, economic and social life is the subject of intense debate in Moscow today.

To appreciate the distinctive trajectory of queer Moscow's evolution, I begin by examining the regulation of sexuality in the immediate post–1945 era. After victory in 1945, and after Stalin's death in 1953, surveillance of queer genders and sexualities was renewed and extended, in the wider context of anxieties about social order. The second section explores the complexities of the period of "political postponement" from 1964 to 1991, when Soviet liberals and conservatives were locked in a frozen conflict over social values, and yet the appeal of the West's "sexual revolution" challenged all. A final section of the essay looks at the post-Communist and post-modern era since 1991, when Moscow became the center of an unprecedented eruption of queer activism and cultural action, and at the same time the focus of new homophobic politics.

After victory, after Stalin

The human losses inflicted in the 1941–5 "Great Patriotic War" confronted the Stalinist leadership with an alarming demographic crisis. Of the 26 million war dead, 20 million were male, and in both sexes most victims were of reproductive age.[4] Implications for post-war reconstruction and for the strength of the Soviet Army were stark. Even before the war's end, Stalin's eventual successor, Nikita S. Khrushchev, conceived and implemented a series of family policies to replace the population losses as rapidly as possible. Khrushchev's law of July 8, 1944 "On increasing government support for pregnant women" gave single mothers state support for the first time; they had previously depended on alimony from absent fathers. Along with tighter divorce and the 1936 abortion ban, the package led to a surge in post-war single motherhood. Within ten years, almost 9 million children were being raised by single mothers.[5]

Such a deep population crisis might have triggered anti-homosexual propaganda campaigns, or a spike in arrests under Stalin's anti-sodomy statute of 1934, but the evidence is inconclusive. Little overt animosity explicitly targeting the Soviet queer appeared in the press. The Stalinist habit, acquired in the 1930s, of silence regarding same-sex love prevailed. Nevertheless it was a constructive silence, with contempt for sexual dissidence in Cold-War themed journalism, as Erica Lee Fraser has demonstrated.[6] In commentaries on foreign affairs, the national satirical journal *Krokodil* typically portrayed capitalist allies of the USA as feminized, weak, and often in queer situations (West German chancellor Konrad Adenauer in drag "marrying" Uncle Sam, in June 1950, for example). Such images contrasted with representations of the broad-shouldered Soviet Man striding away from perverse capitalist blandishments. Fraser argues that these images constructed Soviet masculinity as unproblematically and healthily heterosexual when contrasted with the explicit queering of the capitalist hireling. In post-war cinema too Soviet heterosexuality was presented as fecund, natural, and untroubled by perversion.[7] Queer was an attribute of capitalists, not of the victorious leaders of the world's socialist camp.

Arrests for consensual sodomy between men occurred, but are mostly unrecorded in accessible official documents. The most notorious wartime case took place in 1944 when the Moscow crooner and superstar Vadim Kozin was charged with sodomy and anti-Soviet statements, and sentenced to the Gulag in 1945 (as discussed in Chapter 3). The popular gypsy ballad singer lived indiscreetly, treating young men to dinner and his bed in Moscow's Metropole Hotel, where secret police surveillance was ubiquitous. The accessible record of sodomy convictions is incomplete, with few convictions registered in the civilian courts (as opposed to secret police arrests, discussed in Chapter 7). The immediate post-war years were a time of hunger, sickness, and hard work; opportunities for sex were slim.[8] I have described elsewhere how queer men met in the 1950s in Moscow's public toilets, parks, and bathhouses, for sexual encounters, and how private space also afforded opportunities for same-sex love.[9]

Little is known about secret police actions against homosexuals in the late Stalin years. During this period, secret police terror increased, targeting a range of "counterrevolutionaries" and new "enemies of the people." It seems unlikely that large-scale arrests explicitly for homosexual activity were conducted by the secret police during the post-war years, if only because no memoirists or émigré observers recall any mass operations against homosexuals. Gay men would have been collateral victims of the various campaigns against citizens suspected of disloyalty as the Cold War opened, and as Stalin's illness and paranoia advanced.[10]

After Stalin's death in 1953, living conditions improved and official liberalization sanctioned the pursuit of a relatively unmolested private life. The Party under Khrushchev adopted a tutelary approach, steering citizens toward "communist morality" via public education and social policy reform. Despite the headline trend of official de-Stalinization and political liberality conventionally ascribed to Khrushchev's rule (beginning with his "secret speech" denouncing Stalin in 1956 and ending with his removal by hardliners led by Leonid I. Brezhnev in October 1964), recent scholarship has noted the regime's nervous responses to the forces unleashed by liberalization, and its search for new methods of control.[11] Decisions about how to treat queer men and women in this period are a heretofore unknown example of renewed authoritarianism during the Khrushchev years.

The dismantling of the Gulag camps during this period, and the renewal of Stalin's anti-sodomy law as Khrushchev's legal reforms developed, both examined in Chapter 1, shaped the new regime's approach toward homosexuality. Recorded prosecutions for same-sex relations between men rapidly increased, and the police began routinely monitoring homosexual haunts in parks and public toilets, and used informants threatened with prosecution to incriminate others.[12] Moscow cruising grounds acquired notoriety as places where one might be entrapped by a pretty stranger working for the KGB. Yet this was a national strategy, as the 1959 re-arrest of Vadim Kozin in a hotel room with a young police decoy, in distant Khabarovsk demonstrated.[13] Male homosexuality would remain a crime until after the fall of Soviet rule.

While male homosexuals were pursued with new vigor, lesbians, apparently ignored under Stalin, were not criminalized during the Khrushchev era either, but instead subjected to new psychiatric scrutiny. Medical "treatment" of lesbians in the late-Soviet decades might entail the prescription of libido-deadening drugs, and compulsory registration as a psychiatric outpatient with unpleasant consequences in daily life.[14] The assignment of the lesbian to medicine coincided with the Khrushchev state's turn to psychiatry to control other forms of dissent, although a direct connection in the thinking of the authorities between sexual and political dissent remains elusive.[15]

The situation for "free" lesbians in Moscow of these years remains obscure. The codes of femininity, and the general lack of eligible men, licensed much female intimacy and allowed women to mask same-sex love as conventional friendship. The Moscow actress Faina Ranevskaya (1896–1983) lived in a long partnership with her mentor and lover, the actress Pavla Vulf (1878–1961). After wartime evacuation to Tashkent, they returned to Moscow and lived separately, but took holidays together. Through the 1950s, Ranevskaya nursed Vulf who died in her arms; later she admitted that Vulf had been the only love of her life.[16] Ranevskaya's queer persona reportedly found expression in the faintest of hints: a stirring performance in a Moscow 1945 production of Lillian Hellman's "The Little Foxes"; her invention of a gender-troubling name for her character "Lev Margaritovich" in the 1947 comedy film *Vesna* (Spring).[17]

Not all lesbian lives during the period were so successful. The poet Anna Barkova (1901–76), survived three periods of imprisonment (1934–9; 1947–56; 1957–65).[18] Her lesbianism was not illegal but her sexuality nevertheless underpinned her conflicted relationship with Soviet power; Barkova's first arrest was for writing an ironic poem about Stalin. Released in 1939, she settled in Moscow province with an ex-prisoner and lover, Tonya (her surname is unknown) and they survived the war years together, although often quarreled; Barkova agonized over her sexuality in her diary: "Maybe this is the nature of a decadent orientation: perhaps healthy people never feel this way. But does that mean that they are in the right?" She considered moving to Moscow to live with other female friends; jealous at this betrayal, Tonya denounced Barkova. She was arrested in 1947, sentenced to ten years for anti-Soviet statements. Released in 1956, she settled with another ex-inmate lover in Ukraine, but they were both re-arrested the following year for writing anti-Soviet material. Barkova was released in 1965, and only fully rehabilitated in 1967 thanks to the intervention of a leading literary liberal, Aleksander Tvardovsky, but her work was excluded from his journal, *Novyi mir*. In 1967, Barkova settled in a communal flat in Moscow; she insistently re-wrote her diary after each confiscation and left a body of work reflecting on the nature of homosexual desire that remains almost unknown.

Queer solidarities in late-Soviet life

Between 1964 and 1985, under Party leader Leonid I. Brezhnev, and two short-lived successors, neo-Stalinists and bureaucrats seeking predictable government curtailed the Khrushchev experiment in "liberal" de-Stalinization. "Liberals" given hope in the early 1960s (the so-called *shestidesiatniki*, "people of the sixties"), and "conservatives" terrified of losing privileges or of being called to account for their crimes, confronted one another in every sphere of political, social, and economic endeavor. Brezhnev mediated with the close assistance of the KGB, normally, in favor of stasis between these camps. Even as political decision-making froze to a halt, economic and social transformation accelerated: by 1965 city-dwellers in the USSR finally outnumbered rural ones for the first time, and Moscow expanded from a dusty metropolis of 4.8 million in 1957, to a global capital of at least 9 million in 1990. Huge new residential districts of concrete apartment towers appeared, linked to the historic heart by an impressively efficient Metro. Private car ownership grew, although traffic jams would not appear until the twenty-first century.[19] The pinnacle of Soviet government, industry, arts, sciences, and education, Moscow was a magnet for ambition and talent, and queer Soviet citizens were disproportionately motivated among migrants in search of a better life. For sexual and gender dissidents, Moscow offered possibilities and even freedom unmatched elsewhere in the USSR.

Probably the most important factor in creating a sense of opportunity was the expansion of housing, as the majority of families were now able to obtain private flats – after decades in communal apartments, shared by multiple households. As new housing complexes sprang up, the prospect of an end to the mutual surveillance of the communal flat held obvious attractions for queers. Moscow got more investment in modernized accommodation than other cities, and yet supply never met demand, with priority given to newlyweds. A new sector of quasi-private, "cooperative" housing was an expensive alternative available to senior managers and professionals, and some gay men appear to have benefited.[20]

A more likely route for the gay man or lesbian seeking a private apartment in Moscow was to marry heterosexually and join the faster queue of couples entitled to housing. By the 1970s a "veritable industry" in marriages of convenience operated in the capital.[21] This "industry" was not exclusively homosexual; it was the result of internal passport and residency registration barriers, devices introduced to socially engineer the populations of major cities.[22] It was impossible to live legally in Moscow or other "regime" cities without official permission, granted by an employer, university, or when a resident married a non-resident. Thus, to gain a foothold in the capital, straights *and* queers from the provinces sought sympathetic or credulous Moscow spouses.[23] Russian gays and lesbians married each other too, fully aware of their partners' orientation, in order to jump the housing queue. Fictive marriages also conferred respectability on queer participants, satisfying family curiosity and deflecting official suspicions. Divorce rates soared after relaxations enacted early in Brezhnev's tenure, and marital breakdown was as much a badge of heterosexuality as an enduring alliance.[24] Soviet queer men (reports do not mention women) also sought to marry foreigners, and leave the USSR permanently. The marital route out of the country could be one of the easiest "escape routes" for determined queers. Until the 1980s, obtaining exit visas entailed lengthy paperwork and administrative penalties. Another option, for queers with a Jewish connection, was to seek an exit visa to Israel, but this route came with additional harassment and anti-Semitism.[25]

Not everyone could find private space, and sex in public, which had long played a role in straight and queer intimate life in Moscow, continued to assert itself, particularly for gay men. So too did public courtship and socializing, following traditions established in the late nineteenth century.[26] By the 1970s and 1980s, the principal public meeting places for queer men stretched in an arc around the Kremlin and Red Square, producing a celebrated *marshrut* or "circuit" for the adventurous.[27] An underground toilet in the Alexander Gardens near the Kremlin Wall and just steps from the busy Lenin Library metro station was a notorious place of assignation. Ten minutes' walk from this public convenience, facilities in GUM department store on Red Square itself, or in the basement of the Central Lenin Museum just off Red Square and directly above the Revolution Square metro, served as the next ports of call. Leaving the museum and crossing Sverdlov Square, one passed a monument of Karl Marx glaring down upon the epicenter of Soviet queerdom: a little garden in front of the Bolshoi Theatre, with its benches facing each other in a circle surrounding a low fountain, forming the northern half of Sverdlov Square. The ensemble was partially shielded from the street by shrubs and gardens. Winter and summer this square – with a plethora of queer nicknames, but commonly known as "the bald patch" or *pleshka* – was a popular spot for cruising and socializing.[28]

The *pleshka* as queer site endured from perhaps the 1930s until the late 1990s when renovation, and then the Internet, largely killed it off.[29] That such a visible and central meeting place for queers, in the heart of the capital, lasted so long may seem odd, but the authorities evidently came to tolerate it as a way to monitor a normally secretive minority of non-conformists. Rumors even circulated on the *pleshka*, evidently attempting to explain the existence of this gathering place, that in the early 1970s, the state had secretly decreed a hiatus in the persecution of homosexuals.[30] Perhaps this was disinformation, circulated by *agents provocateurs*. Official statistics released later show no decrease in prosecutions.[31] Moreover, the clean-up of Moscow's streets before the 1980 summer Olympics, which hit the "circuit's" gay men as well as prostitutes and the homeless, showed that any such tolerance was conditional.[32]

Continuing the "circuit" in its arc around the heart of the capital, following Marx Prospect uphill to KGB headquarters on Dzerzhinsky Square, one passed the Children's World department store and side-streets harboring the Sandunovskie and Central Baths: traditional steam-baths where "[a]s in the toilets, furtive glances and sidelong looks pass between the gay customers, who, having found each other, get acquainted and go elsewhere for consummation."[33] The busy, well-staffed municipal baths of the capital made it impossible for queer men to colonize them as they had before the Revolution.[34] Later in the 1990s, the "circuit" extended even farther around the arc, to Staraya Square, where a monument to tsarist Russian victory over the Turks provides a focal point for gay cruising even today.

The "circuit" of queer spaces surrounding Moscow's heart did not exhaust the city's queer possibilities. A major artery running north from Red Square, Gorky Street, ran into Pushkin Square, popular with all types of non-conformists, and Mayakovsky Square, where lesbians sometimes met. Cruising spots could also be found in Gorky Park, on the south-west fringe of the center, and farther afield on Lenin Hills, near Moscow State University.[35] There were numerous public toilets used by queer men, near the Kazan Railway Station, on Trubnaya Square near the old State Circus, in Hermitage Park, and on Gogol Boulevard steps from a monument to the queer nineteenth-century writer Nikolai Gogol.[36] Moreover, late Soviet Man, if he was one of the 15 percent of householders with a private car in 1985, used it for sexual trysts, although cars were still so rare that no notorious queer parking spots developed in Moscow's suburbs.[37]

At least as striking as the extent of queer men's space in late Soviet Moscow were the audibility of queer language, and a new feeling of shared injustice. Queer language of course circulated throughout the Soviet Union, and it had its roots in the pre-revolutionary homosexual underground, Gulag slang, and contemporary criminal and street jargon.[38] Gender inversion was its most enduring characteristic. From at least the nineteenth century, same-sex oriented men used Russian's rich store of gender inflection to refer to self and comrades ironically (as seen in Chapter 2, they would use for example, "*ya poshla*," "I went," in feminine gender, instead of "*ya poshel*" masculine gender). Also popular were feminizing sobriquets; such queeny inversions persisted during the early twentieth century and, with great discretion, during and after the Stalin era.[39] The *pleshka* and its perverse comradeship seemed to license a degree of linguistic liberty; consider the shock of a friendly heterosexual visitor to the square in the mid–1970s. The writer Alexander Dymov was introduced to the scene there by Alyosha, a gay friend. On one early visit, Dymov was present when a friend of Alyosha's in a military uniform arrived and addressed them:

> In a high-pitched voice that cracked from time to time, he sang, "My little dears! If only you knew what a cock I've just sucked!" I was shocked on three levels. *Primo*, he was a genuine air force officer in an impeccable uniform, blue epaulettes and gold buttons. *Secundo*, despite the masculine sex of those present, he addressed them as "little dears" [using feminine gender]. *Tertio*, he spoke of himself in the feminine gender . . .[40]

Dymov might have added that to make such a flagrant pronouncement in his presence, someone not known to the speaker, showed confidence in the security of this milieu.

The sensibilities of the *pleshka's* habitués merit closer attention than they have received. Some, reflecting the intelligentsia prejudice that held open queerness to be criminal, have tended to associate life on the "circuit" with law-breaking, a lack of education, and the dangers of the Soviet street, dismissing it as hazardous and coarse. They distinguish between intellectual gays who avoided the "circuit", and working-class queer life on the streets. Intelligent young people supposedly hung around on the "circuit" only as long as it took to find a partner, then they abandoned it for the safety of private spaces.[41] There is much truth in this characterization, given the fear of KGB entrapment, and the violence meted out by homophobic gangs, that *pleshka* stalwarts evidently encountered. However, all was not fear, degradation, and empty pleasure-seeking, and the division between stay-at-home educated gays, and rough boys who roamed the streets in search of sex, was never so absolute. Observers noted serious attempts among *pleshka* denizens to create camaraderie (if not "community") and to puzzle out the meaning of gay existence in Soviet circumstances.[42] The gay "manifestos" of Yury Trifonov (1977) and Evgeny Kharitonov ("Listovka") lambasted Soviet homophobia, and similar thinking was easy to find on the street.[43] In the early 1970s, the lexicographer Vladimir Kozlovsky interviewed "Mama Vlada," a man said to be "the chief homosexual of Moscow," and a member of the "elite" frequenting the *pleshka*. In a conversation rich with scabrous wordplay, "Mama Vlada" argued bitterly against the persecution Russian homosexuals suffered because they were "nonconformists":

> I don't understand our fucking leaders, who can lock me up and work me over as much as they like, but they will never get me to change. It's no fault of mine. I was born this way . . . Oh, if only the authorities up there knew how many celebrated names there are in our ranks . . . How many of [us there are among] their own KGB, police officers, people in the government, and People's Artists, important cultural figures, award-winners in various fields, scientists, painters, poets.[44]

Repeating apologetics familiar to Russians since before 1917, "Mama Vlada" argued that Sigmund Freud discovered "bisexuality" and "was the first to see in the liberation of humanity from sexual prohibitions the path to spiritual liberation and personal development." Moreover, "we have always existed – and what people there have been in our midst: Shakespeare, Tchaikovsky, and Proust . . ." To Kozlovsky, "Mama Vlada" was a "major creator of homosexual folklore and mythology," and evidently someone who commanded authority on the *pleshka*.[45]

A growing solidarity was emerging among queers who met in private apartments, in the closely knit circles of trusted friends (*kruzhki*, singular *kruzhok*) that were ubiquitous in urban society in these years, not confined to homosexuals alone. (Other designations for such groups were *salony*, "salons," and *tusovka*, "the scene.") A gay male Russian-speaking U.S. graduate student who lived in Moscow for several months in 1979 noted that "[a] strong sense of camaraderie results from the peculiar situation of Soviet gay people, a loyalty and devotion not only to one's lover but to one's circle of friends (*kruzhok* or *salon*). Most often, gay people meet other gay people through their friends and acquaintances; this is true, of course, outside Russia, but due to the lack of alternatives, it is much more important in Moscow."[46] A queer New Left visitor from Boston saw in Soviet loyalty to friends and lovers a positive alternative to Western gay life saturated in pornography, consumerism and promiscuity.[47] Dymov, active in illegal publishing (*samizdat*), saw parallels and crossovers in the solidarities between political and sexual dissidents. *Samizdat* relied upon trusted groups to copy (by typewriter) and distribute (by hand) works of banned literature and journalism; he once found himself delivering such material to a gay *kruzhok*.[48] Gay *kruzhki* often circulated whatever reading matter about homosexuality they could obtain.

Significantly for the rise of open gay and lesbian activism in Moscow on the threshold of the 1990s, the queer *kruzhki* of the 1970s–80s developed a sharpening understanding of Soviet homophobia. Virtually all observers commenting on late Soviet gay life mention encounters with charismatic personalities leading their own *kruzhki*, expounding their pet theories of homosexuality, its persecution and prospects.[49] Soviet queers had an increasingly detailed awareness of how Western gay activism was making an impact on the other side of the Iron Curtain, and a sense of how implausible gay liberation might be in the USSR. Some queer Russians argued that Eastern European people's democracies were more likely to produce a form of queer activism permissible under socialism. As Sasha, a perceptive engineer from Moscow put it in 1977 when asked if there was any prospect of a Soviet gay movement:

> Definitely not for the foreseeable future. First, we do not have the gay subculture that exists in the West, and it is very difficult to develop the idea of a gay identity, and still less a consciousness of our oppression. Second, even if a group solidarity existed, it would be impossible to organize ourselves, given the political repression. The [Soviet] state has this matter well under control, in contrast, say, to the situation in Poland, for example. And just as a movement for democratic socialism has more chance of emerging in Poland than here, I think that a movement for sexual politics will arise first in one of the people's democracies [rather than here].[50]

Foreign leftist gay activists expressed similar views, even as they made concerted and sometimes daring efforts to establish ties with gay and lesbian "leaders" in Moscow and Leningrad.[51] The opinion of the Russian-speaking U.S. graduate student writing in 1980 was pessimistic:

> Soviet society changes with glacial speed; the enormous advances in gay rights during the 1970s in America and western Europe have not begun

to happen here, nor are they likely to happen for generations to come. More important, even the small improvements that have occurred are not necessarily permanent. Who knows what will happen after Brezhnev?[52]

There was little or no anticipation of the momentous changes that were about to engulf the Soviet Union's queer citizens.

If same-sex oriented men constituted the most visible element in the diverse strands of queer Moscow life, they were nevertheless not alone. Women who loved women continued to come to self-awareness in isolation, although by the late 1970s there were opportunities to experiment in the underground scene. Elena Gusiatinskaya (born 1946) studied French at the capital's Institute for Foreign Languages. She recalls:

> I sensed my untraditional orientation from a rather early age, in my youth . . . but because in the 1960s this subject was under a total taboo, I did not reflect on it particularly deeply. Since I read foreign languages easily, I had access to a degree of information on the theme. But in general my homosexuality was deeply buried in my subconscious. On one hand, I sensed it, but on the other, I lived a traditional way of life: I got married, I divorced . . .[53]

Another Moscow woman who later gained notoriety as the first Soviet lesbian activist, Evgenia Debrianskaya, also married heterosexually in these years.[54] Olga Krauze was born into a Leningrad professional family in 1953. As a youngster, she wore trousers in the streets and changed into her school dress on the sly. Qualifying as a designer in the late 1970s she was lucky to find a *kruzhok* of gays and lesbians in Leningrad. "We shuttled back and forth between Moscow and Peter[sburg]. Later I got involved in activism, the underground, mutual aid. I remember very clearly how we organized marriages of convenience with gay men, when they needed saving from prosecution."[55] Krauze's experience illustrates how artificial it is to divide a history of queer Moscow from that of the Soviet Union's second city, Leningrad. Rail and airfares were very cheap, and shared contacts between the two Russian capitals expanded the circle of trusted friends.[56]

Soviet intersex and trans people emerged from obscurity in this period as a result of the expansion of medical research, centered on Moscow. Professor Aron I. Belkin of Moscow's Institute of Psychiatry, in cooperation with colleagues from the Institute of Experimental Endocrinology, experimented with "correcting" the sex of intersex persons, and changing the sex of transgender patients. These experts were ignorant of the many Soviet experiments in these areas during the 1920s–30s, but well versed in Western developments since 1945.[57] In the fifteen years after 1961, the endocrinology institute operated on 684 hermaphrodites to "clarify" their sex, in seventy-one cases, resulting in a change of passport sex. In the 1970s, many Soviet intersex patients were teenagers and adults; there were no standard protocols for treating intersex infants, and local doctors hesitated to intervene. Patients had to journey vast distances to seek advice from Moscow's specialist clinics.[58] Changing the passport sex of a Soviet citizen was apparently harder than "giving the hermaphrodite an unambiguous sex by means of surgical and hormonal therapy." Despite new regulations introduced in 1974, to change patients' identity documents, doctors had to write dozens of unofficial letters to bureaucrats, falsify medical records, and conduct long-term pastoral relationships with many intersex patients to ensure their successful integration.[59]

Belkin and his colleagues also began sex-change operations during this period. Little is known about these patients and their experience. Igor Kon (1928–2011), the nation's foremost sexologist, noted that the psychiatrist Belkin conducted sex changes without the psychological testing considered standard in the West; there was simply no one he could confidently entrust with the task.[60] Later at the end of the 1990s, surgeons and endocrinologists were versed in the full range of Western procedures including psychological filtering of prospective patients, and their post-operative pastoral care.[61] As with intersex patients, ordinary Soviet physicians had scant acquaintance with Western medical approaches to the transgendered subject. Some doctors knew about sex change operations and thought they ought to be prescribed for women presenting as lesbians (according to one woman's autobiography published in a queer journal).[62]

Post-communist, post-modern

In 1985, with the accession of Mikhail S. Gorbachev as leader of the Communist Party, "political postponement" came to an end. Increasingly bold bids to revitalize the Soviet system flowed from the Kremlin, guided by "new thinking," "restructuring" (perestroika), "openness" (glasnost), and crucially, "democracy" as watchwords. The political results – the end of the Cold War (1989), the collapse of Communist rule, the largely peaceful disintegration of the Soviet Union into fifteen sovereign states (1991) – are well known. The former socialist bloc abandoned socialist economics and embraced capitalist globalization. The change was seismic, experienced by Russians as liberating, euphoric, and deeply unsettling as well.

A discursive "sexual revolution" accompanied the wider political revolution. With increasing boldness, in the late 1980s the Soviet media broke with past censorship and talked openly and explicitly about sex, to an audience that was amazed, titillated, shocked and disgusted – and could not, it seems, get enough of it. Glasnost in the realm of sexuality brought stunning media openness to Western ideas and values, frank reflection on the anxieties and joys of ordinary citizens, and even crude attempts to arouse audiences. Sex became a badge of "post-ness," post-Sovietness, of life after Communism, however it might take shape. All sex became in late Soviet and early post-

Soviet culture a credential marking out one's text or product as non- or anti-Soviet, new, fresh and democratic. Homosexuality was publicly acknowledged as one of the social "problems" that the Soviet system had swept under the carpet. More daringly after 1991 it became a symbol for a spectrum of social and cultural preoccupations (many of them having little to do with queer experience). Yet at the same time notes of anxiety and fear accompanied these stirrings: HIV/AIDS was a new threat apparently from outside the USSR, and "non-traditional" sexuality (a label for queer sex that has stuck) was to blame.[63]

Moscow was the center of these developments. However, one should not ignore the vast provincial hinterland in the evolution of post-Communist queer Russia. In political and cultural terms, the late 1980s and the 1990s were a moment of decentralization, when Russia's regions re-discovered their voices. The provinces and republics of Russian Federation (independent from late 1991 and led by President Boris Yeltsin until 1999) displayed greater confidence and threw up new leaders on the national stage. This was as true in Russia's LGBT culture and politics as in any other field in the 1990s. From 2000, with paramount leader Vladimir V. Putin, a counter-trend towards the re-centralization of power and wealth began that has not yet run its course. However, the rise of digital technologies and networks has challenged Putin's agenda, with significant consequences for queer Russians.

On the eve of Communism's collapse, sophisticated and well-prepared Soviet queer voices took advantage of democratic politics to speak out with a fresh, uncompromising frankness about homosexuality in the USSR. The first Soviet gay and lesbian magazine, *Tema* (The Theme – a common tag for same-sex love), appeared in December 1989, edited by Roman Kalinin (born 1966) and Vladislav Ortanov (1953–2011), assisted by the politically experienced Debrianskaya, who devised a front-organization to support the publication, the Association of Sexual Minorities (ASM). The ASM hosted several Moscow media conferences in 1990–1, well attended by Western journalists and soon by Russian ones too; its first, in February 1990, saw *Tema*'s associates condemn the persecution of sexual minorities and call for the decriminalization of male homosexuality.[64] Early attempts to develop an organization representing all Soviet lesbians and gays came to nothing, but *Tema* itself galvanized young activists from across the Soviet Union. They had support from international friends, who invited Kalinin to San Francisco in late 1990 on a speaking and fundraising tour. The diminutive blond made an impression on U.S. audiences, and the funds raised went to support a major international conference of gay and lesbian rights, held in Moscow and Leningrad in summer 1991. In June 1991, Kalinin stood in the elections for Russian president as a candidate for the tiny Libertarian Party, and if his chances of winning were non-existent, the media publicized his demands for an end to gay persecution with a degree of bemused curiosity.[65] Activists around *Tema* participated in the public agitation that followed the August 1991 attempted coup against Gorbachev. They printed an extra four thousand copies of the magazine, with Boris Yeltsin's proclamation denouncing the coup, and distributed them to crowds and soldiers in tanks at the Moscow demonstrations.[66] In retrospect, the small band of activists who gave voice to the demands of homosexuals in the last months of Soviet power now appear braver and more successful than many at the time were prepared to concede. While male homosexuality was still illegal, the KGB still threatening gay men, and when the social taboo against coming out publicly as gay or lesbian remained extremely strong, a core of Moscow radicals dared to organize a campaign for queer rights and to publish their demands in the country's first queer magazine and in the national media.[67]

Decriminalization of gay male sex came soon after, in April 1993, in an omnibus package of laws rushed through the Russian legislature by the Yeltsin administration. The influence of the "first generation" of Russia's queer activists on the legal change was probably very limited. Instead, Russia's "shock therapy" reformers were keen to enact as much legislation to comply with Council of Europe human rights standards as quickly as possible.[68] When one considers how cooperation broke down later in 1993 between the president (who had a strong popular mandate after his June 1991 election) and the legislature (a holdover from the Soviet regime, packed with Communists), it seems remarkable that the administration managed to get its way on this controversial measure. Nevertheless the decriminalization of voluntary sodomy between adults was confirmed by legislators in Russia's first post-Soviet criminal code in 1996–7.[69]

Moscow's lesbian and gay activist and cultural groups came and went rapidly during the economically turbulent 1990s. The Moscow Association of Lesbian Literature and Arts (Russian acronym *MOLLI*) was founded like *Tema* before the Soviet collapse, and carried on until 1995 hosting literary events and supporting the publishing of lesbian writing. Olga Tsertlikh (born 1952) and Liubov Zinovieva (1958) were among its mainstays; *MOLLI's* participants published Russia's first lesbian literary journals *Adelfe*, *Sofa Safo*, and *Ostrov*.[70] United States and EU sponsorship supported safe-sex campaigning groups like the Aesop Center; and an attempt to establish a national umbrella organization for LGBT activism, the Triangle Center (*Tsentr Treugol'nik*), opened an office, published a newsletter, and held an All-Russian Conference of Lesbians and Gays in June 1996. It was attended by 120 activists, most of whom were Moscow-based (see Figure 4.1). Triangle closed when its foreign sponsorship ended the following year.[71]

Another hybrid organization originated in two Moscow scholars' contrasting visions for Russian queer studies. Elena Gusiatinskaya and Viktor Oboin (born 1950) jointly established an archive and library of LGBT materials in an attempt to preserve and analyze the explosion of documentation appearing after 1990. Oboin, an information scientist, tenaciously chased ephemeral documents from organizations and magazines that emerged and then closed down. He published a newsletter commenting on media homophobia and occasionally positive coverage of queer themes, boldly posting it to every parliamentary deputy and other public figures.[72] Gusiatinskaya, a literary

FIGURE 4.1 *Masha Gessen, Elena Chernykh, Evgenia Debrianskaya at the All-Russian Conference of Lesbians and Gays, Moscow, June 1996.*

scholar and translator, assembled a library of published LGBT materials (novels, stories, autobiographies, non-fiction) and material about queer themes from the mainstream press. She facilitated much queer writing, including an impressive anthology of lesbian prose.[73] Oboin moved his extensive document collection to Amsterdam's Homodok in 2000, and Gusiatinskaya still collaborates with a younger generation of activists.

Much of Russian gay men's publishing originated from Moscow during the 1990s; the emerging erotic market is examined in Chapter 5. *Tema*'s editors fell out, and Ortanov left to set up new projects, including magazines (*RISK, ARGO*) and books, eventually agreeing a partnership with Germany's leading gay press Bruno Gmünder. The deal collapsed in the 1998 financial crisis. Another publisher, Dmitry Lychev, built a successful gay men's magazine, *1/10*, producing twenty-three issues between 1991 and 1998, carrying erotic fiction, news and contact ads, vital in the pre-internet era. Contact ads, local news and views, and erotic fiction dominated the content of many local gay and lesbian periodicals that appeared in provincial Russian towns like Barnaul, Novosibirsk, Tver, and Rostov-on-Don. Nevertheless, except for St. Petersburg's high-brow literary review *Gay Slaviane!*, Moscow dominated Russia's queer publication market. The 1990s offered a short interval – after Communist persecution, but before the digital revolution of the 2000s – when print media were critically important for constructing LGBT communities in Russia. Gay and lesbian magazines, newspapers, leaflets and erotic albums allowed Russians the first chance in decades to speak for themselves, and to leave physical traces of their voices. Recent measures of official homophobia, combined with the general reduction in Russian media freedom, throw this momentary explosion of voices into sharp relief, as a time of unprecedented liberty for LGBT expression in Russia.

Despite these accomplishments, for many reasons, this "first generation" of post-Soviet activists and entrepreneurs generally failed to found lasting organizations and businesses. Ignoring decriminalization and democratization, on "moral grounds" Moscow's city hall denied most of them official registration and thus access to legal personhood; they were condemned to run on a shoe-string from private flats and the corners of host-organizations. St. Petersburg's post-Soviet administration began as more liberal, granting LGBT organizations *Krylia* ("Wings") and later *Vykhod* ("Coming Out") official registration. The Moscow police harassed publishers of erotica and bothersome newsletters; Lychev and Oboin emigrated. Gay and lesbian conferences and cultural festivals were harder to mount especially in the wake of the 1998 financial crisis. During the 1990s, homophobic responses to the new visibility of same-sex love grew louder in the media but remained largely untapped by politicians, while the country's leadership wrestled with economic and political crises.[74]

The tougher stance adopted since 2000 by Vladimir Putin's presidency, leading in his second term to his formula for "managed democracy," would eventually drive politicians to revisit the question of LGBT citizenship and to set limits on queer visibility. Chapter 6 examines the attempts by parliamentary politicians to mobilize homophobic sentiment in the early Putin years. A "second generation" of queer activists emerged during the first decade of the twenty-first century, from a rising young professional and entrepreneurial class.[75] This generation's activism was primarily directed "inward" toward building community and less aimed "outward" at mainstream society; it took advantage of the new digital technologies to operate virtually and reach more diverse and geographically scattered constituencies. Yet, as this chapter has shown, whatever the novelty of the environment the "second generation" emerged from and the tools at its disposal, these activists built on achievements won by successive generations' struggles against Stalinist terror, late-Soviet authoritarianism, and the chaos of political collapse and economic transformation. The "political postponement" of democratic freedom until 1989–91 did not prevent Soviet citizens from developing home-grown queer voices. Even before the flowering of Gorbachev's perestroika and glasnost in the late 1980s, a Soviet gay male and lesbian self-consciousness was well-established, and if it lacked Western-style "community" it nevertheless acquired, preserved, and passed on important assets: a sense of solidarity, of cultural heritage, and physical and social spaces in which to combat isolation and invisibility. Late-Soviet queers were cautious and often victimized, yes; but they were also resourceful and ambitious, and when freedom arrived they lost no time in speaking out, and they had plenty to say. The queer voices that burst on the scene in the 1990s in Russia were "Made in the USSR," not manufactured in the USA or Europe. The battles still ahead for the next generation of queer Russians are daunting, and yet the distance that Moscow's queers have traveled in the space of a single lifetime inspires respect and hope.

5

Active, Passive, and Russian:

The National Idea in Gay Men's Pornography

Russia's transition from a closed society under Communist rule to an open one under President Boris Yeltsin was marked by a rupture with the sexual values of the Soviet era. Those "traditional" Soviet values included a relative, but never absolute, silence about sex. Beginning in the late 1980s, the last Communist leader, Mikhail Gorbachev, opened the floodgates to debate about sex with his policies of perestroika and glasnost. Russia experienced a belated discursive "sexual revolution" that accompanied the democratic wave of the late 1980s and early 1990s. That revolution gathered more speed when Communism collapsed in 1991, and Russia began a dash to capitalism. Debates raged in the Russian media over sex education in schools, family planning clinics funded by Westerners, the rise of AIDS and the need for safer sex, and the sexualization of television and cinema. Meanwhile, the state made basic reforms to sexual regulation. Homosexuality between men was decriminalized in 1993, and a new criminal code enacted in 1997 redefined rape and the age of consent.[1]

After 2000, conservative-nationalist critics, long upset by these trends but emboldened by the presidency of Vladimir Putin, denounced this sexual revolution. In the troubling context of cultural globalization, with its appeals to individuals across and beyond national borders, conservative-nationalists saw the nation and state as threatened from a hyper-sexualized marketplace and its new conduit, the internet.[2] Sexual values became a critical battleground for national regeneration. Conservatives and nationalists turned their attention to Russia's then-prevailing demographic implosion and prescribed the re-regulation of sexuality. Putin put the rapidly shrinking population on the national agenda, and marshaled support in Russia's parliament, the Duma, to promote family values and to boost marriage and the birthrate, and to stigmatize divorce.[3]

The situation of Russia's homosexuals did improve, thanks to the 1990s "sexual revolution"; yet Putin's conservative-national politics sought to set clear limits to progress. As Chapter 6 discusses, Russia has apparently accepted the decriminalization of homosexuality, obliquely confirmed during Duma debates in 2002; even conservatives now reluctantly agree that gays and lesbians are an undeniable if unpalatable fact of national life.[4] But Russia has bluntly rejected the wider range of legal and social reforms enacted in the European Union. Anti-discrimination laws, gay marriage, and gay pride parades are denounced as un-Russian, a danger to the birthrate and to morality, and adherence to reforms like these – and the visibility of homosexuality they herald – has come to distinguish a European-Union-led "Europe" from a geopolitically independent "Russia" as political constructions.[5] A cultural battle is underway to establish how far an open homosexual identity is compatible with Russian citizenship. Well before Putin's return to the presidency in 2012, disputes over Moscow gay pride parades and the 2009 Eurovision Song Contest (held in Moscow) showed that the political establishment refused to concede public space to queer Russians.[6] In the face of the homophobic conservative politics of national regeneration, one is tempted to paraphrase courageous British Communist Harry Whyte's question to Stalin about the status of the homosexual in 1934, and ask, "Can an open homosexual be considered a person fit to be a citizen of the Russian Federation?"[7]

Confinement of queer life, a disturbing new "global" form of self-expression, to private and commercial space has been the rule. Putin-era prosperity, itself heavily reliant on access to global capital and markets, initially saw the maturation of Russian gay entrepreneurship and some improvement in the quality of queer private spaces. Russia began to develop lively gay and lesbian internet meeting places and websites; a handful of periodicals led by the glossy lifestyle magazine *Kvir* (Queer, first published in 2003) appeared in Moscow; and a small collection of gay shops, bars, nightclubs, and saunas opened in both cities.[8] Indeed, some queer voices, allied to the new generation of gay entrepreneurs, criticized the Moscow pride parade organizers as misguided. These critics claimed that Russia was "not ready" for Amsterdam-style gay pride, that such events would alienate the average citizen and provoke extremists to violence.[9] The pride parade debate has compelled the authorities to engage in a public conversation with queer citizens and, while public space has not been conceded, the fact of that conversation is something new. During the 1990s, despite the élan of the "sexual revolution," the "first generation" of Russia's divided gay and lesbian movement largely failed to ignite a national discussion about queer citizenship.

Yet Russians did talk about homosexuality during the 1990s: after the collapse of Communism they puzzled over it in literature, in cinema, in popular music, and on the stage. Scholars have observed that culture – rather than politics – has served as the privileged sphere in Russia where the problem of same-sex desire can be elaborated. They have argued persuasively that this privileging of the cultural sphere as the place where homosexuality can be contemplated is an old tradition in Russian life, pre-dating the 1917 Revolution and re-emerging since 1991 with surprising force. They generally argue that the homosexual has served as a symbol of national abjection or impotence (in the action-thriller *boevik* novel, for example).[10] Paradoxically, they have also noted how proximate to key values in Russian culture the homosexual figure comes when imagined as suffering martyr, or as tortured soul with spiritual gifts or refinement.[11] These observations derive from readings of "legitimate" genres rather than deliberately "pornographic" ones: best-selling novels, films, television serials, and other mass-market popular culture.

Although Russia's heterosexual pornography has attracted some attention from scholars, they have seldom examined gay men's pornography for insights into Russian culture.[12] Gay porn has featured, if at all, as a sidelight to Russian porn studies. If scholars of Russia are no longer deterred by pornography's disreputable aura, and its power to excite condemnation and ridicule, their reluctance to examine gay porn has perhaps been not intellectual but logistical: finding it could apparently be difficult. In a commentary on Russian pornography, Helena Goscilo, following second-wave anti-pornography feminist critiques, offers a tendentious reading of all gay porn as structured by violent top-bottom inequalities, positing that the "top" in male homosexual relations (typically, the insertive partner) always dominates and exploits, while the "bottom" (the receptive partner) suffers and is subordinated. By analogy, homosexual roles allegedly mirror a heterosexual, patriarchal pattern of exploitation. Content with this sweeping dismissal, Goscilo does not look at a single example of Russian homo-porn.[13] In the same volume, in a chapter discussing male sexuality in print and visual media of the 1990s, Luc Beaudoin devotes a paragraph to two early gay porn films made in Russia; he notes their success on the U.S. market and the "imperialistic fetishism" they signaled.[14] These films' place in the wider contexts of gay erotica, Russian and foreign, is unexplored. Using a much larger archive of materials sourced more systematically from Russia and the West, and drawing upon queer theory and pornography and film studies, it is possible to offer an analysis of Russian gay porn that moves beyond reductive readings to place it nearer the heart of studies of erotica, and of Russian culture.

This chapter seeks to explore a number of questions that previous accounts have been unwilling or unable to address. Is there an emerging Russian gay pornographic tradition with its own esthetic? How do global and domestic gay porn styles interact and influence each other? Can gay men's porn construct or re-construct gay desire as Russian – and if so, how? To answer these questions, I first sketch the atypical pre-history of gay erotica in Russian culture, and turn to review the explosion of print-based gay pornography that appeared in the 1990s in Moscow and St. Petersburg.[15] After establishing some themes prevalent in indigenous printed porn, I then examine representations of gay sex in Russia in pornographic films. Following the definition used by Richard Dyer in his seminal 1985 essay on gay men's videos, I define gay cinematic pornography as erotic film deliberately intended to evoke sexual arousal in gay men.[16] I approach these materials in the feminist but frankly appreciative spirit pioneered by Linda Williams twenty years ago; I cannot agree that gay porn is simply an extension of hetero-patriarchal hegemony, with reductive and ahistorical readings of who's on top and what that means.[17] The films I examine were produced principally in Russia between 1995 and 2005. Their "Russianness" is not unproblematic; many of these films were made by "outsiders" about "Russia," however imagined, and even the more "indigenous" films display the influence of European or U.S. makers of pornography. This is a discussion of an as yet emerging, hybrid esthetic.[18] I argue that this global intercourse is a critical feature of the genre. The exchange between Westerners and Russians of cinematic techniques, sexual choreography, and scenarios of gay life has run in two directions; it has not simply been a colonial project imposed on a Russia "innocent" of gay desire. Taking a cue from globalization theorists, and the insightful work by Eliot Borenstein on nationalism and Russia's heterosexual pornography, I further argue that these exchanges operate, sometimes laboring against considerable homophobic resistance, to "embed" gay desire in Russia's national ethos.[19]

"Hard to imagine" à la russe: a brief history of Russian gay men's erotic imagery

The storehouse of Russian visual culture holds plenty of images that same-sex oriented men have responded to enthusiastically, although documenting that response is more difficult than listing the images themselves. Alexander A. Ivanov's nineteenth-century drawings and paintings of the male nude often linked spirituality with male beauty, while Kuzma Petrov-Vodkin's early twentieth-century nude youths were less religiously inspired but no less erotically charged. Sergei Eisenstein's homoerotic camera-eye lingered lovingly on the Russian sailor and worker.[20] Among official socialist realist artists, the best-known celebrant of male beauty who managed to combine Soviet patriotism with echoes of earlier traditions was Aleksandr A. Deineka. Boys, youths, and adult men as "future pilots," as workers, and as defenders of the motherland all came under his remarkably ambiguous gaze, perhaps best captured in his 1935 canvas *Lunchbreak on the Donbass*, in which five nude men run through sun-dappled water toward the viewer.[21] Contemporaries of Deineka and later socialist realist artists made the square-jawed, half-naked muscle-bound worker a cliché to such an extent that a walk through many civic spaces of the late Soviet era was a lesson in the discreet charms of the proletariat.[22]

These "legitimate" images appeared publicly and sustained erotically ambivalent readings. Images deliberately designed to arouse the gay viewer also circulated clandestinely. The drawings that accompanied poet Mikhail A. Kuzmin's 1920 gay sex-themed verse cycle "Veiled Pictures" rendered the erotic imagery of the poetry visual in an explicitly phallic way.[23] Eisenstein's secret phallic drawings of the 1930s–40s are now well known, and probably represent the tip of an iceberg: images made covertly by gay men for their own pleasure.[24] Such sexual *samizdat* was part of Western gay (and straight) pornographic traditions, and it seems likely that gay men made similar images themselves in the Soviet Union. As in the West, few of these images have probably survived, and yet perhaps in the collections of Soviet-era sexopathologists and private individuals one day more material of this type may surface.[25]

Another series of explicit sexual images created in Gulag camps and prisons were less concerned with expressing desire (although this cannot be excluded) than with cementing hierarchies of power. As noted in Chapter 1, by the 1950s–60s, tattoos branded members of Russian prisons' most "degraded" (*opushchennyi*) caste, known as *petukhi*, men and youths deemed sexually accessible for oral and anal intercourse to all "real men" (*muzhiki, patsany*).[26] Not images expressive of a freely chosen gay desire, these tattoos, and the nightmare world of coercive and humiliating male same-sex relations they signaled, nonetheless exist as a significant specter that haunts the ways in which physical love between men is imagined in post-Soviet Russia. Male prison homosexual experience is hard to imagine for Russian gays as erotic fantasy (in contrast to Western pornographic representations), and the "disgust" it arouses exerts a significant influence over the way sex between men is depicted by Russians.[27]

With the publication of the first Russian gay periodical, *Tema*, in 1990, a decade of liberty opened which saw numerous gay and lesbian magazines appear and disappear, often after just a single issue.[28] These print publications of the 1990s, later greatly diminishing in number in the 2000s by the shift to digital media, and intensifying political homophobia, constitute a unique archive of Russian LGBT freedom and visibility. Early publications pirated erotic images (normally, male nudes without erections and not engaged in sex) from the Western gay press. *Tema* and its earliest competitors and imitators (such as *Partner(sha!)*, and *Ty*) combined these photographs with varying degrees of political news, HIV awareness campaigning, safer sex instruction, erotic and coming-out fiction, poetry, historical sketches, and contact ads.[29] Also common were drawings by Russian artists, usually more explicitly sexual than the foreign photographs. Stylistically, the drawings mirrored the graphic modes of late Soviet publications or – and this was perhaps more popular – reflected a nostalgia for the pre-revolutionary Silver Age (as in Mikhail Anikeev's publications including *Partner(sha!)* and *Uranus*).[30]

By the mid–1990s, and after some early battles between the authorities and street traders selling erotica, a clearer division emerged between publications designed to educate, and those designed to provoke an erotic response. According to Borenstein's account, by 1994 Moscow city authorities resolutely suppressed "straight" pornographers with pretensions to "high culture"; in order to survive, pornography had to remain obviously "low" in the cultural hierarchy.[31] A similar distinction emerged with Russia's gay publications. The Moscow periodicals *RISK, Zerkalo, Gay, Slaviane!*, and the lesbian magazine *Adel'fe* were among those which took the high road, focusing on literary, social, and historical material, and avoiding explicit visual erotica.[32] The publishers of *RISK* also launched a sister-magazine, *ARGO*, billed in a fashion that betrays the Soviet education of its originators (and the bureaucrats who licensed its registration) as an "Illustrated erotic literary-publicist and advertising journal for gays."[33] The duality of the *RISK-ARGO* enterprise deftly compartmentalized the enforced division between "high" and "low" sexual cultures. *ARGO* reviewed gay films, presented news of the gay scenes of Europe and America, and offered Russian-produced nude centerfold photography under the rubric "the first steps of the *ARGO* photo studio." Before collapsing as a result of the 1998 financial crisis, *ARGO* made links with the leading European gay publisher Bruno Gmünder of Berlin.[34] Meanwhile, Russia's most successful gay magazine, *1/10* (*Odna desiataia*), survived most of the 1990s and reached some 10,000 subscribers, with a winning formula of domestically produced soft-porn photographs and drawings, erotic fiction, and a light mix of national and foreign gay news.[35] It was published by Dmitry Lychev, who had collaborated with *RISK* and *ARGO*. Before internet access was widespread in urban Russia, *1/10* offered a rich array of contact ads. It also published what could be described as Russia's first recognizably pornographic publications aimed at a gay male audience. In 1996, *1/10* issued a magazine of photographs by Vitaly Lazarenko with an English-language title – *Hot Russian Soldiers* (Figure 5.1).[36] In and out of uniform, the youthful soldier was eulogized in this comparatively tame collection. In it, *1/10* announced new pornographic publications: its own *Dimka*, billed as a "hard erotic" periodical and issued in illustrated, chap-book format; plus two collections of pornographic fiction released by *ARGO* and distributed by Lychev's network.[37]

By the end of the Yeltsin era, *1/10* had ceased publication and the Moscow authorities had compelled publisher Lychev to seek asylum in the Czech Republic; the financial crisis had closed *ARGO* as well. Nevertheless, the basics of a Russian gay men's porn esthetic had been established, to be perpetuated in other media. Its visual language depended on a few ready-to-hand scenarios. The centrality of the soldier and military themes reflected the near universality of young men's experience in serving in the Russian Army – or evading such service. The military theme appeared early and often in these publications, and evidently appealed to Russian consumers of porn.[38] The notion that it could attract foreign interest was apparently behind the appearance of *Hot Russian Soldiers*, with its captions in Russian,

FIGURE 5.1 *Hot Russian Soldiers (Moscow, 1996).*

English, and German, in 1996. The military male was a significant subject in drawings too (see Figure 5.1).[39]

Another key theme was that of male love in the Russian countryside. *ARGO*'s first photographic experiments featured a series of shots evidently taken at Serebriannyi Bor on the Moscow River, a popular gay cruising and naturist sunbathing spot in the 1990s. Similar locations were featured in *Hot Russian Soldiers*, domesticating army personnel by draping them among birch trees and alongside tributaries of the Moscow River. On occasion, erotic drawings invoked peasant Russia's architecture and visual grammar, a sort of homosexualization of peasant kitsch.[40]

Gay effeminacy, vulnerability, and martyrdom furnished an unusual current running through Russian visual representation of homoerotic desire during the period. As in other genres of popular culture, the suffering and pain endured by gay men, and in particular gay youth, was mobilized to ennoble the subject; what was perhaps uniquely Russian was the eroticization of weakness, effeminacy, and martyrdom. In the earliest publications, this theme was often linked to AIDS-awareness and safer sex campaigning. A striking example is the centerfold of *Partner(sha!)* no. 6–7–8 (1994) with its reclining Christ, tastefully draped, with the slogan, "For the sake of my love for you, please – a condom" (see Figure 5.2). This could shade into images of horror and violence, such as the drawing accompanying an article on "AIDS-terrorism" (see Figure 5.3), or the bondage theme in the illustration accompanying the short erotic story "Rodnaia krov'."[41] The effeminate gay man might be paired with a more masculine buddy, for example, in representations of gay weddings, or be depicted as an artist.[42] The distinction between "active" and "passive" sex acts and the gender role play that might accompany such acts seemed to matter less in these images than the power and allure seemingly invested in the feminized partner. In a subculture where perhaps rather few men considered themselves exclusively gay, but lived "bisexual" lives serially or simultaneously with women and men, the effeminate partner might offer a bridge between men's sexual experiences with women and their explorations in gay sexuality.[43] Here too was a subtle message that coded effeminacy and submission as powerful, because of the desire it evoked in the viewer; the specter of the abject prison bottom was implicitly countered with a more positive understanding of masculine submissiveness and its attractions.

The short, rapid evolution of Russia's gay print pornography and its visual language contrasted with the gradual development of gay porn esthetics in the West.[44] In the United States and Europe over the twentieth century, photographers and artists had produced a lively canon of gay erotica, beginning with invocations of Classical Greece and Rome, and moving, toward the middle of the century, to less highbrow muscle-worship. The cult of body-building served as a front to dignify Western gay pornography, and it is striking to observe the virtual absence of the body-builder or athlete in 1990s Russian gay porn.[45] U.S. mail-order companies

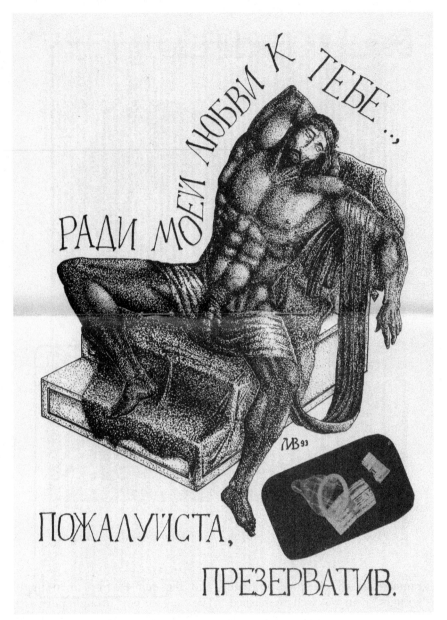

FIGURE 5.2 *"Radi moei liubvi . . .," illustration by "M.V."*

distributed nude photographs to thousands of subscribers during the 1940s–60s, always under threat of prosecution. At the same time, erotic imagery in underground cinema was becoming more homosexually explicit (in the films of Jean Genet, Kenneth Anger, and Andy Warhol); by the time U.S. censorship of cinematic porn began to relax in the 1970s, a visual

Подготовил *Сергей Щербаков.*

FIGURE 5.3 *"AIDS terrorism," illustration by Viktor Putintsev.*

grammar based on muscle-worship and the cult of the (un)attainable "straight" man was well established.[46] The "gay for pay" straight porn actor appearing in gay porn videos arose in the 1980s, when a star system emerged in U.S. gay production houses.[47] During the 1970s and 1980s, a gay pornographic film industry took off, alongside a far larger straight one, in California, Germany, and the Netherlands. With the 1989 collapse of the people's democracies of Central and Eastern Europe, gay porn movie makers (like straight ones) opened in Prague, Budapest, and Riga, led by the Czech "Bel Ami" brand. By the 1990s, U.S. and European gay men's porn constituted a globally dominant genre, just as Russian gay men's pornography was taking its "first steps" in the pages of *Dimka, ARGO,* and *1/10*.[48]

A combination of global and local factors emerged at the end of the 1990s to challenge and transform Russia's gay pornographic landscape. Wider access to the internet made the production of paper-based media less urgent: online social networking replaced contact ads in gay magazines. The Putin roll-back of the perestroika-inspired sexual revolution led publishers producing gay print erotica to leave an often difficult market.[49] In their place, Ed Mishin's slick website gay.ru appeared in 1999, and his glossy magazine *Kvir*, with its tastefully discreet imagery, hit the newsstands in 2003. Before President Putin's third term, the authorities appeared to tolerate Mishin's relatively visible magazine, for sale on the newsstands of Moscow. Since 2012, the glossy has reverted to a virtual, internet-only publication. Even before then, *Kvir* had always been an outlier in a country where gay and lesbian visibility was significantly restrained by comparison with Western societies. Yet inside Russia and beyond it, the impulse to make porn films with Russian men and Russian scenarios attracted foreign and domestic producers.

The Russification of gay sex on screen

During the wild 1990s, a few gay porn films were made in Russia, by European and American directors, using Russian men as actors. The most notorious were the *Military Zone* series (Zigmar Anatof, running to at least four sequels between 1996 and 1999). As Luc Beaudoin has pointed out, these films trained a Western, colonizing gaze on the Russian male body.[50] The sexual identities of these men were indeterminate, and this exotic inflection of the "unattainable straight" trope heightened the *Military Zone* series' appeal. The earliest *Military Zone* films were set in ex-Soviet Army barracks, and were undeniably monotonous, relying upon what Richard Dyer labeled the simplest of plots used in gay porn: the "encounter – sex – orgasm" storyline bereft of emotional complexity. Yet this series established the "hot Russian soldier" as an internationally recognizable type on the gay porn supermarket shelf in Berlin, Amsterdam, and San Francisco, and stimulated more imaginative attempts to deploy the type. The director of the *Military Zone* series shot at least one other film, *Last Train to Moscow* (1997), which featured a sequence of wordless railway encounters between eleven "Russian studs ... filmed entirely in Russia."[51] *Last Train* drew on the pool of actors first assembled for the *Military Zone* series, apparently appealing to Western viewers because they did not resemble the sleekly groomed men prevalent in U.S. and European gay porn.

Russia's potential evidently caught the eye of one very popular U.S. porn producer, Kristen Bjorn, who has specialized in filming "gay travelogue pornography" using foreign locations, scenarios, and actors.[52] The Bjorn effect globalizes a painstakingly choreographed, "vanilla" style of American gay sexuality that seems to be available anywhere on the planet. Making films for the U.S. gay porn market, Bjorn worked during the 1990s in Brazil and Central Europe. In 2001, Barry Gollop, a long-time Bjorn protégé, directed *Moscow: The Power of Submission* with the assistance of a Russian partner, Andrei Sharko of St. Petersburg's Kalina Studios.[53] This film made far more sophisticated use of the soldiers theme than the *Military Zone* series had done. It relied on a classic version of Dyer's model of a complex gay porn plot: two men, who are fated to fall in love and have spectacularly hot sex, are prevented from meeting as the movie unfolds. In flashbacks, fantasies, or parallel storylines, they have sexual adventures with other men, before they finally hook up. Dyer said that this complex plot line mirrored the contradictions of gay male sexuality, offering "a utopian reconciliation of the desire for romance and promiscuity, security and freedom, making love and having sex." *Moscow: The Power of Submission* is structured around this tension. It also offered an example of what John Burger has called a "revisionist history" of gay experience, by writing gay sex into depictions of familiar Russian institutions.[54]

The action is set in 1986, the Soviet era, when male homosexuality was still a crime. The hero, Corporal Slava Petrovich, is a KGB informant spying on Red Army private Alexander (Sasha) Byazrov and his comrades. Slava's job is to denounce their sexual antics, but his growing love for Sasha compels him to abjure the role of informer. Thrown in a KGB cell for insubordination, Slava meets a sympathetic jailer, but he is later dumped from a speeding Volga on a Moscow River embankment. As he tumbles into the snow, an address on a slip of paper falls from his pocket. (In the storyline, the address turns out to be Sasha's; but it is in fact that of the State Duma, a gag inserted by the local production team, and apparently an allusion to rumors about the "untraditional" sexuality of liberal, westernizing deputies.)[55] After a digression involving a black-marketeer and a shivering soldier for rent, the Slava–Sasha drama resumes with Slava seeking out the address; he finds Sasha there. Slava the corporal stops Sasha the private on his doorstep and receives a smart salute; he invites himself upstairs to Sasha's flat and the passionate embrace that has been delayed for over two hours finally ensues. The finale between Slava and Sasha won a "Hard Choice Award" as 2001's "Most Romantic Sex Scene."[56]

This film, made in Moscow by an American bringing Western production values and by Russians imparting local talent and knowledge, illustrates the complexity of cultural globalization: flows of culture do not operate in a single direction from center to periphery, and transfers of standard scenarios and narrative frameworks result in complex new formations and spin-offs.[57] Gollop's Russian collaborators learned how to make porn films for a global market: in a "making of . . ." DVD, we see Gollop choreographing the actors and explaining to his cameramen the glossy look he sought to achieve.[58] The Kalina Studio director Andrei Sharko recruited the actors (approved by

Bjorn, who vetted them from the USA via fax), and found the locations, but Gollop disagreed with Sharko over costs and they parted company. Gollop had advice about Russian life from his cameramen, actors, and interpreter.[59] It was not long before the Russian "periphery" made use of these skills, using national motifs and historical references to communicate to global and domestic audiences.

An émigré Russian who straddles the divide between cultural center and global periphery made two films under the English-language title *To Moscow with Love* (Michael Lucas, 2001, 2002). Lucas, born and raised in Soviet Russia, worked as a male escort in Germany before moving to New York in the 1990s and establishing his own gay porn production house.[60] These films are loosely organized around Lucas (as director and performer) acting the jet-setting gay Russian returning to Moscow to enjoy man-to-man sex. Moscow itself frames the action: *flâneur* Lucas takes in the town before a sequence of sex scenes in the Ukraina Hotel with Russian men, some of them soldiers. Two are actors who appeared in *Moscow: The Power of Submission*, including Sasha Byazrov, who is quizzed for gossip about that movie in the DVD "bonus extras" of Lucas's film.[61] Following John Burger's reading of gay porn set in the present as "revisionist," these Lucas films might be said to document contemporary gay experience, making gay desire visible, "real" and central rather than marginal.[62] The Lucas films depict a globalized gay Russia at ease with the technology, travel, and (implicitly at least) male prostitution associated with affluence. Lucas resembles Zygmunt Bauman's ideal global "tourist," the traveler free to choose his destination and sate every desire.[63]

Probably the first indigenously produced Russian gay porn film is *Kazaki* (Cossacks), released in 2004 by Kalina Studio in St. Petersburg by the well-established and prolific producer of Russian heterosexual porn films Sergei Prianishnikov, and director Andrei Sharko, Gollop's sometime collaborator on *Moscow: The Power of Submission*.[64] *Kazaki* in its confident boldness recalls the self-assured tone of that earlier St. Petersburg product, Mikhail Alekseevich Kuzmin's path-breaking 1906 novel *Krylia* (Wings) (Figure 5.4). *Kazaki* is set in a Cossack village, in an indeterminate past, where a band of brothers in plausible Cossack costumes ride and tend horses, pitch hay with wooden rakes, and do their other farm chores; they live communally in log huts decorated with embroidered towels and rough-hewn benches. The film unites two of the key themes seen in the Russian gay porn esthetic of the 1990s: the all-male military utopia, and the idyll of gay sexuality in the countryside. Its use of the Cossack historical setting puts gay sexuality at the heart of an important national myth. The Cossacks extended the Russian nation by opening Siberia to European conquest in the sixteenth and seventeenth centuries, and later, as military colonists, they served the tsarist regime as elite troops for keeping public order.[65] Moreover, there is a contemporaneity to this setting: Cossack communities are enjoying a renaissance in the troubled border region of southern Russia, with pageants staged by Cossack brotherhoods performing

FIGURE 5.4 *Kazaki, dir. Andrei Sharko, St. Petersburg, 2004.*

military parades and re-enacting battles becoming popular pastimes.[66] To set a gay utopia in a Cossack village may seem a provocative gesture for a Russian director in the prevailing nationalist climate. Yet it follows the logic traced by Borenstein in his examination of Russian heterosexual porn: in allegories of the anxieties confronting a shattered nation-state, national motifs and concerns are allied to graphic representations of sexuality. In pornography, national pride and sexual arousal intersect.[67] The deployment of national motifs to garland gay sex nevertheless has to work hard to square a circle: how to represent gay desire affirmatively in a culture that has previously treated it with disgust and silence?

Mutuality and the power vertical: constructing gay desire in Russian porn

Richard Dyer, John Burger and other critics argue that gay porn works to "educate" and repair gay men's psyches – damaged by homophobia – by showing men how the "struggles of the self" might be handled. Dyer went so far as to celebrate porn as constructing the liberated self:

> Gay porn asserts homosexual desire, it turns the definition of homosexual desire on its head, says bad is good, sick is healthy and so on. It thus defends the universal human practice of same-sex physical contact (which our society constructs as homosexual). It has made life bearable for countless millions of gay men.[68]

Beyond the affirmative value of gay porn in a homophobic world, Dyer readily admits its limits: it is as racist, sexist, and class-bound as the culture that makes it. But it is also essential to recognize that porn is not a conduit of an authentic sexuality; for Dyer, following Michel Foucault, it produces in its audiences a "knowledge about the body" which is culturally and historically specific.[69]

The chief "knowledge about the body" these theorists discerned is the conventional hierarchy between active and passive, top and bottom. They generally discern an evolution in the past thirty-five years in how this top-bottom hierarchy, which I shall call the "power vertical," has been depicted in Western gay men's porn. The AIDS emergency between the mid–1980s and mid–1990s was a key to this evolution, and divides the epoch of Western cinematic gay porn into a pre-AIDS (1970–83), "AIDS crisis" (1983–95), and "post-crisis" (1996+) periodization. Writing before the full impact of AIDS (unwittingly at the time, about the pre-AIDS era), Richard Dyer observed that the gay porn narrative was organized around the will to orgasm, with the gay "top" as the imagined agent of the directorial gaze. Influenced by then prevalent second-wave feminist analysis, Dyer argued that the gay top displayed a male sexuality little different from his heterosexual counterpart.

In 1995, having systematically reviewed hundreds of gay porn films, John Burger qualified Dyer's view, arguing that in the years after gay liberation but before the AIDS era (1970–83), mutuality held sway in American gay porn. He defined mutuality as tops and bottoms swapping roles, sometimes accompanied by overtly romantic gestures and stories. For Burger, the AIDS epidemic of the mid–1980s curtailed such mutuality. He suggestively linked the 1980s rise of a star system based on actors' reputations as "top" or "bottom" in the gay porn industry to the AIDS crisis. Fear of AIDS had the effect of rigidifying top-bottom distinctions. Marketing celebrated the straight male actor who turned "gay for pay" as a top, never bottoming in anal intercourse, and (in the dubious reasoning then prevalent) thereby evading the danger of HIV infection.

Burger's 1995 analysis only just pre-dated the appearance of combination therapy that made HIV infection a manageable rather than fatal condition. Arguably, since that time, directorial styles have shifted again. The mutuality characteristic of the pre-AIDS era, a "romantic" willingness to be both top and bottom, is now often combined in a post-modern mixture with elements of a conventional "power vertical." Conventionally powerful "tops" and submissive "bottoms" engaged in serial promiscuity no longer prevail exclusively, or command popularity and critical acclaim, in contemporary gay porn.[70] Indeed, the erotics of the gay top-bottom dyad are no longer as predictable in "post-crisis" Western gay porn films; shy tops are frequently seduced by bossy bottoms. To Dyer's complex model of porn emplotment, with its "utopian reconciliation of the desire for romance and promiscuity" can now be added the qualification that sexual mutuality and a power vertical coexist and interact in the genre today. This complex and queerer emplotment has been globalized in porn for gay consumers of the developed world.[71] The critique of gay porn's top-bottom relations as merely replicating the worst features of hetero-patriarchal norms is unsustainable if one takes account of the shifting historical meanings implicit in gay men's sexual roles.

Russia's gay print porn of the 1990s was only loosely connected to these emerging global currents. It was certainly the case that erotic stories and sexual imagery worked within the *aktiv/passiv* binarism, and during the 1990s, the term *universal* joined *kombain* to indicate the man who was happy to pitch and catch.[72] The eroticization of the effeminized male partner, necessitating an evidently masculine counterpart, appeared in drawings and photographs. Yet in the 1990s, the aggressive top man, an alpha-male with only one sexual posture in his vocabulary, was not an obvious feature of Russia's print-based gay erotica. The "hot Russian soldier" was as likely to be a youthful virgin, like "Konstantin (19) . . . [who] for the moment has no sexual experience, since he is under the strict eye of his mother."[73] In depictions of the military fantasy produced by Russians in the 1990s, soldiers were often figured as physically strong but spiritually vulnerable:

perhaps a projection, via some alchemy, of Russians' despair over the waste of young men in the first war in Chechnya. There is also a note of popular sentimentality for the transition from youth to adult manhood that national military service has long represented in Russian culture.[74] This vulnerable "top" man also approached the other important trope of this indigenous esthetic – the gay man as martyr, as suffering for his essence, as spiritually elevated being.[75]

Another explanation for the weak development of the aggressive alpha-male top in this porn points to the difficulty in Russia of eroticizing prison homosexual encounters. Well-established U.S. gay porn scenarios long featured prison as a site of "maximum visibility" and a predictable power vertical of jailer-top dominating prisoner-bottom.[76] Russian gay pornographers evidently find this thematic, and with it the "straight" top-man who rapes other men in places of confinement, too unsettling to assimilate. Prison rape scenes figured prominently during the 1990s in *boeviki*, best-selling popular action novels set in the criminal underworld; they were not erotic but the stuff of nightmare, part of the black excess of *chernukha* or sadistic, violent cynicism typical of post-Soviet popular culture.[77] For a potential gay audience, the traumatic memory of victimization, at least as old as the Gulag, and shrouded in homophobic "disgust," stubbornly resists eroticization.[78] The few affirmative novels and short stories set in the prison and army written by gay men make the terror of stigmatization, of becoming the object of disgust, the chief dilemma of the self for each protagonist. In Gennady Trifonov's prison novel *Setka* (The Chain-link Fence), young Korolenko struggles to understand how his relationship with the slightly older and more self-assured Obraztsov can be different from those of prison *petukhi*, the brutalized "passives" who are his only exemplars of gay sexuality.[79]

In the earliest gay porn films made about Russia by Westerners and Westernized Russians, the simple power vertical of top-bottom relations did prevail. The colonial gaze was apparent here – Russia was offered as the sexually available Other for the Western porn consumer. The Michael Lucas *To Moscow with Love* series presented a hybrid of power-vertical and mutuality models, but according to a semi-colonial hierarchy. Ideal "tourist" Lucas, despite his long career in the West, presents himself in his own films as exclusively "top." The Russians he meets in Moscow exist to "service" him as willing bottoms. Despite this adherence to the power vertical, the sequel gestures towards mutuality, as one scene without Lucas involves swapping of roles, albeit with this production house's trademark emotional *froideur*.

Moscow: The Power of Submission integrated the two paradigms of gay male sexuality in a commentary on Russia's politics and history. The U.S. director also imported the prison scenario, in a move that a Russian director would have found hard to imitate. Slava, the unfortunate informer in the KGB brig, is abused by a "General" and his minions exclusively as a bottom in an explicit equation between being the bottom and being subordinated. Slava's refusal to betray his beloved Sasha exacts a cost in the form of submission to a series of alpha-male tops (including the KGB jailer, who pities him and passes him Sasha's address – an example of the "power of submission" upon which the plot turns). The sexual tastes of the KGB are unorthodox and cruel, alluding to the depravity often ascribed to the Soviet secret police, and the black marketeer is also depicted as mildly depraved.[80]

Moscow: The Power of Submission contrasts the moral confusion of power vertical relations with scenes of emotionally positive mutuality. In a dream sequence when Slava recalls spying on Sasha and his three soldier friends, their comradely banter is complemented by friendly symmetrical trade-offs in which all are top and bottom in turn. In the final love scene between Slava and Sasha, a progression to mutuality is plotted, with military rank initially honored (corporal Slava tops private Sasha) and then inverted in the emotional and prize-winning climax. This "revisionist history" proposes a scale of values in which sexual mutuality accessed through genuine love, or true comradeship, triumphs over the exploitative power vertical of the KGB and the black marketeer. Of course, this moral is the romantic conception of an American director. Arguably, his all-Russian production team absorbed the lessons of this moral fable, for some like director Sharko and actors Byazrov and Petrovich went on to make Russian and foreign porn films that display some of these features.[81]

Kazaki, a totally Russian product, includes elements of the top-bottom power vertical, and the prospect of mutuality, showing that producer Prianishnikov and director Sharko are alert to globalizing trends even as they try to hail a local market of Russian men who have sex together. In *Kazaki*, a film without dialogue that proceeds through a series of carefully composed scenarios, the casual observer notes the prevalence of power vertical-style relations, from the opening sequence of the film with its public flogging of a miscreant Cossack. A youthful blond messenger, whose presence links most of the film's scenes, witnesses this scene as he arrives in the Cossack village on horseback. The messenger enters the cottage of the Cossack hetman (chieftain), only to find him having intercourse with his wife (the only woman in the film); he sees the hetman's impressive endowment and immediately offers himself as a passive alternative to the wife – which the hetman accepts with relish. Subsequent scenes involve the messenger's and others' non-reciprocal "servicing" of a "top" who is at the centre of the directorial gaze. Some of these are presented as sexual comradeship, while one scenario involves a degree of coercion, with the bottom bound to a tree trunk in the forest.

Yet the power vertical does not simply dominate this Cossack idyll. Romance between Cossacks is also possible, even if the emotional dimensions of gay love in a film without dialogue are inherently limited. In a dreamlike central sequence lit by a campfire, pairs of Cossack warriors kiss passionately and make love. Using much gentler background music than the frantic dance beat employed elsewhere, this scene pushes beyond representations of sexual comradeship to gesture toward romance and even love between men. As if this nighttime romance was too hot to handle, the final scene shows the sheepish Cossacks waking up with hangovers in the hetman's cottage. In the ensuing orgy, the men adopt as their collective bottom a particularly hung-over alpha-male (and the man with the biggest physique in the cast) whom they drag out from under a bench. Close-ups reassure us of his consent: he smiles and laughs as he makes himself available to the entire Cossack brotherhood. Even the messenger-bottom gains the "right" to top this alpha-male, as the directorial gaze turns to him.

For a Russian gay audience, familiar with prison culture's stigma of the passive homosexual, the final scene of *Kazaki* is potentially haunted by the nightmare of male rape in places of confinement. As a work of gay porn, affirming sex and affection between men, the film works hard to displace that specter with a fraternal and consensual fantasy. The apparent inversion of the power vertical, with a top willing to bottom and a bottom who finally gets to be on top, disrupts (but cannot entirely dispel) phobias about sexual passivity. In a film without dialogue, the working-out of such dilemmas of the self can only be hinted at. *Kazaki* does not reject the power vertical, but struggles with the lurking stigma of bottom-status, a stigma that threatens to undermine the affirmative erotic purpose of the film.

Pornography, Russian nationality, and the politics of gay visibility

Can we see a genuinely Russian esthetic evolving in gay men's porn films? With so few films to draw upon, it is too soon to tell, and the "Russianness" of the films discussed here is far from straightforward. I have argued that gay Russian visual pornography did not develop in a vacuum, but is emerging with its own iconography and is engaged in an exchange with well-established Western styles of erotic imagery and cinema. Foreigners or émigrés have taken the lead in defining the cinematic esthetic so far, starting from a colonial gaze and but also sifting a unique cultural heritage with the help of local agents. Furthermore, Russians themselves are now also making the genre their own, and in the process they are implanting something utterly novel in Russian culture.

In porn studies, there is still relatively little work on the impact of globalization on erotic cinema. Existing scholarship considering porn's colonial gaze tends to focus on the U.S. erotica industry as a "center" dominating racially distinct global "peripheries."[82] This view fails to take into account the recent rise, for example, of a post-communist Czech or Latvian porn industry where concepts of "race" are less significant than local economic inequalities, historical legacies, and regulatory freedoms that make such an industry viable. Where Russia is concerned, one might well ask: with so much "product" available from "the West," why have an indigenous porn industry at all? Eliot Borenstein answers this question by reminding us of Western pornography's origins in the Enlightenment as a form of political satire, and referring to the "project of postsocialist liberation" that indigenous pornography heralded and embodied, even as an entire culture was "pornographized."[83] For the Russian heterosexual male at least, and for a brief period at the height of the 1990s democratic wave, the freedom to depict desire explicitly represented an emancipatory rupture with the Soviet past, and endowed pornography with political meaning. With the passing of the euphoric moment, the Russian porn industry has matured, tastes have differentiated, but the "self-conscious . . . preoccupation with Russia's status as a nation and as a culture" persists.[84]

Porn depicting Russian gay desire expresses this preoccupation in distinctive ways. Anxiety about national collapse does not seem to hang over gay fantasy about the Russian military with the same ubiquity found in the straight porn reviewed by Borenstein and Beaudoin. If anything, demoralization in the ranks is a projection of Western gay pornographers depicting the end, or the revival, of the Cold War.[85] Russian-made gay erotic fantasies of the military domesticate the "hot Russian soldier" as a mama's boy, a cultivated and powerful physique to drape over birch trees, or a historical type (the Cossack) with a crucial place in the national epic. Here a popular view of the military as a key forge for Russian manhood meets the official, rose-colored view of Russia's army, and the realities of *dedovshchina* (hazing culture) and Chechnya find no place in the gay porn esthetic.[86]

The emergence of indigenous gay pornography is significant for what it suggests about the evolving politics of nation and queer visibility. A pressing "dilemma of the self" for same-sex desiring men (and women) in Russia is the question of how publicly to express that desire while still being considered a good citizen. "European" openness beckons from the global "center," but Russian conservatives repulse this appeal and insist on Russia's specificity. The question remains unresolved, and like Trifonov's young Korolenko in the novel *Setka*, battling his demons – his internalized homophobia – to find an acceptable definition for his gay desire, individual Russians are forced to search for their own answers.[87]

Does gay porn offer a serious answer? Dyer wrote that "gay porn asserts homosexual desire" and that it "made life bearable" for millions of gay men. Russia-centered depictions of gay sex go some way to fulfilling the porn-maker's task of exploring the chief "dilemmas of the self" that trouble the Russian gay psyche. Those dilemmas have deep roots in a legacy of "disgust" and victimization, a legacy of homophobia. How to write into a resistant national culture the story of eros and love between men: that is the reparative work that gay men's porn might do in Russia, as it has done elsewhere. Yet, paradoxically, as pornographers radically inject gay visibility into Russian culture, they also align same-sex eros with national myths, unsettling the heterosexual foundations of those myths, and challenging the narrow nationalist view of Russian sexual citizenship.

6

"Let Them Move to France!":

Public Homophobia and "Traditional" Sexuality in the Early Putin Years

The national-patriotic mood of Vladimir Putin's first two terms as President was characterized by high anxiety about Russia's fitness to meet the challenges it faced. For new nationalists the decline in the nation's population during the 1990s and early 2000s, and its enduring gender imbalance, were not merely tragic effects of disastrously managed economic transition, but threats to the nation's existence. In particular, the prospect of a deficit of men to recruit into the army, police and emergency services loomed as a significant obstacle to the Putin administration's aspiration to revitalize and strengthen the state. In the demographic curve current at the time, nationalists fixed upon gender relations as a political sore point. Nationalist gender rhetoric, whether discussing "sexual morality," teenage sexual behavior, or homosexuality, struggled to articulate a resonant and persuasive appeal to counter the "sexual revolution" of the post–1991 "reform" era. In the early Putin presidency, compared to what would later emerge, national-patriotic criticism of the "sexual revolution" was secular in tone and language. Often it relied on experts steeped in the paternalistic and patriarchal habits of Soviet medical science for support. Politicians across the spectrum also displayed a distinctly blind spot when it came to evaluating men's role in the demographic crisis. For nationalists seeking to forge a new conservative gender consensus, masculinity was the unexamined factor that no one wanted to analyze. Instead, talk – and blame – turned to the abject: single mothers, teenagers out of control, sex criminals, and homosexuals.

During 2002 the State Duma resounded with debate over changes to the criminal code, proposed in a bill entitled "On the defense of morality." The draft bill incited vigorous discussion about the nation, its potential to defend itself, and the gender order best suited to this task. New voices from the nationalist and old-style Soviet wings of society gained confidence as liberal understandings of sexuality were challenged in a combination of "managed" debate and less predictable but equally powerful political carnival. In the process anxieties about sexuality were aired in ways that were new for Russia's political culture. An important result of the debate over this law was the realization by nationalist conservatives that a more sophisticated political language of homophobia would be needed to win support for further projects against LGBT freedom. The focus on male homosexuality presented a foil to the masculinity of "simple Russians" and offered a distraction from the dilemmas facing the "normal" man. The path to the invention of "traditional sexual relations" as a political weapon in Russian politics began with this first campaign for "traditional sex."

The draft bill "On the defense of morality" proposed a range of measures to protect young people from sexual exploitation and harm believed to be caused by early sexual activity.[1] The principal measures included raising the age of consent for sexual acts from fourteen to sixteen; harsher penalties for sex with underage persons; and an extension of the 1997 Russian Criminal Code's definition of "persons . . . [with] responsibility for the education of minors" expanding the list of occupations subject to harsher penalties in child sex abuse cases. The draft bill also widened the definition of pornography and imposed a harsher regime of penalties for possession of pornography depicting persons under eighteen.[2]

The origins and fate of the bill can be quickly traced: it began as a proposal in the Duma Committee on Women's, Family and Youth Affairs, sponsored by its chairperson, then-Communist Svetlana Goriacheva (Figure 6.1). On February 4, 2002, Goriacheva presided over a day of hearings on the bill in parliament's Legislation Committee. During spring 2002 Russia's media discussed the hearings and the bill, and Duma deputies supplied a range of colorful copy. In late June 2002 the bill passed first reading by a vote of 414 in favor and 0 against (with three abstentions). Thereafter, the bill disappeared from view. Much later, in November 2003, the Duma passed an omnibus bill of changes to the 1997 Criminal Code and on December 8, 2003 President Putin signed it into law. This legislation raised the age of consent to sixteen, and made possession of child pornography illegal; yet it did not include the new definition of pornography or the new list of occupations subject to harsher penalties for child sexual abuse.

It is not clear how the Duma debates influenced the behind-the-scenes work of Kremlin lawmakers. The ultimate result of the public debate, however, would be a marked re-invigoration of Russian conservative discourse about homosexuality and gender. By examining the motives and contributions of the participants in the Duma sex debates the rise of this rich discourse can be charted. A closer look at the statements and silences around masculinity can then serve to illustrate the patriarchal and nostalgic elements underpinning this discourse. This now-forgotten political controversy marks

FIGURE 6.1 *Svetlana Goryacheva. Photo by Anton Novoderezhkin\TASS. Source: Getty Images.*

an important moment in the invention of "traditional" Russian sexuality during Putin's first term.[3]

Sounding off about sex

Four sets of social and political actors promoted "On the defense of morality" with differing motives and emphasis. President Putin's domestic political agenda was enhanced by association with the draft bill; Duma deputy Svetlana Goriacheva vaulted to prominence thanks to her sponsorship of the law; the conservative medical establishment found a platform for its views on sexuality; and finally nationalists inside and beyond the Duma drew inspiration from the debate. Liberals managed to score some victories in this contest, even considerable ones, but the response to these gains would eventually be the amplification of obscurantism, misogyny and homophobia in Russian sexual politics.

Vladimir Putin's concern about Russia's demographic crisis quickly became a signature issue of his early administrations. Population decline, mentioned in the president's first "state of the Federation" address to both houses of parliament in 2000, was proceeding at a rate of 800,000 per year, and statisticians were warning then that the country's population of approximately 145,000,000 could fall as low as 120,000,000 by 2025.[4] Poverty and its effects were taking their toll, as economic regeneration was in its early stages and the benefits were spread unevenly. While waiting for the economy to rebound, Putin's concern for population renewal has focused on the protection of young people as the engine of national renewal.[5] But his policies began as illiberal ones: the Kremlin's support for measures to protect the sexual development and inviolability of the nation's youth appeared to derive not from European models of individual sexual citizenship but from an instrumentalist view of youth as a resource to be cultivated in the service of the state.

Svetlana Goriacheva felt so passionately about "On the defense of morality" that she resigned her senior position in the Communist Party in early 2002 so that she could continue to chair the Duma Women's Committee and steer the bill into law.[6] Goriacheva presided over a day of hand-picked presentations to the Legislation Committee when experts and laypersons spoke virtually unanimously in favor of the bill. By the time the bill came to its first Duma vote she said she had received 50,000 letters of support from the public. A carefully spoken lawyer with a long Communist Party service record before and after 1991, Goriacheva has since joined the Kremlin-supporting A Just Russia Party and now sits in parliament's upper house, the Council of the Federation, representing a district of the Pacific-coast Primorsky Region. She projected an image of maternal concern for the nation in her explanation of the legal changes she promoted.[7] Goriacheva's language of analysis was secular and sociological, possibly a legacy of her Communist political past; her campaign did not appeal to religious values. Arguing that the liberal "sexual revolution" after 1991 had left Russia vulnerable to new forms of exploitation, she condemned the "uncontrollable proportions" that prostitution was now reaching thanks to contact magazines and especially the internet. "Under the influence of propaganda for a beautiful life" even mothers "sold [their daughters] into factual sexual slavery to men." Claiming half the child pornography then available on the internet was produced in Russia, she warned that the nation's laws protecting children from exploitation are "unjustifiably liberal and markedly divergent from the legislation of other countries."[8] Indeed the legislation she sponsored did seek to recognize how the internet and globalization had changed the nature of commercial sexual exploitation even since the first post-Soviet criminal code of 1997. Anxieties raised by cultural and commercial globalization were at the forefront of this early "traditional sex" campaign.

Goriacheva's proposals to raise the age of consent found particular favor with Russia's conservative, Soviet-trained medical establishment. In the February 2002 committee hearing, medical experts propounded a scientific view of teenage sexuality little changed since the Stalin era. Medical authorities in the late Soviet period routinely denied that teenage sexuality existed or that if it did exist, that it could be healthy. They were influenced by medicolegal discourse about "sexual maturity" as a biological resource in the population, a platform for healthy reproduction that had been protected by Soviet criminal legislation for the collective good.[9] Young persons in this view were not citizens with liberal democratic rights to sexual inviolability, sexual knowledge, and sexual freedoms; instead they were biological and social subjects of a Soviet regulatory regime shaped by medical experts and police, for the collective socialist society. The legacy of that regulatory regime survives in contemporary Russian expert views.

A typical statement to the committee came from Dr Viktor Ostroglazov, a Moscow specialist in psychosomatic disorders:

> During the so-called years of reform [since 1991] instead of acceleration we have seen a retardation of the process of sexual maturation [in teenagers]. Consequently the current average age of sexual maturity is now over eighteen, or at least, it should not be less than that. It is not necessary or natural in the teenage years to feel desire for a sexual life. It is the cultivation of artificial desire that leads to its arousal and to pathological forms of it, too.[10]

Goriacheva herself reported on seventeen expert opinions from child psychiatrists, physiologists and pediatricians who stated "unanimously . . . that full sexual maturity in today's young persons is not achieved until, on average, eighteen years of age." She summarized their findings:

> The specialists are unanimous in their views about young people's premature sexual activity. They confirm that it is a powerful stress factor on the formation of the organism that can lead not only to negative consequences for general health, but also to the formation of anomalous sexual behavior, inclinations to rape, sadism, pedophilic behavior, homosexuality and so on.[11]

Hence, early teenage sexual activity damages the body during a crucial period of growth, and leads to frightening perversions. The leap from physiological derailment to psychosexual disorder remains a frequent reductionism practiced by conservative Soviet sexology. There is also a liberal current in Russian scientific sexology, which was best represented by Professor Igor Kon (1928–2011). Goriacheva, however, "forgot" to invite him to the February hearing. He tried to intervene by writing an open letter to the Duma, arguing against raising the age of consent, and against the attempt to define pornography in law – his plea was ignored.[12]

The Women's Committee chair skillfully recruited nationalists of various stripes to furnish dramatic testimony to the hearing on her draft bill. They spoke entirely in favor of raising the age of consent, while their language revealed a rich seam of anxieties, as this sample of their comments illustrates:

- "Society is undergoing a pathological mutation"
- "A national betrayal of unprecedented scale, in favor of the fallen nature of adults, is taking place in the country"

- "The decline of feelings of shame, the removal of psychological barriers and the propaganda for a beautiful life – are these the prime 'achievements' of the sexual revolution?"
- "The sexual despoliation of children is destroying the gene pool of the nation!"
- "Seducers [of children] are guilty of spreading HIV infection, moral vices, and the destruction of all of us ourselves as a nation"
- "It's time to begin the repression of those who are destroying our nation!"[13]

Soviet discourse about threats to the "sexual maturity" of the next generation fused in the minds of Goriacheva's conservative-patriotic supporters with anxieties about Russia's decline. Their powerful metaphors of pollution (of the gene pool, of childhood innocence) dramatized a national crisis. (Similar rhetoric had been deployed against attempts to reform attitudes toward family planning.)[14] Linked to this was a mistrust of economic reform – embodied in the stock phrase "propaganda for a beautiful life," that is, the improbably affluent lifestyles peddled on television and in the marketplace during the harsh economic transition to capitalism after 1991.

The draft bill and the heavily managed hearing stimulated spontaneous national-populist outbursts aimed at the sexual depravity apparently threatening the nation. Leading the charge was Gennady Raikov, an engineer and leader of a small faction of Kremlin-supporting People's Deputies in the Duma as then constituted.[15] In the wake of the February hearing, Raikov grabbed media attention with his draft bill to restore Stalin's 1934 ban on male homosexuality (which President Boris Yeltsin had scrapped in 1993). Raikov's gesture fostered two follow-up proposals, one to ban consensual lesbian relations, and another to make masturbation an administrative offence.[16] It was indicative of the anxiety provoked specifically by male homosexuality that neither of these secondary gestures yielded the response that the anti-sodomy proposal generated. Raikov argued that a law against "sodomy, pederasty" was needed "to facilitate the fight against venereal diseases and AIDS" and that it would save the Russian nation from population decline. "[Sodomy] is against the spirit of the Russian people," he declared, observing that it also violated the teachings of most of Russia's recognized faiths.[17]

An interview that spring with Oleg Rashidov of *Komsomolskaya Pravda* permitted Raikov to elaborate the nationalist motives behind his proposal – and explain why he voted for sodomy decriminalization during the debate over the 1997 Criminal Code. Asked about the individual's right to privacy, Raikov replied, "We're not in France! . . . If someone wants to do this, let them move to France, let them move to Holland. But here just go to the countryside, they don't even know the words for those things there." Rashidov asked then why he, as one of the Duma deputies who voted for the

1997 penal code, had agreed to decriminalize homosexuality. Raikov responded: "Well we didn't know back then! . . . it turned out that this old chestnut in the old Criminal Code was a beam holding up a barrier against international organizations of homosexuals with their powerful finances." "You mean – there's a conspiracy . . .?" asked Rashidov. "Before, they [homosexuals] were afraid. But now. . . you can't even turn on the television!" Raikov responded.[18]

Kremlin strategists had intended that Raikov's People's Deputies faction would imitate the Communist Party (CP) by sounding the same nationalist and socially conservative notes to attract an ageing electorate away from the CP; but in fact while the anti-sodomy proposal got Raikov plenty of publicity, it was slapped down by the Kremlin and ridiculed across the political spectrum, from the Communists to the Union of Rightist Forces (URF). And indeed, one of the surprising aspects of this public discussion was the historically unprecedented (if often only implicit and qualified) support for the decriminalization of male homosexuality that Russian politicians expressed in the media.[19]

In one April commentary, a source from the Presidential Administration reacted nervously when asked point-blank if Raikov's anti-homosexual proposal originated with the Kremlin: "We don't think up anything for him. He's not a little boy. If he can be of use for something besides idle chatter, we'll help him. If not – we'll drop him as quickly as we picked him up." Even the Communists' own spin doctors found Raikov's proposal ludicrous, and took the opportunity to link his obsession with homosexuals to the Kremlin. "Who in Russia is upset about homosexuals at the moment? Sure the ordinary working man never ever sees them. And everything else Raikov says is pure nonsense. Let him repeat word for word everything [leader of the CP Gennady] Ziuganov says, everyone still knows that a politician so close to the present leadership cannot seriously claim to be a defender of the toiling people. He's probably making it up. And nobody's fooled. Everyone knows that he's singing someone else's song."[20]

On the opposite end of the political spectrum, the leader of the URF, liberal Boris Nemtsov (1959–2015) had this to say in April when Kazan University students quizzed him about the proposed ban on sodomy: "Although it's a very important issue, and the Duma hasn't slept for three days because of it, I am against the idea of the state getting into bed with the people."[21] Property developer Vladislav Reznik, then deputy leader of the powerful Unity faction in the Duma's pro-Kremlin coalition, at the same time poured scorn on Raikov's proposals.[22] They would "surely bring sharp condemnation from the Council of Europe, and it is difficult to think they were entirely rational." Reznik's further comments were noteworthy for their historical perspective: the same law [that Raikov was proposing] had been enacted in the USSR in 1933 "in unison with analogous laws introduced in fascist Germany," and that in 1936 "it was proclaimed that homosexuality was a product of the demoralization of the exploiting classes, that it was the equivalent of counterrevolution. After that they filled up the Gulag." Reznik contemptuously dismissed Raikov's initiative as a publicity stunt and a pre-election ploy. His was the first and only public statement by any Russian politician of the rationale behind Yeltsin's decriminalization of male homosexuality, citing both Council of Europe norms, and Soviet regime's unjustifiable use of terror against gay men.[23] Other senior politicians regretted how the uproar brought parliament scant respect from a public impatient to see more pressing economic issues resolved.[24]

Masculine evasions and fears of national decline

If an outright ban on homosexuality was laughed off by an unlikely combination of parliamentary forces, the same legislature nevertheless eagerly passed Goriacheva's "On the defense of morality" on first reading in June 2002. In doing so it was persuaded by arguments put by the moralizing camp about demographic implosion, national decline, and the exploitation of what progeny Russians were producing. A striking feature of these political arguments about national decline was the absence of any responsibility attributed to men. Men's refusal of responsibility as parents, their role as customers of commercial sex, the patriarchal yearning to suppress sexuality in youth, women and "sexual minorities": none of these themes was aired in the new nationalist-conservative discourse of demographic decline that developed during Putin's first term.

To understand this reluctance to address male behavior it can be helpful to consider the intensifying of male alienation that accompanied late-Soviet and 1990s Russian economic and social transformation. When thinking about the evasion of male responsibility for Russia's demographic downturn, the observations of Elena Zdravomyslova and Anna Temkina, gathered at the end of the 1990s, about the late-Soviet "crisis of masculinity" as a historical legacy weighing on post-Soviet man, are useful.[25] Zdravomyslova and Temkina argued that Soviet sociologists and commentators in the 1970s–80s already perceived a grave crisis of masculinity in society. According to these experts, man in the contemporary USSR was "the passive victim of his own biological nature, or cultural and structural circumstances." War and terror had reduced the proportion of men in the population with grievous consequences for families; modernization and "bad habits" (smoking, alcohol, poor diet) had turned men into "the weaker sex"; Soviet family law had given women so much power over the domestic unit that men were alienated from it. There were no credible positive models of masculinity available to late Soviet man. Stalin-era "heroic Soviet masculinity" was an exhausted relic; pre-revolutionary aristocratic manliness held a certain charm for intellectuals but was hardly a model for most daily lives; and before the collapse of Communism in 1991, the self-made, patriarchal Western-style male was politically inaccessible. In place of these types arose a widely observed countertype, a perverse late- and eventually post-Soviet variant of the *muzhik* (literally, "peasant man," but now, more colloquially, a crude-mannered lower-class lout) who rejected the woman-dominated domestic sphere. The *muzhik* escaped to the company of brothers who displayed their autonomy in homosocial drinking binges and sexual adventures with women who were easy to exploit or abuse.[26] By the late 1990s, the liberal intelligentsia's hopes for meaningful renewal of masculine identities was foundering on the tenacity of the *muzhik* and the persistence of his anti-social traits. In Zdravomyslova and Temkina's optimal reading of gender ideals during the transition to capitalism of the 1990s, "[t]he new real man contrasts himself with the Soviet past and the criminal present" and his task was to realize the "hegemonic masculinity of Western man: autonomous, rational, property-owning subjects with liberal rights."[27] Yet shaking off both Soviet legacies and reform-era criminality and degradation proved more difficult than liberals imagined.

Indeed, the prestige of the *muzhik* never went away. Instead, Vladimir Putin's early appeal as strong leader tapped elements of the *muzhik* persona to "remasculinize" the presidency as the twenty-first century dawned. A renewed war in Chechnya saw Putin flying to the warzone posing as a fighter pilot, invoking traditional military machismo to stiffen the prestige of the presidency, while his periodic media statements couched in coarse street-language burnished his alpha-male swagger and connection to "ordinary" Russians.[28] Increasingly, liberal property-owning subjects who leaned too far toward the West were characterized as insufficiently patriotic and in extreme cases, a threat to the national interest: the arrest of Yukos oligarch Mikhail Khodorkovsky in 2003 saw a redrawing of the state's relationship with Russia's most powerful businessmen. To suborn the country's top capitalists, the president used Russia's hellish prisons – or the threat of them, not excluding the threat of male rape – and won their submission to his authority. One oligarch, Vladimir Gusinsky, signed over his shares in an independent media empire to the state's proxies after "a few days in prison in a cell with common criminals, some of whom were thought to be infected with HIV."[29] As Elizabeth Wood and others have noted, Putin's political persona relied on a complex amalgam of masculine "types," with elements of the *muzhik*, the patriarchal chief, the virile pop-star, and even the wealthy sophisticate with European tastes. Yet the critical factor Wood points to is the highly contrived "naturalness" of Putin's masculinity, its presumption of authority: as she writes, "masculinity for Putin became a way of showing power without having to explain it."[30]

The 2002 debate over the draft law "On the defense of morality" took place against the backdrop of this patriotic-nationalist scenario of political machismo. On the ascendant was a masculinity that refused to explain itself or consider the male role in the demographic slide. Commentators and politicians sought other scapegoats for the precipitous decline in the birthrate and the threat it posed for Russia's future. Men's role in the restoration of the Russian population was overlooked as women, youth and male homosexuals were diagnosed as at fault.

One persistent source of support for the new conservative morality was the *Parliamentary Newspaper* (*Parliamentskaia gazeta*), the legislature's journal of record, with its unabashedly lurid photo-montages and headlines on the topic of sexual morality. The demographic crisis fueled nostalgia for Stalin's family policies of the 1930s–40s, and the *Parliamentary Newspaper* concentrated its fire on women's reproductive role. "A Boycott on Posterity" (September 5, 2002), noted Russia's population implosion and quoted the Labor Minister worrying that "not only will there be no reinforcements for the army, but for the police, the emergency services and other bodies as well." Readers were invited to imagine the Russian state starved of the manpower (and in these male-heavy services it is *man*power) all because of the selfishness of one sex:

> Remember when in Soviet times long lists of women awarded the Hero-Mother and Maternal Glory prizes were published in the newspapers? That was when the state really worried about the future generation. There was an intelligent demographic policy. Now that's all gone without a trace. Our women have declared a de facto boycott on posterity.[31]

If (as the author claimed) Russia's women in 1875 normally gave birth seven times each, and until recently, twice or thrice, by the dawn of the twenty-first century, they were barely bringing a single child each into the world. Still worse in the eyes of these experts, the ones who survive in contemporary Russia, in contrast to the past when only the fittest lived, were frequently "neurotics and allergic types." According to sociologist Igor' Bestuzhev-Lada, "In fact the genetic fund [*genofond*] is worsening sharply, and it is a direct path to degeneration."[32]

Setting aside the wildly anachronistic appeal to degeneration theory, here the evasion is obvious – men clearly share some responsibility for this supposed "boycott on posterity." Decisions about whether to terminate pregnancies, and about the living conditions parents raise children in, are taken not only by mothers. The evasiveness of this message was even greater when one recalls that Russia's demographic slide began in the 1970s. Post-Soviet man was looking back to the generation of his grandfather, not his father, for solutions. Nostalgia for Stalinist intervention in private life (discussed in Chapter 4) made sense to many commentators with their view of "our women" who should be obedient, passive, fertile and content with Hero-Mother medals. Implicitly, men's duty is to create a posterity worth bringing children into and the article argued that economic liberalization tempered by welfare measures would bring this about. Even so, reform-era man recalled the heroic masculinity of the 1930s and worried that he could not measure up to the manliness of his grandfather, because he could not impose "an intelligent demographic policy" on "his" women. Unlike the heroic Stalinist New Soviet Man, whose epoch-making sacrifices secured superpower status for the Soviet Union, reform-era man was threatened with national impotence, a depletion of the "genetic fund" and the state's organs of force because of "his" women's boycott on posterity.

In articles stimulated by Goriacheva's campaign, the demographic crisis was the backdrop for the horrors visited on the nation's youth by the sex business. A tragic rise in abandoned and homeless youngsters, occasioned by family poverty, was said to have created a pool of children exposed to sexual exploitation.[33] Yet this cruel social trend was also framed in terms that evaded any male responsibility. In "Flowers of Life Grow on Asphalt" (another *Parliamentary Newspaper* exposé, of April 1, 2002) Duma press officer Natalia Dolgushina discussed the hundreds of girl prostitutes held in a Moscow remand center for minors, and a huge increase in prostitution rings around Russia; Dolgushina also noted a rise in the exploitation of young homeless children by "pornobusiness."[34] Another report began sensationally by recounting a Tula-district case of kidnapping and mutilation, using the case to call for the reforms backed by Goriacheva.[35] Yet the character of the customers of these prostitutes and pornographers is seldom examined at length. If they do appear (as in the Tula case) they are distinctly labeled as outsiders, as "pedophiles," "pimps," and "brothel-keepers." The Russian fathers who abandon their children, the men who buy child sex, who make, sell and use pornography were virtually absent from these articles. They existed as shadows behind abstract phrases such as "the exploitation of young people," but this discourse failed to confront the aspects of contemporary Russian manliness, of the post-Soviet *muzhik*, that shaded into this criminal world. A politics seeking legitimation through a particularly aggressive form of masculine theatrics, as scholars have pointed out, would scarcely invite a searching critique of manhood.[36]

A further feature of the masculine evasions of conservative nationalist discourse were the patriarchal views about sexuality espoused in this campaign by Soviet-educated medical experts. Denying that childhood and teenage sexual desire exists or can be healthy was a mainstay of their arguments. Indeed, it had been a longstanding tactic in the Stalinist medical channeling of sexuality into the vessel of heterosexual marriage.[37] In the month following the February hearings on Goriacheva's package of sex crime reforms, *Parliamentary Newspaper* slated the liberal sexual values of the 1990s reform era; it directed its ire at an "infamous 'Plan for sexual education of school children'" framed by the Russian organization "Planned Parenthood." This program would have introduced children at ages twelve to fourteen to concepts of sexual anatomy, functions and emotions; its authors were said to offer information for older pupils about "group sex and petting" and later "homosexualism, homophilia, homoeroticism, bisexuality, [and] transsexualism." In the late 1990s (with the intervention of a U.S. anti-abortion lobby, "Pro-Life"), Russian Planned Parenthood's curriculum was rejected by the Duma.[38] In the same item, Ostroglazov expanded on his concept of "sexual maturation" leaving no doubt that teenagers should not be experiencing these sexual feelings, "needless at their tender age," otherwise "the development of the personality will be crippled. . . [a]s it would be from alcohol or narcotics." "Only full sexual and psychophysical maturity can guarantee the birth of citizens of a society instead of neglected 'Mowglis'," Ostroglazov said, thrusting the blame for child neglect not on the fathers of unwanted children – but on teenagers who might experiment with or be forced into sex at an early age.[39]

The conservative medical backlash against Western style sex education highlighted the same experts' resistance to the relaxation of the taboo on homosexuality. Leaders of conservative sexual politics found in 2002 that their attacks on the reform-era decriminalization of male homosexuality produced unexpected reactions. In May 2002 Raikov complained that "influential circles" tried to silence him and he was receiving threatening telephone calls.[40] His draft bill to recriminalize sodomy was regarded as a joke. Conservative opinion-making on the issue was apparently in disarray. A sexologist with a folksy prose style and a doggedly antigay agenda rapidly supplied a far more sophisticated and dangerous critique of tolerance. In early 2003, Dilia Enikeeva, psychiatrist-sexopathologist and graphomane author of self-help guides and detective novels, published *Gays and Lesbians*, a 411-page polemic against "devotees of untraditional sex who are actively lobbying for the interests of sexual minorities, bolstering corporate interests, protecting 'their own' and fostering propaganda for homosexualism in the media."[41]

Addicted to aphorisms, jokes, and frilly hats, Enikeeva's chatty style and media persona might appear lightweight, but her interventions in the debate (she contributed to the Legislative Committee hearing) and her analysis of the problem of homosexuality in *Gays and Lesbians* purveyed a dark message. Arguably, it supplied conservatives with a homophobic political rhetoric that crystallized and focused popular attitudes. As Enikeeva wrote, only one in ten of contemporary Russia's gays and lesbians is a "true homosexual." The other nine are "ex-straights" who have been gradually, voluntarily groomed to accept homosexual advances from the "true homosexual." These homosexuals created "by compulsion" become gay for a variety of reasons: some acquiesce to further their careers; some are "mentally immature, subordinated, dependent people"; and many discover a truth Enikeeva apparently could not deny, that "same-sex sex is more attractive than heterosexual sex."[42] The danger to young people is obvious: "transitory . . . teenage homosexualism" is exploited by the "true homosexual" to recruit. The sexopathologist warned that the current law allowed adult "true gays" to seduce the unsuspecting teenager, and that a coterie of "pedophiles and ephebophiles in the circles of power" lobbied in the 1990s to drop the age of consent to fourteen as part of "the accomplishments of our democracy." She herself would gladly strangle any seducer who recruited her child into homosexual behavior, but she noted sourly that the law would imprison her for murder and not the corrupter of her offspring.

Enikeeva maintained that "simple Russians" had been distracted by a malign conspiracy of liberal sexologists and politicians who were themselves concealed members of the "sexual minority."[43] These villains were named as liberal politicians from parties such as the URF, and the sexologist Igor Kon, whom Enikeeva attacked as an amateur in her profession. Enikeeva diagnosed Raikov as "a homophobe and a rather limited man who obediently fulfilled an order he received" to "attract attention to the problem of homosexuality." Raikov's orders supposedly came "from above," from "homosexuals themselves" who sought to initiate a "'gay' scandal" in order to demonstrate "how many defenders of homosexuals would immediately appear!"[44] He was thus rapidly branded a "fascist." Discerning a media permeated with "gayness" (*golubizna*) and claiming that journalists are paid to promote gay opinion, Enikeeva called for an end to "gay censorship" in the media. To save heterosexuality, she argued that the age of consent should be raised to eighteen. As well, Enikeeva presciently pointed toward the next conservative homophobic project, noting that forbidding one form of gay sex, anal intercourse, as Raikov had suggested, would be pointless, but that the state should ban "homosexual propaganda."[45]

Although Enikeeva's book ostensibly dealt with both male and female homosexuality, the overwhelming thrust of her argument was directed against gay men as a distinctly dangerous, conspiratorial influence on the Russian body politic.[46] The sexopathologist turned political commentator mobilized homophobic rhetoric in an essentially new way for Russia, by offering apparently sophisticated medical justifications for curbing the social acceptance of same-sex love.[47] (Her critique was entirely secular, not referring to religious morality at all; this is one of the most striking things about Enikeeva's book seen from the perspective of the Kremlin's official campaigns against feminism and LGBT activism since 2012.) Her book refocused conservative arguments about the dangers of underage sex by training attention on male homosexual contacts, when in fact the vast majority of sex assaults against young persons are perpetrated by men on girls.[48] In the debate about age of consent reform, *Gays and Lesbians* increased the evasion of masculine responsibility for sexual crime and disorder by directing attention towards an abject group that supposedly works insidiously against the vast majority of "simple Russians."

Enikeeva's medical theory of the origins of homosexuality was primarily a nurture-, not nature-, based model but in this it reflected a long-standing tradition in Russian medicine to ascribe non-heterosexual practices to "mental infection" and the dangers of bad examples breeding perverse imitation.[49] Nevertheless, metaphors of "mental infection" quickly elide into more biologized language. The rhetoric heard in the February 2002 Duma Legislation Committee hearings showed that Soviet-trained experts and conservative commentators thought in medicalized terms of a Russia undergoing "pathological mutation." In the same session the claim that the "sexual despoliation of children" was polluting the "gene pool of the nation" brought the image of sexual disorder squarely into the biological realm (as did Bestuzhev-Lada's archaic discourse of "degeneration"). Women's role as biological carriers of the nation was only indirectly mentioned, but the repeated metaphors of the nation as a biological entity (or, a mutating genetic fund) suggested a passive, feminized Russian body, the victim of active "outsider" agents. Such imagery obscured the role of ordinary Russian men as contributing to the supposed pollution, infection and pathology of the national body.

The rise of a new moral rhetoric warning of national infection was accompanied by some developments that amplified its reach. Less than a month before Enikeeva's book was published, a government decree on the medical inspection of military conscripts appeared to extend a new ban on gay men in the Russian army.[50] The decree actually refined regulations on mental disorders disqualifying conscripts for service. Men experiencing "disorders of sexual identification and sexual preference" were deemed to be of "limited fitness" for military service. The decree specifically stated "in this regard sexual orientation in and of itself is not considered a disorder"; the text of the decree did not use the words "homosexuality," "homosexual" or "homosexual orientation."[51] A commentary on the decree from legal and psychological experts points out that the regulation is framed according to World Health Organization medical definitions of "disorders of sexual preference" that have not included homosexuality since the early 1990s.[52] The army ostensibly did not intend a blanket ban of homosexuals, yet the decree was widely reported as such in Russian and foreign media.[53]

Apparently the decree's author felt the need to explain the army's position after journalists used it to supply a spicy hook to their seasonal stories on the autumn draft (and how to avoid it). In November 2003 Major-General Valery Kulikov of the army's medical services clarified that international norms were indeed the basis for the decree: "In medicine there is no such thing as a diagnosis of homosexualism." So long as homosexuals are physically and mentally healthy, they will be judged "fit and will go and serve" he said, continuing, "but I would not advise these persons to declare their sexual orientation while in the army – such people are not liked and they will just get a beating."[54] On one hand, Russia's army adapted to international standards, including the de-pathologization of homosexuality, while on the other hand it affirmed the "everyday homophobia" of conscripts and society as a whole. Kulikov suggested that no one responding to the draft, or sending their son to the reception center, need worry about "mental infection" from openly homosexual soldiers. In fact, in this ultra-masculine environment "openly homosexual" conscripts would hardly make themselves visible. Same-sex relations, when visible in the army, assume a far more brutal character.

Fragmentary evidence from Russian anthropologists suggests that brutal male rape in this all-male institution has long been a widespread threat. Violent *dedovshchina* (hazing of new recruits by older conscripts) in the army is sometimes enforced by sexual exploitation and assaults, in a close parallel to Russia's prison culture discussed in Chapter 1. Little is known about the sexual dimensions of military hazing, and its links to prison culture are even more obscure. As a social problem, military hazing only began to attract the notice of the Soviet press in the late 1980s, with only a few exposes mentioning sexual assaults. During the 1990s when press freedom was widest, reports of male rape in Russia's conscript army apparently increased, and military prosecutors suppressed rather than pursued cases, according to one close observer of army life.[55] The role of male rape and sexual abuse in the ranks receives very little attention because the task of reconstructing the "sexual culture" of the average recruit implies an almost unimaginable transformation of everyday masculine attitudes in wider society, and in the Russian Army itself.

Soon after Enikeeva's book identified an "anti-propaganda" law as an objective for Russia's conservatives, proposals rapidly found sponsorship in the Duma, and quickly acquired a religious gloss too. In September 2003 Aleksandr Chuev, then deputy chair of the legislature's Committee on Religious Congregations and Public Organizations, submitted a draft bill to suppress with criminal sanctions any "demonstrations of the homosexual way of life and homosexual orientation" in the media and in public. Chuev claimed the support of the Russian Orthodox Church, and named the protection of children from propaganda for same-sex love as his primary purpose.[56] The fate of his various "gay propaganda" proposals is discussed in the Introduction. Chuev was returned to the Duma in the December 2003 elections, along with Raikov and Goriacheva, who found that the morality ticket worked to their electoral advantage. In early 2004 the three deputies formed a thirty-strong cross-party association in the new legislature with the slogan, "To support traditional moral and spiritual values in Russia." The lobby group called for a ban on erotic broadcasts, films and publications, "mandatory instruction in religious discipline" for schoolchildren, and "encouragement for Russians to get married."[57] Conservative Russian politicians learned the lessons of 2002 and began to explore ways of relaunching their homophobic and moralizing political projects. The results included the local and eventually national "gay propaganda" bans that would proliferate as President Putin returned to power in 2011–12.

Towards "traditional sex"

The Russian conservative concept of "traditional sexual relations" that was so prominent in the political homophobia project of 2013 had a pre-history in the early years of the Putin presidency. Responding to rising anxiety about the influence of the internet – a new and virtually unregulated medium – and the impact of economic, social, and cultural globalization, many Russian politicians began to seek ways to counter the free-for-all atmosphere of the

1990s "sexual revolution." Their first efforts were hardly crowned with success: Raikov's bid to recriminalize sodomy was laughed off, along with his colleagues who proposed the criminalization of lesbian sex, and fines for masturbation; and even Goriacheva's more serious bill disappeared for a long period, when it underwent significant revision and ultimately survived only as amendments in a larger package of changes to the criminal code. Many of its broader aspirations – to define "pornography," to punish sex offenders from certain professions more harshly – failed to make the cut in the law President Putin eventually signed in 2003. But the core project, to raise the age of consent from fourteen to sixteen years, had been achieved.

Goriacheva had staged a moral panic, with the apparent blessing of the Kremlin, the active participation of Duma colleagues and the Legislation Committee, as well as selected Soviet-trained medical experts and the editors of the *Parliamentary Newspaper*. Her political project chimed with the new president's concern for demographic decline and the threat this posed to Russia's future. The protection of the sexuality of young people, envisioned as a collective resource rather than an individual right, also chimed with medical expert knowledge inherited from the Soviet era. If the homophobic and moralizing initiatives from Raikov and his allies were rejected by the Kremlin and cooler heads in the Duma, that was because Putin's presidency in its first term still adhered to a model of cooperation with the Council of Europe and to a wider sense that Russia shared common interests with Europe. That orientation, already strained as Putin came to power, would be severely tested and eventually abandoned as confrontations with the West accumulated: over the 2003 Iraq War and other strategic tensions; and especially over the color revolutions in Georgia (2003) and Ukraine (2004). Confrontation with the West over LGBT rights at Sochi in 2014 was in this sense rooted in a geopolitical turn that originated during and after Putin's first term in the Kremlin.

And yet the project of a "return" to "traditional sex" was also built on the new president's use of gender as a tool of legitimation. Putin's masculine theatrics, playing the war hero, talking like a streetwise *muzhik*, and casting himself in a variety of patriarchal and rock-star guises, was already well established by the time Goriacheva's initiative was launched in 2002. Fascinatingly, Goriacheva's embryonic "traditional sex" project was remarkably silent about men's bad behavior that was at the root of so many of the problems she highlighted, especially child sexual abuse, and child abandonment, as well as the "boycott on posterity" which was wholly blamed on mothers. With tough-guy masculinity acquiring political traction and men's bad behavior celebrated in the Kremlin, "a way of showing power without having to explain it," there was no oxygen for a campaign that looked critically at male attitudes toward parenting and family responsibilities. In this early "traditional sex" campaign, men's irresponsibility and bad behavior were simply "priced in" as a given, and were not put under the microscope. The Kremlin would eventually spot this gap, and "traditional sex" would be given a positive gloss. Its various youth-movement projects such as "*Nashi*" (Ours), political summer camps, and campaigns for stable love and marriages, would try to foster a more family-friendly if still patriotic and martial masculinity, paired normatively with a submissive and fertile femininity.[58]

The homophobic outbursts that accompanied this early "traditional sex" project were perhaps spontaneous. It was striking how little traction they acquired. Duma politicians across the spectrum seemed to decry the attempt to limit an important sexual freedom won in the reform era, and more importantly, most referred to the fact that the public had more pressing economic concerns on its mind. For conservatives opposed ideologically to LGBT visibility and the expansion of sexual freedom, the 2002 Duma debate demonstrated that more refined political objectives, and more carefully calibrated language, would be needed before another homophobic political project could be launched.

PART III

Writing and Remembering Russia's Queer Past

In Part III, my attention turns from sketching some origins of contemporary Russian homophobia, to exploring the obstacles to uncovering the LGBT past in Russia today, and asking what opportunities lie ahead for the next generation of historians, biographers, and activists.

A crucial means to legitimation and full citizenship is to write one's social group into the national story, as LGBT activists, scholars, and ordinary citizens have done for over half a century and more in the Western world. Russia's national narratives of the twentieth century are, for obvious reasons, particularly fraught with trauma, political conflict, and continuing controversy. There was no "Nuremberg" trial of Stalinism or Communism after the fall of the Soviet Union, and there is no agreement on how the violent past under Stalin and his successors should be commemorated. Unlike the clearly identifiable victim groups targeted by political terror elsewhere, in the USSR violence was used against a broad spectrum of national, ethnic, social, and economic groups. There are now multiple "remembering collectives" in Russian society, based on varied ethnic and social identities, and, arguably, there are many collectives of interested parties who would prefer to forget. LGBT Russians, striving to write themselves into the national narrative, struggle to constitute themselves as one of the country's recognized "remembering collectives."

One aspect of the struggle for recognition focuses on documenting the damage done to gay, lesbian, bisexual, and transgender citizens under the Soviet regime. Here the problems faced by historians and ordinary citizens in tracing the legacy of Stalinism and late-Soviet oppression in Russia's archives and documentary collections are huge. Despite a quarter-century of "archival revelations" and serious scholarship, little is yet known about the mechanisms of state repression against gay men under the Stalinist anti-sodomy law; less understood still is the suppression of lesbians by psychiatric medicine. Barriers to access to certain collections continue to hobble investigation of these questions. Yet more serious is the failure of professional historians and archivists in Russia to view the LGBT histories of their country as a legitimate part of their own national heritage.

Recognition is also blocked by a widespread cultural and intellectual resistance in Russia to the idea of a distinct homosexual heritage, history, and culture. Even Russian democrats and liberal intellectuals (at least until the "gay propaganda" debates of 2013) find the notion of a homosexual community with a specific culture and experience, never mind entitlement to rights and recognition, impossible to accept. This refusal is perhaps most vividly evident in the practice of Russian biography and life-writing about queer artists and poets, where the sexuality of the subject is widely regarded as irrelevant to a critical evaluation of the person and his or her creativity. The Russian queer artist is almost always described using what I call the "heteronormative voice."

The 2013 "gay propaganda" law launched an assault on queer knowledge in Russia. In a cultural war over the production and distribution of queer knowledge, Russian LGBT communities need new tools to help them shape a happier future. In the final chapter, I explore some ways that Western queer theorists have conceived of historical memory work, and how some LGBT communities in Russia and the region are developing their own tools, in their own cultural settings, to write their own histories and with that, their own futures.

7

Stalinist Homophobia and the "Stunted Archive":

Challenges to Writing the History of Gay Men's Persecution in the USSR

The use of political terror against homosexual men in the USSR began as a specific feature of Stalinism. During the 1930s, Joseph Stalin and his Politburo colleagues enthusiastically welcomed the use of secret police repression against so-called "pederasts," and embedded homophobic terror in their system of rule. So integral was homophobic prejudice to the system that Stalin built, that after his death in 1953, Soviet authorities thought it was entirely natural to continue persecuting homosexuals. In fact, they "renewed the struggle against sodomy," modernizing and expanding systems of police surveillance that remained in place to the end of the Soviet Union. Despite this apparently straightforward story of persecution, great difficulties exist in documenting, interpreting, and explaining this history.

Historians trying to chronicle political terror against Soviet homosexuals work with extremely difficult, but interesting, challenges. The anti-sodomy law of 1933–4 was adopted with an unusually high degree of secrecy, especially when compared with other Stalin laws that punished aspects of social life such as petty theft, abortion, or juvenile crime. Sources about Soviet terror against homosexuals remain carefully concealed, thanks to document-production practices of the 1930s, and later archival classification. Under Stalin, there was an unwritten taboo on speaking in government documents about homosexuality. This taboo went beyond the convention of using euphemisms for heterosexual sexuality found in Stalin-era documents. Only in secret police files and in occasional high-level Party correspondence intended for a tiny readership was homosexuality explicitly discussed. While state and Party archives in the Russian Federation reveal a great deal about state terror, very little of the material that these archives made available to researchers after 1991 discusses homosexuals as victims. Fuller and freer access to the archives of the Federal Security Service (FSB, successor to the Soviet KGB), and the Archive of the President of the Russian Federation (APRF, the "Presidential Archive") is essential before historians can fill in this historical "blank spot" of the Stalin era.

Defining "political terror" and other forms of state persecution is not simple for historians of the USSR. Types of state violence against populations varied enormously over the seventy-four years of the Soviet regime, and involved a spectrum of measures from summary execution without trial, to sentencing to the Gulag system of forced labor camps, and forced deportation and exile in "special settlements."[1] Under Stalin, the regime framed these measures in its ideology variously: as deliberate and supposedly "planned" population transfers and restructuring to facilitate projects like the collectivization of agriculture; as preventative forms of social and national cleansing to make cities "socialist" or to secure border regions; and as punishment for imagined or genuine anti-Soviet treachery.[2] Some forms of terror, such as the mass executions and imprisonments under the infamous secret police Order No. 00447 of July 30, 1937, which launched the "Great Terror" of 1937–8, were obviously "political" in the commonly accepted sense – that is, directed from the Kremlin by Stalin and the Party elite against specific categories of political "offenders."[3] There were other forms of state terror that did not begin with orders from the top leadership, but which emerged from secret police activities and proposals.[4] The adoption of a law against male homosexuals in 1933–4 was apparently one of those police initiatives. Despite its origins at this time in the increasingly intrusive surveillance and population categorization practices of the secret police, the Stalinist anti-sodomy law quickly acquired a politicized justification in Soviet ideology.

Moreover, our knowledge of how police monitored, arrested, and imprisoned homosexuals during Stalin's rule, and after his death, is also very limited. It is a symptom of the silence in the available archives that weighty recent studies of Stalin's policing fail to say anything about roundups of homosexuals in Soviet cities as the new anti-sodomy statute was adopted.[5] Accounts of wartime and postwar policing say nothing about the persecution of male homosexuals.[6] What is more, for the years after 1953, we do not know anything about what political decisions were taken about the status of the homosexual. Who made the decisions? In which state or party body? When? On what rationale? We know very little about how the KGB interacted with the regular police (the "militia") when dealing with homosexuals. We do not know which agencies gave the orders for infamous Brezhnev-era arrests under the anti-sodomy law that had a political dimension: those of film director Sergei Paradzhanov, in 1974; poet Gennady Trifonov in 1976; and archaeologist Lev Klein in 1981. We do not have an accurate and full count of the numbers of men sentenced under the anti-sodomy law. (Between 25,688 and 26,076 men were convicted of sodomy offenses between 1933 and 1991 in the USSR, but these figures include no statistics for twenty-two years of the period and include no secret police statistics. The likely total is probably something approaching 60,000.)[7] Would-be historians of the Communist state's repression of homosexuality, whether for the Stalin era or the late Soviet decades, still have many unanswered questions.

The "stunted archive" of this history, created by heteronormative Soviet and Russian information regimes, is not the only problem facing historians.[8] There have been releases and disclosures of state documents that hint at the contours of the story, but the way these have come to light, the manner of their presentation, and, crucially, their interpretation have marginalized their impact. Sometimes, a critical document has been seen only by a single researcher with privileged access to closed archives, and we only know of the material through the medium of that researcher's publications. We have often learned of these documents through the ubiquitous post-Soviet genre of sensational "archival revelations" rather than serious scholarship. Frequently enough, unfortunately, these documents have been subject to homophobic, simplistic, or unprofessional readings by scholars, journalists, archivists, and curators. Many similar problems arise with the provenance and interpretation of non-official sources: Vadim Kozin's diary, for example, is unsympathetically edited and scholars cannot consult the original text. Questions about its provenance, whereabouts, and the integrity of the full document, have not been answered.[9] Even where scholars have access to such documents, as in the case of Nikolai Kliuev's letters, they frequently lack the will to read homosexual content empathetically and professionally.[10] The tattoos gathered from the bodies of Soviet ex-prisoners by Danzig Baldaev present a wealth of information about same-sex relations in the camps and prisons of the USSR, but their presentation in the compendia published by an art house, with an eye to the commercial market, is sketchy about their provenance.[11] Both official and unofficial records of LGBT existence in Russia and the USSR are frequently mistreated by scholars and critics who fail to engage with LGBT historiography, reading practices, and source criticism. When it comes to the specific question of Soviet terror, there has been a general failure in the historical profession, in Russia and beyond it, to recognize homosexuals as victims of Stalinist violence, to consider where and how the records of this persecution are concealed in the archives, and to press for fuller disclosure of the archival record. Poor reasoning and faulty conceptualization of homosexual existence governs much interpretation of the question and the available documents. The entire picture needs an overhaul with fresh research and re-conceptualization using queer theory, informed and professional source criticism, and empathetic "queer eyes" in the archives.

These issues are not merely narrow questions of historical technicalities. I would argue that this relative lack of historical information about the mechanisms and scale of Soviet homophobic persecution affects contemporary debates about the status of the Russian LGBT community. In a cultural war over the production of queer knowledge, the "stunted archive" of Soviet queer history has political consequences. When we speak about the gay victims of Soviet persecution, we are forced by the current information famine to deal in conjecture and assumptions. For today's LGBT Russians, this historical blank spot makes it that much harder to identify LGBT citizens as fellow victims of Stalinist oppression; and with very few biographies of named victims to discuss, the consequences of state oppression are difficult to concretize. With more historical examples of injustice, and clearer understanding of the specifically Soviet mechanisms of homophobic repression, Russian LGBT citizens could more easily explain the dangers of official homophobic persecution to their fellow countrymen. European advances in the protection of LGBT citizens' rights in the 1980s and 1990s were assisted by historical research and reflection. A significant change in public and elite perceptions in Germany, France, and other nations came as historical knowledge of the scale of Nazi violence against gay men and lesbians became known, thanks to independent and academic scholarly investigations that built a body of evidence about the human rights violations against LGBT Europeans in the 1930s–40s. Historians produced a "history of homophobia," and the concept of "homophobia" underpinned political discussions.[12] Of course, the situation in contemporary Russia is different; and as I argue throughout this book, there is no "correct path" to full LGBT citizenship that Russians must follow. Nevertheless, more careful scholarship about the history of the oppression of sexual and gender dissent in the USSR would provide a much-needed evidence base for arguments in favor of strengthening the human rights of LGBT citizens in Russia.

This chapter takes stock of what we now know about state persecution of male homosexuals from Stalin's decision to make sodomy a crime in 1933–4 to the annulment of his law in 1993. The focus is on documentary evidence of homophobic state decision-making, and of the policing of the sodomy ban once it was introduced. While treating the repression of gay men, I do not minimize the ways in which the state also persecuted lesbians, but those methods were very different, and they must be the subject of a separate study.[13] By examining the background to 1933–4 and the decisions made during Stalin's homophobic turn, further questions arise about the rationale for official Soviet homophobia. The political changes and policing methods introduced by Stalin's successors after 1953 are also investigated, as they suggest ways in which future research might shed more light on the evolution of late-Soviet popular and official homophobia. Many sources have come to light since I published my book on this subject in 2001; much of the research for that book was conducted under very different conditions than those which now prevail in Russia.[14] Some new sources have emerged because the de-classification of Soviet state and Party documents is a slow and continuing process subject to resource and political constraints. These documents were not yet declassified in the 1990s when I was working on my 2001 book. Others have come to light thanks to scholars who shared their finds with me, responding to my research. Some researchers began to read the archives more queerly; I call their attention to LGBT issues the "queer eye" in the archives. The digital revolution in many of Russia's archives has also made finding relevant documents somewhat easier. With keyword searches it is sometimes possible to identify queer material without the laborious needle-in-a-haystack trawls I used in 1995–6. The result of this stocktaking shows where gaps remain in our understanding of this story, and can assist LGBT Russians in their production of queer knowledge as they do battle with homophobes who would silence them.

The road to 1934

Scholars have described the persecution of same-sex relations in Muscovy, but much of this "homophobia" was generated by the Russian Orthodox Church and less so by the state.[15] The Russian state began to punish male same-sex sexuality later than in Europe. In the early eighteenth century, as part of military modernization, Peter the Great banned sodomy in the Imperial Russian army and navy; it seems that after this time, without a formal ban, sodomy between civilians was punished judicially too.[16] In 1835, Nicholas I explicitly extended the ban on male same-sex relations to wider society, in a new criminal code. He was supposedly motivated by reports of vice in the Empire's boarding schools, but we still do not have a modern, queer-studies informed scholarly investigation of this episode and the tsar's reasoning. Under this law, men who engaged in voluntary "sodomy" (*muzhelozhstvo*) were exiled to Siberia; sodomy with minors or the use of force netted exile with hard labor. The law remained in force until 1917, although the punishment for consensual relations was relaxed from Siberian exile to imprisonment for four to five years, in 1900. There was no law against lesbian sex acts.

When revolution came in 1917, the Bolsheviks abrogated all tsarist law in November 1917. Until 1922 there was no written criminal law. During this interval the Soviet government drafted and discarded a series of criminal codes.[17] All of these drafts, beginning with the first, written in early 1918 by the Bolsheviks' coalition partners, the Left Socialist Revolutionaries, and continuing with versions drafted in 1920–1 by Bolshevik jurists and a consultant from the Cheka (secret police), decriminalized male homosexuality. The first Soviet Russian criminal code of 1922 and the revision of this code in 1926 both confirmed the legality of voluntary same-sex relations.

The early Soviet regime never explained why it relaxed the law, but jurists looked to the tradition of the French Revolution. In 1791, sodomy and other religiously inspired "crimes" like heresy were repealed to secularize criminal law and separate church from state. In Bolshevik Russia, the first

People's Commissar of Public Health, Nikolai Semashko, believed the "sexual revolution" demanded a scientific approach to the question of homosexuality. However, he expressed this view in 1923 not in Russia, but while paying a visit to the socialist sex-reformer Magnus Hirschfeld's Institute for Sex Research in Berlin. Leading Communists Vladimir Lenin and Lev Trotsky wrote nothing explicitly about homosexuality. Lenin probably thought it was an insignificant question, and he dismissed narrow sexual interests and politics in his 1920 interview with Klara Tsetkin.[18] Internationally, sex reformers led by Hirschfeld hailed the Soviet government as progressive for lifting the ban. It *was* progressive: male homosexuality remained a crime in Britain until 1967 and in Germany until the late 1960s.

It is difficult to say how "enlightened" official, expert, and popular Soviet attitudes toward homosexuality were in the 1920s. Much more research needs to be done in several directions, including using the techniques of the history of emotions and subjectivity, to establish the depth and extent of the early Soviet "sexual revolution" in general, and as it related to homosexuality in particular.[19] We know that parts of the Soviet state resisted decriminalization, with a particularly sharp confrontation coming in Petrograd in January 1921, when police raided a "pederasts' party" and arrested ninety-five men, some dressed as women. It appears that the entire operation was based on faulty intelligence: the authorities thought they were uncovering a counterrevolutionary conspiracy, not a threat to public morality. The case was abandoned after a considerable set of archives – psychiatric and legal – was compiled, and at least one jurist in the new government argued unsuccessfully that the men should be charged with hooliganism.[20] New work on this fascinating case is forthcoming from Olga Khoroshilova and Irina Roldugina.[21] The most thrilling discovery made by these researchers is of a photograph from archives of the case, of a group of men later arrested; they are dressed in a variety of wedding and fancy-dress costumes, with fourteen out of seventeen men in women's attire. Khoroshilova, a historian of St. Petersburg's cross-dressing entertainment scene, reading the record of the case held in the city's archive, uncovers the likely identities of these men and shows their cross-class origins.[22] Roldugina's work on the same case confirms the diversity of their class and cultural backgrounds, and observes the "openness with which the men spoke about their homosexuality," positing that the 1917 Revolution had aroused in these men a more defiant consciousness evident in their interrogations with the authorities.[23] This new work on the "pederasts' party" of 1921 demonstrates how determined sleuthing in the archives, with queer eyes, can produce fresh understandings of gay subjectivities in revolutionary Russia.

In the period of sodomy decriminalization from 1922 to 1933, the voices of homosexuals themselves did not appear in officially sanctioned publications, except as "patients" in psychiatric case histories, or in small print runs of the poetry of Mikhail Kuzmin, Nikolai Kliuev, and Sophia Parnok, for small, déclassé audiences.[24] There is no historical scholarship investigating popular "straight" attitudes toward homosexuality during this period, but it would be possible to read archival and medico-legal sources against the grain to examine this question. However defiant the 1921 "pederasts" of Petrograd may have felt, once the Soviet regime stabilized, Russia's queer men and women largely chose to hide their sexual identities (however they understood them). Clearly they did not feel "emancipated" to the degree that Berlin lesbians and gay men, the denizens of the world's most developed homosexual metropolis in the 1920s, did. The eradication of civil society in the Soviet state over the course of the 1920s narrowed the possible sites for the exploration of Russian queer existence. In Weimar Germany, by contrast, sex reformer Hirschfeld's pleas for acceptance of the homosexual on the basis of a medical-biological explanation for sexual variation had emancipatory effects in the 1920s. Such arguments opened a space for a gay and lesbian civil society in a liberal-democratic political system, even if Weimar formally continued to punish male homosexuality in law. Of course Hirschfeld's medicalization argument was controversial then, and his opponents within the homophile community of Germany developed alternative models to explain homosexual love.[25] The intellectual currents running through the thinking of Soviet homosexuals, and the cultural, national, and transnational reference points to which they looked remain unexplored opportunities for future research.[26]

Medicalization of sexualities in Soviet Russia led to some avant-garde proposals, but without the Weimar German emphasis on individual freedom. In February 1929, leading psychiatrists and physicians in the People's Commissariat of Health held a long discussion about homosexuality, "transvestites," and women passing as men. The discussion was prompted by a request for a surgical and passport sex change from a Soviet citizen; but the conversation quickly overran the bounds of this single case. The experts considered the medical and social issues, both positive and negative, associated with "passing" women, with male homosexuality observed in Russia and Central Asia, and they also shared their knowledge of early Soviet attempts to change sex with surgery (pre-dating the now well-known 1930 case of Lili Elbe in Germany). With some reservations, in the context of discussion of "passing" women, they proposed allowing same-sex marriages under psychiatric guidance. They wanted women "dressed as men" to be allowed to marry the women they loved: whether these experts imagined they were helping subjects we would now describe as "lesbian" or "transgender" is impossible to gauge. Their proposal was forgotten and evidently abandoned.[27] We know too that Soviet doctors' attitudes toward the psychological and sexual problems of the intersex patient were among the most humane medical views in the world in the late 1920s and into the 1930s.[28] Nevertheless, the Soviet "sexual revolution" was a revolution for the collective, not for the individual, with distinctively medical and technocratic notes. When we discuss and investigate the early Soviet "sexual revolution," we need to purge our analysis of decades of Western Freudian, feminist and gay liberationist retrospective projections to grasp just how unfamiliar this revolution was.[29] Additionally, cultural historians have noted just how much anxiety, fear, patriarchal contempt, and even violence the Soviet "sexual revolution" inspired in the gradually Stalinizing Communist Party of the 1920s.[30] Enlightened medical thinking among men of science meant little when the political landscape was shifting, as it began to rapidly in the late 1920s and early 1930s.

Stalinist homophobia and repression

In 1933, Stalin and his secret police laid the foundations of modern Russia's state-sponsored homophobia with their terror campaigns, legislation, and policing routines. Evidence points to the origins of this homophobic turn in the roll-out of internal identity documents ("passports") for the inhabitants of major Soviet cities in 1933; but the source of the specifically anti-homosexual drive remains unclear. In this section I discuss the evolution of Stalin's 1933–4 anti-sodomy law as it now appears, from sources new and old. How historians and others have handled these sources is sometimes contentious, and that aspect is examined here too. Many questions remain unanswered and there are still critical archival holdings about Stalinist homophobia largely closed to historians; the prospects and challenges for researchers and activists are also addressed in this section.

What we know about the origin of the anti-sodomy law comes principally from a very limited release of correspondence between the secret police and Stalin, from the Presidential Archives, loosely timed to coincide with the abolition of this law by President Boris Yeltsin's reforming administration in spring 1993. It was published in the archive's journal.[31] The anonymous archivist or editors who published the documents said nothing to explain why they were being published or in what documentary context they are held (and there is no public catalog to the Presidential Archive). It appears that the archival file upon which the publication is based comes from a fond devoted to the secret police, and relates specifically to the anti-sodomy law. It may be that this file is part of an entire "thematic folder" of files on homosexuality, for use by Stalin and the Politburo.[32] The 1993 release of this material effectively constituted a Soviet-style "signal" to the reader to connect the dots: Stalin made this law, and therefore Yeltsin's reforming regime was getting rid of it.

On September 15, 1933, deputy chief of the OGPU (secret police) Genrikh Yagoda proposed to Stalin that a law against "pederasty" was needed urgently. Stalin and Yagoda used the crude term *pederastiia* to discuss male homosexuality; but government lawyers revived the tsarist term *muzhelozhstvo* (sodomy) for the published law that was eventually adopted in March 1934. Yagoda reported that in August–September 1933, OGPU raids had been conducted on circles of "pederasts" in Moscow and

Leningrad, and other cities of the Soviet Union. Yagoda wrote that these men were guilty of spying; they had also "politically demoralized various social layers of young men, including young workers, and even attempted to penetrate the army and navy."[33] From a recent collection of FSB archive documents of political cases against young Communists, it is clear that during the early 1930s, the secret police were obsessed with detecting counterrevolutionary moods among young people.[34]

Stalin forwarded Yagoda's letter to Politburo member Lazar Kaganovich, noting that "these scoundrels must receive exemplary punishment" and directing a law against "pederasty" should be adopted. In the months that followed, Yagoda the secret policeman steered its passage through the various legislative drafts. He argued that "sodomy ... for payment, as a profession, or publicly" ("*muzhelozhstvo ... za platu, po professii ili publichno*") deserved particularly stiff punishment. The word "publicly" caught Stalin's eye and, late in the legislative process, he intervened. According to research by David Brandenberger in declassified archives, sometime between February 20 and March 7 1934, Stalin personally underlined the word "publicly" and then struck out the whole phrase about male prostitution *and* public sex from the draft law.[35] Oddly, in Ukraine in January 1934, where the law was adopted very rapidly after the Politburo and the central Soviet legislature (*TsIK SSSR*) published their draft decrees on the sodomy ban, this phrase about public sex and male prostitution remained in the law as adopted. We still do not know why the phrase stayed in the Ukrainian version. Was this merely an example of chaotic and hasty law-making, not unusual for the period? Or, did Stalin, Yagoda, and the Politburo believe that male prostitution was more prevalent in Ukraine than in Russia? Indeed, was the law more urgently "required" in Ukraine by the secret police, who were perhaps manufacturing a "homosexual conspiracy" there? The Ukrainian "factor" in the story of the anti-sodomy law surfaces in a range of memoir and official archival accounts discussed below. In Boris Nicolaevsky's "Letter of an Old Bolshevik," the launch of the anti-sodomy law is explained as a response to a "homosexual conspiracy" originating in a late–1933 "German propaganda" operation among homosexual circles in Moscow, Leningrad, and the Ukrainian cities of Kharkov and Kiev.[36] The "Letter's" explanation might have a bearing on the circumstances that triggered the wider Soviet anti-homosexual purge. In the 1993 APRF document releases, references to Ukraine would have been removed to avoid offending Russia's newly independent neighbor. Notwithstanding these factors, with the major exception of Ukraine, by March 7, 1934, all Soviet republics had adopted the Stalin-edited version of the sodomy ban.[37]

Stalin's editorial pencil also inserted a *minimum* sentence of three years for consenting male homosexuality – the maximum was five years, already established in earlier drafts of the law.[38] Stalin's purpose in fixing a minimum penalty for sodomy was not stated but can be guessed. From 1930, those offenders sentenced to three years or more were sent to the Gulag system's corrective-labor camps (*ispravitel'no-trudovye lageria*, ITL) which were isolated from central Russia in the far north and east. They were places of hard labor and sometimes very high mortality, seen as the ultimate punishment short of execution. In the early 1930s, these camps, many of them canal-building, forestry, and mining sites, were chronically short of labor and the Gulag was pressing Stalin for more prisoners. Many ended up there on falsified "political" charges; but the worst recidivist criminals were sent there too. Meanwhile, prisoners with sentences of less than three years went to corrective-labor colonies (*ispravitel'no-trudovye kolonii*, ITK), closer to centers of population. Inmates of colonies were usually petty criminals, often workers who had been given a "proletarian discount" in their sentences; Soviet criminology taught that these people were most likely to be "reforged" into good citizens.[39] By setting a minimum sentence of three years, Stalin evidently intended that male homosexuals should end up in Gulag camps as opposed to colonies and be exposed to much harsher conditions as a result. Such a decision also sheds light on Stalin's conception of "pederasts" in the Soviet social taxonomy: as "socially alien" to the Soviet system, by comparison with the "socially friendly" prisoners who could be "reforged" in prison colonies.[40] Whatever the reasoning, what Stalin wanted and what really happened did not always coincide. My own study of sentencing patterns drawn from a limited sample of Moscow city sodomy cases of the 1930s shows that many men, not just workers, were sentenced to less than three years and presumably did time in colonies rather than camps.[41] In the very fragmented court records surviving in the archives, it is normally impossible to trace the fates of individuals once they left the courtroom. Local court records only reflect individuals who were handled by the conventional justice system, not the hidden administrative organs of the secret police. We have virtually no access to their deliberations and we know almost nothing about their treatment of victims of this law.

Historians know very little about the OGPU's raids against homosexuals that Yagoda says were conducted in late summer 1933. These raids are not described or recorded in the documents about Soviet state terror that have been published in authoritative archival document collections since 1991.[42] Only a few foreign sources mention these raids, including works by Wilhelm Reich, Sidney and Beatrice Webb, and the "Letter of an Old Bolshevik" previously mentioned.[43] This "stunted archive" has produced the impression among historians of Stalinist state terror, working in the archives opened to us since 1991, that homosexuals did not constitute a specific category of Stalin's "victims." But it has recently become clear from hard-to-access documents of the archives of the FSB that secret police discussions of persecution of homosexuals took place during the early 1930s, in the context of the social purging of the cities in these years of crisis and upheaval. Additionally, fragmentary evidence has come to light of attempts in the 1930s by the secret police and judicial organs to endow the crime of male homosexuality with a politicized narrative.

In 2013, a St. Petersburg history journal published an article, "Counterrevolutionary Organizations among Homosexualists [sic] of Leningrad in the early 1930s."[44] The author was Viktor Ivanov, then head of the History Department of the St. Petersburg University of the Ministry of Internal Affairs (i.e. a police academy). Enjoying privileged access to the local archive of the FSB, he used operational and individual case file documents about the raids in Leningrad on homosexual men conducted in 1933–4. It must be said that despite this article's title, there are no traces of genuine "counterrevolutionary organizations among homosexualists" in the documents presented. Professor Ivanov's lack of empathy for the victims of this repression, and his failure to conceptualize their experience except through the secret policeman's lens, are among the many technical weaknesses this article displays. Struggling without the appropriate language and knowledge to contextualize his archival "nugget," Ivanov writes in a bemused tone about "pederasts," "clients," and husbands bored with their wives who therefore succumb to "their lowest desires." (The decision to publish this clumsily homophobic article during the 2012–13 local debate about the status of St. Petersburg's LGBT organizations and their supposed "propaganda for homosexuality" seems opportunistic to say the least.) But reading against the grain of his analysis and terminology, it is possible to glean some interesting facts about the operations against homosexuals and about the perceptions of the secret police regarding "homosexualists" of that time. From this it is possible to speculate on the future research directions that queer eyes in the archives may and will take.[45]

First, it is apparent that a critical mechanism for identifying those engaged in homosexual relations was the filtration of the population as the police distributed internal passports for city residents in early 1933. Ivanov notes that the police compiled "compromising" information about residents during the passportization operation and he infers that this included information about non-standard sexual relations.[46] He notes that those defendants who figure in the case files against homosexuals in Leningrad in summer and autumn 1933 were residents who had successfully passed through the passport filtration process, receiving passports and with that the right to live in Leningrad. Only during summer 1933, when the attention of the secret police seems to have turned to homosexuality as a form of anti-social activity, was use made of this "compromising material." Ivanov says that the police processed this material in the standard bureaucratic ways, deciding which people to arrest immediately and whom might be left under observation. Second, Ivanov points to the extraordinary secrecy with which the 1933 anti-homosexual operation was conducted in Leningrad. It was not handled by regular police ("militia") and was not widely discussed; instead it was initiated by the Secret-Political Department of the local secret police. Third, he quotes from case file documents that display the police's diverse perceptions of male same-sex relations. Some give descriptions of the streets and parks where low-class gay male cruising takes place; still others mention sailors who beat gay men when invited to have sex. The majority of the defendants figuring in the case files that Ivanov cites are white-collar workers and artists, some of whom are said to think that homosexuality constitutes a special caste, a "Bohemian" lifestyle more elevated than philistine male–female relations. Others express consternation at the police's new political construction of homosexuality as anti-Soviet. Interrogators quote one Lev Konstantinovich Lisenko, arrested in August 1933, arguing that not all homosexuals can be disloyal: "How can it be that all of them were so terrible? Surely pederasts [sic] are people too, they are workers in the very same factories, members of the same trade unions, and sometimes, of the Party? It can't be that all pederasts were 'Cutie Pie-Sergeys' [Serezhami-Pupsikami], conducting their counterrevolutionary agitation under the eyes of the police in Catherine Square?"[47] In Ivanov's documents, Lisenko appears as a thoughtful individual who has much to say about the condition of gay men in Soviet society, and his case file merits a more sophisticated reading than Ivanov was capable of supplying.[48]

Professor Ivanov's exposition evades the question of where the initiative for an anti-homosexual crackdown originated. Did it come locally, from social-purging operations linked to passportization, or centrally, in orders from the secret police leadership in Moscow? Irina Roldugina, who examined the principal file in the St. Petersburg FSB archive four years after Ivanov used it, reports that the relevant pages on operational matters were not open to view; by the time she saw the file, they were sewn into the standard blue envelope that conceals classified pages from the researcher.[49] The locus of the operation in the Secret-Political Department appears to suggest direction from Moscow; but whatever the origins, the two rationales (social purging and national security concerns) reinforced each other. Ivanov makes clear that the secret police began their raids against Leningrad's "pederasts" during a wave of social and political purging of the city and environs. Indeed we know from painstaking Western research in the open archives of the Soviet state that this wave of urban social purging, a filtration process that accompanied passportization, was directed nationally by the secret police, and first targeted the USSR's most important centers, designated "regime" cities.[50] Compromising information on suspect individuals was collected as passports were issued, and entered in police card-indexes.[51] During 1933, internal directives of the secret police articulated categories of citizens to be denied passports and thereby forced to leave regime cities, and while male homosexuals were not explicitly enumerated, the category of "antisocial" and "declassed" persons, often those with ties to street crime and prostitution, are mentioned explicitly.[52] Moreover, "oral instructions" given to agents working on passportization early on in 1933 facilitated "excesses" of zealous enforcement that conceivably extended the range of suspect categories to male homosexuals with gregarious networks that crossed class and occupational boundaries to include male prostitutes.[53] Yet we remain in the realm of speculation; the source of the impulse to move from what may have been random and spontaneous police notations about individual homosexuals to a national ban on "pederasty" remains unknown, and can only be traced with freer access to secret police archives.

When in mid-September 1933 Yagoda wrote to Stalin, recommending the adoption of a formal law against sodomy, he apparently cited a figure of 130 arrests of "pederasts" for the operations in "Moscow and Leningrad."[54] According to Ivanov, the archives of the St. Petersburg FSB reveal that during August–September 1933, 175 men were arrested on grounds of homosexual relations in Leningrad alone.[55] The raids on "pederasts" continued and probably expanded to the principal "regime" cities, including Kharkov and Kiev. It appears that somewhere inside the central secret police machinery, an order originated in late July or early August 1933 to begin arrests of "pederasts" known to the authorities on their card-indexes either as "anti-social" or "declassed" elements, or as a security threat with international dimensions.

Evidence of probable police fabrication of an ideological basis for the law emerges later, in documents Ivanov seems to have obtained from the FSB. In January 1934, an "Open Letter from Moscow and Kharkov Homosexualists to Mr Marinus van der Lubbe" appeared in Leningrad. Ivanov writes that Leningrad military counterintelligence found this letter in the possession of a local homosexual during an investigation of a conspiratorial group. The accused supposedly obtained it from a Moscow gay man. Ivanov concludes that few, if any, Leningrad homosexuals saw or knew of this letter.[56] Van der Lubbe was the Dutch anarchist accused and later executed for starting the Reichstag Fire. His homosexuality became a political weapon in the propaganda war between socialists and fascists, discussed in the "Brown Book" on the "facts" of the Reichstag fire, written by exiled German Communists, and translated and published in September 1933 in the USSR in a print-run of 20,000. Soviet homosexuals no doubt read with alarm the condemnation of van der Lubbe's homosexuality that in this account was tied to his political betrayal. He was said to have abandoned Communist comrades in Holland, met a gay associate of Ernst Roehm, and become "materially dependent" on these "homosexual connections with National Socialist leaders."[57] Whether they were so daring as to address an open letter to van der Lubbe seems highly unlikely as a rational political act; in any case, the letter's anti-Communist language looks calculated to incriminate anyone tied to it. The letter blames the Reichstag fire on Communists, criticizes Soviet living conditions, indicts Soviet educational policy as inspiring depravity in young people, and argues that police ignorance and lack of culture are to blame for the pogrom being waged against Soviet homosexuals. "How could we, the third sex, with our tender hearts and feelings [tretii pol, s nashei nezhnoi dushoi i chuvstvami] be capable of the destruction of culture, order, civilization? No, no, a thousand times no. . . . We are for culture, civilization, order," it concludes. The "Open Letter of Moscow and Kharkov Homosexualists" was perhaps the foundation for a secret police-manufactured "homosexual conspiracy" against Soviet power – the conspiracy later mentioned in the "Letter of an Old Bolshevik."[58] I believe that the "Open Letter" is a Soviet secret police fabrication, but without queer eyes in the archives, and freer access to secret police operational files, the question remains open.

Ivanov's article and Roldugina's recent probing of the sources he used demonstrate an important fact about archival material on the Stalinist anti-homosexual campaign: local FSB archives, in former "regime" cities and beyond, will probably contain the most detailed and interesting materials about the persecution of homosexual men, and about police perceptions of dissenting sexualities. In certain cases where the biography of a particular victim of the Stalinist anti-homosexual campaign was known, e.g. the poet Nikolai Kliuev, or the singer Vadim Kozin, the most important materials about their experience were found by researchers in local, not national, FSB and police archival collections.[59] This fact suggests, however, that researchers need to know the names of victims, and their eventual whereabouts in the Gulag system, before their case files and any surviving personal documents attached to their cases might be located. The dispersal of the archives of the victims of the anti-sodomy law across the breadth of the Soviet Union poses enormous hurdles for historians. Yet it also suggests that most regional urban secret police archives in the former Soviet Union, and secret police archives for Gulag districts, will contain some traces of the persecution of homosexuals in this period, if one could only engage in a trawl of these records. Of course such trawls are currently impossible in the Russian Federation, but some post-Soviet countries have more open access policies in the secret police archives they hold, and therein lies an opportunity for further exploration.

Reactions, and the geopolitics of Stalin's homophobic turn

In the 1993 release of correspondence between Yagoda and Stalin leading to the sodomy ban, one other significant document was published from the same file in the Presidential Archive. It is a sixteen-page letter to Stalin, from a homosexual British Communist, Harry O. Whyte (1907–60), an ex-patriate journalist living in Moscow who loved a man who was a Soviet citizen. His Soviet lover was arrested sometime during late 1933 or early 1934. The release of the Whyte letter said little about its provenance and the author.[60] It was typical of the 1993 publication that this document also appeared without commentary, but was labeled "Humor from the Special Collections" by archivists or editors who failed to show any historical empathy or intellectual curiosity.

Whyte, who worked for the English-language *Moscow Daily News*, wrote to Stalin, in May 1934, asking him to justify the new law. The journalist boldly explained why it violated the principles of both Marxism and the Soviet revolution. He argued that persecution of the law-abiding homosexual was typical of capitalist regimes and fascist ones: Nazi Germany's "racial purity" drive was just the most extreme example of the push in both systems for "labor reserves and cannon fodder." "[C]onstitutional homosexuals, as an insignificant portion of the population . . . cannot present a threat to the birth rate in a socialist state." Their position was analogous to that of other unjustly persecuted groups: "women, colored races, national minorities" and the best traditions of socialism showed tolerance of the relatively insignificant number of naturally occurring homosexuals in the population. He asked Stalin, "Can a homosexual be considered a person fit to become a member of the Communist Party?" In a revealing reaction, Stalin scrawled across the letter, "An idiot and a degenerate. To the archives." Whyte got a blunt answer to his question: he was expelled from the Communist Party; he hastily left the Soviet Union for England in 1935. His passionate commitment to socialism was undimmed and he continued his career in journalism in Britain and abroad.[61] Stalin's brusque ascription of social-Darwinist "degeneration" to this letter-writer reflected the widespread credence then given to theories of the heritability of so-called social "diseases" such as suicide, alcoholism, and tuberculosis.[62] Bolsheviks reveled in terms of abuse like "degeneration," "degenerate," and "perversion," to denigrate the political ideas and reputations of opponents regardless of their Marxist propensity to construct social and environmental causes for all things human.

The fact that Stalin even read the Whyte letter was significant: only a fraction of the thousands of letters addressed to him actually crossed his desk and the dictator controlled the filtering process. He paid close attention to letters addressing "theoretical" questions but much less often to those from "enemies" of the regime.[63] Thus Whyte's letter appears as an exceptional case that seems to have compelled Stalin to commission an explanation about the purpose of the anti-homosexual law, with an eye to world left-wing opinion and, in particular, to the Soviet Union's propaganda war with European fascism. One wonders how far the geopolitical and international-communist ideological dimensions of the official homophobic policy had been anticipated before the receipt of this letter, by those who decided to embark upon the internal, domestic, anti-homosexual campaign. To judge from the January 1934 appearance of the "Open Letter of Moscow and Kharkov Homosexualists," the secret police had prepared the outline of a narrative. Now it needed filling in.

The dictator turned to his cultural spokesman Maxim Gorky, to explain the law's rationale for Soviet and European readers (Figure 7.1). Gorky wrote an article that appeared in *Izvestiia* and *Pravda* on May 23, 1934, and later in a German-language socialist newspaper in Switzerland, in which he compared healthy Soviet youth to the degenerate youth of Nazi Germany. "Destroy the homosexuals – and fascism will disappear" he concluded, propounding the genocide of a social group on the grounds of sexuality.

FIGURE 7.1 *Maxim Gorky (right) with Andrey Zhdanov, a Party cultural ideologue, 1934. Source: Fine Art Images/Heritage Images/Getty Images.*

(Incidentally, scholars often mistranslate this slogan as "Destroy homosexuality . . ." and its genocidal intent is lost.) Later in 1936, People's Commissar of Justice Nikolai V. Krylenko gave a speech to the central Soviet legislature in which he explained that the law was necessary because homosexuals were not healthy workers but "a declassed rabble, or the scum of society, or remnants of the exploiting classes."[64] These were rare public statements about the law, again demonstrating how Stalin's regime preferred to shroud its introduction in secrecy. During the 1939–41 interval of the Hitler–Stalin Pact, the Soviet regime apparently considered breaking that silence. Roldugina's energetic archival trawls reveal that a show-trial of homosexuals was prepared in late 1939, but the plans were shelved. The documents about it are held in files associated with "Stalin's prosecutor" Andrei Y. Vyshinsky, who at the time directed the legal affairs of the secret police.[65] Vyshinsky only briefly supervised secret police legal matters in the wake of the Great Terror, and the idea of a public airing of the theme of international homosexual conspiracy appears to have been considered and dropped in less than four months. One suspects it was raised during the era of Nazi-Soviet cooperation with its public relations demonstrations of harmony between the Nazi and Soviet regimes. No doubt Vyshinsky found a suitable anti-homosexual narrative difficult to construct, since previously both sides had ascribed homosexuality to the other. Whatever the fate of this individual case, once the Hitler–Stalin Pact was ruptured with the Nazi invasion of the Soviet Union in June 1941, the extreme secrecy surrounding the anti-sodomy law remained a settled feature of Stalinist rule.

Arrests and trends in enforcement to the end of Stalin's rule

As mentioned, the number of men arrested, prosecuted, and convicted under Stalin's anti-sodomy law between 1933 and 1993 remains difficult to fix. The number of convictions for the Stalin era up to 1953 is particularly impossible to establish satisfactorily, given archival limitations. No Russian or foreign historians, no non-governmental organizations, no political parties, and no individual politicians have ever asked the FSB to supply information on this question.

Tracing Stalin-era victims of the anti-sodomy law will be complicated; careful study of the mechanisms of Stalinist terror is required to find these victims. In the first weeks of Yagoda's raids against "pederasts" in Soviet cities, before the anti-sodomy law was in place, many homosexual men were probably arrested on charges of counterrevolutionary crimes, some apparently in combination with existing sex-crime articles, cited "by analogy." This much-criticized Soviet legal principle allowing the prosecution of a non-criminal act "by analogy" to a defined crime, was used in these cases to serve in place of the sodomy ban, still then in the process of formalization. Indeed, Roldugina reports from the St. Petersburg FSB files that the earliest cases in Leningrad, considered in late 1933, were brought under the infamous article 58 of the Soviet Russian criminal code that punished counterrevolutionary actions or speech, sometimes in combination with articles that punished infecting someone with sexually transmitted disease (article 150), or compelling a woman into prostitution (article 155).[66] New data from the Siberian case file of poet Nikolai Kliuev illustrates the point well. Kliuev was denounced to Yagoda by literary bureaucrat Ivan M. Gronsky in February 1934 for his homosexuality; and he was charged "by analogy" with article 151, which punished "sexual intercourse with persons not having achieved sexual maturity," and article 58.[67] Even after the anti-sodomy law was enacted, we see combined charges – suggesting that investigators linked sodomy to anti-state intentions along the lines Yagoda proposed when he drafted the law. Probably, secret police instructions about the law, still inaccessible to us, circulated to explain this linkage to lower-level operatives. Two 1935–6 cases against a party official and an NKVD employee recently noted by Jonathan Waterlow in the relatively open former central Communist Party archives combine denunciations of homosexuality with charges of supporting "Trotskyism."[68] Secret police embedded in state and party organizations seem to have been the transmission-belts for action against networks of queer men in the immediate aftermath of the homophobic law, but traces of their activity in the available archives are confined to rare documents that went to the highest police and party leadership.[69] The policeman's view of an inherent relationship between unconventional sexuality and "crimes" of counterrevolution is often presumed in LGBT histories of Stalinist homophobia, but we do not have any studies of documentary sources that could demonstrate how that relationship was explained to police and investigators, and what official procedures fixed the links between sexual and political deviation.

Understanding how the anti-sodomy law was applied during and after the Second World War in the USSR requires more research. For the war years 1941–5, there are barely any recorded convictions found in the available records.[70] Invasion, evacuation, plummeting food supplies, and mass mortality shocked the Soviet Union such that the authorities probably paid little attention to same-sex relations during the national emergency. Most citizens were starving, laboring in extreme conditions, or on the move.[71] (The contrast with Anglo-American experience of the war as a time that brought a modern homosexual identity into being for millions could not be greater.)[72] The only mass institution that was generously fed in wartime was the Red Army, and as Arthur Clech correctly observes, it was "perhaps the institution most productive of homosexual practices" at the time.[73] The regulation of sexual relations in the army was reportedly slack, and current research on wartime sexuality says little about what Army rules as recorded in military archives actually said about sex; most attention focuses on heterosexual affairs as remembered in memoirs (900,000 women served in the Red Army, of whom 120,000 were combatants).[74] This "heterosexual" research unaccountably ignores the homogenic effects of largely homosocial life at the front. Clech astutely notes that fear, generous alcohol and food rations, and intense comradely bonds in the face of ubiquitous violent death must have produced same-sex affairs in the ranks that were deliberately overlooked by commanders. He also points to the presence of Gulag penal battalions at the front, ex-prisoners who may have brought their violent, hierarchical homosexual practices to the battlefield with them.[75] The memory of these stigmatized male same-sex practices and relationships was suppressed in post-war memoirs that expressed a "stubborn, bordering on monolithic . . . heterosexual fantasy" about wartime relationships that were heroic, patriotic, and, if not chaste, then resolved successfully in marriage.[76]

Soviet annexation of the independent Baltic republics – Estonia, Latvia, Lithuania – during the Second World War brought the USSR's legislation including the Soviet version of the ban on male homosexuality. It seems extraordinary that in the violent tumult of the sovietization of Latvia, for instance, the Central Committee of the Latvian Communist Party found the time to discuss the prosecution of "pederasts," as reported in the emerging research of Ineta Lipša.[77] In fact, of the interwar Baltic republics, Latvia and Lithuania had retained a form of the Imperial Russian sodomy ban, and it was now sovietized; only Estonia had decriminalized sodomy and had the full Soviet ban imposed with annexation.[78] Other annexed territories (Western Ukraine, Moldova) also had the Soviet anti-sodomy legislation imposed, although more research is needed to understand the impact in these regions.

Trends in policing homosexuality in the late Stalin years also remain difficult to chart. Conviction statistics for the years 1945–60 are fragmentary at best; for the RSFSR we have nothing for 1951–60. Rather anomalously, we know that 130 men were convicted in 1950 in the RSFSR under the anti-sodomy law, with a regional and quarterly breakdown that testifies to possible raids on queer networks: the manufacturing city of Tula, 173 km south of Moscow led the way (twenty convictions all in the fourth quarter), Sverdlovsk had thirteen convictions, and finally the capitals Leningrad (nine) and Moscow (six) fell some distance behind, perhaps suggesting that little attention was paid to cases in the larger cities.[79] To judge from cases in the archives of the Moscow People's Courts, and from Leningrad Province, for the period, arrests were the result of denunciations by neighbors, or passersby who happened upon public encounters between men; and they could also result when other crimes were reported.[80] In the last eight years of Stalin's life, only eleven men were convicted of sodomy in Soviet Latvia.[81] In the more rural Belorussian SSR, only eight men were convicted under the analogous law in these years.[82] Despite the fact that terror against the population was renewed between 1945 and 1953, there are no memoir reports of coordinated raids on male homosexual circles, similar to those of 1933–4, for the last years of Stalin's rule. One possible exception surrounds the 1948 arrest of film student and later internationally renowned director Sergei Paradzhanov. In the summer of that year, he was part of "a small coterie of young men in Tbilisi" arrested because of their association with a secret police official, who also worked in the Georgian Society of Cultural Liaisons with Foreign Countries, an international front organization.[83] Perhaps the link between foreign spying and homosexuality was being revived in postwar security apparatus scenarios. No access to secret police discussions about the danger from "pederasts" in the era is possible in the case of Russia, and nothing has thus far emerged from other republican secret police archives.

A final point about Stalin-era persecution of homosexuals as reflected in the archival records is the difficulty of charting the experience of prisoners in the Gulag, discussed in Chapter 1. The documents of that experience in the Gulag are apparently confined to still-classified secret police papers. In the Stalin era, same-sex relations were virtually never mentioned in the Gulag's official documents to which we have access; rare exceptions refer to the rape and sexual abuse of juvenile male prisoners. In a published document of the Central Archive of the FSB, one mentions how, at the Solovki "special purpose" camp, a 1920s prototype of the Gulag system, teenaged male prisoners "are demoralized morally and physically by the adults among the prisoners (the use of them as passive pederasts flourishes)." The Shanin Commission that inspected Solovki after international criticism of Soviet penal camps made this observation in 1930.[84] Probably, secret police operational files at the local camp level record the cases that came to the attention of camp authorities, but these will be in regional FSB archives. Local court records may hold trial records for homosexual rape in nearby camps and colonies; I have found one such case, involving a teenage rapist and victim, for a penal colony in Leningrad Province in 1954, when procedures were in flux.[85] As noted in Chapter 1, only after the death of Stalin in 1953 did Gulag administrators begin to record their discussions about homosexuality in the camps.

Renewing "the struggle against sodomy" in the 1950s–80s

After Stalin's death, "political terror" changed as Party leader Nikita Khrushchev promoted de-Stalinization. Khrushchev and his successors evolved an authoritarian regime that still used political persecution, but more selectively, and without deliberate killing, against a narrower spectrum of targets. Nationalists, religious believers, and political "dissidents" were subjected to secretive police actions that abused their human rights. Where did sexual minorities fit in this reforming environment? The civilian police, KGB, and Soviet leadership apparently could not decide. Sometimes they treated homosexuals as simple sex-criminals, and at other times as social or political "dissidents" following definitions established in Stalinist ideology in the 1930s. Sometimes the two ideas fused when arrests targeted homosexuals with a "political" past. What is becoming evident from new research is that policing routines modernized and became enmeshed with other forms of surveillance.

In the 1950s, at Khrushchev's instigation, Soviet jurists reviewed and abolished hundreds of Stalin-era statutes. As described in Chapter 1, in 1958 an order of the Interior Ministry of the RSFSR "on the strengthening of the struggle against sodomy" was secretly issued. It evidently told police they should make greater efforts to crack down on homosexuality between men. We have no access to records that could explain why it was adopted, nor what conceptions of male homosexuality informed the discussions surrounding it in the Interior Ministry, or the Communist Party. From the archives of the Gulag of the 1950s, we know that authorities were greatly concerned about the homosexuality and sexually transmitted infections (STIs) they observed in the camps. With millions of prisoners being released, the public reacted angrily to the appearance of "criminals" in the streets, and the government worried about the crime waves that followed these amnesties.[86] It seems likely that the Interior Ministry, the KGB, and the Party believed that the "contagion" of homosexuality (and the STIs they associated with queer sex) also threatened Soviet society as these prisoners were freed, and that this rationale explains the 1958 renewal of the Stalinist anti-homosexual law in the RSFSR. In the new Russian criminal code of 1960, the sodomy ban remained in place, this time with Stalin's minimum sentence removed; but the maximum sentence for voluntary relations would remain for five years until the law's repeal in 1993.[87]

In other Soviet republics, analogous orders were probably given to civilian police. From archival research, Ineta Lipša suggests that the KGB oversaw the process by which local republican police forces discussed the law's renewal. A significant variation in the maximum sentences for sodomy appeared in the 1961 criminal codes adopted in the Baltic republics, from Estonia's low two-year limit, to Lithuania (three years) and Latvia (five years).[88] Perhaps these limits mirrored interwar leniency in Estonia and traditional severity in the other two republics. What seems indicative of some central KGB or Party direction in the legal drafts is the rejection of proposals from Riga's civilian police to penalize all "satisfaction of sexual desire [between] same-sex individuals" – a major extension of the law that would have banned even lesbian sex. Nevertheless, Lipša found no records of KGB, expert, or Party comment on this proposal – and the law adopted in 1961 banned "sodomy" alone. Such processes were replicated around the USSR and could be investigated in each republic's archives.

Recorded prosecutions for same-sex relations between men rapidly increased throughout the USSR. From 1961 to 1981, 14,695 men were convicted of sodomy in the RSFSR, constituting between 0.10 and 0.17 percent of all criminal convictions each year.[89] In the rest of the USSR, 7,468 men were convicted during the same period. Lipša, Teet Veispak, and Uladzimir Valodzin report analogous surges in convictions for Latvia, Estonia, and Belorussia, respectively; Valodzin also confirms surges in the Soviet republics of Ukraine and, to a lesser extent, Lithuania and Moldavia.[90] New routines of civilian policing of gay men appeared in the late 1950s and were solidified during the 1960s, curated and occasionally enhanced by the KGB. The police in cities and towns monitored homosexual haunts in parks and public toilets, and used informants who were blackmailed with the threat of prosecution to incriminate others.[91] One intricately documented case from rural Estonia in 1966 (part of an extraordinary artists' project incorporating historical and artistic methods) demonstrates that a single denunciation could trigger an extensive civilian police investigation running to 167 documents including interrogations, medical and psychiatric opinions, and prosecution reasoning. Collective farm chairman Juhan Ojaste, a Party member, was let off lightly for a first offense – he was dismissed from his position but not arrested. Even with this blot on his biography, he was only given eighteen months' jail time after a sex partner denounced him a few years later.[92]

Historians have not yet uncovered the official policies adopted towards the gay male subculture in late Soviet cities. Such research would require needle-in-a-haystack searches for key discussions in Party, Komsomol, and city government archives, as well as unfettered access to police and KGB records. The Estonian historical project's interviews with older gay men show that Tartu and Tallinn had lively cruising grounds where gay men met, made love, and forged friendships; the interviews give the impression police attention to these meeting spots was infrequent but fear of prosecution was not forgotten.[93] Lipša's archival study shows that from 1965, as part of all-USSR health ministry measures to control STIs, surveillance of homosexuals in Soviet Latvia was modernized, with queer men "registered in at least two filing systems": a card-index of male homosexuals maintained by the Riga police, and another index of "spreaders of venereal diseases" run by Latvia's republican STI treatment and monitoring center.[94] An ad hoc group of police and venereologists cross-referenced data on possible queer STI carriers whose names were then passed to police for monitoring or detention and medical treatment. A similar system with a police bureau monitoring homosexuals, both those reported by STI treatment clinics and those noted by surveillance of cruising spots, is said to have operated in Leningrad in the 1970s–80s, although we do not have archival confirmation of its activity.[95] This report says that the KGB led "gay hunting" entrapment campaigns in the city, training civilian police and even setting up gay meeting spots in saunas in the 1980s to catch queers red-handed. Anecdotal sources for Ukraine and Siberia confirm that as in Leningrad, police and KGB kept card-indexes of known homosexuals, and compelled young men to serve as informants to avoid prosecution; gay men got early release from imprisonment if they agreed to infiltrate and denounce gay networks.[96] One Novosibirsk queer man, who served a total of eighteen years for homosexual offenses, recalled that "a special group of police assigned to gays" whose commander "got promoted on the backs of gays" ran in the city from the 1950s. He personally saw its card index with nicknames of male homosexuals and the usual biographical detail too.[97]

During the late Soviet years, artists and intellectuals were prosecuted under the sodomy laws in cases that carried political significance. The Soviet authorities used the sodomy law to harass these figures and destroy their reputations. As noted in Chapter 3, in 1959 the singer Vadim Kozin was arrested in a Khabarovsk hotel room with a young male informer while on tour with the Magadan Musical-Drama Theater.[98] Kozin only served a few months in prison, but he interpreted this second conviction as a signal that the authorities would not allow him a free career, and indeed this would be the case until the late 1980s. Even after the end of the Soviet regime, Yeltsin's democratic regime denied Kozin full rehabilitation. His friends campaigned unsuccessfully to have Kozin named a Merited Artist of the Russian Federation. His biographer Savchenko suggests that Ministry of Culture officials blocked the honor because of his criminal record, and that the KGB's successor continued to view Kozin as a "'natural pederast [who] perverts our youth!'".[99]

Director Sergei Paradzhanov, who like Kozin had already been convicted once in the 1940s for a homosexual offense, was imprisoned again in 1974 for homosexual acts. He was released in 1977 after foreign artists ambushed Communist Party leader Leonid Brezhnev at a public event, to plead for his freedom.[100] Another sentence on trumped-up charges, for bribery this time, followed in the early 1980s, again terminated early after international campaigning.[101] Paradzhanov's extravagant non-conformism, bisexuality, and refusal to work within ideological constraints imposed on Soviet filmmakers were the obvious reasons for this persecution. He left behind a body of prison writing, including letters, and a film scenario, "Swan Lake. The Zone," alluding to a guard's love for an inmate. As James Steffen points out, after imprisonment, Paradzhanov's notoriety as queer was inescapable, and his work in the 1980s with its flaunting of "oriental" and exotic elements irritated nationalist critics determined to purge Georgian and Armenian cultures of non-heteronormative motifs.[102]

Another infamous case from this period involves the Leningrad poet Gennady Trifonov. From 1973 he worked in Lenfilm Studios and was forced by blackmail to collaborate with the studio's KGB minders; driven to desperation, he tried to emigrate and appealed to Heinrich Böll in Germany for assistance. The authorities took their revenge when plainclothes police dragged Trifonov off the street in Leningrad and beat him in spring 1976. Later that year, he was arrested and sentenced to four years under the anti-sodomy law. When international protests called for his release, the authorities responded by adding other charges to his case (hooliganism, giving alcohol to minors) to damage his reputation. Trifonov served the full four years in prison. On his release, Soviet authorities used administrative resources to punish him for his literary non-conformism and his open poetry about homosexuality.[103] Similarly, Lev S. Klein, an archaeologist with a dissident past, was arrested and held for eighteen months on sodomy charges. After his release, he was stripped of his academic degrees and career. He later refused to deny or admit a homosexual orientation, arguing that his sexuality was a private affair.[104] The author and drama teacher Evgeny Kharitonov was never arrested for his homosexuality, but he was interrogated by the KGB in the murder investigation of a gay friend; he died at the age of forty from a heart attack that was perhaps brought on by this incident. He was certainly under police surveillance and in danger of arrest.[105] In the 1970s, Trifonov and Kharitonov each penned underground manifestos, distributed in the West, defending homosexuality and criticizing its persecution in the USSR; in the run-up to the 1980 Moscow Olympics, Trifonov, then still in prison, was evidently penalized for this outrage with long confinement in punishment cells.[106]

The same-sex relations of these intellectuals and artists served as a convenient pretext to arrest them. We lack confirmation of how they came to be persecuted on the basis of their sexuality. As the Trifonov and Paradzhnov cases suggest, it was axiomatic that the cultural industries in late Soviet life labored under the gaze of KGB surveillance, and it is logical that the security police initiated these investigations. Yet the many thousands of ordinary gay and bisexual men who were arrested and convicted under the sodomy law were probably not so closely observed by the KGB. The collective farm chairman Ojaste was a Party member and his "spoilt biography" was known to the Communists; yet his convictions arose from routine police work and, it seems, denunciation from an aggrieved (or coerced?) sex partner. Many others, whose stories are unknown, probably were caught in the matrix of surveillance that was apparently curated by the KGB but run by urban sub-departments of the civilian police force, in tandem with STI clinics. The operation of these modern police and health-professional card-index, contact-tracing, and surveillance- and informant-systems merit further investigation, to understand more fully how and why ordinary victims of state-sponsored homophobia were identified and persecuted. In Russia and in the West, LGBT communities commemorate the talented and educated victim of state oppression enthusiastically, but we tend to forget the ordinary, unexceptional victims of the same state oppression.[107]

Towards a better historical understanding

To understand the use of political terror against lesbians and gay men in twentieth-century Russia requires more sophisticated thinking about the concept of homosexuality in the past. Also needed is a more empathetic attitude toward the objects of investigation. We need more "queer eyes" in the archives and less of the hostile, amateurish and badly informed analysis that we find in the work of some who have had privileged access to secret documents, especially those of the FSB. Russian men and women who were persecuted for their same-sex inclinations were not alien from the rest of society. Homosexuality is not confined to a specific set of sexual acts, but had and has a far more important emotional and intellectual dimension. It is gross historical malpractice to read the archives of Soviet "homosexualism" solely through the policeman's lens. The victims of Stalin's anti-homosexual law were fellow citizens, and it does not take much imagination to infer that until 1934, Russia's same-sex feeling people did not consider themselves a criminal element. Many, like the Leningrad "pederast" Lev Lisenko, arrested in August 1933, or Harry Whyte boldly writing to Stalin in the following year, believed themselves to be innocent biological variants of humanity, entitled to respect and dignity, and indeed "protection" in the world's first socialist society.

Apart from empathy and more intelligent conceptualization of same-sex relations, historians and activists urgently need a rich and sophisticated account of the history of popular homophobia in Russia, Ukraine and the other societies of the USSR. "Homophobia" is a problematic concept to apply to past societies, but more work on the history of attitudes to same-sex love in the Russian Empire and Soviet Union is undeniably necessary. In part we need this work to understand the roots of the Stalinist political turn against male homosexuality. Upon what pre-existing social and cultural substrate did Stalin and the Communist Party build its modern homophobic sexual politics? We scarcely know. I believe we also need a historical account of popular Soviet homophobia to explain the long continuities we see in social attitudes in the former Soviet Union. In order to combat present-day hostility to LGBT citizenship, activists must be equipped to explain how Russian/Soviet prejudices were constructed and evolved, as part of a modern heteronormativity. Human rights activists also need more stories of individual persecution and endurance, to enrich a threadbare narrative and to inspire the next generation of young LGBT citizens and democrats of all sexualities.

To understand better the fate of the victims of political terror or police persecution because of their sexual non-conformism, we also need a more detailed picture of techniques of power that the state used against homosexuals. There are many obstacles to research here, starting with the virtual inaccessibility of secret police archives and the incomprehension and active hostility of archivists and officials, even in archives that are open. A comparative approach, exploiting the differentiated archival regimes of peripheral post-Soviet states, would seem to be the most promising way to address this problem. Research collaboration between scholars in the Baltic Republics, Ukraine, Georgia, Moldova, and other non-Russian republics may allow us to enrich our sources on, and understanding of, the Soviet state's persecution of sexual and gender dissent. Such a project would extend the reach of "queer eyes" in the archives by uniting disparate and often isolated scholars into a powerful team of investigators.

More systematic and scholarly research on these and many related questions can be done with the will and resources. A clearer picture of how Stalinists and their heirs conducted political persecution against Soviet gay men and lesbians would be a powerful tool in the struggle for human rights. Without such research, an intelligent, well informed dialogue in post-Soviet societies on the question of the status of LGBT citizens cannot take place.

8

Shame, Pride, and "Non-traditional" Lives:

The Dilemmas of Queering Russian Biography

Dealing with the homosexuality of a given biographical subject is not straightforward when the subject is Russian. Biographers of the Russian queer have long had to contend with the politics of the closet, and particularly its tortuous epistemology in Russian culture. The country's politics of the closet have become much sharper following the 2013 adoption of the national ban on "propaganda [among minors] for non-traditional sexual relations." In the debate about the law in the Russian media, lies, half-truths, and coy spin about Tchaikovsky's homosexuality figured as an apparently light-hearted talking point. Even President Vladimir Putin was drawn into the fray, fighting shy of admitting the indisputable and copiously documented historical truth about the composer's sexuality, a supposedly irrelevant character trait:

> They say that Peter Ilyich Tchaikovsky was a homosexual . . . Truth be told, we love him not because of that, but he was a great musician, and we all love his music. So what? There's no point in making a mountain out of a molehill, there's nothing wrong here, nothing wrong is going to happen in our country.[1]

Only a few days later his Minister of Culture boldly lied in an interview for Interfax, saying "there is no proof that Tchaikovsky was gay" and brushing aside the flaccid challenges of a poorly informed journalist.[2] The brazen denial of historical truth to fit a nationalist neo-traditional fantasy was puzzling in its apparent triviality and unapologetic stupidity. Yet the episode illustrated how politicized "non-traditional" sexuality has become in today's

Russia. The politics of the closet, and the status of information about homosexuality, are no longer social or cultural issues, but matters of state. The culture minister's ignorance of the existence of "proof" of Tchaikovsky's sexual orientation exemplifies, admittedly in extreme form, the will to denial and evasion that typifies Russia's biographers writing the lives of their country's queer historical figures.

These challenges to biography begin with the well-known "difficulties of evidence," i.e. the relative paucity of documentation that historians encounter when trying to discuss the sexually dissident aspects of a subject's life. I shall not dwell on these obstacles at length here; it is an interesting fact of queer historiography in the West after the postmodern turn that historians complain about this less than we used to. It remains, however, a reality when we consider the distant past in our own cultures – and the past and present in a culture like Russia's. Trauma, suppression, erasure, and euphemism all have an impact on the written record. When it comes to evidence of LGBT lives, it is all too true that "manuscripts *do* burn": right now in the Russian Federation, I'm willing to bet that someone somewhere is destroying letters or a diary, deleting emails and text messages, wiping a hard drive or destroying a library to conceal a deceased relative's or their own "non-traditional" sexual and emotional relations.[3] It has long been a simple fact of queer existence that the creation, preservation, and transmission of knowledge about sexuality that does not conform to the ideology of "compulsory heterosexuality" are and were problematic and even dangerous activities.[4]

Here I want to raise three issues that trouble the queering of Russian biography, using examples from biographies I've encountered in my scholarship and activism. The first issue revolves around the purpose of queer biography: why write the queer life, what purpose does an overtly queer life-story serve, and why should we care that such lives are told explicitly? To a Western ear, such questions may seem oddly elementary, but in the contemporary Russian and global political climate, I argue that they have renewed political and critical relevance. A second cluster of questions focuses on the writers of biographies of queer Russians. Who are they, and what are their attitudes toward so-called "non-traditional" sexual relations? Does the sexuality of the biographer matter? Does empathy have a place in the biography of the sexual dissident? Or, to put it another way, how intellectually legitimate is the "heteronormative voice" found in many Russian biographies of gay subjects? A third question focuses on how sexuality is conceptualized in these biographies. How historically sensitive and sophisticated are biographers' conceptions of the sexuality of their subjects?

In thinking about these questions, I returned first to Robert K. Martin's powerful call first issued in 1980 in the pages of New York's influential gay magazine *Christopher Street* for honesty and sympathy in Anglo-American biographies of gay artists.[5] His essay shone a light on the routine falsification, silences, and homophobia evident in biography at that time. I propose to call the practices that he criticized the construction of a "heteronormative voice" in biographical writing. Brian James Baer's recent work on contemporary Russian literature is another important influence on my approach: he describes how Russian culture seems institutionally incapable of accepting visible LGBT identities. Literary and cultural attitudes make it "difficult if not impossible to reconcile gay activism with Russian cultural citizenship."[6] He argues that translators, editors, and critics who "package" Western literature for the Russian market engage in strategies of erasure, estheticization, and Russification to veil or suppress unwelcome attention on queer sexualities.[7] I suggest that domestic biographers of Russia's queers perform similar homophobic moves as well.

In this chapter I examine the purpose of queer biography, the significance of the empathetic biographer, and the understanding of queer sexuality in life writing, and conclude with remarks about the relevance of these issues for Russian queer biography. My argument is that the heteronormative voice about the lives of queer Russians in history is not only a Putinist postmodern media sideshow, but has its roots in long-standing Russian scholarly and intellectual practices. We need to attend to those practices to understand how information regimes around homosexuality operate in Russia today; and we have to do that while remembering how we Westerners arrived at the point where frankness about the queer subject in biography has become a norm. I should state at the outset that "Russian queer biography" is not a terribly satisfactory term; in this essay I use it to specify biographies of Russian figures in history and culture who are known to be (or have been), or are represented as, lesbian, gay, bisexual, or transgender. The examples I draw upon are of men who loved men: the poet Nikolai Alekseevich Kliuev (1884–1937), poet and diarist Mikhail Alekseevich Kuzmin (1872–1936), and singer-songwriter Vadim Alekseevich Kozin (1905–94).

Gay pride, shame, and the purposes of queer biography

"Queer" children, growing up almost always in "straight" families, receive very little information about the history of their tribe. Unlike children of religious, ethnic, linguistic, or cultural minorities, queer children (and I am going to dispense with the scare quotes) are seldom offered any cultural capital to help them understand their predicament. As Martin wrote in the 1970s, "We [gay and lesbian people] see heterosexually because we have been taught to and because our survival depends on it."[8] Indeed, where children are concerned, not much has changed since then. One does not need to live in Russia to think that it is undesirable or foolhardy to expose a child to queer knowledge. Even today, in our own societies, the idea of giving children access to this cultural capital to build their self-esteem as queer people is controversial. It would be more prudent, runs the argument, to wait until young people are "sure" of their orientation and not risk "turning" them lesbian or gay. We are still influenced in this thinking by Freudian ideas of the bipolarity of sexuality (as distinctively hetero or homo) and the notion that children pass through a bisexual "phase" on the long climb to a healthy heterosexuality from which, once attained, they never then waver.[9] Such ideas dominate mainstream thinking as well in Russia, promoted by sexologists and child psychologists reporting to the state Duma and making recommendations to the government's internet regulator.[10]

Thus one important purpose of explicitly queer biography is to foster pride in being differently oriented by sexuality or gender. "Gay pride" is almost half a century old as a political idea, a product of the post-Stonewall ferment of gay liberation. Nevertheless, queer moderns, mostly Europeans, have been arguing for some form of "gay pride" since the late 1860s, among them the St. Petersburg poet, composer, and diarist Mikhail Kuzmin (see Figure 8.1). Yet the epistemology of the closet – the knowledge regime created by ideologies of compulsory heterosexuality (or, heteronormativity) – is more tenacious than Eve Sedgwick suspected in 1990, when she first identified the concept.[11] In the current global context, events in Africa, some Muslim countries, and Russia show that the capacity of ideologies of heteronormativity to generate new regimes of knowledge and information control is, if anything, increasing. The law banning "propaganda [among minors] for non-traditional sexual relations" is just one example of recent attempts by states confronting globalization's discontents to obstruct *information* about same-sex love and queer genders. In 2014, Uganda toughened its already draconian anti-homosexual laws with the criminalization of "promotion" of same-sex love, and curbed speech freedoms for LGBT organizations and non-queer NGOs. Nigeria punishes not just the act of same-sex love but the organization, registration, or supporting of LGBT societies. Cameroon recently imprisoned a man for sending a text message to another man reading, "I'm very much in love with you."[12] The trend toward the imposition of new knowledge regimes to silence queer desires and histories also has a clear post-colonial inflection that bears comparison with the Russian case. In Asia and Africa, many countries inherited anti-sodomy laws imposed by colonial powers in the nineteenth century; these laws implanted a modern European homophobia in cultures that often had pre-existing traditions of accommodation (if not tolerance) of same-sex relations and gender variation. European and U.S. Christian churches in Africa, having successfully attracted millions of adherents, are the main transmission belts of a politicized and often violent homophobia. In Russia, the sources of homophobia are mostly local, but the Kremlin justifies its new information regime for "non-traditional" sexuality by citing the supposed "threat" from globalizing or European forces that, during the 1990s, allegedly "imported" LGBT-rights discourses to a weakened Russia.[13]

FIGURE 8.1 *Mikhail Kuzmin.*

In such a political environment, queer biography cannot be taken for granted as an academic exercise in inclusiveness, a species of box-ticking "good practice" in life-writing. We have to remember Martin's impassioned call for openness and analytical sophistication in queer biography as a political tool. Writing life-stories queerly should be an engaged way to forge and transmit important social and cultural capital with urgent political significance for those who experience same-sex desire or gender difference. Stories of the queer self help the individual to wrestle with the dilemmas of being queer, and they enable positive and healthy self-realization. Theorists of "gay shame" have recently observed how "shaming operations" conducted against individuals voicing queer desires have been and continue to be psychologically devastating.[14] Russian psychologists have documented the damage that shame and homophobia does in Russia, to its own citizens, even before the 2013 political campaign against "gay propaganda."[15] The knowledge that others have endured and survived these assaults is an important weapon, and the beginning of a sense of non-pathologized identity and supportive community. We might not wish to go as far as Sedgwick, who recently argued that gay shame is a "keystone affect" in the constitution of the queer self; shame's stigma, some U.S. queer theorists contend, marks the personality of the individual and embeds itself in the person's developmental history. Queer shame is "integral to and residual in the processes by which identity itself is formed."[16] Shame interrupts identification with a wider world of which the individual desires to be part (the "sacred center" of society, as Erving Goffman termed it). It thereby threatens sociability, but it potentially creates new identifications with other "shamed" beings.[17] "In fact people are always a little ashamed of being proud of being homosexual," to use Hocquenghem's pithy phrase.[18]

Historical life stories can counteract the sense created by queer theoretical writing that shame is an inescapable trap. George Chauncey, writing of gay male diarists of mid-twentieth-century New York City, observes that they "developed ideological resources to counteract the dominant culture's insistence that they should be ashamed, some of them tried to help troubled men overcome their shame, and most of them commented on men who had succumbed to shame."[19] In the diary of singer Vadim Kozin for the years 1955 and 1956 while on tour with the Magadan Musical Theater in the Soviet Far East, we see him creating the same resourceful responses to the relentless homophobia of his colleagues in the theater troupe. (As discussed in Chapter 3, his homosexuality was public knowledge, since he was sent to Magadan as a victim of Stalin's anti-sodomy law.) In December 1955, resting with colleagues after a concert in Omsk, Kozin complains in his diary about the indiscreet behavior of a gay man in his troupe, and how this indiscretion reflects on him:

[Kabalov, drunk,] conducted a conversation with my guests that left me speechless with amazement. His behavior is going to land him in a prison camp. Now I understand why he ran away from Moscow. After he went off to the canteen, I apologized to my comrades for Kabalov's behavior, blaming all the oddness and tactlessness of his speech on his insobriety; his boldness staggers me. I will have to tell him straight out that his sexual adventures must not in any way concern me and still less, my acquaintances. I do not want to have people thinking of me like that again. I would rather suffer alone. But all this shocks me. Where is the justice at the end of the day? A man with a Party card does whatever comes into his head, and he gets away with everything because his membership card is his miraculous invulnerable shield.[20]

Aghast with all the spectrum of shamed emotion, the singer nevertheless turns his ire on the Party and its homophobic hypocrisy – the ultimate source of his shame. Kozin's diary offers Russian queers a rare example of an individual victim of the Stalin-era repression of homosexuals who survived that assault, and coped with the social oppression that followed in its wake. "Not all shaming operations succeed," Chauncey reminds us, and Vadim Kozin's diary vividly illustrates the point in a context familiar to contemporary Russia's queers.[21]

Writing explicitly queer biography has historically been an important part of the LGBT movement's strategy, and after the collapse of communism, Russia's queer intellectuals certainly made contributions to the genre of popularized, LGBT-proud or at least positive, life stories.[22] Writing one's people's story into the national and global narrative creates a common minority identity, ties the "minority" to the desired "sacred center" and its values, and begins a dialogue with the "majority." That at least is how one can generalize from half a century's progress in the struggle for LGBT human rights in the West. Whether Russian LGBT activists "need" to follow this formula, and how they might adapt its characteristics, are matters for them to decide; I am not making a homonationalist claim to know what's best for Russians.[23] My intention is to point out how Russian writing about the lives of the country's queer artists tends to deny, obscure, or estheticize homosexuality rather than treat it sympathetically and analytically. For the Russian LGBT movement, certain problems also issue from the paucity of historical and biographical work available to mine for politically instructive examples; currently, historiography on Russian LGBT experience remains shallow.

The shallowness of Russian LGBT historiographies is probably a temporary problem, but it does limit the purchase that LGBT arguments have on the national story and therefore on the process of domesticating queerness in Russia. An interesting aspect of this problem is the lack of more than a handful of biographies of victims of Stalin's 1934 anti-sodomy law. We suspect that tens of thousands of men were convicted for voluntary sodomy during Stalin's lifetime. Yet of all these people, we have only the stories of a few notables: Nikolai Kliuev, arrested in 1934 and eventually executed in 1937; Vadim Kozin, arrested in 1944 and sentenced to eight years' imprisonment in 1945; and Sergei Paradzhanov, arrested in 1948 and imprisoned for a few months before being released in an amnesty.[24] Queer scholars and activists have paid little attention to the few documents they produced that reveal anything of the experience of a Gulag queer; in any case, these letters and diaries have only been published in small print runs.[25] For a lack of biographical data about repressed individuals, LGBT activists in Russia have struggled to write themselves into a core narrative of twentieth-century Soviet experience, the victimization of gay men and lesbians as one of the myriad target groups of Stalin's terror. Without a more richly evidenced story to tell about the fate of thousands of shamed men who suffered under this law, there is a gap in the LGBT movement's narrative that might otherwise tie LGBT rights struggles to wider struggles for democratic rights in Russia.

Writers of biography and the heteronormative voice

Who writes the queer biography? Does the biographer's sexuality matter when the biographical subject is queer? Are writers of "authentic" lives of poets and artists obliged to acknowledge the sexuality of their subjects? Are they obliged to engage empathetically with the sexuality of the subject? How far should the heteronormative voice govern biography?

In Western literary criticism, these questions have been so comprehensively answered in favor of the honest, sympathetic, and "homonormative" approach that it seems extraordinary to raise them. Nevertheless, they remain relevant to students of life-writing in Russia. In the 1970s, at the dawn of Western gay liberation, engaged gay and lesbian critics castigated existing biographies of Oscar Wilde, Hart Crane, Walt Whitman, and other queer icons as insufficiently imbued with a sense of honesty and sensitivity about the sexuality of the subject. Robert K. Martin indicted biographers for their lack of empathy, their embarrassment around unfamiliar sexuality, the "failure of the straight imagination." In contrast to extensive research into, and description of, the sexual lives of straight subjects, which was held to be indicative of the "truth" of a subject, Martin found biographers keen to dismiss the homosexuality of a subject as "irrelevant" to their lives or art. "The lives of most gays, as they are written, revolve around a central void. The biographers, believing that they are simply eliminating the sex from the life, have eliminated the heart."[26] Denial, falsification, and dismissal characterized life-writing that lacked empathy and sensitivity regarding the impact of dissenting sexuality on the biographical subject. This sexuality had to be examined "*on its own terms*" (Martin emphasized) and in its carefully reconstructed historical context. Furthermore, where the subject was an artist, their creative work had to be reinterpreted sensitively through the prism of sexuality; homosexual existence in a heterosexual world was not merely a trivial "character flaw" or private "detail," but an experience that shaped artistic expression.

More methodological issues agitated Martin. He charged that formalist criticism, focused on esthetics, and denying links to the artistic life as lived, worked to obliterate queer experience and an understanding of queer creativity. Additionally, it was necessary for archives to be read empathetically, and for papers to be accessible to later scholars without concealment or alteration. It was not necessary, Martin argued, for the biographer of the queer subject to be queer himself or herself:

> . . . we must ask the straight biographer to make a leap of the imagination. Gay lives cannot be examined through straight spectacles. This is not to say, of course, that one must be gay in order to write a gay life, but it does mean that our lives must be treated with the same respect that we are called upon to give theirs [heterosexuals']. Every biographer must at some point become his or her subject; it is precisely at that point of sympathy and identification that biographies of gays have failed, because their authors have not been willing to imagine a gay life from within.[27]

In a similar fashion, albeit discussing the "ghosting" of lesbian lives in fiction, Terry Castle argued in 1993 that failures of frankness and sympathetic imagination dogged Western representations of the lesbian life, making such lives "apparitional," "spectral," and barely visible.[28] Thus the dismissal of the subject's queer sexuality as "irrelevant," the outright fabrication of a heterosexual identity for the subject, the obscuring of the sexual life of the subject to make homosexuality "apparitional," and the formalistic treatment of artistic work all served to suppress the queer subject, and to produce the heteronormative voice.

In the 1980s and 1990s, in the Anglo-American world the truth-telling biography that recuperated the subject's homosexuality became the new standard: think of Andrew Hodge's painstaking reconstruction of the life of British mathematician and Second World War code-breaker Alan Turing (1912–54) that recast him as a gay hero.[29] Today in the global West, the queer biography is most likely to be a queer *autobiography*, a truth-telling, confessional exercise in the pursuit of authenticity that allows for no vocal appropriation, ventriloquism, or mediation between "deviants" and "the normal."[30] The biographical presentation of the queer subject using a heteronormative voice is now regarded as inauthentic, as misrepresentation. Western queer biography, regardless of the sexual subject position of the biographer, speaks with empathy and respect, and with an understanding that queer experience shapes the subject's life and creative activity.

Queer biography in Russia retains features of the heteronormative voice that largely reigned before Stonewall in the West.[31] The obscuring or outright denial of the homosexuality of Tchaikovsky merits a specific study in its own right from the perspective of queer theories of epistemology. The most authoritative biographer of the composer, Alexander Poznansky, traces the history of the construction of Tchaikovsky's closet from the earliest editorial trimming conducted by his brother (and also homosexual) Modest, through the interesting variations in early Soviet, Stalinist, and post–1953 textual scholarship, to the notorious homophobic fable of Tchaikovsky's death as a suicide allegedly commanded by a "court of honor" composed of notables disgusted by his sexual misadventures.[32] The 2013 Russian media and political denials and dodges about the composer's sexuality were reflections of well-established habits of obfuscation and outright fabrication, the result of efforts of private individuals, scholars, and biographers to construct a less troubling and more conventional national hero.

In Russian-language biographies of Kliuev, Kuzmin, and Kozin, there are similar evasions and obfuscations that create a heteronormative voice. Some of the most strikingly heteronormative language occurs in scholarship about Nikolai Kliuev, a poet whose verse is heralded by an unlikely combination of radical Russian nationalists, sentimentally patriotic schoolteachers, and LGBT activists.[33] Kliuev was a "neo-peasant" poet of the pre–1917 Silver Age of Russian literature, and of the 1920s Soviet era, a calculating eccentric who appeared at Petersburg and Moscow salons in peasant garb and whose verses sang of the Russian people's bond to the soil (see Figure 8.2). By the time of Stalin's collectivization, launched in 1929, his lyrics were deeply out of step with the times, and he was labeled a "father of kulak literature." (Kulak was the regime's name for peasants, allegedly wealthy, opposed to collectivization.) Kliuev was also unabashedly homosexual, and wrote openly of his love in his poems, especially celebrating his deepest love for the young illustrator Anatoly Yar-Kravchenko, whom he met in 1928. Scholarly publications in the 1990s of their correspondence and Kliuev's secret police files demonstrated that the homoerotic voice in Kliuev's poetry had its basis in his everyday life and desires. U.S. scholar Michael Makin reports on Russian academics' tendency, despite their own investigative work, to treat Kliuev's homosexuality coyly or evasively, although he does see some evolution toward franker acknowledgments in the first decade of the twenty-first century.[34] A particularly blatant example is found in the landmark 1995 study of the KGB's literary archives by Vitaly Shentalinsky.[35] During the democratizing era of perestroika in the late 1980s, by dint of campaigning as a member of the Union of Soviet Writers, Shentalinsky obtained privileged access to the KGB archival files of a series of writers repressed under Stalin's rule. He deliberately silenced critical information about Nikolai Kliuev's sexuality and its impact on his fate, despite the fact that it was crucial to the poet's treatment in state hands.[36] Kliuev was arrested in February 1934 in Moscow after denunciation by a high literary bureaucrat who found his homoerotic love-poems distasteful. The arrest took place just as the Stalin anti-homosexual law was being enacted; the

FIGURE 8.2 *Nikolai Kliuev.*

poet was charged with sodomy, and with anti-Soviet agitation, and exiled from Moscow to Siberia.[37] Kliuev was later executed in Tomsk during the Great Terror as a counterrevolutionary. When privately challenged by Michael Makin, Shentalinsky, the democrat from the Writers' Union, admitted that he excised all mention of the sodomy charge from his account so that his Russian readership would not dismiss him as "some kind of faggot" (*kakoi-to pedik*).[38] Later, in 2004 at a Kliuev studies conference,

Shentalinsky did declare that a franker assessment of the poet's homosexuality and its impact on his work was overdue, although Makin reports that this call was met with silence and was unlikely to be taken up.[39] Even the most balanced and scholarly biographer of the poet, Konstantin Azadovsky, still handles Kliuev's sexuality evasively.[40] A recent critical edition of the correspondence between the poet and his lover treats their relations in "apparitional" fashion, designating their love as "friendship" or "intimacy" and erasing its flesh-and-blood manifestations; the result is a total "failure of the straight imagination" that buries same-sex love under euphemism and flaccid critical analysis.[41]

Other literary scholars have been blatantly hostile toward Kliuev's sexuality. The anti-Semitic, radical nationalist critics Stanislav and Sergei Kuniaev note that "Kliuev, like [Mikhail] Kuzmin and his circle . . . was liable to a vice that was extremely widespread in the cultural elite of that era: the sodomitical sin."[42] Kliuev's relationship in 1915–16 with the young neo-peasant poet Sergei Esenin – the subject of much speculation about a possible homosexual element – is treated as a pathological and even semi-pedophilic episode in the Kuniaevs' popular biography of Esenin in the "Lives of Remarkable People" series. The twenty-year-old Esenin was "in a ridiculous situation," dependent on the older bard for introduction to the capital's literary salons, but "as a young, handsome boy with healthy masculine instincts, of course he could not" submit to Kliuev's intimacies. Kliuev's "womanish" jealousy provoked the youth to threats of violence, in the circumstances a reaction entirely justified according to the Kuniaevs, who presume their readership will agree. Yet ultimately Esenin was able to cultivate detachment from the "unhealthy pestering of his brother poet" and laugh off "Kliuev's pathological weakness" in a kind-hearted fashion.[43] The nationalist critics call upon on a much-used trope of contemporary homophobic discourse, the notion that the "simple Russian" is not violently anti-gay but has a generous capacity to laugh off homosexuality as merely "comic."[44]

A peculiar example of the operations of erasure, euphemism, and evasion pervades the several successive biographies, in Russian and in English, of Mikhail Kuzmin, by the collaborative team of Kuzminists, Nikolai Bogomolov and John Malmstad.[45] Kuzmin was a composer, poet, prose-writer, and author of a diary from 1905 to 1931 (with a further volume in the fateful year 1934). His short novel *Krylia* (Wings, 1906) was the first European gay Bildungsroman with a happy ending, a supremely confident manifesto for homosexuality in a hybridized Russian and European cultural context.[46] His diary, with its Proustian reportage of Petersburg–Petrograd–Leningrad's shifting homosexual coteries, and its reflections on the dilemmas of queer existence, constitutes the single most important gay document of modern Russian culture, and it remains untranslated and still largely unpublished.[47] Kuzmin's life and work are rightly situated at the core of Russian queer studies, and the successive editions of the Bogomolov and Malmstad biography of their subject reflect the profound scholarship they have invested in this captivating figure over at least four decades. One can imagine the conversations between them – both in their own rather different ways committed to frankness about their shared subject's homosexuality – that resulted in some strikingly differing passages between the two versions. In the first chapter of the English version, we read that "Same-sex love is the defining fact of Kuzmin's life and art."[48] In Russian, the same passage prevaricates: ". . . the intimate side of life played an unusually important, and often, defining role in the creative work of Kuzmin." It is only several sentences later in the Russian version that the reader learns that Kuzmin's private life was distinguished not merely by the "extraordinary intensity of experiences of love" but the fact that this passion was directed "exclusively . . . toward men."[49] In contrast to the English version, the Russian text never uses the word "*gei*" (gay), and often evades explicit statements about homosexuality, apparently deferring to the prejudices of its readership. For example, "gay society" is used in English to describe Kuzmin's hopes to form a gay coterie, while in Russian these sentences simply do not appear.[50] The writer Evdokia A. Nagrodskaya, in Kuzmin's circle, is described as a "fag hag" in English, while in Russian a necessary explanation stands in for this misogynist characterization: "One must obviously seek the reason [for their awkward relationship] in the ambiguity of these relations."[51] Here we have an apparently reversed case of Baer's "packaging" of translation, in this case, from a Russian original text – where euphemism, erasure, and evasion prevail, to the English variant, which yielded a "gayer" Kuzmin for a Western readership.[52] In this case, neither voice is satisfactory. The evasiveness of the Russian text resembles the heteronormative treatments of Kliuev and pre-Stonewall Western biography that made the queer subject invisible; while the 1970s-style identity-bound labeling of the English version jars with its anachronism and insensitivity.[53]

An insistent case of the heteronormative biographical voice belongs to Boris Savchenko, a journalist from Magadan whose publications about the Stalin-era gypsy romance crooner and composer Vadim Kozin have done much to rescue the artist's reputation from oblivion. In 1944, Kozin was arrested in Moscow on charges of both sodomy and counterrevolution; he served five years in Magadan camps, albeit working most of the time for the central theater of the Gulag city.[54] In the early 1960s, Savchenko was a young writer for the *Magadan Komsomolets* newspaper, when he first met the singer in the town's public library. This encounter came not long after Kozin's second brief imprisonment for a homosexual offense in 1959. They developed a friendship over the subsequent decades, and Savchenko began to publish material based on the artist's reminiscences in the 1980s. The association with a notorious homosexual, even if he was also Magadan's greatest surviving artist, apparently cost the young Savchenko some anxiety. In his most recent explanation of their relationship, published in his introduction to Kozin's diary in 2005, Savchenko is quick to disabuse readers of any suspicion that he had sex with Kozin:

I rejoiced at the thought that I was going to be a guest of the famous artist, but suddenly my joy faded, and everything was struck with an unexpected feeling of strange awkwardness. By the time I got home I was already very doubtful about whether it was worthwhile visiting Kozin's apartment. No doubt it was under surveillance, since the owner of the flat had such a "reputation" (many years later I learned that the flat opposite was occupied by a KGB employee, so draw your own conclusions!). And the question tortured me: "Why then did he invite me to visit him? Why me? Maybe I look to him like that 'stamp collector' who got him arrested in 1959?" I was young, good-looking, the girls fancied me. It was likely that he fancied me too . . . Then I suddenly remembered.

My hero was already sixty-five years old. With that physiology, with what feelings . . .

And something else worried me. What would people think – my friends, my boss at work? In a word, "What would Princess Maria Alekseevna say?"[55] "He visits Kozin?! He's 'gay'?!" All the same I overcame that psychological barrier and set off for the singer's.

I will immediately assuage the reader's curiosity: did anything happen? . . . I answer: no, nothing happened. In those days I belonged to the class of "honored masters" of bedroom contests with the opposite sex, however bombastic it sounds; I became a regular "visitor" [to Kozin] and eventually I calmed down, and every incident of masculine interest there nauseated me to the point of vomiting. True, during one of our first meetings, in the middle of a game of chess, from the lips of the maestro emerged a delicately veiled hint at . . . With equal intelligence I firmly rebuffed his "move" (in the style of the modern American cliché, "Don't even think about it"), and our later conversations – at first sporadic, later more frequent – bore a strictly business-like character, with my aim concentrated on the article, sketch or book [that I would one day write] about the forgotten singer.[56]

Savchenko works strenuously here to establish his heteronormative voice, while justifying his excursion into sensationally deviant territory. In his introduction, a complex set of responses are at work. The mature biographer's insistence on his heterosexual credentials is paramount; but the retrospective reflection of the danger he put himself in in pursuit of a story over a quarter of a century also displays his curiosity about a forbidden form of sexuality that was evidently part of his fascination with the singer from the outset. What did Kozin represent for this provincial youngster from Kolyma's frozen wastes with an interest in the theater, but a connection to the stages of Imperial St. Petersburg and jazz-age Soviet Leningrad, 10,000 km away? (The pretext for their first meeting was the singer's invitation to his flat to consult his private collection of pre-revolutionary periodicals.) In his editorial commentary accompanying Kozin's diary, we see an attitude of fascination and repulsion with the singer's intimate life that shields the diary's radioactive homo-desire in a heteronormative lead casing while reveling in voyeurism.[57] Savchenko cannot empathize with the dilemma of writing a queer diary in a homophobic time and place; but as a fan, and a journalist with bills to pay, he cannot resist publishing the document. His is a tragic "failure of the straight imagination" when entrusted with one of the Soviet period's most important documents of a queer voice.

How to do the history of Russian homosexuality?

Historians and queer theorists have argued at great length on the ways in which we can describe same-sex relations in the past. These scholars generally agree that early post-Stonewall assumptions about an essentialized, trans-cultural and trans-historical "homosexuality" make little sense when we examine contexts whether they be quite recent historically or more distant. Same-sex acts in the past carried different meanings, and few societies beyond the modern global West reified "homosexual" acts to the point where they become the marker of a relatively fixed identity category and personality type (homosexuality/homosexual). Contemporary categories of "homosexuality" and "heterosexuality" are very recent constructs that owe much of their explanatory power to medical, scientific, and sociological discourses.[58] These categories are also not uniformly present even in "modern" societies – many troubling blends, overlaps and temporal and generational transitions, cross-overs, and reversals of sexual identity persist and resist ironing out.[59] The trouble for most historians of sexuality is that identity-based discourses are very hard to forget when we search for evidence of same-sex relations in the past. The theoretical move in the early 1990s from identitarian "gay" and "lesbian" toward the post-modern "queer" was meant to shatter the templates we work with, and to de-familiarize the subjects we encounter in the archives of past sexual behavior. Yet historians of the queer past, even sophisticated social constructionists, find it hard not to imagine that the evidence we work so hard to find in the archives of "gay," "lesbian," or "queer" lives in the past, is proof of a bond, a link, a tie between "them" and "us." The healing and recuperative project of "restoring" the "gay past" is still a strong impulse for most queer historians, myself included.[60]

More recently, Western queer theory has inspired some historians to challenge this assumption that our task is to find people "like us" in the past. In particular, they ask whether people in the past – even individuals like Alan Turing, who lived and loved relatively recently – thought of themselves as "sexual beings" or imagined that they had a "sexuality" at all. They ask how someone as complex and intelligent as Turing would respond to the monument erected in his honor in Manchester's "gay village." The world of fixed sexualities was not one he might recognize. In his biography of the mathematician, Andrew Hodges did a magnificent job of reconstructing the inner homoerotic impulses of his subject on the basis of mere scraps of evidence, but he leaves us wondering how Turing conceived of same-sex desire; it is especially puzzling since Turing was so inquisitive about nature and the world in almost every other respect.[61] Some historians propose queering not just the identities we seek in the archives among historical subjects, but a more profound queering of method as well, to enable us to shake off "a gaze defined by presentist preoccupations."[62] The questions that drive our research into historical sexualities need refinement, our gaze must become more empathetic and imaginative, and we must not simply assume that we will find people like ourselves, or indeed people that we want to emulate, in the past.

Historians of Russian homosexuality appear to be behind the curve in this debate. We are aware of the awkwardness of our global Western categories and questions when applied to the Russian case, but we seldom problematize this discomfort frankly. The difficulties come in trying to situate Russia somewhere within European modernity but always, also, at a distance from it.[63] Our queer biographies and histories ride roughshod over the complexity, even the unknowability, of sexual and social identity as experienced in Russia and the Soviet Union. Documents such as the Kliuev and Yar-Kravchenko correspondence, Kozin's diary, and of course the celebrated diary of Kuzmin, merit re-reading from these more rigorous perspectives. For example, Kliuev's letters to his lover repeatedly frame his devotion for the younger man in archaic-religious terms ("My own dearest child, I send you my eternal blessings and kiss you on your sweetest of lips!").[64] The combination of religious ecstasy and homoerotic sensuousness is well known to scholars of Russian homoerotically inflected literature and culture, but it is seldom glimpsed in daily life settings.[65] Similarly, Kliuev's carefully confected 1922 "autobiographical" account of his capture and seduction by a gang of Caucasian lads, one of whom eventually killed himself in despairing love for the poet, "seems to provide highly significant markers in the construction of identity," as Makin has observed – yet what that identity *was* has not been the object of queer examination.[66]

More careful scrutiny of the "bisexuality" of figures like Sergei Esenin, Yar-Kravchenko, Kuzmin's long-term partner Yuri Yurkun, and the film director Sergei Paradzhanov, could introduce more complexity to our "gay" histories by considering the gender relations and unstable subjectivities that framed Russian and Soviet same-sex love. Recent work by sociologist Francesca Stella offers a more sophisticated approach to the complexity of the queer life that women lived in late-Soviet and post-Soviet Russia. Stella points to the fact of "parallel heterosexual [and homosexual] relationship[s]" in many of her respondents' Soviet-era biographies. Noting the strategies for concealment and disclosure these women adopted, she questions whether the Western assumption that "coming out" and speaking honestly about her subjects' sexuality is the only pathway in contemporary Russia to a securely and authentically lived life. She asks whether Soviet and Russian "modernity" has to be measured against Western judgments about "the closet" and the supposed "false consciousness" that it embodies.[67] In his currently in-progress doctoral research, French historian Arthur Clech is taking a similarly skeptical, de-familiarizing approach to the lives of late-Soviet men who had sex with men.[68] We could do a better job of trying to listen to our subjects in the past for what they say about themselves, rather than hoping to hear what we would like them to say about us.

Reclaiming Russian LGBT lives

"They have taken away our lives, and we have paid for the loss," concludes Robert K. Martin in his essay on "reclaiming our lives." He was commenting in 1980 on a set of Anglo-American intellectual and scholarly practices that evolved organically over many years to yield the "heteronormative voice" in biography. What Russian scholars and LGBT activists confront today is more calculated, novel, and blunt. The Kremlin's official homophobia, with its assault against *knowledge* of same-sex love and queer genders, is a critical problem facing those who would write queer biographies of Russians. The country's internet regulator Roskomnadzor has recently commissioned a report by psychologists that, among other things, proposes to censor lists of famous "gays and lesbians" of the past and present, found on LGBT websites: they could harm the child's developing sexual psychology by conveying the impression that homosexuality is a positive attribute.[69] In the wake of the anti-propaganda law, gay activists in Arkhangelsk and other cities have been arrested and fined merely for holding signs with lists of well-known Russian queer historical figures: Tchaikovsky, Kliuev, Kozin, and Kuzmin among them. Of course, the weapons of gay pride will only get you so far. As one U.S. activist recently commented at a conference on "gay shame," "shame isn't the problem: homophobia is.... [L]ooking on the bright side is only effective up to a point: it can't replace the work of making sure that there is, in fact, a brighter side to look on."[70] Queer biography is not a panacea to stem the tide of homophobia in Russia. Nevertheless, in a cultural war over the production of queer knowledge, it has already been identified as a weapon – by the enemies of queer freedom.

Whatever the recent political developments, the task of reclaiming Russian queer lives requires not just a fight with novel and sinister state initiatives. It also demands a confrontation with conventional scholarly and cultural practices. Well before the state Duma began to discuss the new, homophobic information regime in 2013, well-established intellectual habits did much to "take away" Russian queer lives. Falsification, evasion, silence, trivialization, mistranslation, contempt, voyeurism: the spectrum of strategies that have been used to construct the "heteronormative voice" in biographies of Russian lesbian, gay, bisexual, and transgender subjects did not come from politicians; these strategies came from literary and cultural scholars, from historians and archivists, from literary executors and translators. Michael Makin, one Western scholar who has thought carefully about this problem, sums it up very clearly: "Many Russians would respond with surprise or even distress to the suggestion that a person's sexuality and sexual preferences might be an integral part of an identity accessible to public discussion, and even more so to the suggestion that such matters might be directly or indirectly related to the creative impulse and its realization in works of art."[71] This assessment, published in 2010, significantly predates the Putinist "homosexual propaganda" debate and reflects Makin's long engagement with Kliuev scholars in the Russian Federation. Brian Baer's work on the queer politics of translation, and Kevin Moss's on the cultural politics of queerness in Russian film, echo these sentiments. A "universalist conception of Russianness" or "Russian cultural citizenship" prevails among intellectuals, who find the idea of a separate community identified by sexual orientation threatening and perplexing.[72] Here is the liberal critic Mikhail Zolotonosov commenting, in the country's most authoritative cultural journal, on a rare attempt to compose a "gay folklore" of St. Petersburg, K. K. Rotikov's *The Other Petersburg* (1998):

> There is no such thing as homosexual literature, neither fiction nor folklore, nor any other type, and there cannot be . . . Homosexuality as a form of sexual life, as an ethos (based on play, in which men play roles of active and passive), as a psychology — that exists. But there are no means available for the construction of some particular literary form on the part of homosexual authors. There are particular thematic concerns, but no special literature or culture as a whole.[73]

On such foundations is the intellectual case for homophobia built.

And finally, as queer scholars of Russia, we need to seek more than a recuperative "truth" about the biographical subject as "gay," "lesbian," or "bisexual." Our questions need updating, our methods need queering, our frames of reference need greater sophistication. It is not simply enough to "tick the box" of homosexuality in the subject's life story, and feel that the issue of sexual identity has been addressed satisfactorily. We need to ask more searching questions about the nature of same-sex love and same-sex consciousness shared by the Russian and Soviet subjects we investigate. Such investigations need to attend carefully to the heterosexual impulses and experiences, and the gender relations that these subjects constructed for themselves. A more profound understanding of queer subjectivities in Russian and Soviet history should also lead us to a richer, more complexly queer analysis of same-sex oriented art, literature, and culture in Russia. As well, it would begin the project of destabilizing and undermining fixed notions of a "traditional" heterosexuality – an invented tradition, now utterly politicized – in Russian history and culture.

9

On the Boulevards of Magadan:

Historical Time, Geopolitics, and Queer Memory in Homophobic Russia

Magadan is about as far from continental Europe as you can get on the Eurasian landmass and still be somewhere notionally thought of as "European." It lies on Russia's northern Pacific coast. It is eight time zones from Moscow, and from the Russian capital, passengers in modern Boeings can fly non-stop for eight hours to arrive on the cracked and windswept concrete runway of its "Sokol" airport. In Stalin's time, Gulag prisoners took months to get there by a combination of Trans-Siberian rail transport, the Vanino Port Transit Camp, and a treacherous sea passage; Stalin forbade even the imagining of a direct rail link. The city was founded in 1931 as the gateway to the Gulag's Kolyma River gold mines, the "profitable" jewel in the secret police economic empire. Almost 900,000 prisoners were shipped here between 1932 and 1956, and over 127,000 of them died in custody, according to official records.[1]

Magadan today is a city of 95,000 residents, the descendants of prisoners, plus the children and grandchildren of "free" Soviet citizens who moved there in the 1960s and 1970s, when "normalization" transformed the capital of a prison empire into a "company town" paying generous salaries and benefits to draw labor from the "mainland" of European Russia and Siberia. If the population of Magadan has dropped slightly from the late Soviet years, it remains a going concern after capitalist transition: gold has not gone out of fashion. Inhabitants still enjoy the enhanced benefits (higher salaries, earlier retirement) associated with working in the Russian Far North. While the shopping and dining opportunities are rudimentary, and the finest hotel in town has the hardest beds I have ever encountered, its residents are welcoming and its library, regional museum, provincial archive, and other cultural facilities are impressive for such a remote place. A new Orthodox cathedral, a stand-out anachronism in a city born in the era of Communist atheism, rises on the main square in place of the usual statue of Lenin. There is a hardy sense of local pride: "Magadan is, was, and will be!" declared a 2009 billboard sponsored by the city government. Another billboard, showing a pair of newlyweds (heterosexual, of course), claims that "Magadan is the city of our hopes." Indeed, the place feels like a young person's town, with energetic men and women piling up cash, looking perhaps to early retirement to the "mainland" in a sunnier climate, and living life to the hilt in the meantime. Kseniya Melnik's stories of the city and its schemers and dreamers ring true.[2]

In 2013, the city erected a monument to its most famous artist, the singer-songwriter, and Gulag queer, Vadim Kozin (see Figure 9.1). The bronze sculpture is located in a small square on Karl Marx (formerly Joseph Stalin) Street, in the heart of the city next to the apartment-museum where the singer lived until his death in 1994. It presents us with a life-size figure of Kozin dressed in a winter coat and traditional Russian long felt boots, sitting on a park bench, one of his beloved cats on his lap. A music portfolio by his side on the bench bears the inscription "Singer and Composer Vadim Kozin."[3] Kozin of course became a Magadan "resident" involuntarily in 1945 when he was convicted for sodomy and anti-Soviet agitation, deported from Moscow, and sent to serve his sentence in the Kolyma camps. Mainstream Russian

FIGURE 9.1 *Monument to Vadim Kozin, Magadan.*

media "sanitized" his biography (described in Chapter 3), ignoring the singer's sexuality and the reason for his persecution when they reported the inauguration of his memorial: for websites as diverse as the news agency RIA Novosti and the principal Vadim Kozin fan site, his sexual orientation and the state persecution he suffered for it was irrelevant.[4] An unusual example of candor about the reason for the singer's convictions came from Aleksandr Krylov, a photo-blogger and former member of the Magadan Provincial legislature's "Chamber of Youth" (a civil society conduit for future politicians and business leaders); Krylov's blog explains how the singer arrived in Magadan as a result of his conviction for sodomy, and he praises Kozin's artistic independence and creativity.[5]

The irony of this event was not lost on LGBT activists in Russia. Magadan Province was one of the early adopters of the "gay propaganda" local ordinances that proliferated across Russia in 2012. Gayrussia's news page noted, "In gay propaganda-banning Magadan, a monument to Soviet gay singer Vadim Kozin has been unveiled." Despite the law against propaganda for homosexuality, the site continued, both the mayor and deputy mayor led the festivities and cited the historical significance of Kozin for Magadan.[6] While ignoring the singer's homosexual "sins," he is viewed as an important symbol for the city; and his museum reportedly attracts 4000 visitors each year.

British readers familiar with the bronze monument in Manchester, England, to Second World War codebreaker, mathematician, and "gay icon" Alan Turing might see many uncanny parallels and some wide distinctions with the Kozin sculpture on the other side of Eurasia. Unveiled in 2001, the Turing memorial also depicts its subject seated on a park bench, surrounded by tokens of his career (see Figure 9.2). A plaque defines him as "Father of Computer Science, Mathematician, Logician, Wartime Codebreaker, Victim of Prejudice." He holds an apple, symbol of his reputed suicide: in 1954, two years after his conviction for homosexual offenses, he is thought to have injected an apple with cyanide and consumed half of it. The memorial in Manchester is located between the city's "gay village," and the university where Turing worked, and it is often seen garlanded with flowers during LGBT Pride celebrations.

The most striking difference between the two memorials is the candor with which Turing's site of memory explicitly appeals to at least two "remembering collectives": the public interested in the war and science on the one hand, and the LGBT community on the other.[7] Turing's wartime codebreaking feats, of major significance for Allied victory, were secret at the time and long after, and were brought to public attention when gay activist and mathematician Andrew Hodges began work on his definitive biography in the 1970s; his book appeared in 1983. Hodges also exposed the injustice of Turing's prosecution and framed his presumed suicide as a martyrdom to the homophobic prejudice of that age.[8] Such has been the impact of Hodges' biography and subsequent popularization of the Turing story on stage and

FIGURE 9.2 *Monument to Alan Turing, Manchester.*

screen that the mathematician received a posthumous Royal Pardon in 2013. "Rehabilitation" by the British state has come as a result not simply because his original crime is now regarded differently: his story fits into a contemporary national narrative of the Second World War in which an increasing number of social, ethnic, and institutional groups, even unrecognized ones of the era, are accorded acknowledgment for service.[9] Turing's "rehabilitation" complements Britain's self-image as inclusive, tolerant, and forgiving.

The contrasts with Kozin's monument and the approach to his commemoration could not be starker. As we shall see, the singer's memory is caught between Russian culture's resistance to the visibility of the queer, and the same culture's ambivalence about Stalinist violence and its commemoration. The sculpture to the singer in Magadan makes no reference to his persecution – far harsher than Turing's – and the laconic inscriptions mention only his public career. His contributions to culture before and during the war – less weighty than Turing's in his field, but still of Russian national importance – are virtually the sole focus of public memory about him. As I explained in Chapter 8, his biographer, Boris Savchenko, has told the story of Kozin's persecution for homosexual offenses without empathy, using the "heteronormative voice" common to Russian life writing, which continues to resist overt acknowledgment of the non-normative sexuality of the biographical subject. Only one "remembering collective" was allowed to speak at the unveiling ceremony. Mainstream music fans and city officials have monopolized Kozin's commemoration and sanitized it, both as it is reflected in the singer's memorial sculpture, and in the museum devoted to his life in Magadan.[10]

My juxtaposition of these two memorials and their two worlds – Manchester and Magadan, Russia and "Europe" – is deliberate. The presumptions implied by the juxtaposition, that Russia is "backward," not adequately "European," that it is lagging behind in recognizing its LGBT people as full citizens, are verdicts that deserve greater scrutiny. They are commonplaces that shape our understanding of gender and sexual politics in Russia today. Here I want to reflect on the historical temporalities and contemporary geopolitics that shape our assumptions about "Europe" and LGBT "progress." Post-colonial and queer theorists, historians, and political scientists have valuable insights that can be applied to the unique position of Russia, simultaneously part of Europe but also on the global "periphery." Progress in LGBT rights has no obvious technocratic formula or roadmaps. We can refer to Western historical experience in LGBT emancipation when considering other regions, but our own histories cannot dictate pathways to progress elsewhere. One feature of Western experience – encapsulated in the Turing memorial, and absent in Kozin's monument – is the long development, and strategic mobilization by Western LGBT communities, of a "usable past."[11] A consideration of queer memory studies, an emerging field of scholarship, can also assist us in thinking about LGBT political strategies for building community and combating homophobia that might fit in post-Soviet contexts. How Russians will fight homophobia, and what a post-homophobic Russia might look like, are matters for Russians to decide, not for outsiders to dictate. Nevertheless, outsiders can comment and reflect on these issues – the purpose of this chapter and this book.

Time, geopolitics, and LGBT progress

Juxtapositions of geography – Magadan versus Manchester, Russia versus Europe – imply in our imaginations gaps in historical time. In *Provincializing Europe*, Dipesh Chakrabarty describes how the coming of "'political modernity' – namely the rule by modern institutions of the state, bureaucracy, and capitalist enterprise" to non-European societies initiates of a process that implants European enlightenment values and engenders a contestation about their adaptation to the new society.[12] Progressive modernization in history, whether told by liberals or Marxists, dictated a story that ran "first Europe, then elsewhere," that put some societies in the vanguard of "historical time," conceived as a story of the inexorable Europeanization of the globe, while others languished in "history's waiting room," "not yet" ready to be modern.[13] Russia, part of an imaginary "Orientalized" Eastern Europe, sits somewhere between the "metropole/peripheral colony" dichotomy of Chakrabarty's post-colonial scheme; one might revise it as "first Europe, then Russia, then elsewhere."[14] As I explained in the Preface, Russia's relationship to the idea of "Europe" and to processes of "Europeanization," has been, since the eighteenth century especially, one of reflexive contestation and adaptation, of successful attempts and tragic failures "to overtake and surpass" Europe, and moments of rejection of "European" ideas as unsuitable to Eurasian conditions. Historical time, measured in Chakrabarty's terms of "achieving" European-style modernization, always seemed slow in Russia, or if it was accelerated (as one might argue it was "from above" under Stalin), the lunge was too exhausting to be sustained.[15] The imperial and then Soviet state differed in character and structure from the European ideal of the nation-state so significantly that power, as expressed in successive Russian and Soviet gender and sexual orders, flowed in distinctive channels and left distinctive legacies in its wake.

In the contemporary period, after the collapse of Communism and the Soviet Union in 1991, with the depredations of the hasty transition to capitalist markets, and the weakening of the state in the 1990s, Russia's sense of its geopolitical position has taken a beating. So too has the timeline of history as moving toward "Europeanization." The post–1991 notions of a "transition" to a known "European" destination – a civil society, a "normal" market, the rule of law – no longer apply so optimistically. And it appears that any transition to a presumed "liberal" gender order recognizably like those in the West is currently off the table.[16] (Moreover, in the 1990s with the diffusion of LGBT rights including hate crime protections and civil partnership or equal marriage, the Western, liberal gender order that post-Communist societies were supposedly modeling themselves after was changing radically. Russians pursuing "transition" in this area were chasing a moving target in the 1990s.) No longer a superpower in a bipolar Cold War world, promoting its own ossified Marxist gender politics, the Russian state in the twenty-first century now seeks a place in a multipolar world where it argues for a unique geopolitical status and credentials as part of a revised international order. In this context, as I explained in the Introduction, the Kremlin has mobilized gender and sexual politics in a conservative-modern direction, domestically and internationally.

The Russian authorities have taken an ambivalent line on the relationship between LGBT rights as a feature of "European" values. The dominant tone of government-controlled television commentary was, crudely put, that Russia is not part of a U.S.-dominated "Europe" (often reduced to the EU), but as a nation it is exceptional, with its own "traditions." Extended LGBT rights are follies of European origin, and do not belong in Russia.[17] A more sophisticated tone is taken, occasionally, by President Putin in his discussions of the country's European vocation. With its defense of "traditional values," Russia is reminding Europe of its core values, "including the Christian values that constitute the basis for Western civilization," values that Europe has supposedly forgotten.[18] Such comments find appreciative audiences among far-right sympathizers in European publics. Ultimately, the Kremlin's destination with these initiatives remains unknown, and the capacity of the government of Russia, even in partnership with the Russian Orthodox Church and other faith communities, to dictate matters like family size and character, sexual behavior, and social identities inside its own borders is limited at best. Society, in other words, will contest, reject, and adapt to official policies. Whether Russia can dictate such matters beyond its borders is also not clear.

The geopolitical dimension of Putin's gay propaganda law cannot be ignored, even if the results of this apparent attempt at "soft power" projection have largely stalled or failed.[19] Politicians friendly to Russia in former Soviet republics, the "near abroad" of Eurasia, have harnessed the Kremlin's gender politics to promote "gay propaganda" laws protecting minors from LGBT-neutral or positive information. The result is a regional version of anti-homonationalism, a refusal of the EU's and the West's supposed promotion of the virtues of their human rights regimes for LGBT citizens. These contests play out in a context of geopolitical jostling for influence over the region between Russia (promoting a "Eurasian Economic Union" economic space, the EEU); and the European Union (through its European Neighborhood Policy), which sharpened drastically after the Ukrainian crisis of 2014. Draft bills have been proposed to legislatures in Ukraine (2012), Armenia (2013), and Kazakhstan (2015). All of these were withdrawn, on different grounds. Currently Belarus and Kyrgyzstan have draft laws under consideration. The legislatures of Latvia and Lithuania, countries in the European Union, have dallied with similar laws, a signal that EU membership is no inoculation against the Kremlin's political homophobia and that its "soft power" projects are not confined, necessarily, to the countries of the former Soviet Union that remain unaffiliated with the EU or EEU.[20]

Russia, then, is no longer sitting patiently in "history's waiting room," if it ever was. What is more, the story line that dictates "first Europe, [then Russia], then elsewhere" has been challenged by the Kremlin and that challenge strikes a deep chord in Russian society. The presumption based on the Eurocentric story line, found in Western reactions to Russia's official homophobia, that progress toward full LGBT citizenship is inevitable and that it is clearly mapped by Western examples and playbooks, must be tempered with humility, and a deeper understanding of the societies under consideration. In this spirit, how might LGBT communities in Russia speak to their "mainstream" and what strategies can they use to expand the realm of tolerance and acceptance in their society? One strategy involves the mobilization of queer memory to challenge conventional, heteronormative, histories of Russia's "traditional sexual relations."

Archives, histories, and insurgent projects of queer memory

The two memorials to Kozin and Turing resonate with very different public values, expressive of very different geopolitical and historical reference points. If the Turing memorial writes the "gay" mathematician into the core national myth of modern Britain – victory in the Second World War – the Kozin sculpture alludes strongly to one of the central stories of the Soviet twentieth century: the violence inflicted on the people by Stalin's dictatorship. The Russian mainstream's resistance to recognition of the queer dimensions of Kozin's persecution presents Russian LGBT activists with a problem. In the commemorative practices surrounding Vadim Kozin, the politics of the collective memory of Stalinist terror collides with the politics of queer visibility and citizenship in contemporary Russia. This collision of two political realms prompts the question: can queer victims ever join the Russian pantheon of martyrs to Stalinist terror?[21] This prompts another: who are these "martyrs" and how are we to identify them?

For those who do not specialize in Russian studies, it may seem surprising that the Russians still do not agree about what happened to them under Soviet rule and how they should remember it. After all, Stalin died almost a lifetime ago and successive political rulers and a regime change in 1991 have offered ample opportunities for reconsidering the impact of Soviet terror, with new and richer sources from the state's archives. As well, since Stalin's death, educators, museum curators, cultural authorities, and politicians have sought to recast the story of violent modernization under Stalin (or, under Lenin and Stalin, or, under the Communist Party and Soviet system) to explain to subsequent generations how to think about this tragic and brutal past.[22] Yet there remains no consensus, no settled or official view on these events, and instead there is a considerable degree of confusion, dispute, and politicization of the memory of state violence. Despite what some historians seem to assume, Germany's successful "coming to terms" with the Nazi past and the Holocaust does not supply a readily transferable roadmap to "mature understanding" of a violent past; there were too many differences between the Nazi regime and the Soviet one.[23]

Many observers agree that in Russia, the uncertainties of the politics of memory of the Soviet terror flow from the extremely diffuse and varied nature of state violence: no single nation or ethnicity, no clearly demarcated social group stands out as the only suffering community. In Russia, victimhood is not the preserve of any one easily defined group. Moreover, perpetrator- and victim-status are intertwined in many individual biographies; few occupy the moral high ground.[24] Since 1991, in Alexander Etkind's view remembering has become a process of identity formation: "a struggle between myriads of collective subjects, who constructed themselves according to a variety of principles, from the ethnic to the political to the generational to the memorial."[25] Russia's LGBT activists are also one of these new "collective subjects" constituting themselves in part via the commemoration of Soviet oppression, but cultural resistance to the queer impedes mainstream recognition of this claim to victim-status in the national narrative of Communist violence.

Integrating LGBT victims into mainstream narratives of Stalinist or Soviet oppression was not automatic after Stalin's anti-sodomy law was rescinded in

1993. As I have explained in Chapter 7, the state has not fully released the documentary record of the repression of gay men under that law, and conventions of historical work in Russia block queerer understandings of the effects of the Stalin law. LGBT communities in the present are not able to draw upon the full range of biographies of the oppressed; as Chapter 8 showed, life-stories of gay and lesbian Russians remain obscured by the same historical and cultural conventions. The country's democrats in the 1980s and 1990s, and today's democratic opposition, did not automatically question the "everyday homophobia" bequeathed to them from Stalinism and late-Soviet dissident memoir literature; instead, at least until 2013, they continued to regard their LGBT fellow citizens "with a shade of disgust."[26] The Kremlin's more aggressive recent gender politics have shifted attitudes among at least some of its opponents. Signs are that the country's most important civil-society organization devoted to commemoration of the victims of Soviet oppression, the Memorial Society, increasingly understands the link between homophobia and other forms of political violence. Memorial has held occasional seminars devoted to exploring the repression of gay male and lesbian citizens under the Soviet system; in April 2016 it hosted a seminar on new research conducted by feminist historian Irina Roldugina in the St. Petersburg archives of the FSB (the secret police).[27] The 2013 "gay propaganda" law appears to have cemented a connection for some in the "mainstream" democratic movement between sexual oppression and other forms of political oppression.

Western queer theorists and historians have recently explored the problems of cultural resistance to the queer in public memory; these queer scholars have been affected by the turn in the humanities to the study of memory, commemoration, trauma, and the limits of historical practice.[28] While much of this work concentrates on concerns that preoccupy queer communities of the United States – the AIDS crisis of the 1980s–90s; traumas of violence based on race and sexuality – insights from this scholarship can suggest some opportunities available to LGBT Russians engaged in building communities and forging alliances through memory work. At stake in U.S. theoretical debates are several relevant issues: how to do the history of homosexuality? Is the "discipline" of history too "straight" to accommodate queer pasts? Is there such a thing as queer time and how does it differ from "straight time"? Are the archives (of governments, public bodies, and private collections) reliable enough resources for the re-construction of a usable past? Is queer memory, shaped by queers and by present-day concerns, of more value to "remembering collectives" than traditional history?

Twenty years ago Lisa Duggan challenged LGBT scholars to relax their disciplinary boundaries and some of the methodological constraints that bolster them. Historians, she claimed, ought to think less rigidly about the queer past, and queer theorists, most of them scholars of literature and culture, ought not to be so quick to dismiss history and its possibilities.[29] Other critics agreed. Conventional "lesbian and gay" historical work of the 1970s and 1980s, conforming to the rigors of the influential trend of social history, and trying to document "the real," had done much to recuperate and restore past lives, and in the process build communities. But the discipline's empiricism, and its alleged default setting to narratives of progress, were said by queer theorists to have constrained the imagination and limited affective connections with the past.[30] As well, professional gay and lesbian historians' reliance on what Duggan terms a "stunted archive," one that queer historians complained was created and policed by a heteronormative world, confined us to a history written in that world's terms.[31] Professional historical caution about anachronism, about reading the past through presentist lenses alone, and distorting or misreading past lives in the pursuit of identification with "sisters and brothers" in the queer past, came under new critical scrutiny too. As David Halperin admitted, "Identification [with same-sex relations found in the past] gets at something, something important: it picks out resemblances, connections, echo effects."[32] Careful identification across time, "strategic anachronism," challenges "straight" narratives that regulate temporality (as in "gay is just a phase you are going through" or "first Europe, then elsewhere") and offers the prospect of a richer understanding of the queer predicament in the straight world.[33]

Queer theorists thinking critically about LGBT history, and queer memory work, have drawn on this sensibility to propose new means of public commemoration. Work that relies upon a more relaxed approach to the rigors of professional historical writing might offer alternative ways of understanding, of "coming to terms," with pasts scarred by homophobia-induced trauma and damage. Memory work might be archive-creating, artistic, popular, and documentary about the past, without necessarily being professionally "historical."[34] "Insurgent commemoration" can contest conventional and mainstream public memory and makes possible new ways of articulating political projects for queer communities.[35]

How have Russian LGBT communities worked with archives, history and commemoration to bind themselves together and to write themselves into the national past? The first point to make is that conventional historical work is far from exhausted as a method in Russia. "History" remains a powerful tool for persuading both queer communities and a wider public schooled, for better or worse, in respect for the discipline as an objective social "science." This impulse is not merely following a Western playbook. Recall that in the 1980s–90s, LGBT Russians turned enthusiastically to the preservation, re-construction, and remembering of their queer pasts almost the moment the opportunity appeared as the country democratized. Soviet lesbian and gay voices were "Made in the USSR," not imported from the USA and Europe (as discussed in Chapters 4 and 5). There is still a lot of historical reconstruction and recovery work to be done to write the history of queer experience in Russia and the USSR. Yet the persistence of the "stunted archive" and the heteronormative voice in interpretation of its contents remains, as I have described in Chapters 7 and 8. The heteronormative atmosphere of Russia's state-run archives is another deterrent to deeper research; no one in the archival system advocates for LGBT materials, researchers, or approaches. As well, there are huge costs to the careers of researchers wishing to write LGBT histories in the Russian academic sector, and since the 2013 "gay propaganda" law the costs have only escalated.

Let us focus on archives. One of Russia's longest lasting LGBT institutions is the Moscow Archive of Lesbians and Gays, curated by retired French literature specialist Elena Gusiatinskaya. It originated not long following Yeltsin's 1993 decriminalization of sodomy: it seemed vital to Gusiatinskaya and her colleague, information scientist Viktor Oboin, to gather systematically the growing flood of discussion about queer subjects in mainstream newspapers and magazines, supplemented with the outpouring of Russian gay and lesbian publications.[36] They also assembled a collection of LGBT literature, both Russian-language works, and international works in Russian translation, as the flow of these publications burgeoned during the 1990s. Additionally, Oboin collected the correspondence and ephemeral documentation of Russia's gay and lesbian organizations, and published a newsletter, *Zerkalo* (The Mirror).[37] The Archive's impact has arguably been strongest in community-building, conscious-raising, and forging literary projects. Opening most Thursday nights in a private flat, it created a friendly, welcoming, and intellectually free space for reading, thinking, and writing about LGBT experience. Particularly significant have been the lesbian literary projects that emerged from the groups of women who gathered there, including the magazine *Ostrov* (Island) and an anthology of lesbian prose.[38]

Critically important for the future of the queer past in Russia is the extensive archive of publications produced by gay and lesbian authors, editors, and organizations in the democratic interval of the 1990s. Many of these publications have been digitized by the Moscow Archive of Lesbians and Gays, to be preserved for the future and made accessible to a wide readership inside and beyond Russia. The last decade of the twentieth century presents a window after Communist persecution, but before the digital revolution of the 2000s, when print publications helped to build a Russian LGBT community. Gay and lesbian magazines, newspapers, leaflets and erotic albums allowed Russians the first chance since 1917 to speak for themselves, and leave physical traces of their voices. These were not just Moscow voices (discussed in Chapter 4) but periodicals from activists and organizations in provincial towns of European Russia and Siberia: Barnaul's *Sibirskii variant* (Siberian Version; 1992); Nizhnii Tagil's *Gei-dialog* (Gay Dialogue, 1993–6); Tver's *Spektral* (Spectral, 1993–4), and many others.[39] In these short-lived magazines and newsletters gay men and lesbians reflected on the nature of homosexuality; called upon the government to repeal the ban on male homosexuality, and improve AIDS-prevention work; discussed the history, literature, and culture of same-sex love in Russian and world history; and talked about the challenges of organizing locally. The fate of ex-prisoners convicted under the anti-sodomy law was a preoccupation of Valery Klimov, publisher of *Gei-dialog* and organizer of a gay men's group in the Urals region. These publications, especially those from the provinces, remain an untapped archive of freedom that has the potential to illustrate how in an unfettered information regime, LGBT Russians raised their own voices and identified their own priorities with little Western influence and relying solely on their own resources. They also demonstrate that the "first generation" of post-Soviet gay and lesbian activists valued their history and thought legitimation as a community through the "recovery" or the "creation" of a shared past was an important goal.

More recent Russian attempts to mobilize a "usable past" as memory in queer communities have seen historians, still adhering to recognizably "historical" disciplinary forms, working in partnership with activists. To mark the twentieth anniversary of the decriminalization of male homosexuality, feminist historians Irina Roldugina and Nadia Plungian produced an outstanding booklet published for Kvirfest 2013, a celebration of queer arts in St. Petersburg, organized by *Vykhod* (Coming Out), the city's principal LGBT organization.[40] The purpose of the lavishly illustrated forty-page booklet and the exhibition that accompanied it was to describe:

> ... the history of LGBT in Russia and the USSR: from medicalization and social exclusion, to the formation of subcultures and the struggle for political rights. [. . .] The movement for the rights of sexual minorities in our country, [. . .] was assisted by the gradual rise in interest in the history of LGBT in Russia and the USSR and the appearance of publications on the topic. [. . .] Although this publication is popular rather than scholarly in character, we hope that it will become part of the movement to include queer-problematics in the field of historical knowledge.[41]

Here we see that the power of "History" to mobilize the LGBT community is invoked, while at the same time the authors aspire to speak to wider audiences ("to include queer-problematics") and transform their discipline. This is not the only such collaboration between historians and activists, and the digital world, despite the limits Russian authorities attempt to place on it, remains one of the key sites where LGBT histories will continue to be told, for example on the website "*Deti–404*" (Children–404) aimed at LGBT children, with its pages and video clips offering queer histories.[42]

One of the most exciting recent attempts to construct a queer archive that I have witnessed in the region comes not from Russia but its "totalitarian" partner in the EEU, Belarus. This queer archive broke with rigorous historical practice to capture something less concrete but not less "real" for its affective and provocative impacts. In May 2015 to mark the International Day Against Homophobia, Trans- and Biphobia, queer artists in Minsk staged an art project entitled "*My est*'" (We exist) that featured an "Unstraight Museum." Visitors were invited to donate objects they considered "unstraight" to the exhibition, and to explain their choices. The exhibits ranged from posters for a rare Gay Pride celebration in 2001 in

Minsk, to a Michael Jackson fridge magnet, queer comics and books, photographs of friends, and old gay magazines. Alongside these "artefacts," paintings, photographs and art objects created by queer artists presented another take on the dilemmas of unstraightness.

The mood in the hall at the opening party combined a giddy sense of youthful freedom, undercut at the same time with Belarusian modesty and a nervous sense of the ephemeral possibilities of a fleeting "liberal" political moment. (Approaching national elections, and the state's uncertain reaction to the Ukrainian crisis, opened this "liberal" moment of the dictatorship's turn toward "Europe," but there was no faith that it would last among the LGBT activists I spoke to.) The historical possibilities of the "Unstraight Museum" were foreseen by exhibition curator Darya Traiden, who wrote,

> Others are those who are not described in the normative framework, who cannot feel their existence, who are absent in space, time, history, culture. And today they say, "We exist." This exhibition in honor of the Day Against Homophobia and Transphobia, is an attempt to re-think our discursive practices and to escape from the verbal into the language of images, impressions, and feeling. We exist via our relationship to the world. We exist via our thoughts and creativity. We even exist via attempts to deny us.[43]

For Traiden, queer existence as history cannot simply be told within the "normative framework" because queers are excluded from it. Instead "images, impressions, and feeling" offer channels for the expression of histories of desire. In this event some of the intuitions of queer theory – that historical methods constrain memory, that normative "time" does not recognize queer existence, and that self-constructed archives are more meaningful – are at the heart of a community's attempt to re-constitute itself.

At the same time, Belarusian LGBT activists also rely on more familiar techniques of story-telling and historical commemoration to bring queers together and to communicate with the wider world. "Makeout" is a collective cultural initiative that screens films, offers anti-homophobia training sessions, and runs a web portal for news, events and history.[44] Makeout's "*Retra*" (Retro) webpages offer interviews with earlier generations of LGBT activists recalling Minsk Pride parades in the 1990s; a story about how the Belarusian mainstream press dealt with LGBT teens' letters in the same period; younger queers reminiscing about "The Balcony," a rooftop gathering space in Vitebsk, and much more.[45]

What time is it in Russia?

In the recent debate over the status of LGBT citizenship in the Russian Federation, one extraordinary gesture of official homophobia (among the many) stands out for its invocation of "historical time." In spring 2012, the city council of Moscow decreed a ban on gay pride parades not just for the coming May, but for the next *one hundred* years. According to the resolution, no applications for pride-day marches will be considered until May 2112.[46] Behind this panicky measure lies nostalgia for the Soviet era when queer voices went unheard and when, conservatives claim, "traditional sexual relations" reigned unchallenged. The epic timescale that the city council imposed is a tragicomic echo of the millenarian aspirations of both Soviet Communism, which propounded the Marxist end of history in a communist utopia, and Russian Christianity, which once claimed that Moscow was the "third Rome," the final bastion of the faith after Constantinople (representing eastern Christianity) split with Rome's papal authority, and the subsequent fall of Constantinople to Islam. Both Christian and Marxist ideologies offered Russia's successive leaders powerful narratives of imperial exceptionalism. Perhaps Moscow's lawmakers thought that Russia was "not ready" for LGBT rights, but might be at some point long into the future. However they were acting, the appeal to "historical time" in their gesture was unmistakable.

What I have tried to show is that expectations regarding Russia should not be calibrated with a presumption of progress imagined as working toward some uncomplicated template of "European values." "Historical time," in other words, is not necessarily running to a European timetable in Russia or anywhere else for that matter, and while defending loudly the human rights of Russia's LGBT citizens, we would do well to reconsider presumptions of a "timetable" of "transition" for the Russians as they contend with modernity's challenges. We need to recall that "European" values, when it comes to LGBT rights – however we imagine them – were long in their historical development, are endlessly under construction, remain controversial even within the European Union, and are not set out on a technocrat's roadmap. One day, I very much hope the Russian state will drop its policies of official homophobia and reverse the damage it has created, if that is possible. What seems fairly certain is that when that day arrives, the Russian embrace of LGBT rights will be the result of cultural evolution from within society and not some off-the-peg downloading of a "European" formula.

Russia's LGBT citizens will continue to contend with their society's ideological resistance to queer visibility. In a cultural war over the production of queer knowledge, they are creating and exploring new ways to remain visible, unite their communities, and give hope and support to queer youth. This effort involves trying to work in all realms of knowledge production and distribution that are not currently blocked to them: academic life, publishing in books and articles, oppositional broadcast media, and especially the virtual world of social media. The porosity of the Russian-language information sphere gives reasons to be hopeful. The Russian-speaking world is far larger than the Kremlin-dominated Russian Federation alone, and in the "Russian world" many different knowledge regimes apply, as the examples even from "totalitarian" Belarus attest. In the geopolitical jostling for influence in the region "between" Russia and the EU, official homophobia as soft-power initiative has not proved as successful as the Kremlin probably hoped. Instead, an incitement to discourse, the public discussion and debate about the status of LGBT citizens across the region, has been launched. If fresh queer memory work is building the LGBT communities in the region by strengthening awareness of a common heritage, the new mainstream public debate about the status of queer citizens has the potential to work not only in negative directions but in positive ones as well.

The consequences of that stirring of national discussion cannot be predicted but the fact of these conversations has caused more people in these societies to think about, develop opinions on, and to argue about, LGBT lives and their value. More knowledge has been produced, and that has already altered the status of LGBT lives in the region: probably first for worse, but later, potentially, for better. What the proliferation of discussions about queer lives has also done is to widen the archive available for queer contention and mobilization. The endless stream of homophobia experienced by queer youth is documented online by *Deti–404*'s Letters pages. The "stunted archive" of official records is challenged by oppositional probing and discussion. New archives of trauma, memory, and resistance left in the trail of the 2013 "gay propaganda" debates online and in print media are potentially available to new generations of queer artists and activists. The Belarusian "Unstraight Museum" and "Makeout's" impressive online "Retro" pages offer exciting models for breaking the frustrating and repetitive cycle of generational rupture that structures queer knowledge transfer from older activists to younger ones. However brutal the official homophobia inside Russia, organizations like the Moscow Archive of Lesbians and Gays and St. Petersburg's Coming Out remain active, and they are redoubling their efforts to compile the archive and speak to power.

Official homophobia has made Russia queerer – not straighter. LGBT Russians will not magically evaporate from the population because of political homophobia. Intensify the pressure, and more LGBT citizens will conceal themselves in heterosexual marriages, with tragic consequences for some unwitting spouses and offspring. Drive queer citizens underground and some will most likely seek to emigrate; others will choose self-destructive behaviors (alcoholism, drug addiction, suicide) and still others will sublimate their desires and live in depression or more serious mental illness. Yet I believe that queer Russians will do more of what they are already now doing: arguing forcefully for the value and dignity of their lives and their families, and in the process creating space for themselves in society and culture in ways that the Kremlin, whoever may occupy it, will have to accommodate.

NOTES

Preface

1   Annette F. Timm, and Joshua A. Sanborn, *Gender, sex and the shaping of modern Europe: a history from the French Revolution to the present day* (London: Bloomsbury, 2016).

2   On the "burdens" of Russia's imperial project, see Alexander Etkind, *Internal colonization: Russia's imperial experience* (Cambridge: Polity, 2011).

3   Geoffrey Hosking, *Russia: people and empire, 1552–1917* (London: HarperCollins, 1997).

4   On homosocial space in pre-Petrine Russia, see Dan Healey, "Can We Queer Early Modern Russia?" in *Siting Queer Masculinities*, eds Katherine O'Donnell and Michael O'Rourke, (Basingstoke: Palgrave, 2005).

5   On Peter the Great's orders for mixed-sex socializing and the adoption of European marital norms, see Nancy Shields Kollmann, " 'What's Love Got to Do with It?': Changing Models of Masculinity in Muscovite and Petrine Russia," in *Russian Masculinities in History and Culture*, eds Barbara Evans Clements, Rebecca Friedman and Dan Healey (Basingstoke and New York: Palgrave, 2002).

6   Dan Healey, *Homosexual Desire in Revolutionary Russia: The Regulation of Sexual and Gender Dissent* (Chicago: University of Chicago Press, 2001), 78–81. For an excellent new analysis of pre-Petrine regulation of same-sex acts, see Marianna Muravyeva, "Personalising Homosexuality and Masculinity in Early Modern Russia," in *Gender in Late Medieval and Early Modern Europe*, eds Marianna Muravyeva and Raisa Maria Toivo (London: Routledge, 2012).

7   Healey, *Homosexual Desire in Revolutionary Russia*, 78–81. On Nicholas and masculine values, see Rebecca Friedman, *Masculinity, autocracy and the Russian university, 1804–1863* (Basingstoke: Palgrave Macmillan, 2005).

8   See David N. Collins, "Sexual imbalance in frontier communities: Siberia and New France to 1760," *Sibirica* 4, no. 2 (2004): 162–85; Alan Wood, "Sex and Violence in Siberia: Aspects of the Tsarist Exile System," in *Siberia: Two Historical Perspectives*, eds John Massey Steward and Alan Wood (London; Great Britain-USSR Association; School of Slavonic and East European Studies, 1984). On the administration of Siberian exile populations see Andrew A. Gentes, *Exile to Siberia, 1590–1822* (Basingstoke: Palgrave Macmillan, 2008); idem, *Exile, Murder and Madness in Siberia, 1823–61.* (Basingstoke: Palgrave Macmillan, 2010).

9   See Healey, *Homosexual Desire in Revolutionary Russia*, 78–79; idem, "Can
    We Queer Early Modern Russia?" Space – and a lack of research – does not
    permit an exploration of the attitudes toward homosexuality of other faiths
    of tsarist Russia: Islam, Judaism, Protestantism, Catholicism, Buddhism, and
    animism.

10 Healey, "Can We Queer Early Modern Russia?" 110–13.

11 Gregory Freeze, "Bringing Order to the Russian Family: Marriage and Divorce
    in Imperial Russia, 1760–1860," *Journal of Modern History* 62, no. 4 (1990):
    709–46.

12 Laura Engelstein, *The Keys to Happiness: Sex and the Search for Modernity in
    Fin-de-Siècle Russia* (Ithaca & London: Cornell University Press, 1992), 245.
    On pre-revolutionary theological ferment, see e.g., Vera Shevzov, *Russian
    Orthodoxy on the Eve of Revolution* (Oxford & New York : Oxford
    University Press, 2004); Stephanie Solywoda, "Internal Visions, External
    Changes: Russian Religious Philosophy, 1905–1940," D.Phil thesis, University
    of Oxford, 2014.

13 It is striking how infrequently Engelstein, *The Keys to Happiness,* refers to the
    Russian Orthodox Church as a participant in debates about sexual morality in
    late Imperial Russia.

14 On German churches' modernizing views, see Dagmar Herzog, *Sex after
    Fascism: Memory and Mortality in Twentieth-Century Germany* (Princeton &
    Oxford: Princeton University Press, 2005).

15 Orthodox theologians in exile developed an anti-Communist and to some
    extent anti-secularist theology: Christopher Stroop, "The Russian Origins of
    the So-Called Post-Secular Moment: Some Preliminary Observations," *State,
    Religion and Church* 1, no. 1 (2014): 59–82. On the Church after 1991, see
    John Gordon Garrard, and Carol Garrard, *Russian Orthodoxy Resurgent:
    Faith and Power in the New Russia* (Princeton & Oxford: Princeton University
    Press, 2008).

16 Wendy Z. Goldman, *Women, the State, and Revolution: Soviet Family Policy
    and Social Life* (Cambridge: Cambridge University Press, 1993).

17 Healey, *Homosexual Desire in Revolutionary Russia*, 223–27. See also the case
    of Anna Barkova discussed in Chapter 4.

18 Dan Healey, "The sexual revolution in the USSR: dynamic change beneath the
    ice," in *Sexual Revolutions*, eds Gert Hekma and Alain Giami (Basingstoke:
    Palgrave Macmillan, 2014).

19 Francesca Stella, *Lesbian Lives in Soviet and Post-Soviet Russia: Post/socialism
    and Gendered Sexualities* (Basingstoke: Palgrave Macmillan, 2015), 65.

20 Clech is working on a doctoral dissertation (EHESS, Paris) based on dozens of
    interviews with homosexually experienced men who came of age in the
    1960s–80s in the USSR.

21 On the new visibility of sexuality in the public sphere, see Eliot Borenstein,
    Overkill: Sex and Violence in Contemporary Russian Popular Culture (Ithaca:
    Cornell University Press, 2008); Brian James Baer, *Other Russias:
    Homosexuality and the Crisis of Post-Soviet Identity* (New York: Palgrave
    Macmillan, 2009).

Introduction: 2013 – Russia's Year of Political Homophobia

1   See http://ria.ru/incidents/20130513/937002026.html#ixzz2WkJ5gUm7 (accessed July 16, 2015).

2   In Russian, there are two translations for "homosexuality": *gomoseksualizm*, for which I use the somewhat archaic sounding "homosexualism," and the more neutral *gomoseksual'nost'*, which I render as "homosexuality." "Homosexualism" is regarded by Russia's LGBT community as a homophobic term, originating in medical and Stalinist political usage (although in fact its use in political contexts predates Stalin's rule). The form taking "-izm/ism" as its suffix is seen by some as reducing an individual's sexual orientation or personal identity to a mere ideology. (There is no analogous "heterosexualism" – *geteroseksualizm* – in the Russian language, only *geteroseksual'nost'*.) Russian jurisprudence and legislation routinely refer to "homosexualism" as do the state-controlled media.

3   One of the first to be fired for speaking out in support of LGBT rights was Il'ia Kolmanskii, a biology teacher in Moscow; he was fired just four days after the draft bill banning "propaganda for homosexualism" was given first reading in the Duma. See http://www.novayagazeta.ru/news/62543.html (accessed July 16, 2015).

4   See http://lenta.ru/articles/2013/05/23/volgograd (accessed July 16, 2015).

5   Russian law does not recognize hate crime against LGBT citizens as a protected social group. On silence as a deliberate judicial strategy against LGBT citizens' rights, see Alexander Kondakov, "Resisting the Silence: The Use of Tolerance and Equality Arguments by Gay and Lesbian Activist Groups in Russia," *Canadian Journal of Law and Society* 28, no. 3 (2013): 403–24. "Homosexual panic" is my paraphrase for Smolin's self-justification; on the "homosexual panic" defense in Soviet practice, see Chapter 2. For the sentences, see http://www.newizv.ru/accidents/2014–07–03/204166-koryst-vmesto-nenavisti.html (accessed July 16, 2015).

6   My discussion of the origins of the concept draws upon: Barry D. Adam, "Theorizing Homophobia," *Sexualities* 1, no. 4 (1998): 387–404; Daniel Borillo, *L'homophobie. Que sais-je?* (Paris: Presses Universitaires de France, 2000); Louis-Georges Tin, ed., *Dictionnaire de l'homophobie* (Paris: Presses Universitaires de France, 2003); Daniel Wickberg, "Homophobia: On the Cultural History of an Idea," *Critical Inquiry* 27, no. 1 (2000): 42–57.

7   Wickberg, "Homophobia," 47–52; Adam, "Theorizing Homophobia," 387–9.

8   See Michael J. Bosia, and Meredith L. Weiss, "Political Homophobia in Comparative Perspective," in *Global Homophobia: States, Movements, and the Politics of Oppression*, eds Michael J. Bosia and Meredith L. Weiss (Urbana, Chicago, Springfield: University of Illinois Press, 2014); on sexuality's changes in the globalization era, see Dennis Altman, "Sexuality and globalization," *Sexuality Research & Social Policy* 1, no. 1 (2004): 63–8.

9   The classic text is Jasbir K. Puar, *Terrorist Assemblages: Homonationalism in Queer Times* (Durham: Duke University Press, 2007); and see also Joseph Andoni Massad, *Desiring Arabs* (Chicago: University of Chicago Press, 2007).

10   Corinne Lennox, and Matthew Waites, "Human rights, sexual orientation and gender identity in the Commonwealth: from history and law to developing activism and transnational dialogues," in *Human Rights, Sexual Orientation and Gender Identity in the Commonwealth: Struggles for Decriminalisation and Change*, eds Corinne Lennox and Matthew Waites (London: Human Rights Consortium, Institute of Commonwealth Studies, 2013).

11   See Dagmar Herzog, "Hubris and Hypocrisy, Incitement and Disavowal: Sexuality and German Fascism," *Journal of the History of Sexuality* 11, no. 1/2 (2002): 3–21; idem, *Sex after Fascism: Memory and Mortality in Twentieth-Century Germany* (Princeton & Oxford: Princeton University Press, 2005); idem, *Sexuality in Europe: A Twentieth-century History* (Cambridge & New York: Cambridge University Press, 2011).

12   Herzog, *Sexuality in Europe*, 122–9.

13   Erik N. Jensen, "The Pink Triangle and Political Consciousness: Gays, Lesbians, and the Memory of Nazi Persecution," *Journal of the History of Sexuality* 11, no. 1/2 (2002): 321–32.

14   Ibid., 337–9.

15   Russia has long given off mixed messages about its European vocation. Russian President Vladimir Putin has trod an ambivalent line, emphasizing Russia's sovereignty and great power status while claiming to remain truer to Europe's fundamental values – usually characterized as "Christian"; see e.g. Roderic Lyne, "Russia's Changed Outlook on the West: From Convergence to Confrontation," in *The Russian Challenge*, eds Keir Giles, Philip Hanson, Roderic Lyne, James Nixey, James Sherr and Andrew Wood (London: Royal Institute of International Affairs, 2015).

16   See http://www.theguardian.com/world/2013/nov/15/life-as-out-gay-russia (accessed August 24, 2015).

17   Conor O'Dwyer, "Gay Rights and Political Homophobia in Postcommunist Europe: Is there an 'EU Effect'?" in *Global Homophobia: States, Movements, and the Politics of Oppression*, eds Meredith L. Weiss and Michael J. Bosia (Urbana, Chicago and Springfield: University of Illinois Press, 2013).

18   See e.g. Narcisz Fejes and Andrea P. Balogh, eds, *Queer visibility in post-socialist cultures* (Bristol: Intellect Books, 2013); Robert Kulpa and Joanna Mizielińska, eds, *De-centering Western Sexualities: Central and East European Perspectives* (Farnham: Ashgate, 2011); Roman Kuhar and Judit Takács, "Homophobia – a unifying experience?" *Druzboslovne razprave* 29, no. 73 (2013): 7–10.

19   The following paragraph builds on Altman, "Sexuality and globalization"; Bosia and Weiss, "Political Homophobia in Comparative Perspective"; Lennox and Waites. *Human rights, sexual orientation and gender identity in the Commonwealth*; Michelle Rivkin-Fish and Cassandra Hartblay, "When Global LGBTQ Advocacy Became Entangled with New Cold War Sentiment: A Call for Examining Russian Queer Experience," *Brown Journal of World Affairs* 21,

no. 1 (2014): 95–111; Ryan Thoreson, "From Child Protection to Children's Rights: Rethinking Homosexual Propaganda Bans in Human Rights Law," *Yale Law Review* 124, no. 4 (2015): 1327–44; Valerie Sperling, *Sex, Politics, and Putin: Political Legitimacy in Russia* (New York & Oxford: Oxford University Press, 2014).

20 An example of an entirely descriptive approach is Byrne Fone, *Homophobia: A History* (New York: Metropolitan Books, 2000).

21 Source: World Bank GDP Growth, http://data.worldbank.org/indicator/ NY.GDP.MKTP.KD.ZG?page=1 (accessed July 16, 2015).

22 The Putin political system is described in Alena V. Ledeneva, *Can Russia Modernise?: Sistema, Power Networks and Informal Governance* (Cambridge: Cambridge University Press, 2013). On media control and "imitation democracy" see Dmitrii Furman, *Dvizhenie po spirali. Politicheskaia sistema Rossii v riadu drugikh sistem* (Moscow: Ves' Mir, 2010), 101–16.

23 See https://www.youtube.com/watch?v=nS48UuVXbjQ (accessed July 17, 2015). For an argument that Putin has since achieved a "remasculinization" of the presidency, see Oleg Riabov and Tatiana Riabova, "The Remasculinization of Russia?" *Problems of Post-Communism* 61, no. 2 (2014): 23–35.

24 Vera Tolz, and Sue-Ann Harding, "From 'Compatriots' to 'Aliens': The Changing Coverage of Migration on Russian Television," *The Russian Review* 74, no. 3 (2015): 452–77.

25 See Cai Wilkinson, "Putting 'Traditional Values' Into Practice: The Rise and Contestation of Anti-Homopropaganda Laws in Russia," *Journal of Human Rights* 13, no. 3 (2014): 363–79; note also Gulnaz Sharafutdinova, "The Pussy Riot affair and Putin's démarche from sovereign democracy to sovereign morality," *Nationalities Papers* 42, no. 4 (2014): 615–21. The wider logic of the conservative turn is sketched in Marlene Laruelle, "Conservatism as the Kremlin's New Toolkit: an Ideology at the Lowest Cost," *Russian Analytical Digest* 138, no. 8 (2013): 2–4. On the Church in politics, see Irina Papkova, *The Orthodox Church and Russian Politics* (Washington: Woodrow Wilson Center Press; New York: Oxford University Press, 2011); John Gordon Garrard and Carol Garrard *Russian Orthodoxy Resurgent: Faith and Power in the New Russia* (Princeton & Oxford: Princeton University Press, 2008). On the exchange of political ideas between U.S. and Russian Christians, see e.g. John September Anderson, *Conservative Religious Politics in Russia and the United States: Dreaming of Christian Nations* (Abingdon & New York: Routledge, 2015); and http://www.thenation.com/article/how-us-evangelicals-fueled-rise-russias-pro-family-right (accessed September 3, 2015).

26 On Russia's sexual revolution of the 1990s, see Dan Healey, "The sexual revolution in the USSR: dynamic change beneath the ice," in *Sexual Revolutions*, eds Gert Hekma and Alain Giami (Basingstoke: Palgrave Macmillan, 2014). Homosexuality in culture, and as "foreign import" is analyzed in, e.g. Brian James Baer, "Now You See It: Gay (In)Visibility and the Performance of Post-Soviet Identity," in *Queer Visibility in Post-socialist Cultures*, eds Narcisz Fejes and Andrea P. Balogh (Bristol: Intellect, 2013); and Vitaly Chernetsky, *Mapping Postcommunist Cultures: Russia and Ukraine in the Context of Globalization* (Montreal & London: McGill-Queen's

University Press, 2007), 146–81. On Stalin's anti-sodomy law and the status of lesbianism in the Soviet Union, see Dan Healey, *Homosexual Desire in Revolutionary Russia: The Regulation of Sexual and Gender Dissent.* (Chicago: University of Chicago Press, 2001).

27 See http://www.guardian.co.uk/world/2007/may/28/russia.gayrights (accessed July 23, 2015); on the Moscow pride parade confrontations more generally, see Francesca Stella, "Queer Space, Pride, and Shame in Moscow," *Slavic Review* 72, no. 3 (2013): 458–80.

28 The early LGBT movement in post-Soviet Russia is described in Chapter 4. On this generation's visibility and public responses, see Baer, "Now You See It," 39–42.

29 I draw the distinction in directions of address in LGBT activism from Jensen, "The Pink Triangle and Political Consciousness," 326. On activist tactics, see e.g. Sergei Mozzhegorov, "'. . . Zabyt' Queer!' ili diskursy govoreniia/umolchaniia v deiatel'nosti LGBT-dvizheniia v sovremennoi Rossii," in *Vozmozhen-li "kvir" po-russki. LGBT-issledovaniia,* ed. Valerii Sozaev (St. Petersburg: LGBT Organizatsiia Vykhod, 2010); and also the essays in Svetlana Barsukova and Valerii Sozaev, eds, *LGBTK issledovaniia: aktual'nye problemy i perspektivy. Materialy mezhdunarodoi mezhditsitsiplinarnoi nauchno-prakticheskoi konferentsii posviashchennoi pamiati I. S. Kona. Sankt-Peterburg, 27–9 oktiabria 2011 g.* (St. Petersburg: LGBT Organizatsiia Vykhod, 2011).

30 Quoted in Bosia and Weiss, "Political Homophobia in Comparative Perspective," 4.

31 The UK law was repealed in 2000 in Scotland but not until 2003 in England and Wales; see Thoreson, "From Child Protection to Children's Rights."

32 See http://asozd2.duma.gov.ru/main.nsf/%28SpravkaNew%29?OpenAgent& RN=311625–4&02 (accessed August 3, 2015). Chuev was deputy chair of the Duma Committee on Social Associations and Religious Organizations; he was a member of Motherland Party and from 2006, A Just Russia Party. He lost his Duma seat in 2007 but remained associated with parliament as an advisor to the leader of A Just Russia; see http://lenta.ru/lib/14160404/#42 (accessed August 5, 2015).

33 Valerii Sozaev, "Analiz pravoprimenitel'noi praktiki zakonodatel'stva o zaprete propagandy gomoseksualizma sredi nesovershennoletnikh," http://www. ihahr-nis.org/dokumenty (accessed August 3, 2015).

34 Ibid. On the significance of the invocation of tradition see Marianna Murav'eva, "'(Ne)traditsionnye seksual'nye otnoshenii' kak iuridicheskaia kategoriia: istoriko-pravovoi analiz," in *Na pereput'e: metodologiia, teoriia i praktika LGBT i kvir-issledovanii [sbornik statei],* ed. Aleksandr Kondakov (St. Petersburg: Tsentr nezavisimykh sotsiologicheskikh issledovanii, 2014). Fedotova pursued a complaint to the UN's Human Rights Committee and won a favorable decision in October 2012; see http://www.gayrussia.eu/russia/5280 (accessed August 3, 2015).

35 Space does not permit a full examination of the circumstances in which these laws were debated and adopted; in order of adoption the regions are:

Arkhangel'sk Province (September 30, 2011); Kostroma Province (December 27, 2011); St. Petersburg (March 17, 2012); Novosibirsk Province (June 7, 2012); Magadan Province (June 9, 2012), Krasnodar Region (June 20, 2012); Samara Province (June 26, 2012); Republic of Bashkortostan (July 23, 2012); Kaliningrad Province (January 24, 2013); Irkutsk Province (May 13, 2013). Other regions that considered banning "gay propaganda" include Moscow City, Kirov and Vladimir Provinces, Perm' Region and the Republic of Iakutiia (Sakha). A useful introduction to the local laws is found on Russian Wikipedia: https://ru.wikipedia.org/wiki/%D0%97%D0%B0%D0%BA%D0%BE% D0%BD%D0%BE%D0%B4%D0%B0%D1%82%D0%B5%D0%BB%D1 %8C%D0%BD%D1%8B%D0%B5_%D0%B7%D0%B0%D0%BF% D1%80%D0%B5%D1%82%D1%8B_%D0%BF%D1%80%D0%BE%D0 %BF%D0%B0%D0%B3%D0%B0%D0%BD%D0%B4%D1%8B_%D0% B3%D0%BE%D0%BC%D0%BE%D1%81%D0%B5%D0%BA%D1%81 %D1%83%D0%B0%D0%BB%D0%B8%D0%B7%D0%BC%D0%B0_% D0%B2_%D0%A0%D0%BE%D1%81%D1%81%D0%B8%D0%B8#. D0.90.D1.80.D1.85.D0.B0.D0.BD.D0.B3.D0.B5.D0.BB.D1.8C.D1.81.D0. BA.D0.B0.D1.8F_.D0.BE.D0.B1.D0.BB.D0.B0.D1.81.D1.82.D1.8C (accessed August 4, 2015).

36 Adam, "Theorizing Homophobia," 398–9.

37 See http://www.vz.ru/society/2011/9/28/526071.print.html (accessed August 4, 2015).

38 In September 2011 Aleksandr Diatlov, Arkhangel'sk legislature deputy and chair of its youth and sport committee, said he was actively seeking such contacts through United Russia channels (Ibid.). On misogyny and homophobia in the youth wings of Russia's political parties, see Chapter 3 of Sperling, *Sex, Politics, and Putin*.

39 See http://www.novopol.ru/-matvienko-v-rossii-mojno-zapretit-propagandu-gomoseks-text112668.html (accessed August 4, 2015).

40 See e.g. http://www.specletter.com/obcshestvo/2013–05–30/vera-dlja-menja-uzh-izvinite-vyshe-zakona.html (accessed August 4, 2015).

41 See e.g. http://www.huffingtonpost.com/2013/12/19/russia-to-free-pussy-riot-mikhail-khodorkovsky_n_4472756.html (accessed August 5, 2015); Sperling, *Sex, Politics, and Putin*, 222–39. Sperling notes the feminist credentials of Pussy Riot remain contested, with some Russian feminist critics seeing too much violence and patriarchal rhetoric in their lyrics and tactics.

42 Sebastian Buckle, *The Way Out: A History of Homosexuality in Modern Britain* (London: I. B. Tauris, 2015), 104–15.

43 Dorofeev was a member of both the Novosibirsk Provincial legislature and the federal Duma. See http://www.mn.ru/politics_law/20120330/314570931.html (accessed August 13, 2015). On petitions from regions, I am grateful for the advice of Ben Noble.

44 See http://www.duma.gov.ru/news/273/235815 and http://www.bbc.com/russian/russia/2013/01/130125_duma_gay_propaganda_law.shtml?print=1 (accessed August 13, 2015). It appears the one opposing vote was down to a new United Russia Party deputy's pushing "the wrong button": http://grani.ru/people/1752 (accessed August 13, 2015).

45 Explanations for the change in wording have been minimal and evasive. In an
    interview after the publication of the new draft law Mizulina suggested the
    revision was a direct result of representations from the LGBT community; she
    also emphasized the pedigree in Russian jurisprudence of the concept of
    "traditional/non-traditional sexual relations." See http://www.gazeta.ru/
    politics/2013/06/10_a_5375845.shtml (accessed August 13, 2015).

46 "Our plans have not been affected by the talk about homophobia spreading
    through society in the wake of the incident in Volgograd," she told RIA
    Novosti on 14 May 2013. "That's just stupid. It's a so-called objective opinion,
    and I absolutely reject it." See http://lenta.ru/articles/2013/05/23/volgograd
    (accessed August 13, 2015).

47 I first discussed the myth of Russia's sexual innocence in Healey, *Homosexual
    Desire in Revolutionary Russia*, 251–7.

48 See http://www.gazeta.ru/politics/2013/01/25_a_4940585.shtml (accessed
    August 13, 2015).

49 See http://www.gazeta.ru/politics/news/2013/06/07/n_2959549.shtml (accessed
    August 13, 2015).

50 For an example of her attribution of the power of the "pedophilia lobby" to
    the lack of progress on a bill to refine child pornography law, see http://www.
    vesti.ru/doc.html?id=975240; and note commentary on the non-existence of
    such a lobby by her peers and experts, http://www.aif.ru/politics/russia/40239
    (accessed August 13, 2015).

51 See "Kontseptsiia gosudarstvennoi semeinoi politiki Rossiiskoi Federatsii na
    period do 2025 goda," http://www.komitet2–6.km.duma.gov.ru/site.
    xp/050049124053056052.html (accessed August 14, 2015).

52 "Kontseptsiia gosudarstvennoi semeinoi politiki Rossiiskoi Federatsii na period
    do 2025 goda," 4–5, 14. The 25-page document uses the words "tradition/
    traditional" 33 times. The "concept" was greatly modified before its adoption
    as official state policy in 2014; for a thorough analysis, see Marianna
    Murav'eva, "Traditional Values and Modern Families: Legal Understanding
    of Tradition and Modernity in Contemporary Russia," *Journal of Social
    Policy Studies* 12, no. 4 (2014): 625–38.

53 Andrey Makarychev and Sergei Medvedev, "Biopolitics and Power in Putin's
    Russia," *Problems of Post-Communism* 62, no. 1 (2015): 48.

54 See http://www.bbc.com/russian/russia/2013/06/130611_duma_gay_propaganda.
    shtml?print=1 (accessed August 13, 2015).

55 See http://russian.rt.com/article/12821, http://www.segodnia.ru/content/
    125604, and http://www.interfax-religion.com/?act=news&div=10639
    (accessed August 18, 2015).

56 For a summary of the first year's impact, see http://www.slate.com/blogs/outward/
    2014/10/09/russian_lgbt_activists_on_the_effects_of_gay_propaganda_law.html
    (accessed August 18, 2015).

57 See http://www.deti–404.com/; https://www.hrw.org/news/2015/04/02/russia-
    court-hearing-against-lgbt-group; http://www.pinknews.co.uk/2015/07/29/
    russia-fines-owner-of-lgbt-teen-support-network-for-gay-propaganda/;
    (accessed August 18, 2015).

58 See http://www.newrepublic.com/article/117896/vladimir-medinsky-russias-culture-minister-putin-toady (accessed August 19, 2014); Alexander Poznansky, *Tchaikovsky: The Quest for the Inner Man* (New York: Schirmer Books, 1991). On the problems of writing queer life histories in Russia today, see Chapter 8.

59 See http://www.gay.ru/news/rainbow/2013/10/11–27253.htm (accessed August 19, 2015).

60 See http://www.nytimes.com/reuters/2014/11/03/technology/03reuters-russia-gay-apple.html?ref=reuters&_r=0; and https://meduza.io/en/lion/2015/08/12/this-bus-stop-might-be-too-gay-for-russia (both accessed August 19, 2015). The anti-Apple gesture came as the Ukrainian crisis yielded economic sanctions, and melded homophobia with anti-Americanism.

61 See e.g. http://www.themoscowtimes.com/news/article/anti-gay-vigilante-groups-face-backlash/484774.html, http://www.ft.com/cms/s/0/71eaa49e–0580–11e3–8ed5–00144feab7de.html#axzz2pLypgrfO (accessed January 3, 2014).

62 See e.g. the UK's Channel 4 documentary: http://www.channel4.com/news/gay-russian-sochi-hunting-season-we-are-the-hunted (broadcast February 5, 2014); Australia Broadcasting Corporation's *Foreign Correspondent*, http://www.abc.net.au/foreign/content/2013/s3879592.htm (broadcast October 10, 2013).

63 Reports of LGBT victims of violence: 2011 = 3; 2012 = 12; 2013 = 25; 2014 = 8; 2015 (to 1 August) = 2. See the Sova Centre's database http://www.sova-center.ru/database/violence/?tip1=301&tip2=303&date_start=01%2F01%2F2011&date_end=01%2F10%2F2015&phenotype=658&xfield=phenotype&yfield=y&victims—in&show=1 (accessed August 18, 2015).

64 For examples of the new fear and self-concealment, see Masha Gessen, Joseph Huff-Hannon, Bela Shaevich, Andrei Borodin, Dmitri Karelsky, and Svetlana Solodovnik, *Gay Propaganda: Russian Love Stories* (New York: OR Books, 2014).

65 See http://rt.com/news/church-same-sex-unions–404 (accessed August 18, 2015). On allegations of ex-KGB links, see e.g. http://www.thetimes.co.uk/tto/faith/article2100100.ece; on his taste in wristwatches, see e.g. http://www.bbc.com/news/world-europe–17622820 (both accessed August 18, 2015).

66 Note e.g. Chapter XII section 9, "Problems of bioethics," in the Church's 2005 "Fundamentals of the Social Conception of the Russian Orthodox Church," http://www.patriarchia.ru/db/text/141422.html (accessed August 4, 2015).

67 The program had first been aired in April 2013, but when repeated in August it caught the attention of bloggers, who raised unsuccessful complaints against Kiselev with the Procuracy; see http://tvrain.ru/teleshow/novosti_sajta/blogosfera_vozmutilas_prizyvom_dmitrija_kiseleva_szhigat_serdtsa_geev–349742; and http://top.rbc.ru/society/04/04/2014/915620.shtml (both accessed August 20, 2015).

68 See http://www.theguardian.com/world/2013/dec/09/putin-appoints-homophobic-presenter-kiselyov-head-news-agency-homosexuals; on Russian media's new tendentiousness, see e.g. Ivan Tsetkov, "Russian Whataboutism vs American Moralism," http://www.russia-direct.org/opinion/russian-whataboutism-vs-american-moralism (accessed August 20, 2015).

69 The anniversary year was marred by "violations" of diplomatic immunity with a sexual undertone, in October, with Dutch authorities detaining a Russian embassy official on suspicion of child abuse, and a few days later the mysterious break-in at a Dutch official's residence in Moscow where attackers drew a pink heart and the Russian letters LGBT on a mirror; on the arrest in The Hague, see http://www.bbc.com/news/world-europe-24448147; on the Moscow attack, see http://www.bbc.com/news/world-europe-24547823 (both accessed August 19, 2015). This "exchange" of insults took place after a month of tensions over Russia's detention of the "Arctic Sunrise," a Dutch-registered Greenpeace ship, with its crew.

70 See http://www.kremlin.ru/transcripts/17850 (accessed January 6, 2014).

71 On the decriminalization of male homosexuality under Lenin in 1918–22, see Healey, *Homosexual Desire in Revolutionary Russia*, 100–25. On Khrushchev's policies, see Chapter 1.

72 The highly controversial Dutch pedophile advocacy association "Martijn" did indeed exist at the time Putin spoke; it has lost recent appeals against legal orders to shut down: see http://www.nltimes.nl/2015/02/03/pro-pedophile-association-loses-eu-court-bid (accessed August 20, 2015). Putin's reference to a party rejecting women as politicians is presumably to the ultra-Calvinist Reformed Political Party (SGP) which elected its first female deputy in 2014, after losing battles with the European Court over sex inequality policies: http://nos.nl/artikel/625641-sgp-vrouw-komt-in-raad-vlissingen.html (accessed August 20, 2015).

73 See http://ria.ru/politics/20130904/960605375.html (accessed January 6, 2014).

74 On these myths see Dan Healey, "'Untraditional Sex' and the 'Simple Russian': Nostalgia for Soviet Innocence in the Polemics of Dilia Enikeeva," in *What is Soviet Now? Identities, Legacies, Memories*, eds Thomas Lahusen and Peter H. Solomon Jr. (Berlin: Lit Verlag, 2008).

75 See http://en.kremlin.ru/events/president/news/19243 (accessed August 20, 2015).

76 The argument that Russia stood as the last defender of Western Christian values, with implications for its homophobic and anti-migration demographic policies was commonly circulated by Russian TV commentators in 2013; see Tolz, and Harding, "From 'Compatriots' to 'Aliens'", 462–3.

77 Source: http://eng.kremlin.ru/transcripts/6402 (accessed January 6, 2014).

78 Quoted in Helen Jefferson Lenskyj, *Sexual Diversity and the Sochi 2014 Olympics: No More Rainbows* (Basingstoke: Palgrave Pivot, 2014), 71–2. See also Richard Arnold and Andrew Foxall, "Lord of the (Five) Rings," *Problems of Post-Communism* 61, no. 1 (2014): 3–12.

79 The "Olympic Industry" is Lenskyj's characterization; on the impact of new social media, see Lenskyj, *Sexual Diversity and the Sochi 2014 Olympics*, 77, 79, 86.

80 Swedish track and field athletes deliberately staged a "silent protest" by painting their nails; see http://sverigesradio.se/sida/artikel.aspx?programid=2054&artikel=5617678 (accessed August 20, 2015).

81 See e.g. http://stadium.ru/news/19–08–2013-vnimanie-fotografov-privlek-potselui-ksenii-rizhovoi-i-tatyani-firovoi; and http://www.thenation.com/article/was-kiss-just-kiss-medal-stand-smooch-heard-round-world (both accessed August 20, 2015).

82 See http://america.aljazeera.com/articles/2013/11/20/putin-warns-againsthomophobiaassociolympicsapproach.html (accessed August 20, 2015); Lenskyj, *Sexual Diversity and the Sochi 2014 Olympics*, 76.

83 Patrick B. Miller, "The Nazi Olympics, Berlin 1936: Exhibition at the U.S. Holocaust Memorial Museum, Washington D.C. [Review essay]," *Olympika* V (1996): 134; cited in Lenskyj, *Sexual Diversity and the Sochi 2014 Olympics*, 68.

84 The others were the enormous cost and linked corruption, and security problems relating to conflicts in the region; see Arnold and Foxall, "Lord of the (Five) Rings"; Karen Dawisha, *Putin's Kleptocracy: Who Owns Russia?* (New York: Simon & Schuster, 2014), 314.

85 The interview took place in Sochi with BBC journalist Andrew Marr, ABC's George Stephanopolous, and leading Russian broadcasters Sergei Brilev and Irada Zeinalova; see http://kremlin.ru/events/president/news/20080 (accessed August 20, 2015).

86 He emphatically and repeatedly said the law's title was "On the banning of propaganda for pedophilia and homosexualism"; it is in fact "On the introduction of changes to Article 5 of the Federal Law 'On the protection of children from information harmful to their health and development' and specific legislative acts of the Russian Federation in order to protect children from information propagandizing the denial of traditional family values." At no time during its passage through parliament did the bill contain the word "pedophilia."

87 See http://www.rt.com/politics/russian-adoption-same-sex-couples–854 (accessed August 27, 2015).

88 On Parnok see Diana Lewis Burgin, *Sophia Parnok: The Life and Work of Russia's Sappho* (New York & London: New York University Press, 1994).

89 Francesca Stella, *Lesbian Lives in Soviet and Post-Soviet Russia: Post/socialism and Gendered Sexualities* (Basingstoke: Palgrave Macmillan, 2015), 16–21, 45–66.

90 For a study of selfhood in 403 Ukrainian bisexual men that suggests their different- and same-sex relations are asymmetrical and marked by significant internalized homophobia, see Maksim Kasianchuk, "Internal'naia gomofobiia biseksual'nykh muzhchin," in *Na Pereput'e: metodologiia, teoriia i praktika LGBT i kvir-issledovanii*, ed. Aleksandr Kondakov (St. Petersburg: Tsentr nezavisimykh sotsiologicheskikh issledovanii, 2014). For Western bisexuality theory's critique of "monosexuality" and the role of "bi" as a "portal" that queers rigid binarisms, see Serena Anderlini-D'Onofrio and Jonathan Alexander, "Introduction to the Special Issue: Bisexuality and Queer Theory: Intersections, Diversions, and Connections," *Journal of Bisexuality* 9, no. 3–4 (2009): 197–212.

91 Stella, *Lesbian Lives in Soviet and Post-Soviet Russia*, 106.

92 Healey, *Homosexual Desire in Revolutionary Russia*, 12, 63–4; 162–71.

93 See e.g. Dmitrii Isaev, "Konstruirovanie gomoseksual'noi i transgendernoi identichnosti," in *LGBT issledovaniia: aktual'nye problemy i perspektivy. Materialy mezhdunarodnoi mezhditstsiplinarnoi nauchnoprakticheskoi konferentsii posviashchennoi pamiati I. S. Kona. Sankt Peterburg, 27–9 oktiabria 2011 g.*, ed. Valerii Sozaev (St. Petersburg: LGBT Organizatsiia Vykhod, 2011); Dmitrii Isaev and F. A. Kuznetsov, *Mify i fakty o transseksualakh* (St. Petersburg: LGBT Organizatsiia Vykhod, 2012); Tat'iana Zborovskaia, "Spetsifika formirovaniia kartiny mira transgenderov v zavisimosti ot sotsiokul'turnykh realii: issledovanie assotsiativnykh norm na primere russkogo i anglisskogo iazykov," in *Na Pereput'e: metodologiia, teoriia i praktika LGBT i kvri-issledovanii*, ed. Aleksandr Kondakov (St. Petersburg: Tsentr nezaivisimykh sotsiologicheskikh issledovanii, 2014).

Chapter 1: Forging Gulag Sexualities: Penal Homosexuality and the Reform of the Gulag after Stalin

1   See http://lenta.ru/articles/2013/05/23/volgograd (accessed September 10, 2015).

2   For a suggestive analysis of contemporary attitudes see Marina Yusupova, "Masculinity, Criminality and Russian Men," *Sextures: E-journal for Sexualities, Cultures, and Politics* 3, no. 3 (2015): 46–61.

3   See http://www.gazeta.ru/politics/2011/05/25_a_3628401.shtml; http://www.vanityfair.com/news/politics/2012/04/vladimir-putin-mikhail-khodorkovsky-russia (accessed October 17, 2015).

4   Estimates of the Gulag population remain contested; see e.g. Otto J. Pohl, *The Stalinist Penal System: A statistical history of Soviet repression and terror, 1930–1953* (Jefferson, N.C.: McFarland, 1997), 5; Anne Applebaum, *Gulag: A History of the Soviet Camps* (London: Allen Lane, 2003), 515–22.

5   See e.g. Alexander Solzhenitsyn, *The Gulag Archipelago 1918–1956: An Experiment in Literary Investigation.* 3 vols. (London: Collins & Harvill Press, 1974, 1975, 1978), 2: 227–50; Applebaum, *Gulag*, 284–306; Emma Mason, "Women in the Gulag of the 1930s," in *Women in the Stalin Era*, ed. Melanie Ilic (Basingstoke: Palgrave Macmillan, 2001); Veronica Shapovalov, *Remembering the Darkness: Women in Soviet Prisons* (Lanham, Md.: Rowman and Littlefield, 2001), 279–81.

6   For studies that ignore the theme, see G. M. Ivanova, *GULAG v sisteme totalitarnogo gosudarstva* (Moscow: Moskovskii obshchestvennyi nauchnyi fond, 1997); Oleg Khlevniuk, *The History of the Gulag: From Collectivization to the Great Terror* (New Haven, & London: Yale University Press, 2004); Cathy A. Frierson and Semyon S. Vilensky, *Children of the Gulag* (New Haven and London: Yale University Press, 2010). For a voyeuristic discussion, see Viktor Berdinskikh, *Istoriia odnogo lageria (Viatlag)* (Moscow: Agraf, 2001), 180–7.

7   Wilson T. Bell, "Sex, Pregnancy, and Power in the Late Stalinist Gulag," *Journal of the History of Sexuality* 24, no. 2 (2015): 198–224.

8   See e.g. Steven Anthony Barnes, *Death and Redemption: the Gulag and the shaping of Soviet society* (Princeton: Princeton University Press, 2011), 98–105, 121.

9   Bell, "Sex, Pregnancy, and Power in the Late Stalinist Gulag," 200, 223.

10   Jane Caplan, "Gender and the concentration camps," in *Concentration Camps in Nazi Germany: The New Histories*, eds Jane Caplan and Nikolaus Wachsmann (London & New York: Routledge, 2010); Anna Hájková, "Sexual Barter in Times of Genocide: Negotiating the Sexual Economy of the Theresienstadt Ghetto," *Signs* 38, no. 3 (2013): 503–33.

11   Vladimir Kozlovskii, *Argo russkoi gomoseksual'noi subkul'tury: Materialy k izucheniiu.* (Benson, Vt: Chalidze Publications, 1986), 87–146.

12   Ol'ga Zhuk, *Russkie amazonki: Istoriia lesbiiskoi subkul'tury v Rossii XX vek* (Moscow: Glagol, 1998). On this work see Dan Healey, "Olga Zhuk, *Russkie amazonki: Istoriia lesbiiskoi subkul'tury v Rossii XX vek.* [review]," *Kritika: Explorations in Russian and Eurasian History* 3, no. 2 (2002): 362–8.

13   Dan Healey, *Homosexual Desire in Revolutionary Russia: The Regulation of Sexual and Gender Dissent* (Chicago: University of Chicago Press, 2001), 230–44. For documentary sources, see e.g. Kevin Moss, ed. *Out of the Blue: Russia's Hidden Gay Literature* (San Francisco: Gay Sunshine Press, 1996), 258–61.

14   Adi Kuntsman, " 'With a Shade of Disgust': Affective Politics of Sexuality and Class in Memoirs of the Stalinist Gulag," *Slavic Review* 68, no. 2 (2009): 308–28; idem, "Between Gulags and Pride Parades: Sexuality, Nation, and Haunted Speech Acts," *GLQ: A Journal of Lesbian and Gay Studies* 14, no. 2–3 (2008): 263–88.

15   Reading archives "against the grain" is proposed in Ann Laura Stoler, *Race and the Education of Desire: Foucault's History of Sexuality and the Colonial Order of Things* (Durham: Duke University Press, 1995).

16   These came to light during my investigation of the medical care system in the Gulag camps, "Medicine in the Gulag Archipelago"; I am grateful to the UK Wellcome Trust (grant no. 085948) for supporting the project.

17   Hájková, "Sexual Barter in Times of Genocide," 506–7.

18   Ibid., 508. For more on the contextual issues see Chapter 9.

19   On the Gulag's penal-colonial model, see Den Khili, [Dan Healey], "Nasledie GULAGa: prinuditel'nyi trud sovetskoi epokhi kak vnutrenniaia kolonizatsiia," in *Tam, vnutri. Praktiki vnutrennei kolonizatsii v kul'turnoi istorii Rossii*, eds Aleksandr Etkind, Dirk Uffelmann and Il'ia Kukulin (Moscow: Novoe literaturnoe obozrenie, 2012). On the "company town" model of the Gulag, see Alan Barenberg, *Gulag Town, Company Town: Forced Labor and Its Legacy in Vorkuta* (New Haven & London: Yale University Press, 2014).

20   On these points see: Barnes, *Death and Redemption*, 100–3; Bell, "Sex, Pregnancy, and Power." The number of free-standing abortion clinics in the Gulag fell from 22 in 1936 to 15 in 1938; see A. B. Bezborodov, and

V. M. Khrustalev, eds, *Istoriia Stalinskogo Gulaga. Konets 1920-kh – pervaia polovina 1950-kh godov. Tom 4: Naselenie Gulaga: chislennost' i usloviia soderzhaniia*. 7 vols. (Moscow: ROSSPEN, 2004), 4: 487. The Kolyma region's abortion rates in 1949 and 1950 stood between 29 to 50 per live births, with sanitary officials admitting that few cases were passed to the procuracy for punishment: Gosudarstvennyi arkhiv Magadanskoi Oblasti (GAMO), f. 45, op. 1, d. 23, ll. 99–100.

21 The gender imbalance was stark, except when the proportion of women in wartime (1941–5) rose dramatically because of releases of men to serve in the army. E.g. the 1934 percentage of female prisoners was 5.9; 1937: 6.1; 1940: 8.1; 1943: 13; 1945: 24; the percentage fell thereafter. See J. Arch Getty, Gabor T. Rittersporn, and Viktor N. Zemskov, "Victims of the Soviet Penal System in the Pre-War Years: A First Approach on the Basis of Archival Evidence," *American Historical Review* 98, no. 4 (1993): 1017–49, table and commentary at 1025.

22 Bell, "Sex, Pregnancy, and Power"; on VD isolation camps, see GARF, f. 9414, op. 1, d. 2762, ll. 25–31 (1940 order to set up separate camps to treat VD patients).

23 On the Kolyma camps' children's homes, see e.g. Frierson and Vilensky, *Children of the Gulag*, 312–14; and Eugenia [Evgeniia] Ginzburg, *Within the Whirlwind* (London: Collins Harvill, 1989), 3–11.

24 See e.g. David L. Hoffmann, *Stalinist Values: The Cultural Norms of Soviet Modernity, 1917–1941* (Ithaca: Cornell University Press, 2003); Dan Healey, *Bolshevik Sexual Forensics: Diagnosing Disorder in the Clinic and Courtroom, 1917–1939* (DeKalb, Il.: Northern Illinois University Press, 2009).

25 On the shift toward "compulsory heterosexuality" in the late 1930s, see Dan Healey, *Homosexual Desire in Revolutionary Russia: The Regulation of Sexual and Gender Dissent* (Chicago: University of Chicago Press, 2001), 196–202.

26 Barnes, *Death and Redemption*, 69, 71. Similar incentives and penalties were used in the tsarist era; see Daniel Beer, *The House of the Dead: Siberian exile under the tsars* (London: Allen Lane, 2016), 64–8, 242–8.

27 See A. G. Kozlov, "Iz istorii kolymskikh lagerei (1932–1937 gg.)," *Kraevedcheskie zapiski [Magadanskii oblastnoi kraevedcheskii muzei. Magadanskoe knizhnoe izdatel'stvo]*, Vypusk XVII (1991): 79–80.

28 Anxious about the gender imbalance east of the Urals, in 1637 the authorities in European Russia sent 150 "virgins" to live with Cossack conquistadors; a century later Cossacks in Siberia were still "buying" Ostiak native boys for the eloquent sums of 25 bronze kopecks and girls for just 20 kopecks, for sex; see Sergei Vasil'evich Maksimov, "Sibir' i katorga," in *Sobranie sochinenii*. 20 vols (St. Petersburg, 1908), 2: 411–12.

29 Berzin's ten-year plan for the development of Kolyma, thought to be a trigger for his downfall, saw a gradual transition to "free" labor, normalization of administration and through a rail link to the "mainland" all rejected by Stalin in 1939; see Pavel Grebeniuk, *Kolymskii led: Sistema upravleniia na Severo-Vostoke Rossii 1953–1964* (Moscow: ROSSPEN, 2007), 29–30, 35.

30 Only on the eve of Stalin's death did Gulag bosses entertain timid proposals to enable early release (under administrative exile) and the right to bring family members to join ex-prisoners. See Aleksei Tikhonov, "The End of the Gulag," in *The Economics of Forced Labor*, eds Paul Gregory and V. V. Lazarev (Stanford: Hoover Institution, 2003), 69; on Vorkuta's gender imbalance and attempts to address it after 1953, see Barenberg, *Gulag Town, Company Town*, 168–9. In Magadan Province only 18 percent of the population was female in 1954, and it had the lowest incidence of marriage and family formation in the USSR; by 1959 women constituted almost 44 percent of inhabitants and the birthrate had increased rapidly: Grebeniuk, *Kolymskii led*, 81, 171–2.

31 Healey, *Homosexual Desire in Revolutionary Russia*, 126–51.

32 Ibid., 181–204.

33 See the sensitive readings of Dostoevskii's memoir in Andrew Armand Gentes, *Exile, Murder and Madness in Siberia, 1823–61* (Basingstoke: Palgrave Macmillan, 2010), 212.

34 Beer, *The House of the Dead*, 258–9.

35 For a more detailed discussion of late-tsarist and early Soviet male homosexual activity in prisons, see Healey, *Homosexual Desire in Revolutionary Russia*, 230–3. The rest of this paragraph is based on Mikhail N. Gernet, *V tiur'me. Ocherki tiuremnoi psikhologii.* (Moscow: Izd. Pravo i zhizn', 1925), 73–80.

36 D. I. Lass, "Polovaia zhizn' zakliuchennykh," in *Izuchenie prestupnosti i penitentsiarnaia praktika* ed. D. I. Lass (Odessa: Izd. Odesskogo tsentral'nogo DOPRA, 1927), 19.

37 B. L. Bishko, "K kharakteristike iskustvennykh khirurgicheskikh zabolevanii v mestakh zakliucheniia," *Leningradskii meditsinskii zhurnal*, no. 9 (1926): 41.

38 On the patterns of early twentieth-century women's same-sex love, see Healey, *Homosexual Desire in Revolutionary Russia*, 50–73.

39 Mikhail N. Gernet, *V tiur'me. Ocherki tiuremnoi psikhologii* (Leningrad: Iuridicheskoe izdatel'stvo Ukrainy, 1930), 110–11.

40 Dan Healey, "Evgeniia/Evgenii: Queer Case Histories in the first years of Soviet power," *Gender & History* 9, no. 1 (1997): 83–106.; idem, "Unruly Identities: Soviet Psychiatry Confronts the 'Female Homosexual' of the 1920s," in *Gender in Russian History and Culture, 1800–1990*, ed. Linda Edmondson (Basingstoke & New York: Palgrave, 2001).

41 See the extremely brief comments on prison homosex in Federico Varese, "The society of the vory-v-zakone, 1930s–1950s," *Cahiers du monde russe: Russie, Empire russe, Union soviétique, États indépendants* 39, no. 4 (1998): 519.

42 Regina Kunzel, *Criminal Intimacy: Prison and the Uneven History of Modern American Sexuality* (Chicago & London: University of Chicago Press, 2008), 1–14; Christopher Hensley, Cindy Struckman-Johnson, and Helen M. Eigenberg, "Introduction: The History of Prison Sex Research," *The Prison Journal* 80, no. 4 (2000): 360–7.

43 Available treatments before the advent of penicillin after 1945 required long courses of monitoring. Penicillin, once it arrived, was not shared out equally to Soviet populations and prisoners sat at the bottom of a hierarchy of drug

distribution. See e.g. instructions on penicillin use from the Ministry of Health in Moscow, 1951, in GAMO, f. 45, op. 1, d. 23, ll. 38–42a; and interview with Anna Kliashko, Dal'stroi civilian doctor, June 24, 2009 (Montreal, Canada).

44 E. A. Kersnovskaia, *Skol'ko stoit chelovek* (Moscow: ROSSPEN, 2006), 518.

45 Memorial Society, St. Petersburg, Iashenkov, Aleksandr Mikhailovich, "Vorkuta," n.d., no archival citation, 21.

46 Memorial Society, Moscow, video-taped interview of Aleksandr Tsetsulesku, conducted by Irina Stepanova (ca. 2008).

47 On male prostitution, see Dan Healey, "Masculine Purity and 'Gentlemen's Mischief': Sexual Exchange, Barter and Prostitution between Russian Men," *Slavic Review* 60, no. 2 (2001): 233–65.

48 See "Zhenshchina blatnogo mira," (part of "Ocherki prestupnogo mira") in Varlam Shalamov, *Preodolenie zla* (Moscow Eksmo, 2011), 595.

49 Effeminate male homosexuals might use feminine forms of past-tense verbs, which are marked by gender. See Chapter 2.

50 Kersnovskaia, *Skol'ko stoit chelovek*, 518.

51 Iurii Fidel'gol'ts, "Tot Vaninskii port," in *Za chto? Proza, poeziia, dokumenty*, eds. V. A. Shentalinskii and V. N. Leonovich (Moscow: Kliuch, 1999), 126–7.

52 Kozlovskii, *Argo russkoi gomoseksual'noi subkul'tury*, 126–7, 134–6. A peasant-teacher arrested for political crimes was shocked by the obscenity, including similar terms for male and female homosexuality, heard in 1942 in Karaganda; see Memorial Society, Moscow, Zaitsev Aleksandr Georgievich, "Pervyi i vtoroi aresty. Lageria" [Vospominaniia]. Gor'kii, 1989, f. 2, op. 2, d. 32, l. 101b.

53 Rape in prison in the mid-twentieth-century USA followed an analogous pattern; it was often structured on racial lines, with black men targeting weaker and younger white men in a reversal of the "lynch mob justice" whites dispensed to blacks in wider society; see Ian O'Donnell, "Prison Rape in Context," *British Journal of Criminology* 44, no. 2 (2004): 241–55.

54 There were over 3,300 adolescents out of 57,000 inmates; see Bezborodov, and Khrustalev, eds, *Istoriia Stalinskogo Gulaga*, 4: 141.

55 See e.g. Chirkov's sympathetic treatment by Dr. Leonid T. Titov (himself a homosexual); and the dispute over Chirkov between a criminal Fedia and a "political" prisoner, the military officer Antonovich in Iouri Tchirkov, *C'était ainsi . . ..* (Paris: Editions de Syrtes, 2009), 57–9, 60–2.

56 Janusz Bardach and Kate Gleeson, *Man is Wolf to Man: Surviving Stalin's Gulag* (London: Simon & Schuster, 1998), 125.

57 Khlevniuk, *The History of the Gulag*, 234, citing GARF f. R9414, op. 4, d. 12, ll. 24–38.

58 GARF, f. R8131, op. 37, d. 4545, l. 29 (March 1948, "O narushenniakh zakonnosti v ispravitel'no-trudovykh lageriakh i koloniiakh MVD SSSR").

59 I. M. Fil'shtinskii, *My shagaem pod konvoem. Rasskazy iz lagernoi zhizni* (Nizhnii Novgorod: Dekom, 2005), 158.

60 Healey, *Homosexual Desire in Revolutionary Russia*, 235–7.

61 Fil'shtinskii described a "femme" lesbian with the tattoo "Why use boys when
you have fingers!" (*Zachem mal'chiki, kogda est' pal'chiki!*): *My shagaem pod
konvoem*, 157.

62 Memorial Society, Moscow, Konstantin Petrovich Gurskii, "Polovaia zhizn' v
lageriakh Gulaga," f. 2, op. 3, d. 17, ll. 159–66; for another incident in the
1950s in which the author himself was knifed by a jealous lesbian partner, see
Fil'shtinskii, *My shagaem pod konvoem*, 156–60.

63 Memorial Society, St. Petersburg, Mariia L'vovna Kono, "Vospominaniia,"
n.d., 1–4.

64 Memorial Society, St. Petersburg, Aino Andreevna Lotto, [Vospominaniia], n.d.

65 "The *kobly* [butches] always had to be transported with their wives, because it
was very difficult to separate them. Any attempt to do so resulted in very noisy
protests from the spouses, even going so far as suicide.": Memorial Society,
Moscow, Stepan Stepanovich Torbin, "Vospominaniia," Selo Andreevka,
Ukraine, 1993; f. 2, op. 2, d. 91, l. 144.

66 See e.g. Fil'shtinskii, *My shagaem pod konvoem*, 198–204; Zhuk, *Russkie
amazonki: Istoriia lesbiiskoi subkul'tury v Rossii XX vek*, 87–129.

67 Memorial Society, Moscow, Aleksandr Maksimovich Zelenyi, [Vospominaniia]
Moscow, 1964.; f. 2, op 1, d. 64, ll. 172–3.

68 Fil'shtinskii, *My shagaem pod konvoem*, 198–9.

69 See Getty, Rittersporn, Zemskov, "Victims of the Soviet Penal System in the
Pre-War Years," 1030–7; Barnes, *Death and Redemption*, 83–93.

70 Kuntsman, "'With a Shade of Disgust'," 316–21.

71 Of 175 homosexual men arrested in Leningrad between August and October
1933, eighty-nine were white-collar workers, twenty-nine were "actors and
artists," and fourteen were scholarly researchers and teachers; see V. A. Ivanov,
"Kontrrevoliutsionnye organizatsii sredi gomoseksualistov Leningrada v
nachale 1930-kh godov i ikh pogrom," *Noveishaia istoriia Rossiia*, no. 3
(2013): 135. This demographic of victims corresponds to that I found in
Moscow court archives for the mid-to-late 1930s: see Healey, *Homosexual
Desire in Revolutionary Russia*, 227.

72 Memorial Society, St. Petersburg, Mane, Ol'ga Meervona, "Interv'iu s Mane
Ol'goi Meerovnoi." Transcription from cassette-tapes, tape 3, p. 2.

73 Gurskii, "Polovaia zhizn' v lageriakh Gulaga," f. 2, op. 3, d. 17, ll. 163–4.

74 Guzikova, Sof'ia Lazarevna, "Stranitsy vospominanii" Moscow, n.d. Memorial
Society, Moscow, f. 2, op. 2, d. 21, l. 11. Another male pair, a surgeon and his
young assistant, is described in Isaac J. Vogelfanger, *Red Tempest: The Life of a
Surgeon in the Gulag*. (Montreal & Kingston, London, Buffalo: McGill-
Queen's University Press, 1996), 135–7.

75 M. Ulanovskaia, "Konets sroka – 1976 goda," *Vremia i my*, 10 (1976): 153–5,
cited in Kozlovskii, *Argo russkoi gomoseksual'noi subkul'tury*, 114–16.

76 Zelenyi, [Vospominaniia] Moscow, 1964.; f. 2, op 1, d. 64, l. 173 (my
emphasis).

77 Memorial Society, Moscow, Evsei Moiseevich L'vov, [Vospominaniia] Moscow,
1968, 1975, 1982; f. 2, op. 1, d. 84, ll. 44–5.

78 See "Prikaz NKVD SSSR No. 0161 s ob"iavleniem 'Polozheniia ob otdelenii kul'turno-vospitatel'noi raboty GULAGa NKVD' . . ." in A. I., Kokurin, and N. V. Petrov, eds., *GULAG: Glavnoe upravlenie lagerei, 1918–1960* (Moscow: Mezhdunarodnyi fond Demokratiia, 2000), 117–28. Among the articles of the criminal code barring work in the KVCh are nos. 151–5 "(sexual crimes)" – including article 154a against sodomy (Ibid., 120).

79 For histories of Gulag theaters, see A. N. Kaneva, *Gulagovskii teatr Ukhty* (Syktyvkar: Komi Knizhnoe Izdatel'stvo, 2001); Natalia Kuziakina, *Teatr na Solovkakh, 1923–1937* (St. Petersburg: DB, 2009). On newspapers, see A. Iu. Gorcheva, *Pressa GULAGa. Spiski E. P. Peshkovoi* (Moscow: Izd-vo Moskovskogo universiteta, 2009). See as well Julie Draskoczy, *Belomor: Criminality and Creativity in Stalin's Gulag* (Boston: Academic Studies Press, 2014).

80 Miriam Dobson, *Khrushchev's Cold Summer: Gulag Returnees, Crime, and the Fate of Reform after Stalin.* (Ithaca & London: Cornell University Press, 2009); Nanci Adler, *The Gulag Survivor: Beyond the Soviet System* (New Brunswick & London: Transaction Publishers, 2002).

81 See e.g. Melanie Ilic, Susan E. Reid, and Lynne Attwood, eds, *Women in the Khrushchev Era* (Basingstoke: Palgrave Macmillan, 2004); Julie Gilmour and Barbara Evans Clements, " 'If You Want to Be Like Me, Train!': the Contradictions of Soviet Masculinity," in *Russian Masculinities in History and Culture*, eds Barbara Evans Clements, Rebecca Friedman and Dan Healey (Basingstoke & New York: Palgrave, 2002).

82 GARF f. R9414, op. 1, d. 2895, l. 166: from a resume of the conclusions of a conference of medical workers in camps of Sverdlovsk Province, March 3–7, 1959; these are the words of Georgii V. Ustinchenko, the director of the Gulag Medical Department.

83 GARF f. R9414, op. 1, d. 2888, l. 207: from Ustinchenko's boilerplate speech to conferences of Gulag medical workers in Kiev, Leningrad, Sverdlovsk, and Irkutsk in late 1956.

84 Ibid.

85 GARF, f. R9414, op. 1, d. 2894, l. 142: conference of medical workers in Gulag prison colonies, Moscow 1958.

86 Assignment in 1956 to deputy chief of the Medical Department Captain M. D. Chermenev; see GARF f. R9414, op. 1, d. 2888, ll. 131, 153; and to medical inspector A. G. Semichastnaia in November 1957: GARF, f. R9414, op. 1, d. 2896, l. 336.

87 Dobson, *Khrushchev's Cold Summer*, sees a decline in Soviet reformist optimism about redemption of the criminal and a turn towards harsher measures by 1960.

88 E.g. GARF f. R9414, op. 1a, d. 608: conference of penal camp directors, Moscow, May 1959.

89 GARF f. R9414, op. 1a, d. 608, l. 44, comments by the deputy Minister of Internal Affairs of the USSR Kholodkov, about murders in Vorkuta in 1959.

90 GARF f. R9414, op. 1a, d. 608, ll. 103, 114: comments by commandants of various camps.

91   "The struggle against sodomy doesn't happen [in my camp, Usol'lag], because we doctors cannot do anything on our own. The investigating authorities [*operativnye rabotniki*] do nothing with the information we pass to them." (GARF f. R9414, op. 1, d. 2894, l. 144; Moscow, 1958). At the same conference, one comrade Vertriuk from Khabarovsk announced that his venereal disease camp had seen a rise in prosecutions to 16 in the previous two years – suggesting how few had taken place in the past (ibid., l. 156).

92   GARF f. R9414, op. 1a, d. 608, ll. 90–1.

93   I am indebted to Emily Johnson, who brought this passage to my attention.

94   Harold J. Berman, *Justice in the USSR: An Interpretation of Soviet Law* (Cambridge, Ma. & London: Harvard University Press, 1963), 74–7.

95   Healey, *Homosexual Desire in Revolutionary Russia*, 262. The penalties after 1960 for voluntary sodomy varied in each republic's criminal code; see Chapter 7.

96   GARF f. R9414, op. 1a, d. 608, l. 76: opinion of commandant of Karlag at a conference of penal camp directors, Moscow, May 1959.

97   From handwritten comments on a study describing the problems with lesbian relations in the camps, GARF, f. R9414, op. 1, d. 2896, l. 182.

98   GARF, f. R9414, op. 1, d. 2896, ll. 144–144ob., correspondence from Siberian camp to director of Gulag, 1956.

99   We do not know whether lesbianism was discussed by the police ministry in 1958; see Chapter 7.

100 GARF, f. R9414, op. 1, d. 2896, ll. 144–69, 170–238. The autobiography was re-classified as "secrets of personal life" in 2010, as well as portions of Krasuskii's study; I was denied access to the entire autobiography and to a handful of pages of the Krasuskii report. When this material was microfilmed for the Hoover Institution in the late 1990s-early 2000s, these same pages were omitted (although in GARF in 2009, the pages were not yet sewn into blue envelopes to conceal them). Another Gulag-related study of female homosexuals was conducted by Elizaveta Derevinskaia under the supervision of Avram Sviadoshch; this candidate's dissertation discussed ninety-six subjects studied from 1954 to 1965 and of these, eighty-seven came from Karaganda's women's labor camp. See Healey, *Homosexual Desire in Revolutionary Russia*, 240–4.

101 GARF, f. R9414, op. 1, d. 2896, ll. 218–32 ("Forms and methods of prevention and struggle with perverted sexual relations between women-prisoners").

102 This was the Derevinskaia study described in Healey, *Homosexual Desire in Revolutionary Russia*, 240–4.

103 See e.g. Judith Pallot, Laura Piacentini, and Dominique Moran, *Gender, Geography, and Punishment: The Experience of Women in Carceral Russia* (Oxford: Oxford University Press, 2012), 49–55, 96–117; Jeffrey S. Hardy, "'The Camp Is Not a Resort': The Campaign against Privileges in the Soviet Gulag, 1957–61," *Kritika: Explorations in Russian and Eurasian History* 13, no. 1 (2012): 89–122.

104 Abby Schrader, "Branding the Other/Tattooing the Self: Bodily Inscription among Convicts in Russia and the Soviet Union," in *Written on the Body: The Tattoo in European and American History*, ed. Jane Caplan (London: Reaktion, 2000).

105 For the view that in the early Gulag tattoos did not yet constitute a "secret symbolism," see Alexander Sidorov, "The Russian Criminal Tattoo: Past and Present," in *Russian Criminal Tattoo Encyclopedia. Volume III*, ed. Danzig Baldaev (London: FUEL, 2008), 16–43. For arguments that prisoners had long sought to keep tattooing symbolism secret from the jailers, see Schrader, "Branding the Other/Tattooing the Self," 187; and Varese, "The society of the vory-v-zakone, 1930s–1950s," 516.

106 Sidorov, "The Russian Criminal Tattoo," 41.

107 On the degraded "pederast" in tsarist and Soviet prisons see Healey, *Homosexual Desire in Revolutionary Russia*, 231–5.

108 See examples from 1956 in Danzig Baldaev, *Russian Criminal Tattoo Encyclopaedia: Volume II* (Gottingen & London: Steidl/Fuel, 2006), 197, 215.

109 Ibid., 271, 272 (undated).

110 Ibid., 162, 163 (Leningrad, 1971); and also Danzig Baldaev, *Russian Criminal Tattoo Encyclopaedia: Volume III* (London: Fuel, 2008), 208 (undated). On "active" and "passive" dynamics in post-Soviet gay erotics, see Chapter 5; and also Dan Healey, "The Disappearance of the Russian Queen, or How the Soviet Closet Was Born," in *Russian Masculinities in History and Culture*, eds Barbara Evans Clements, Rebecca Friedman and Dan Healey (Basingstoke and New York: Palgrave, 2002).

111 Baldaev, *Russian Criminal Tattoo Encyclopaedia: Volume III*, 276 (an eye surrounded by barbed wire, dated 1966); 309.

112 Ibid., 278; 308 (both 1970s).

113 Ibid., 309.

114 On Soviet gays' awareness of Western gay liberation after 1969, see Chapter 4.

115 On Gulag survivors and their memoirs, see Leona Toker, *Return from the Archipelago: Narratives of Gulag Survivors* (Bloomington & Indianapolis: Indiana University Press, 2000); on the moral authority of the survivors as dissidents, see Philip Boobyer, *Conscience, Dissent and Reform in Soviet Russia* (London & New York: Routledge, 2005).

116 Kuntsman, "'With a Shade of Disgust'."

117 Ginzburg, *Within the Whirlwind*, 101–2.

118 Kuntsman, "'With a Shade of Disgust'," 326.

119 Toker, *Return from the Archipelago*, 96–7; Boobyer, *Conscience, Dissent and Reform in Soviet Russia*, 40–55.

120 Violent and consensual same-sex relations in Soviet military formations are almost entirely ignored by scholars, but for brief discussions see Konstantin L. Bannikov, *Antropologiia ekstremal'nykh grupp: Dominantnye otnosheniia sredi voennosluzhashchikh srochnoi sluzhby Rossiiskoi Armii* (Moscow: RAN Institut etnologii i antropologii, 2002), 139–45; E. A. Kashchenko,

Seksual'naia kul'tura voenno-sluzhashchikh (Moscow: Editorial URSS, 2003), 151–64.

121 Mason, "Women in the Gulag of the 1930s."

122 Yusupova, "Masculinity, Criminality, and Russian Men."

Chapter 2: Comrades, Queers, and "Oddballs": Sodomy, Masculinity, and Gendered Violence in Leningrad Province in the 1950s

1   Leningradskoi Oblastnoi Gosudarstvennyi Arkhiv v g. Vyborge (State Archive of Leningrad Province in the City of Vyborg, hereafter LOGAV), f. 3820, op. 2, d. 4471, ll. 223–4. The case file consists of two volumes, d. 4471 and d. 4471a. All further references are given thus: Morozov, d. 4471 or d. 4471a, l. 123.

2   New social and cultural histories of the 194–64 period include Elena Zubkova, *Russia after the War: Hopes, Illusions and Disappointments, 1945–1957* (Armonk, NY: M. E. Sharpe, 1998); Juliana Fürst, ed., *Late Stalinist Russia: Society between Reconstruction and Reinvention* (London: Routledge, 2006); and Polly Jones, ed., *The Dilemmas of De-Stalinization: Negotiating Cultural and Social Change in the Khrushchev Era* (London: Routledge, 2006).

3   On gender policy, see, for example, Mie Nakachi, "Population, Politics and Reproduction: Late Stalinism and Its Legacy," in Fürst, *Late Stalinist Russia*, 23–45; and for the post-1953 era, Melanie Ilic, Susan E. Reid, and Lynne Attwood, eds, *Women in the Khrushchev Era* (Basingstoke: Palgrave Macmillan, 2004).

4   In addition to essays in the collections cited above, see Lewis H. Siegelbaum, ed., *Borders of Socialism: Private Spheres of Soviet Russia* (New York: Palgrave Macmillan, 2006); Deborah A. Field, *Private Life and Communist Morality in Khrushchev's Russia* (New York: Peter Lang, 2007); Orlando Figes, *The Whisperers: Private Life in Stalin's Russia* (London: Allen Lane, 2007); and Stephen Bittner, *The Many Lives of Khrushchev's Thaw: Experience and Memory in Moscow's Arbat* (Ithaca, NY: Cornell University Press, 2008).

5   On sexualities, see Nakachi, "Population"; K. Roth-Ey, "'Loose Girls' on the Loose: Sex, Propaganda and the 1957 Youth Festival," in Ilic, Reid, and Attwood, *Women in the Khrushchev Era*, 75–95.

6   Dan Healey, "Moscow," in *Queer Sites: Gay Urban Histories since 1600*, ed. David Higgs (London: Routledge, 1999), 38–60, especially 51–7.

7   In addition to Healey, "Moscow," see, for example, Simon Karlinsky, "Russia's Gay Literature and Culture: The Impact of the October Revolution," in *Hidden from History: Reclaiming the Gay and Lesbian Past*, eds Martin Duberman, Martha Vicinus, and George Chauncey Jr. (New York: New American Library, 1989), 348–64.

8   John Howard, *Men like That: A Southern Queer History* (Chicago: University
    of Chicago Press, 1999); Peter Boag, *Same-Sex Affairs: Constructing and
    Controlling Homosexuality in the Pacific Northwest* (Berkeley: University of
    California Press, 2003).

9   Jens Rydström, *Sinners and Citizens: Bestiality and Homosexuality in Sweden,
    1880–1950* (Chicago: University of Chicago Press, 2003).

10 One analyst of murders of gay men in Britain writes: "This raises a set of
    difficult questions for gay analysts and commentators on these murders. We
    have long viewed violence against us by heterosexuals as part of our shared
    cultural history. The current study suggests, however, that we must understand
    gay people not merely as the victims of violence, but also a significant amount
    of the time as perpetrators of that violence, at least in the context of gay sexual
    homicide. A simple division between gay victim and non-gay perpetrator is not
    sustainable" (Peter Bartlett, "Killing Gay Men, 1976–2001," *British Journal
    of Criminology* 47, no. 4 [2007]: 573–95, quoted at 582). For a study that
    integrates intramale violence into a conception of modern homosexual acts
    and identity, see Henning Bech, *When Men Meet: Homosexuality and
    Modernity* (Cambridge: Polity, 1997).

11 Russia's criminal records are dispersed and damaged, and archivists have
    culled them to save space. Not all files are released to researchers. Murders
    registered by Soviet Russian justice authorities fell to just 1,641 in 1943 –
    after two desperate years of war, when administration was strained – but soon
    rose to 4,000 to 5,000 per annum in the postwar decade; in 1945, 5,941
    murderers were convicted. Other crimes against the person (including rape)
    rose from 31,000 in 1943 to 173,000 in 1953; see Gosudarstvennyi Arkhiv
    Rossiiskoi Federatsii (GARF), f. A353, op. 16, d. 20, ll. 6, 9. Although statistics
    are difficult to find, rape evidently increased sharply during the period,
    compelling authorities to raise penalties in 1949, as discussed in note 14.
    Comprehensive statistics on the prosecution of sodomy (a crime from 1934
    to 1993) do not exist, but 130 men were convicted in 1950 in Soviet Russia
    (see Chapter 7).

12 A post-1991 consensus based on archival scholarship and sophisticated
    comparative methodology has prevailed since the bitter disputes between
    "totalitarians" and "revisionists" in the 1980s; see the works by Siegelbaum,
    Field, and Fürst cited above and, for example, the multiauthor discussion
    "Historiography of the Soviet Period in Post-Soviet Perspective," *Russian
    Review* 61, no. 1 (2002): 1–51.

13 The case file: LOGAV, f. 3820, op. 2, d. 3235. All further page references,
    named after the lead protagonist, are given thus: Grishin, l. 123.

14 On sodomy law, see Dan Healey, *Homosexual Desire in Revolutionary Russia:
    The Regulation of Sexual and Gender Dissent* (Chicago: University of Chicago
    Press, 2001), 184–6. According to the decree "On Strengthening Criminal
    Responsibility for Rape" (January 4, 1949), the penalty for rape without
    aggravating circumstances was ten to fifteen years' imprisonment; for rape
    of a minor or by a group of persons, the penalty was fifteen to twenty years
    (D. S. Karev, *Ugolovnoe zakonodatel'stvo SSSR i soiuznykh respublik: Sbornik*
    [Moscow: Iuridicheskaia literatura, 1957], 23). Rape in the late Soviet period

has not been studied, but for the foundations of Soviet legislation and its enforcement, see Dan Healey, *Bolshevik Sexual Forensics: Diagnosing Disorder in Clinic and Courtroom, 1917–1939* (DeKalb: Northern Illinois University Press, 2009), 83–103.

15 Morozov, d. 4471 and d. 4471a.

16 "Homosexual panic" was not a term used by the Soviets. On its use in English law, see Bartlett, "Killing Gay Men," 573–4.

17 By mid-century, many of the "rural" sodomy cases discussed by Rydström for Sweden were in settlements that increasingly resembled urban ones; Rydström, *Sinners and Citizens*, 211–12, 317–20.

18 The settlement was renamed Kirova imeni poselok in 1936, but documents in the case file still use Nevdubstroi; see "Kirova imeni poselok," in *Bol'shaia sovetskaia entsiklopediia*, 2nd ed. (Moscow: Sovetskaia entsiklopediia, 1953), 21: 115.

19 "Rakh'ia," in *Bol'shaia sovetskaia entsiklopediia*, 2nd ed. (Moscow: Sovetskaia entsiklopediia, 1955), 36: 128.

20 N. G. Ivanov, A. S. Georgievskii, and O. S. Lobastov, *Sovetskoe zdravookhranenie i voennaia meditsina v Velikoi Otechestvennoi voine 1941–1945* (Leningrad: Meditsina, 1985), 67.

21 Nakachi, "Population," 26.

22 Ibid., 37.

23 Grishin, l. 329.

24 Morozov, d. 4471, l. 245 ob.

25 Howard, *Men like That*, 64.

26 Boag, *Same-Sex Affairs*, 42.

27 Ibid., 25–39.

28 Rydström, *Sinners and Citizens*, 211–12, 317–20.

29 Ibid., 217–21.

30 For "quiet accommodationism," see Howard, *Men like That*, xix; Rydström, *Sinners and Citizens*, 317–20; Boag, *Same-Sex Affairs*, 40–1; on the internalization of the closet, see, for example, Bech, *When Men Meet*; Eve Kosofsky Sedgwick, *Epistemology of the Closet* (Berkeley: University of California Press, 1990), 246–51.

31 Boag argues that "some men sought transient society as a refuge and did not merely perceive it as a closet" (*Same-Sex Affairs*, 41). Rydström sees both actors in the rural Swedish age-stratified pairing "taking the initiative" in his data, and he concludes that before 1930 sex between men in the countryside was "to a large extent situational" (*Sinners and Citizens*, 319). Rydström charts the arrival of urban discourses of homosexuality from the 1930s in rural Sweden, calling it "a changing paradigm" (219–21).

32 Boag, *Same-Sex Affairs*, 45–86; Rydström, *Sinners and Citizens*, 254–65.

33 Grishin, ll. 397–8. After a decree in 1936, "unregistered" de facto marriages lost much legal status, yet the housing shortage discouraged many from formally registering their union.

34 "Did not experience arousal with women; in his cohabitation with Babenko after the sex act he often felt no satisfaction but only achieved a state of sexual arousal when Babenko was sexually intimate with his partners [male]" (Grishin, l. 233).

35 Grishin, ll. 4–4 ob.

36 In court, Grishin denied sodomy but admitted to fellatio (minet): "Fellatio has been my illness since childhood" (l. 373).

37 Babenko named two more rapists who also had sexual contact with Grishin before or during the sexual assault (Grishin, l. 4 ob.).

38 Grishin, l. 135.

39 For sexual "exchanges" by Soviet women migrants living in similar situations in the pre-war years, see Elena Shulman, "Soviet Maidens for the Socialist Fortress: The Khetagurovite Campaign to Settle the Far East, 1937–1939," Russian Review 62, no. 3 (2003): 387–410. On "treating" more generally, see Kathy Peiss, "'Charity Girls' and City Pleasures: Historical Notes on Working-Class Sexuality, 1880–1920," in Powers of Desire: The Politics of Sexuality, eds Ann Snitow, Christine Stansell, and Sharon Thompson (New York: Monthly Review, 1983), 57–69.

40 Morozov, d. 4471, l. 302 ob.

41 Morozov, d. 4471a, l. 110 ob.

42 On Soviet forensic techniques to detect sodomy, see Healey, Homosexual Desire in Revolutionary Russia, 212–13, 239–40.

43 Morozov's wife told police that she was unaware of her husband's homosexual activities; their sex life was "normal," and "he never tried to commit unnatural sex acts with me" (d. 4471a, l. 25 ob.). By 1959 the couple had two children.

44 Morozov, d. 4471a, l. 111.

45 Morozov, d. 4471, l. 224 ob.

46 In Russian masculine culture, serving as the "passive" partner in anal intercourse had long been considered shameful; see Dan Healey, "The Disappearance of the Russian Queen, or How the Soviet Closet Was Born," in Russian Masculinities in History and Culture, eds Barbara Evans Clements, Rebecca Friedman, and Dan Healey (Basingstoke, UK: Palgrave, 2001), 152–71.

47 On drinking in masculine culture, see Christine D. Worobec, "Masculinity in Late Imperial Russian Society," 76–93, and Steven A. Smith, "Masculinity in Transition: Peasant Migrants to Late Imperial St. Petersburg," 94–112, both in Clements, Friedman, and Healey, Russian Masculinities; on courtship and sexuality between men facilitated by drink, see Healey, "Moscow"; Healey, Homosexual Desire in Revolutionary Russia, 23–6, 43, 94–5.

48 Two other photos from Grishin's collection bore the drinking motif, but neither had inscriptions.

49 The status of fellatio in Soviet law was ambiguous and variable. Investigators in Leningrad in 1951 decided it was not punishable as "sodomy." On 1930s legal constructions of sodomy, see Healey, Homosexual Desire in Revolutionary Russia, 217–19. Elsewhere in Grishin's collection of pictures,

the same policeman annotated one photograph of a fellator and another indicating the subject was in a psychiatric hospital.

50 Dan Healey, "Sexual and Gender Dissent: Homosexuality as Resistance in Stalin's Russia," in *Contending with Stalinism: Soviet Power and Popular Resistance in the 1930s*, ed. Lynne Viola (Ithaca, NY: Cornell University Press, 2002), 139–69; see also Chapter 7.

51 On post-Soviet culture, see Brian James Baer, *Other Russias: Homosexuality and the Crisis of Post-Soviet Identity* (New York: Palgrave Macmillan, 2009).

52 Men did rape each other in the USSR, of course, often in the Gulag. See Chapter 1.

53 Grishin, l. 373 ob.

54 Here I make a leap from sexual "discourse" to sexual practice that Halperin eschews in his carefully argued essay, "How to do the History of Homosexuality," in *How to Do the History of Homosexuality* (Chicago: University of Chicago Press, 2002), 104–37. In rural Sweden, by comparison with urban cases, homosexual practice was "more charged with power" based on disparities of class, age, and gender roles (Rydström, *Sinners and Citizens*, 215).

55 Russia's "pederast for money" was not always a prostitute; the term was used by psychiatrists and lawyers to describe men who serviced the *tetka*. These men did not have their own subcultural label, apparently preserving their masculine credentials behind a mask of silence. See Healey, "The Disappearance," 155–60; and George Chauncey, *Gay New York: Gender, Urban Culture, and the Making of the Gay Male World, 1890–1940* (New York: Basic Books, 1994), 47–97.

56 Grishin, l. 178 ob., 233 ob.

57 Morozov, d. 4471, l. 220.

58 The diaries of Mikhail Kuzmin, gay poet, composer, and author of the coming-out novel *Kryl'ia* (Wings, 1906), display examples of this linguistic queerness. See M. A. Kuzmin, *Dnevnik 1905–1907* (Saint Petersburg: Ivan Limbakh, 2002); M. A. Kuzmin, *Dnevnik 1908–1915* (Saint Petersburg: Ivan Limbakh, 2005); M. A. Kuzmin, *Dnevnik 1934 goda* (Saint Petersburg: Ivan Limbakh, 1998). On Kuzmin, see also John E. Malmstad and Nikolay Bogomolov, *Mikhail Kuzmin: A Life in Art* (Cambridge, MA: Harvard University Press, 1999); John E. Malmstad, "Bathhouses, Hustlers, and a Sex Club: The Reception of Mikhail Kuzmin's *Wings*," *Journal of the History of Sexuality* 9, nos. 1/2 (2000): 85–104. For gay subcultural argot from the 1920s to the 1980s, see Vladimir Kozlovskii, *Argo russkoi gomoseksual'noi subkul'tury: Materialy k izucheniiu* (Benson, VT: Chalidze, 1986).

59 Morozov, d. 4471, ll. 252 ob, 258.

60 Morozov, d. 4471, ll 252 ob.-53.

61 For Soviet examples, see V. M. Bekhterev, "Polovye ukloneniia i izvrashcheniia v svete refleksologii," *Voprosy izucheniia i vospitaniia lichnosti*, nos. 4/5 (1922): 644–746 (case history at 734–5); and A. K. Sudomir, "K kazuistike i sushchnosti gomoseksual'nost'," *Sovremennaia psikhonevrologiia* 5, no. 11 (1927): 371–7 (case history at 375).

62 On these points, see Healey, *Homosexual Desire in Revolutionary Russia*, 26–9; and Tricia Starks, *The Body Soviet: Propaganda, Hygiene, and the Revolutionary State* (Madison: University of Wisconsin Press, 2008), 171, 177.

63 Morozov, d. 4471, l. 297 ob.

64 Morozov, d. 4471, ll. 285 ob., 286.

65 Morozov, d. 4471, ll. 247 ob., 248 ob.

66 Morozov, d. 4471, l. 249 ob.

67 Morozov, d. 4471, ll. 252 ob., 253 ob.

68 Morozov, d. 4471, l. 294 ob.

69 For very similar distinctions made by family members to police and social workers investigating family breakdown, see Field, *Private Life*.

70 On transitions in the popular view of the sanctity of private life after 1945, see Figes, *The Whisperers*, 455–596; and Brian LaPierre, "Private Matters or Public Crimes: The Emergence of Domestic Hooliganism in the Soviet Union, 1939–1966," in Siegelbaum, *Borders of Socialism*, 191–209. In the case of Vadim Kozin, discussed in Chapter 3, a homosexual "outed" and shamed by arrest and imprisonment was treated in a shrill homophobic manner by his co-workers. Once the "secret" of homosexuality was fully exposed it had to be condemned loudly and publicly.

71 Juliane Fürst, "Introduction: Late Stalinist Society: History, Policies and People," in Fürst, *Late Stalinist Russia*, 1–20, at 5.

72 Rituals of young men's transition to military service (song, dance, and drinking on the eve of conscription) are catalogued in Zh. V. Kormina, *Provody v armiiu v poreformennoi Rossii: Opyt etnograficheskogo analiza* (Moscow: Novoe literaturnoe obozrenie, 2005); masculine culture inside the contemporary army is extensively described in K. L. Bannikov, *Antropologiia ekstremal'nykh grupp: Dominantnye otnosheniia sredi voennosluzhashchikh srochnoi sluzhby Rossiiskoi Armii* (Moscow: RAN Institut etnologii i antropologii, 2002); the return to civilian life is less researched, but see Rebecca Kay, *Men in Contemporary Russia: The Fallen Heroes of Post-Soviet Change?* (Aldershot, UK: Ashgate, 2006).

73 Kay, *Men in Contemporary Russia*, 42–72. In the Grishin case, the older skilled defendants earned between 800 and 1,000 rubles per month, while younger workers – and Kiselev, a disadvantaged unskilled worker – earned between 300 and 350 rubles. Kirsanov, a nineteen-year-old plasterer earning 300 rubles per month, told psychiatrists he could not afford to drink on payday (Grishin, l. 183).

74 On the ideological approaches to female prostitution in the 1920s and 1930s, see N. B. Lebina and M. B. Shkarovskii, *Prostitutsiia v Peterburge* (Moscow: Progress-Akademiia, 1994); Elizabeth Waters, "Victim or Villain: Prostitution in Post-revolutionary Russia," in *Women and Society in Russia and the Soviet Union*, ed. Linda Edmondson (Cambridge: Cambridge University Press, 1992), 160–77.

75 Bartlett, "Killing Gay Men," 582.

76 For an analysis of modern homosexuality as deeply implicated by masculine violence, see Bech, *When Men Meet*, 32, 77–82.

Chapter 3: The Diary of Soviet Singer Vadim Kozin: Reading Queer Subjectivity in 1950s Russia

1   For an English-language interpretation of Kozin's repertoire, including "Friendship," see the Marc Almond album, *Orpheus in Exile*, 2009.

2   The diary was published in Russian with a preface, epilogue, and editorial commentary by Boris Savchenko as Vadim Kozin, *Prokliatoe iskusstvo* (Moscow: Vagrius, 2005).

3   Kuzmin's full diary has not yet been published and only brief segments have been translated into English; on him the most comprehensive work in English is John E. Malmstad and Nikolay Bogomolov, *Mikhail Kuzmin: A Life in Art* (Cambridge, Ma. & London: Harvard University Press, 1999).

4   Irina Paperno, "What Can Be Done with Diaries?" *Russian Review* 63, no. 4 (2004): 561–73; Boris Wolfson, "Escape from Literature: Constructing the Soviet Self in Yuri Olesha's Diary of the 1930s," *Russian Review* 63, no. 4 (2004): 609–20.

5   Jochen Hellbeck, "The Diary between Literature and History: A Historian's Critical Response," *Russian Review* 63, no. 4 (2004): 621–9; idem, *Revolution on My Mind: Writing a Diary under Stalin* (Cambridge, Ma. & London: Harvard University Press, 2006).

6   Anna Krylova, "The Tenacious Liberal Subject in Soviet Studies," *Kritika: Explorations in Russian and Eurasian History* 1, no. 1 (2000): 119–46. For an attempt to write histories of queer women that evades such presentism, see Laura L. Doan, *Disturbing Practices: History, Sexuality, and Women's Experience of Modern War* (Chicago: University of Chicago Press, 2013).

7   Matt Cook, "Sex Lives and Diary Writing: The Journals of George Ives," in *Life Writing and Victorian Culture*, ed. David Amigoni (Aldershot: Ashgate Publishing, 2006).

8   Much of this biographical section is based on the publications of Russian journalist and Kozin fan Boris Savchenko. His fullest account is Boris Savchenko, *Vadim Kozin* (Smolensk: Rusich, 2001). I am also indebted to Monica Whitlock for her insights on both Kozin and Savchenko.

9   Louise McReynolds, "'The Incomparable' Anastasiia Vial'tseva and the Culture of Personality," in *Russia, Women, Culture*, eds Helena Goscilo and Beth Holmgren (Bloomington & Indianapolis: Indiana University Press, 1996); on drag shows in tsarist Russia, see idem, *Russia at Play: Leisure Activities at the End of the Tsarist Era* (Ithaca and London: Cornell University Press, 2003), 113–53; and Ol'ga Khoroshilova, "Pervye travesty revoliutsionnogo Petrograda," http://arzamas.academy/mag/166-queer (accessed April 30, 2016).

10 Savchenko, *Vadim Kozin*, 38.

11 On the sailor in the city's homosexual subculture see Dan Healey, *Homosexual Desire in Revolutionary Russia: The Regulation of Sexual and Gender Dissent* (Chicago: University of Chicago Press, 2001), 38, 40–2, 44–6.

12 Kozin claimed the teacher committed fellatio on him, and he associated sex with women afterwards exclusively with oral sex, unless one wanted children. Savchenko quotes extensively from Kozin's 1959 "confession" to police in his Preface to the diary; see Kozin, *Prokliatoe iskusstvo*, 13–16.

13 Kozin, *Prokliatoe iskusstvo*, 15.

14 The Soviet definition of "sodomy" was never securely fixed in jurisprudence and the popular conception of the term as focused on anal intercourse alone influenced defendants and jurists; on excuses, see Healey, *Homosexual Desire in Revolutionary Russia,* 220–3.

15 Savchenko did not quiz Kozin about the veracity of the "confession"; Kozin, *Prokliatoe iskusstvo*, 15.

16 Savchenko, *Vadim Kozin*, 78–9.

17 The incidents in this paragraph are described in ibid., 79–84.

18 Ibid., 80.

19 Ibid., 111–13, 115–16; Savchenko records the Teheran legend as fact, and dismisses challenges to it.

20 Ibid., 129–30. Kozin's streak for self-dramatization is evident in this story, told years later to his trusted biographer. Other explanations are more prosaic: he may have let slip an unguarded remark while pleading to evacuate his mother and sister from besieged Leningrad (they died there); or he was denounced as a traitor for giving a concert to Polish soldiers, on the eve of their release from the USSR to join the Allies. (Ibid., 122–4).

21 Savchenko clarifies gaps in his previous publications by spelling out the 3 charges against Kozin brought in 1944 as article 58–10–2 (counterrevolutionary agitation in wartime); article 152 ("depraved acts," i.e. non-penetrative sexual activity, with minors under eighteen years of age); and article 154-a, sodomy: Kozin, *Prokliatoe iskusstvo*, 17–18. Kozin refused to explain the charges in interviews with Savchenko.

22 Pavel Grebeniuk, *Kolymskii led: Sistema upravleniia na Severo-Vostoke Rossii 1953–1964* (Moscow: ROSSPEN, 2007), 23.

23 Savchenko, *Vadim Kozin*, 198–9.

24 Kozin later claimed the young man needed money to travel home, and that he also traded in stamps – a passion shared with the singer. Again, one cannot sift self-defense from the truth. The fullest account of this case is found in Savchenko's introduction and epilogue to Kozin, *Prokliatoe iskusstvo*, 18, 364–6. Yet even the details offered here are sketchy.

25 Savchenko, "Predislovie," in Kozin, *Prokliatoe iskusstvo*, 18.

26 Victims of the Stalin anti-sodomy law, arrested in the decades after 1953, have left a small body of autobiographical and literary texts. On film director Sergei Paradzhanov, writer Gennady Trifonov, and others, see Chapter 7.

27 Savchenko claims that Kozin kept diaries through most of his adult life, and the biographer may possess further, unpublished, volumes; he also says the singer gave some volumes away, and others are still held in Magadan FSB archives; personal communication, Monica Whitlock, February 23, 2015.

28 Cook, "Sex Lives and Diary Writing," 208.

29 Kozin, *Prokliatoe iskusstvo*, 338 (September 26, 1956). On the renegotiation of the public-private divide in society after 1953, see Chapter 2.

30 Kozin, *Prokliatoe iskusstvo*, 56 (June 20, 1955).

31 Kozin, *Prokliatoe iskusstvo*, 78 (July 12, 1955).

32 Kozin, *Prokliatoe iskusstvo*, 168 (October 28, 1955).

33 Kozin, *Prokliatoe iskusstvo*, 233 (March 24, 1956).

34 Kozin, *Prokliatoe iskusstvo*, 223 (February 9, 1956).

35 Kozin, *Prokliatoe iskusstvo*, 228 (March 4, 1956). Previous elliptical passages suggest that Ershov, a Moscow Bolshoi Theater official, has an "adventurous" sex life with men: see e.g. Kozin, *Prokliatoe iskusstvo*, 73 (July 7, 1955).

36 Cook, "Sex Lives and Diary Writing," 202.

37 Kozin, *Prokliatoe iskusstvo*, 150 (May 29, 1955).

38 For Ives's disparaging attitude towards the overt and especially the promiscuous queen, see Cook, 205–6. On Tchaikovsky's comments about of effeminate queens in his diary in 1888, see Healey, *Homosexual Desire in Revolutionary* Russia, 41.

39 Kozin, *Prokliatoe iskusstvo*, 109–10 (August 26, 1955).

40 Kozin, *Prokliatoe iskusstvo*, 300 (August 3, 1956).

41 Kozin, *Prokliatoe iskusstvo*, 98 (August 11, 1955).

42 See Healey, *Homosexual Desire in Revolutionary Russia*, 71.

43 Kozin, *Prokliatoe iskusstvo*, 313–14 (August 18, 1956).

44 Kozin, *Prokliatoe iskusstvo*, 315 (August 19, 1956).

45 There is no systematic study of gender and friendship in Russia, but on heterosexual male bonding, see e.g. Eliot Borenstein, *Men without Women: Masculinity and Revolution in Russian Fiction, 1917–1929* (Durham and London: Duke University Press, 2000); Thomas G. Schrand, "Socialism in One Gender: Masculine Values in the Stalin Revolution," in *Russian Masculinities in History and Culture*, eds Barbara Evans Clements, Rebecca Friedman and Dan Healey (Basingstoke & New York: Palgrave, 2002).

46 Kozin, *Prokliatoe iskusstvo*, 209, 259, 276, 280–1, etc. On Kabalov, see Savchenko, "Predislovie," ibid., 20.

47 Cook, "Sex Lives and Diary Writing," 201–2.

48 Savchenko, "Predislovie," in Kozin, *Prokliatoe iskusstvo*, 27–8.

Chapter 4: From Stalinist Pariahs to Subjects of "Managed Democracy": Queers in Moscow, 1945 to the Present

1 On the "limits of [state] intervention" in late-Soviet sexual life, and conflict over sex education projects, see Deborah A. Field, *Private Life and Communist Morality in Khrushchev's Russia* (New York, Bern, Berlin: Peter Lang, 2007), 51–66.

2 See the discussion of Russian queer community before 1934 in Chapter 7, and see the new evidence discussed in Irina Roldugina, "'Pochemu my takie liudi?' Rannesovetskie gomoseksualy ot pervogo litsa: novye istochniki po istorii gomoseksual'nykh identichnostei v Rossii," *Ab Imperio*, no. 2 (2016): 183–216.

3 As a contemporary observer described the rise of U.S. gay and lesbian liberation: Dennis Altman, *The Homosexualization of America, the Americanization of the Homosexual* (New York: St Martin's Press, 1982).

4 E. M. Andreev, L. E. Darskii, and T. L. Khar'kova, *Naselenie Sovetskogo Soiuza, 1922–1991* (Moscow: Nauka, 1993), 77.

5 Mie Nakachi, "Population, Politics and Reproduction: Late Stalinism and its legacy," in *Late Stalinist Russia: Society between reconstruction and reinvention*, ed. Juliane Fürst (London & New York: Routledge, 2006), 29–37.

6 Erica Lee Fraser, "Masculinity and the Sexual Politics of Self and Other in Soviet Political Cartoons, 1945–1955," MA thesis, University of British Columbia, 2000.

7 For example, in the 1949 musical "Kubanskie kazaki" (The Kuban Cossacks), discussed in Dan Healey, "'Untraditional Sex' and the 'Simple Russian': Nostalgia for Soviet Innocence in the Polemics of Dilia Enikeeva," in *What is Soviet Now? Identities, Legacies, Memories*, eds Thomas Lahusen and Peter H. Solomon Jr. (Berlin: Lit Verlag, 2008), 184–5.

8 On living standards and hygiene, see Donald Filtzer, *The Hazards of Urban Life in Late Stalinist Russia: Health, hygiene, and living standards, 1943–1953* (Cambridge: Cambridge University Press, 2010); and Ethan Pollock, "Real Men Go to the Banya: Postwar Soviet Masculinities and the Bathhouse," *Kritika: Explorations in Russian and Eurasian History* 11, no. 1 (2010): 47–76.

9 Dan Healey, "Moscow," in *Queer Sites: Gay Urban Histories since 1600*, ed. David Higgs (London: Routledge, 1999), 38–9, 51–2, 54, 56.

10 On arrests and policing during the period see Chapter 7.

11 An excellent guide to the period is Miriam Dobson, *Khrushchev's Cold Summer: Gulag Returnees, Crime, and the Fate of Reform after Stalin* (Ithaca & London: Cornell University Press, 2009); on gender policies, see Melanie Ilic, Susan E. Reid, and Lynne Attwood, eds *Women in the Khrushchev Era* (Basingstoke: Palgrave Macmillan, 2004). On private life, see Deborah A. Field, *Private Life and Communist Morality in Khrushchev's Russia* (New York, Bern, Berlin: Peter Lang, 2007); and Lewis H. Siegelbaum, ed. *Borders of Socialism: Private Spheres of Soviet Russia* (New York: Palgrave Macmillan, 2006).

12 Dan Healey, *Homosexual Desire in Revolutionary Russia: The Regulation of Sexual and Gender Dissent* (Chicago: University of Chicago Press, 2001), 262; police entrapment, see Vladimir Kozlovskii, *Argo russkoi gomoseksual'noi subkul'tury: Materialy k izucheniiu* (Benson, VT: Chalidze Publications, 1986), 196–9; "G" [Harlow Robinson], "The Secret Life of Moscow," *Christopher Street*, June (1980), 15–21. For a trial of two middle-aged men, caught masturbating in a Moscow toilet in the early 1960s, see George Feifer, *Justice in Moscow* (London: The Bodley Head, 1964), 207–8.

13 On Kozin's 1959 arrest see Vadim Kozin, *Prokliatoe iskusstvo* (Moscow: Vagrius, 2005), 18.

14 Masha Gessen, *The Rights of Lesbians and Gay Men in the Russian Federation* (San Francisco: International Gay and Lesbian Human Rights Commission, 1994), 17–18; Healey, *Homosexual Desire in Revolutionary Russia*, 244; A. M. Sviadoshch, *Zhenskaia seksopatologiia* (Moscow: Meditsina, 1974), 165–7.

15 There is still no comprehensive history of Soviet "psychiatric abuse"; on what is known, see Dan Healey, "Russian and Soviet Forensic Psychiatry: Troubled and Troubling," *International Journal of Law and Psychiatry* 37, no. 1 (2014): 71–81.

16 Vladimir Kirsanov, *69. Russkie gei, lesbiianki, biseksualy i transseksualy* (Tver': Ganimed, 2005) 296–302.

17 Ibid., 302, referring to opinions in Ol'ga Zhuk, *Russkie amazonki: Istoriia lesbiiskoi subkul'tury v Rossii* XX *vek* (Moscow: Glagol, 1998). "Lev Margaritovich" is a male name, adopted by Ranevskaya's female character after a psychological shock – her abandonment by a lover. The middle name or patronymic 'Margaritovich' (son-of-Margaret) troubles Russian gender expectations because patronymics are formed from father's names: Margaritovich is a queer, impossible, patronymic.

18 Kirsanov, *69. Russkie gei, lesbiianki, biseksualy i transseksualy*, 312–22. For translations of Barkova's poems see Catriona Kelly, "Anna Barkova (1901–1976)," in *Russian Women Writers*, ed. Christine D. Tomei (New York & London: Garland Publishing, 1999), 943–56; Semyon Vilensky, *Til My Tale is Told: Women's Memoirs of the Gulag* (London: Virago, 2001), 213–20.

19 For statistics see A. Volodin, *Moskva: Sputnik Turista* (Moscow: Moskovskii rabochii, 1957), 15; Evan Mawdsley, *Blue Guide: Moscow and Leningrad* (London: A. & C. Black, 1991), 25. Car ownership: Lewis H. Siegelbaum, "Cars, Cars and More Cars: The Faustian Bargain of the Brezhnev Era," in *Borders of Socialism: Private Spheres of Soviet Russia*, ed. Lewis H. Siegelbaum (New York: Palgrave Macmillan, 2006).

20 For speculation, from a gay Soviet observer, that single homosexuals could buy cooperative flats in Moscow towards the end of the 1970s, see Anon., "International: Extrait de Labour Focus on Eastern Europe (publié à Londres) 'Being Gay in Moscou [sic]'," *Masques: revue des homosexualités*, no. 5 Summer (1980): 60; for examples of single gay men owning their own flats from the same period, see "G," "The Secret Life of Moscow," 18, 20.

21 Anon., "International," 60.

22 On the internal passport and registration system, see David R. Shearer, *Policing Stalin's Socialism: Repression and Social Order in the Soviet Union, 1924–1953* (New Haven & London: Yale University Press, 2009), and the discussion in Chapter 7.

23 On the attraction to Moscow, see "G," "The Secret Life of Moscow," 20–1.

24 I base these claims on personal observation in Russia, and on the confidential autobiographies of gay male and lesbian asylum claimants passed to me in the capacity of expert witness. For late Soviet divorce rates, see Peter H. Juviler, "Cell Mutation in Soviet Society: The Family," in *Soviet Society and Culture:*

Essays in Honor of Vera S. Dunham, eds Terry L. Thompson and Richard Sheldon (Boulder & London: Westview Press, 1988), 42–3.

25 "G," "The Secret Life of Moscow," 18–20; Alexandre Dymov, "Document: les homosexuels russes coincés entre la faucille et le marteau: Homo Sovieticus," *Lui*, fevrier (1980): 104.

26 Healey, *Homosexual Desire in Revolutionary Russia*, 21–49; Healey, "Moscow," 43–9.

27 The "circuit" undoubtedly varied historically, and seasonally (although one should not discount the Russian hardiness in winter), and the following description relies on a range of sources including "G," "The Secret Life of Moscow"; Masha Gessen, "We Have No Sex: Soviet Gays and AIDS in the Era of Glasnost," *Outlook* 3, no. 1 (1990): 42–54, especially 46–7; Kozlovskii, *Argo gomoseksual'noi subkul'tury*; Dymov, "Document," 94. The street and landmark names in this section are those in use before 1991 and many have since changed.

28 "Avenue of Sluts," "Boulevard of Young Gifts," "Homodrome" (after Hippodrome, racetrack), "The Zoo," "Club of Free Emotions," "Place Pigalle," and "The Stroke" were some popular labels for the Bolshoi Theater square; see Kozlovskii, *Argo gomoseksual'noi subkul'tury*, 60, 73.

29 Healey, *Homosexual Desire in Revolutionary Russia*, 216, 339 n. 36; V. Arkhangel'skii, "Konets glavnoi pleshke Moskvy," *ARGO*, 5 (1997): 4–5.

30 Rumors: Anon., "International," 59; Dymov, "Document," 114.

31 The number of convictions for sodomy in the Russian Republic were within the range of 773 and 883 during the 1970s; Healey, *Homosexual Desire in Revolutionary Russia*, 262.

32 The Olympics clean-up is briefly described in "G," "The Secret Life of Moscow," 15–16.

33 Ibid, 16. Side streets near the Bolshoi Theater also harbored the "Sadko" and the "Artistic" cafés that attracted a gay crowd in the late 1970s and early 1980s.

34 Healey, "Moscow," 45, 52; Pollock, "Real Men Go to the Banya."

35 Tom Reeves, "Red & Gay: Oppression East and West," *Fag Rag*, no. 6 (Fall 1973): 5–6.

36 I am grateful to Viktor Oboin, who took me on a tour of these facilities – or their sites, since the Gogol Boulevard toilets had long since collapsed, in the summer of 2000. On Gogol's sexuality, see Simon Karlinsky, *The Sexual Labyrinth of Nikolai Gogol* (Cambridge: Harvard University Press, 1976).

37 Siegelbaum, "Cars, Cars and More Cars," 96, discusses only heterosexual trysts, but suggestively depicts the Soviet car owner's world as solidly homosocial, and therefore, in my view, not without queer opportunities.

38 Kozlovskii, *Argo gomoseksual'noi subkul'tury*, 6–14.

39 See for example Dan Healey, "The Disappearance of the Russian Queen, or How the Soviet Closet Was Born," in *Russian Masculinities in History and Culture*, eds Barbara Evans Clements, Rebecca Friedman and Dan Healey (Basingstoke and New York: Palgrave, 2002).

40 Dymov, "Document," 94; see also Kozlovskii, *Argo gomoseksual'noi subkul'tury*, 18.

41 Gessen, "We Have No Sex," 46–7, reports such views in an article about Soviet gay life at the end of the 1980s.

42 For an argument that "community" in the Western sense was impossible, see Dan Schluter, *Gay Life in the Former USSR: Fraternity without Community* (New York: Routledge, 2002).

43 The "manifestos" were Leningrad's Yury Trifonov's 1977 open letter to Soviet authorities, ignored in Russia but published in the Western gay press; and Moscow's Evgeny Kharitonov's "Leaflet," celebrating "our lightweight floral species with our pollen flying who knows where." See both texts in Moss, Kevin, ed., *Out of the Blue: Russia's Hidden Gay Literature* (San Francisco: Gay Sunshine Press, 1996), 224–5, 230–2.

44 Kozlovskii, *Argo gomoseksual'noi subkul'tury*, 17.

45 Ibid. Appeals to Freudian theory and historical figures, see e.g. Healey, *Homosexual Desire in Revolutionary Russia*, 71; and also note Kozin's invocation of Tchaikovsky in his diary, Chapter 3.

46 "G," "The Secret Life of Moscow," 17.

47 Reeves, "Red and Gay," 3.

48 Dymov, "Document," 114.

49 Reeves, "Red and Gay," 6; "G," "The Secret Life of Moscow," 20; Anon., "International"; Dymov, "Document," 104; Joep Schrijvers, Arto Hyvönen, and Reijo Härkönen, "Les Gais De Leningrad," *Gai Pied Hebdo*, 110 (March 10–16, 1984), 22–5.

50 Anon., "International," 60.

51 For example, a "Gay Laboratory" in Leningrad operated in 1983–4, and smuggled its manifesto and other materials out to Amsterdam via gay members of the Dutch Communist Party; see Schrijvers et al., "Les Gais De Leningrad." On "Gay Laboratory" see also Sergej Shcherbakov, "On the Relationship between the Leningrad Gay Community and Legal Authorities in the 1970s and 1980s," in *Sexual Minorities and Society: the Changing Attitudes toward Homosexuality in 20th Century Europe*, eds Udo Parikas and Teet Veispak (Tallinn: Institute of History, 1991); and note also Reeves, "Red and Gay."

52 "G," "The Secret Life of Moscow," 22.

53 Kirsanov, 69. *Russkie gei, lesbiianki, biseksualy i transseksualy*, 396–7.

54 Ibid., 410–12.

55 Ibid., 418. See also her autobiography, Ol'ga Krauze, *Otpetaia zhizn'* (Tver': Novaia Real'nost', 2009).

56 On Leningrad's underground scene, see Alexei Yurchak, *Everything Was Forever, until It Was No More: The Last Soviet Generation* (Princeton: Princeton University Press, 2006).

57 On medical care for intersex patients in the 1920s–1930s in Russia, see Dan Healey, *Bolshevik Sexual Forensics: Diagnosing Disorder in the Clinic and Courtroom, 1917–1939* (DeKalb: Northern Illinois University Press, 2009),

134–58; on Soviet sex changes in the 1920s, see Healey, *Homosexual Desire in Revolutionary Russia*, 165–70.

58 I. V. Golubeva, *Germafroditizm (Klinika, Diagnostika, Lechenie)* (Moscow: Meditsina, 1980), 100–1.

59 Ibid., 105–7, 148–50 (quote at 102); A. I. Belkin, *Tret'ii Pol* (Moscow: Olimp, 2000).

60 Igor' S. Kon, *Seksual'naia Kul'tura v Rossii: Klubnichka na Berezke* (Moscow: OGI, 1997), 183.

61 N. O. Milanov, R. T. Adamian, and G. I. Kozlov, *Korrektsiia Pola pri Transseksualizme* (Moscow: Kalinkin i K., 1999), 15–17, 125–34.

62 David Tuller, *Cracks in the Iron Closet: Travels in Gay & Lesbian Russia* (Boston: Faber & Faber, 1996), 155–67; Ol'ga Krauze, "Vashi Pis'ma," *Gay, Slaviane!,* 2 (1994): 90.

63 For the delayed sexual revolution, see Eliot Borenstein, *Overkill: Sex and Violence in Contemporary Russian Popular Culture* (Ithaca: Cornell University Press, 2008); on the queer dimensions, see Brian James Baer, *Other Russias: Homosexuality and the Crisis of Post-Soviet Identity* (New York: Palgrave Macmillan, 2009). On AIDS in the Soviet press, Dan Healey, "Can Glasnost Cope with Aids?" *The Pink Paper* (London) (18 March 1989), 2; idem, "Pros & Cons with Professor Kon: Russia's Pre-Eminent Sexologist Dissects Russia's Emerging Lesbian and Gay Movement," *Xtra!* (Toronto) (July 1992), 8–9.

64 See Kirsanov, *69. Russkie gei, lesbiianki, biseksualy i transseksualy*, 412–13, 476–9; Julie Dorf, "On the Theme: Talking with the Editor of the Soviet Union's First Lesbian and Gay Newspaper," *Outlook*, 1 (1990), 55–9.

65 Kirsanov, *69. Russkie gei, lesbiianki, biseksualy i transseksualy*, 479–83; Artur Gasparian, "Gosudarstvu ne mesto v posteliakh svoikh grazhdan," *Moskovskii komsomolets*, 182 (24 September 1991), 1.

66 Rex Wockner, "Heroes of the USSR: Soviet gays and lesbians fight coup," *Capital Gay*, 509 (30 August 1991), 3.

67 Kirsanov, *69. Russkie gei, lesbiianki, biseksualy i transseksualy*, 483, makes this point.

68 Gessen, *The Rights of Lesbians and Gay Men*, 24. Some reformers were queer but hidden; one middle-ranking member of the Yeltsin team who later came out was journalist Andrei Cherkizov (1954–2007) – however, his influence on the repeal of the anti-sodomy law was apparently minimal; see Vladimir Kirsanov, *+31. Russkie Gei, Lesbiianki, Biseksualy i Transseksualy* (Moscow: Kvir, 2007), 119–24.

69 On the 1997 criminal code's flaws, see Healey, *Homosexual Desire in Revolutionary Russia*, 249–50.

70 Kirsanov, *69. Russkie gei, lesbiianki, biseksualy i transseksualy*, 455–60; idem, *+31. Russkie Gei, Lesbiianki, Biseksualy i Transseksualy*, 106–12. *Adel'fe*, Moscow, eds Mila Ugol'nikova and Tat'iana Ivanova (1996–), five issues; *Ostrov* (1999–2014), sixty-one issues; *Sofa Safo* (2003), two issues; and *Labris* (2004–5), five issues (see http://az.gay.ru/books/index_magazines.html, last accessed July 27, 2016).

71 On Triangle see Paul Legendre, *V Poiskakh Sebia: Polozhenie Geev i Lesbiianok v Sovremennoi Rossii* (Moscow: Charities Aid Foundation, 1997), 23; conference: Dan Healey, "'Russky 'Comrades' Nix Commies in Election," *Xtra!*, 304 (20 June 1996), 55.

72 Oboin named his archive GenderDok; the newsletter was *Zerkalo*, "The Mirror" (eighteen issues, 1995–9); on GenderDok see also Legendre, *V Poiskakh Sebia*, 23–4.

73 E. Gusiatinskaia, ed., *Antologiia Lesbiiskoi Prozy* (Tver': Kolonna Publications, 2006); Kirsanov, 69. *Russkie gei, lesbiianki, biseksualy i transseksualy*, 396–400.

74 For a resume of Russian homophobia in the 1990s, see Viktor Oboin, "Gomofobiia v Sovremennoi Rossii: Vse Ottenki Chernogo," in Viktor Oboin, ed., *Gomofobiia v Sovremennoi Rossii 1993–2001 g.g. Dokumenty, Fakty* (Moscow: The author, 2001).

75 The "second generation" of post-Soviet LGBT activists is discussed in the Introduction.

Chapter 5: Active, Passive, and Russian: The National Idea in Gay Men's Pornography

1 For summaries of these developments, see Eliot Borenstein, *Overkill: Sex and Violence in Contemporary Russian Popular Culture* (Ithaca: Cornell University Press, 2008), 24–50; and Igor S. Kon, *Seksual'naia Kul'tura v Rossii: Klubnichka na Berezke* 2nd edition (Moscow: Airis-press, 2005).

2 On cultural globalization, see for example, Martin Albrow, *The Global Age: State and Society Beyond Modernity* (Cambridge: Polity Press, 1996), 140–55; Zygmunt Bauman, *Globalization: The Human Consequences* (Cambridge: Polity Press, 1998), 77–102. Russian commentators resist their country's assignment to a global "periphery"; see Hilary Pilkington "Cultural Globalization: A Peripheral Perspective," in *Looking West? Cultural Globalization and Youth Cultures*, eds Hilary Pilkington, Elena Omel'chenko, Moya Flynn, Ul'iana Bliudina and Elena Starkova (University Park: Pennsylvania State University Press, 2002).

3 While demographic anxieties pre-dated Putin, he made it a biopolitical priority. See Michele Rivkin-Fish, "From 'Demographic Crisis' to 'Dying Nation': The Politics of Language and Reproduction in Russia," in *Gender and National Identity in Twentieth-Century Russian Culture*, eds Helena Goscilo and Andrea Lanoux. (DeKalb: Northern Illinois University Press, 2006).

4 In addition to Chapter 6 see also Dan Healey, "'Untraditional Sex' and the 'Simple Russian': Nostalgia for Soviet Innocence in the Polemics of Dilia Enikeeva," in *What Is Soviet Now? Identities, Legacies, Memories*, eds Thomas Lahusen and Peter H. Solomon Jr. (Berlin: Lit Verlag, 2008).

5 On the broad range of Russian voices rejecting queer visibility, see for example Brian James Baer, *Other Russias: Homosexuality and the Crisis of Post-Soviet Identity* (New York: Palgrave Macmillan, 2009), 43–52; see also his "How

Should We Read Queer Russia?," *Kul'tura* no. 2 (2008): http://www.kultura-rus.de/index.html ("Queer Russia" issue, ed. Dan Healey); and Adi Kuntsman, "Between Gulags and Pride Parades: Sexuality, Nation, and Haunted Speech Acts," *GLQ: A Journal of Lesbian and Gay Studies* 14, no. 2–3 (2008): 263–88.

6   On the pride parade disputes see Francesca Stella, "Queer Space, Pride, and Shame in Moscow," *Slavic Review* 72, no. 3 (2013): 458–80. On Russia's troubled relationship with Eurovision, see Julie A. Cassiday, "Post-Soviet Pop Goes Gay: Russia's Trajectory to Eurovision Victory," *Russian Review* 73, no. 1 (2014): 1–23.

7   Contesting the new law banning male homosexuality in a brilliantly argued letter, Whyte asked Stalin, "Can a homosexual be considered a person fit to become a member of the Communist Party?" Stalin's response was to archive the letter, writing on it "An idiot and a degenerate." Dan Healey, *Homosexual Desire in Revolutionary Russia: The Regulation of Sexual and Gender Dissent* (Chicago: University of Chicago Press, 2001), 188–9; and see Chapter 7.

8   *Kvir*'s publisher, Ed Mishin, launched a website (http://www.gay.ru/) in 1999. It is now a massive guide to Russia's commercial gay space, news and culture. *Kvir*'s publishers launched a lesbian monthly magazine, *Pinx*, in 2006. On Mishin's projects, see Vladimir Kirsanov, *69. Russkie gei, lesbiianki, biseksualy i transseksualy* (Tver': Ganimed, 2005), 538–46. On the dance-club scene of the early 2000s, see Stephen Amico, *Roll Over, Tchaikovsky! Russian Popular Music and Post-Soviet Homosexuality* (Urbana, Chicago, Springfield: University of Illinois Press, 2014).

9   Gaynews RU Elektronnyi zhurnal, "Predstaviteli LGBT-soobshchestva Rossii snova prizvali ne poddavat'sia na provokatsii" (May 18, 2006), http://www.gayclub.ru/news/article.php?ID=2316 (accessed December 19, 2008).

10   Baer, *Other Russias* explores all of these themes; see also his "How Should We Read Queer Russia?"; and on the *boevik*, see Eliot Borenstein's "Band of Brothers: Homoeroticism and the Russian Action Hero," *Kul'tura* no. 2 (2008): http://www.kultura-rus.de/index.html; and idem, *Overkill*, 159–94.

11   Iaroslav Mogutin comments in his introduction to the prose of Evgeny Kharitonov: "If I were to reduce the concerns of Kharitonov's works to the level of a simplified analogy, the literary fate of the homosexual is the fate of the 'insulted and injured,' of the Gogolian 'little man,' of Dostoevsky's 'underground man,' and of Zoshchenko's tragi-comic characters, and of the many, many 'superfluous men' in the Russian literary canon." Cited by Baer, "How Should We Read Queer Russia?" from Iaroslav Mogutin, "Katorzhnik na nive bukvy. Ot sostavitelia," *Evgenii Kharitonov, Slezy na tsvetakh. Kniga 1. Pod domashnim arestom. Glagol* 10, no. 1 (1993): 13–14.

12   See e.g. Helena Goscilo, *Dehexing Sex: Russian Womanhood During and after Glasnost* (Ann Arbor: University of Michigan Press, 1996), especially chapter 6, "New Members and Organs: The Politics of Porn." Note also M. Levitt, and A. Toporkov, eds *Eros i pornografiia v russkoi kul'ture/Eros and Pornography in Russian Culture* (Moscow: Ladomir, 1999).

13   Helena Goscilo, "Porn on the Cob: Some Hard Core Issues," in *Eros i Pornografiia v Russkoi Kul'ture*, eds M. Levitt and A. Toporkov, 553–72;

Goscilo's commentary on gay porn is found on pp. 558 and 564, citing only "the comic strip *Tom of Finland* (1979 and 1981)"; no Russian porn is discussed. Touko Laaksonen ("Tom of Finland," 1920–91), was in fact an artist. A Finnish soldier during World War II, he began drawing gay erotica and sold his first work to U.S. publications in 1956. He became the single most powerful influence on gay men's erotic esthetics in the late twentieth century. Pirated versions of his "Kake" comics circulated in Russia in the 1990s.

14 Luc Beaudoin, "Masculine Utopia in Russian Pornography" in *Eros i Pornografiia v Russkoi Kul'ture*, ed. M. Levitt and A. Toporkov, 632.

15 This account uses an archive of materials collected during successive visits to Russia since the 1980s. I am indebted to colleagues who brought many periodicals to my attention, particularly Elena Gusiatinskaya (Moscow Library of Lesbians and Gays); and Viktor Oboin of the Canadian Lesbian & Gay Archives, Toronto. Most of these materials can be consulted at Amsterdam's International Homo and Lesbian Information Center and Archives: see http://www.ihlia.nl.

16 Richard Dyer, "Male Gay Porn: Coming to Terms," *Jump Cut: A Review of Contemporary Media* no. 30 (1985): 27–9.

17 Linda Williams, *Hard Core: Power, Pleasure, and The "Frenzy of the Visible"* (Berkeley and Los Angeles: University of California Press, 1989); another useful set of essays is James Elias et al., eds, *Porn 101: Eroticism, Pornography, and the First Amendment* (Amherst: Prometheus Books, 1999).

18 Although a straight porn-film industry continues to operate in Russia, as of July 2016 I am not aware of any recent Russian-made gay porn films, and the "Erotika" section of gay.ru now seems to focus only on Western material.

19 On the "disembedding" of social relations from one setting and their transfer to another, in conditions of "chaotic" cultural flows and hybridity characteristic of cultural globalization, see Chris Barker, *Making Sense of Cultural Studies: Central Problems and Critical Debates* (London: Sage Publications, 2002), 131–3; on heterosexual pornography and globalization, Borenstein, *Overkill*.

20 Richard Taylor, *The Battleship Potemkin: The Film Companion* (London & New York: I. B. Tauris, 2000).

21 Christine Kiaer, "Was Socialist Realism Forced Labour? The Case of Aleksandr Deineka in the 1930s," *Oxford Art Journal* 28, no. 3 (2005): 321–45. See 325 for *Lunchbreak on the Donbass*; for Kiaer's interpretation of this painting's figures as the products of "his desiring brush," see 341–4. Deineka's work also abounded with images of the female nude, as noted in Igor' Kon, *Muzhskoe telo v istorii kul'tury* (Moscow: Slovo, 2003), 356.

22 See Mikhail Zolotonosov, "Filosofiia obshchego tela: Sovetskaia sadovo-parkovaia skul'ptura 1930-kh godov," in V. Sazhin, ed. *Sovetskii eros 20–30-kh godov. Sbornik materialov* (St. Petersburg: Literaturnoe obozrenie, 1997).

23 This cycle with its explicit illustrations is reproduced in M. A. Kuzmin, *Stikhotvorenie* (St. Petersburg: Akademicheskii proekt, 1999), 343–79.

24 Joan Neuberger, "Strange circus: Eisenstein's sex drawings," *Studies in Russian & Soviet Cinema* 6, no. 1 (2012): 5–52; M. A. Kushnirovich, "Mir ego myslei:

Risunki Eizenshteina iz sobraniia S. Akchurinoi," in *Erotika v russkoi literature: Ot Barkova do nashikh dnei (Literaturnoe obozrenie. Spetsial'nyi vypusk)*, eds I. D. Prokhorova, S. I. Mazur and G. V. Zykova (Moscow: Literaturnoe obozrenie, 1992), 85–6.

25 For similar speculation, see Kon, *Muzhskoe telo v istorii kul'tury*, 358.

26 On tattoos, prison slang, and homosexuality see Chapter 1; and also, see Healey, *Homosexual Desire in Revolutionary Russia*, 230–5.

27 On U.S. gay porn prison scenarios, see John Mercer, "In the Slammer: The Myth of the Prison in American Gay Pornographic Video," in *Eclectic Views on Gay Male Pornography: Pornucopia*, ed. Todd G. Morrison (Binghamton: Harrington Park Press, 2004). On disgust for the Gulag "queer" in Russian culture, see Adi Kuntsman, "'With a Shade of Disgust': Affective Politics of Sexuality and Class in Memoirs of the Stalinist Gulag," *Slavic Review* 68, no. 2 (2009): 308–28.

28 *Tema*, Moscow, ed. Roman Kalinin, 1990–3, thirteen issues. On the origins of *Tema*, see Kirsanov, *69. Russkie gei, lesbiianki, biseksualy i transseksualy*, 424–5.

29 *Partner(sha!)*, Moscow, ed. Mikhail Gladkikh [pseud. of Mikhail Anikeev] 1993–8, fourteen issues. The most lavishly illustrated of these is the 168-page *Partner(sha!)*, no. 10–11 12 (1995). On Anikeev see Kirsanov, *69. Russkie gei, lesbiianki, biseksualy i transseksualy*, 402–8. *Ty*, Moscow, ed. Gennady Krimenskoi, two issues, 1992, 1993.

30 *Uranus*, Moscow, ed. Mikhail Gladkikh [Anikeev], one issue, 1995.

31 Borenstein, *Overkill*, 70–6 discusses the 1993–4 prosecution of the Latvian, Russian-language, heterosexual but heterodox periodical *Eshche*.

32 *RISK*, Moscow, ed. Dmitry Kuzmin, four issues, 1995–2002; see http://www.vavilon.ru/metatext/risk.html (accessed December 16, 2008). On the pre-history of RISK, see Kirsanov, *69. Russkie gei, lesbiianki, biseksualy i transseksualy*, 425–6; *Zerkalo: Informatsionnyi biulleten' GenderDok*, Moscow, ed. Viktor Oboin (1995–9), eighteen issues. *Gay, Slaviane!*, St. Petersburg, ed. Ol'ga Zhuk, Sergei Shcherbakov, Gennaii Trifonov (1992–4), three issues. *Adel'fe*, Moscow, eds. Mila Ugol'nikova, Tat'iana Ivanova (1996–), five issues. Other Russian lesbian publications include *Ostrov* (1999–2014), sixty-one issues; *Sofa Safo* (2003), two issues; *Labris* (2004–5), five issues; see http://az.gay.ru/books/index_magazines.html (accessed January 4, 2009).

33 *ARGO*, Moscow, ed. Vladislav Ortanov (1994–7), five issues; see http://www.gay.ru/argo/index.htm (accessed December 16, 2008). On Ortanov and the registration of *ARGO*, see Kirsanov, *69. Russkie gei, lesbiianki, biseksualy i transseksualy*, 426–7.

34 A collection of gay erotic stories, with Russian and German photographs appeared in early 1998: Vladislav Ortanov, ed., *Goluboi al'manakh* (Moscow: ARGO-RISK, 1998).

35 *1/10 (Odna desiataia)*, Moscow, ed. Dmitrii Lychev (1991–8), twenty-three issues; on Lychev, and circulation figures, see Kirsanov, *69. Russkie gei, lesbiianki, biseksualy i transseksualy,* 530–6.

36 *Hot Russian Soldiers*, Moscow, ed. Vitalii Lazarenko and Dmitrii Lychev, 1996, one issue.

37 *Dimka*, Minsk/The Netherlands, ed. Dmitrii Lychev, 1993-?, 3 [?] issues. *Dimka* was printed in the Netherlands but gave a Minsk postal address for correspondence in its masthead. The fiction collections were Dmitrii Lychev, ed., *Drugoi: Sbornik gei-rasskazov* (Moscow: ARGO-RISK, 1993); and Werwolf [sic], *Rodnaia krov'* (Moscow: ARGO-RISK, 1994).

38 See e.g. V. Volodin, "Liubov' za stenoi kazarmy," *Partner(sha!)*, no. 4 (1994), 6–7; Efim Eliseev, "Skameika," *Ty*, no. 2 (1993), 63–76; and note the cover of *1/10* no. 19 (1996). Lychev wrote a novel about same-sex relations in the army: *(Intro-)missiia* (Prague: Izdatel'stvo Praga, 1998).

39 One illustrator of Russian gay publications in the 1990s, Viktor Putintsev, whose images became iconic, frequently depicted military men. See e.g. *1/10*, no. 6 (1993), 2; *1/10*, no. 15 (1994), 3, 4; *Partner(sha!)*, no. 10–11–12 (1995), 71.

40 See e.g. "Pervye shagi fotostudii zhurnala 'ARGO'," 40–5; *Hot Russian Soldiers*, 11–14; *Partner(sha!)*, no. 10–11–12 (1995), 154–5.

41 See the illustration by Putintsev depicted a pair of men making love, with one man wearing an armband reading "AIDS": *1/10*, no. 18 (1995), 19; and another Putintsev drawing, in which a masked skeleton proffers champagne with "AIDS" in the bubbles to a young man, *Partner(sha!)*, no. 10–11–12 (1995), 163. See also Werwolf [sic], *Rodnaia krov'*, 85.

42 "Wedding": *1/10*, no. 17 (1995), 7 (another Putintsev drawing); "artists": *1/10*, no. 17 (1995), 8 (a ballet dancer, by Dmitrii Kriuger); *Partner(sha!)*, no. 10–11–12 (1995), 75 (Putintsev's drawing of a sexually aroused violinist).

43 For a discussion of "bisexuality" in Soviet and Russian conditions, see the Introduction. For a working out of this theme, see the film *Ia liubliu tebia* (You I Love), directed by Ol'ga Stolpovskaia and Dmitrii Troitskii, 2004.

44 For this history see Dyer, "Coming to Terms"; Thomas Waugh, *Hard to Imagine: Gay Male Eroticism in Photography and Film from Their Beginnings to Stonewall* (New York: Columbia University Press, 1996); idem, *Out/Lines: Underground Gay Graphics from before Stonewall* (Vancouver: Arsenal Pulp Press, 2002); John R. Burger, *One-Handed Histories: The Eroto-Politics of Gay Male Video Pornography* (New York & London: Harrington Park Press, 1995).

45 It is difficult to account for this absence. Before 1917, body-building and physique photography flourished in St. Petersburg, although homosexual links to this culture are speculative; see Louise McReynolds, *Russia at Play: Leisure Activities at the End of the Tsarist Era* (Ithaca: Cornell University Press, 2003), 131–53. With the collapse of Soviet state support for sport, athleticism was perhaps associated with compulsory military service, not recreation. Recent gender studies say little about sport as a constitutive discourse of Russian manhood; but see Julie Gilmour and Barbara Evans Clements, "'If You Want to Be Like Me, Train!': The Contradictions of Soviet Masculinity" in *Russian Masculinities in History and Culture*, eds Barbara Evans Clements, Rebecca Friedman and Dan Healey (Basingstoke & New York, 2002).

46 On the ironies of athleticism in gay porn films see Brian Pronger, *The Arena of Masculinity: Sports, Homosexuality and the Meaning of Sex* (London: Gay Men's Press, 1990), 150–8, 169–71.

47 See Burger, *One-Handed Histories*, 24–5.

48 On globalization of U.S. gay porn see Clare N. Westcott, "Alterity and Construction of National Identity in Three Kristen Bjorn Films" in *Eclectic Views on Gay Male Pornography: Pornucopia*, ed. Todd G. Morrison (Binghamton: Harrington Park Press, 2004).

49 The law in force when this essay was first published (2010) allowed regional authorities to regulate the marketing of print and cinematic erotica, resulting in wide variations; see V. V. Nagaev, *Erotika i Pornografiia. Kriterii razlichii. Problemy pravovoi otsenki i ekspertizy* (Moscow: IuNITI-DANA, Zakon i Pravo, 2009). My thanks to Marianna Muraveva for this reference.

50 Beaudoin, "Masculine Utopia in Russian Pornography."

51 Anatof has a minimal entry on the Internet Movie Database: http://www.imdb.com/name/nm2804880 (accessed September 30, 2008). Despite the claims on the film packaging, *Last Train* was probably filmed in a Baltic republic. Various Russian-themed films, by a director styled "Alex Clark," and produced between 1998 and 2006 by Dolphin International, originate in Latvia with Russian and non-Russian actors. Note also *Amerikanets v Moskve* (dir. Andrei Lev, 1999; In-x-cess Productions, USA) an apparent co-production: http://www.spshop.ru/cat_view.php?id=sp-0435&series=%E3%E5%E9+%E2%E8%E4%E5%EE&sid=88 (accessed October 2, 2008).

52 The characterization is John Mercer's; see "In the Slammer," 160.

53 Interview with Barry Gollop, April 22, 2008. Gollop lived and worked with Bjorn in Prague and Budapest during the 1990s. Further information comes from *Behind the Curtain: The Making of Moscow* (Sarava Productions; 2001), a "making of . . ." documentary about *Moscow: The Power of Submission*, showing Gollop at work with his Russian team and interviewing the actors.

54 Burger, *One-Handed Histories*, 33–8.

55 Dilia Enikeeva, *Gei i lesbiianki* (Moscow: Astrel'/AST, 2003), 221–47; Baer, *Other Russias*, 49.

56 Gay Erotic Archives biography of "The Bear" (Barry Gollop), http://www.gayeroticarchives.com/01_photo/B/e/Bear_The/index.html (accessed April 21, 2008).

57 See Arjun Appadurai, "Disjuncture and Difference in the Global Cultural Economy" *Public Culture* 2, no. 2 (1990): 1–24.

58 See *Behind the Curtain*. On the conventions of representation in hard-core pornography, and the resemblance of porn to the movie musical, see Williams, *Hard Core*, 120–52.

59 Gollop did not intend to distribute the film in Russia, but he acknowledged it might circulate in Russia in pirate copies (interview, April 22, 2008). The authenticity of the settings and props was the result of input from Russian cameramen, who were moonlighting from day jobs in television.

60 Corey Taylor, *Naked: The Life and Pornography of Michael Lucas* (New York: Kensington Books, 2007).

61 The other star appearing in both the Bjorn/Gollop and Lucas films was Andrei Nemov, who played the black marketeer in *Moscow: The Power of Submission*.

62 Burger, *One-Handed Histories*, 41.

63 Bauman, *Globalization*, 89–93.

64 The author's copy was purchased in 2007 a suburban kiosk in St. Petersburg; thanks to Jill Lewis for bringing it to my attention. It is sold on the studio's website: www.sexvideo.ru (accessed July 25, 2016).

65 Robert H. McNeal, *Tsar and Cossack, 1855–1914* (Basingstoke: Macmillan, 1987). That Cossacks also feature in Ukrainian national myth offers a further layer of complexity to this scenario. I am grateful to Yuri Shevchuk for this insight.

66 Anton Popov, "Cossack Lands: Remembering, Imagining and Enacting Place in Ethnic Revival Movements," paper presented at CEELBAS "Doing Culture. Whose Culture? Exploring the Active Audience," Sheffield University, May 2–3, 2008.

67 Borenstein, *Overkill*, 55–6.

68 Dyer, "Male Gay Porn."

69 Ibid.; Thomas Waugh, "Men's Pornography: gay versus straight," *Jump Cut: A Review of Contemporary Media* no. 30 (1985): 30–8.

70 The shift could be attributed to the end of the HIV/AIDS emergency with combination therapies; and the advance of gay marriage in many Western jurisdictions. The films of Kristen Bjorn, for example, rehabilitate mutuality and romance without discarding promiscuity or the power vertical.

71 See e.g. Daniel Tsang, "Beyond 'Looking for My Penis': Reflections on Asian Gay Male Video Porn," in *Porn 101: Eroticism, Pornography, and the First Amendment*, eds James Elias et al. (Amherst: Prometheus Books, 1999).

72 "*Universal*" is now the contemporary usage; Kozlovskii writing in the 1980s gave "*universalka*" (feminine gender) as a synonym for "*kombain*" and a range of synonyms current in Soviet gay speech in the 1970s: Kozlovskii, *Argo russkoi gomoseksual'noi subkul'tury*, 50, 70. A recent humorous glossary gives "female employee of a department store" [*rabotnitsa universama*] for "*universalka*," a word now depleted from camp-ironic overuse: A. M. Zapadaev, *Slovar' khabal'nykh slov i vyrazhenii: Zhargonnye i slengovye slova, vyrazheniia i oboroty geev Rossii (s fol'klornymi dopolneniiami)* (St. Petersburg: The author, 2001), 147.

73 *Hot Russian Soldiers*, 14.

74 On army service as the threshold of manhood, see for the contemporary period Rebecca Kay, *Men in Contemporary Russia: The Fallen Heroes of Post-Soviet Change?* (Aldershot: Ashgate, 2006), 60–3; and for earlier eras Z. V. Kormina, *Provody v armiiu v poreformennoi Rossii: Opyt etnograficheskogo analiza* (Moscow: Novoe literaturnoe obozrenie, 2005).

75 The film *Sto dnei do prikaza* (One Hundred Days before the Order; dir. Hussein Erkenov, 1990) anticipated these currents in a powerful, plotless meditation on the lives of conscripts. The homoerotic undertones, and an imagined homosexual encounter, haunt the comradely normative surface of the film (Baer, *Other Russias*, 62–6).

76 Mercer, "In the Slammer," 163–4.

77 Borenstein, *Overkill*, 11–13.

78 Kuntsman, "'With a Shade of Disgust'."

79 Gennadii Trifonov, *Setka. Leva. Roman, povest'* (Moscow: Kvir, 2006), 47–53, 59–60, 80. A similar panic about labeling propels a series of short homoerotic stories of *dedovshchina* (hazing) in the army, see Konstantin Efimov, *Zapretnaia tema* (Tver': Ganimed, 2002).

80 For speculation on NKVD chief Ezhov's bisexuality, see Marc Jansen and Nikolai Petrov, *Stalin's Loyal Executioner: People's Commissar Nikolai Ezhov, 1895–1940* (Stanford: Stanford University Press, 2002), 198.

81 The "making of . . ." documentary, *Behind the Curtain*, and Gollop in interview, hint that the actors were newcomers to gay porn and in some cases, gay sex. Lucas makes similar claims about his actors on the *To Moscow With Love II* DVD. In both cases, the directors' claims about the apparently genuinely ill-defined sexual identities of these Russian performers serve a marketing purpose (the "unattainable" straight man turning "gay for pay"). Gollop's "discoveries" Byazrov and Nemov later appeared in Lucas's *To Moscow with Love II*, and Gollop's Slava Petrovich plays the exotic Russian protagonist in *Men Amongst the Ruins* (Kristen Bjorn, 2003), set in a tropical Latin country. Sharko later made another entirely Russian gay porn film about soldiers, *Russkie voennye* (2005).

82 The foundational text on post-colonial perspectives for students of gay porn is Richard Fung, "Looking for My Penis: The Eroticized Asian in Gay Video Porn" in *How Do I Look? Queer Film and Video*, ed. Bad Object-Choices (Seattle: Bay Press, 1991). Note also Tsang, "Beyond 'Looking for My Penis'," and Westcott, "Alterity and Construction of National Identity in Three Kristen Bjorn Films."

83 Borenstein, *Overkill*, 53–5.

84 Borenstein, *Overkill*, 56. The diversity of the Russian porn industry was evident from the remarkable catalog menu at the now-defunct www.spshop.ru; Russian-produced straight porn films include porno-satires on Soviet culture such as *Chapaev*, dir. Tat'iana Taneeva, 2003: "It's got Whites, it's got Reds, only it doesn't have any blues [*golubykh* – slang for 'gays'], because everything's simple in the worker-peasant fashion."

85 For the gloomy mood of Cold-War revival, see Latvian-made gay porn films *Spy Games I & II*, dir. Alex Clark, 2004, 2006. In these movies FSB agents kill Russophobic Baltic nationalists in a covert operation; and later Lithuanian intelligence foils a honeytrap the FSB sets for a Swedish diplomat. Moscow's agents are directed by an old Stalinist in the Lubianka, in scenes shot through a yellow filter to suggest his perversion and even insanity.

86 I am indebted to Anne Gorsuch for suggesting this view. Efimov, *Zapretnaia tema*, eroticizes *dedovshchina* relations but always removes the protagonists from their most brutal features. On military hazing in Russia, see "*Dedovshchina*: From Military to Society" special issue of *The Journal of Power Institutions in Post-Soviet Societies*, 1(2004): http://www.pipss.org/index190.html (accessed July 24, 2009).

87　In the novel, Obraztsov defines his lover Korolenko's desire as "bisexual," and hints that it may be the product of prison life (Trifonov, *Setka*, 80). Although Obraztsov himself appears to eschew bisexuality in favor of a preference for men, the hero Korolenko's apparent freedom to return to "normal" heterosexuality after prison presents him, and readers, with a less confrontational and "fixed" sexual identity and more liberty to explore.

Chapter 6: "Let Them Move to France!": Public Homophobia and "Traditional" Sexuality in the Early Putin Years

1　This discussion of the law in the following two paragraphs is based primarily on news bulletins and analysis posted at http://www.gay.ru/society/authorit/ nravstv (accessed December 15, 2004) and related links at www.gay.ru. These links have since been deactivated, a signal of the chilling effect of recent media regulation for LGBT communities. In 2004–5, Nikita Ivanov and Igor Kon helped me with their own observations about the 2002 Duma sex debates. I have also benefited from comments on an early draft of this piece by Brian James Baer and Sergei Oushakine, but its faults are mine alone.

2　The definition: "Note. Pornographic depiction of minors in the present article is understood to mean the depiction of their sex organs for the purposes of arousing sexual attraction (*vlecheniia*), and equally any depiction of the commission with them of depraved activities, sexual intercourse, sodomy, lesbianism or other activities of a sexual character." (art. 242–1).

　　Post-Soviet Russia's age of consent was set at sixteen in the 1997 Criminal Code; in 1998 in a little-noticed change it was lowered to fourteen. Rumors circulate in Russia's legal community that a high-ranking Kremlin male official managed to have it slipped into a bill of amendments to evade prosecution for a sexual relationship with a fifteen-year-old boy. Setting the age of consent has a long, and unusual, history in Russia and the Soviet Union; see Dan Healey, "Defining Sexual Maturity as the Soviet Alternative to an Age of Consent," in *Soviet Medicine: Culture, Practice, and Science*, eds Frances L. Bernstein, Christopher Burton and Dan Healey (DeKalb: Northern Illinois University Press, 2010).

3　On the "invention" of this tradition, see also Marianna Murav'eva, "'(Ne) traditsionnye seksual'nye otnoshenii' kak iuridicheskaia kategoriia: istoriko-pravovoi analiz," in *Na pereput'e: metodologiia, teoriia i praktika* LGBT *i kvir-issledovanii [sbornik statei]*, ed. Aleksandr Kondakov (St. Petersburg: Tsentr nezavisimykh sotsiologicheskikh issledovanii, 2014).

4　Viktor Bashkin, "Demograficheskii krizis: Potomstvu ob"iavlen boikot," *Parliamentskaia gazeta*, no. 167 (September 5, 2002), 1. In July 2016, government statisticians put Russia's population (including annexed Crimea) at 146.5 million, and it was projected to be 145.7 million in 2025; while natural increase has recently risen as life expectancy, birthrates, and living standards all improve, the demographic shadow of previous declines will have an impact on future numbers. See http://www.gks.ru/wps/wcm/connect/rosstat_main/rosstat/ru/statistics/population/demography/# (accessed August 10, 2016).

5 See "Rossiia molodaia: nadezhdy i slezy," *Parliamentskaia gazeta* (March 15, 2002), 4–5. The two-page special feature includes a photograph of Putin on a visit to an orphanage, with a young girl wearing a traditional headscarf.

6 Svetlana Goriacheva, "Izvrashchenets ne imeet prava na amnistiiu!" *Parliamentskaia gazeta* (June 28, 2002), 5.

7 "Goriacheva, Svetlana Petrovna," in Giancarlo Colombo, ed., *Who's Who in Russia*. (Moscow: Who's Who Strategic Area, 2001), 222–3; and note her biography at http://www.spravedlivo.ru/999_1_6_2020.html (accessed March 21, 2016).

8 Goriacheva, "Izvrashchenets ne imeet prava na amnistiiu!"

9 Between 1922 and 1997, Soviet and Russian law lacked an age-defined threshold for consensual sex. There was no age of consent as such. Instead, Soviet law advanced the medical concept of "sexual maturity" as the legal benchmark for judging the full sexual autonomy of the individual. See Healey, "Defining Sexual Maturity as the Soviet Alternative to an Age of Consent."

10 For information about this hearing see Dmitrii Chernyshev, "Zakonoproekt 'O zashchite nravstvennosti'. Otkliki i kommentarii. Kommentarii k 'popravkam' k UK," http://www.gay.ru/society/authorit/nravstv/chern-uk.htm (accessed December 15, 2004).

11 Goriacheva, "Izvrashchenets ne imeet prava na amnistiiu!"

12 Igor' Kon, "Zamechaniia na proekt federal'nogo zakona 'O vnesenii izmenenii i dopolnenii v Ugolovnyi Kodeks Rossiiskoi Federatsii'," February 19, 2002, http://seksologiya.org/info089.html (accessed March 21, 2016).

13 Chernyshev, "Zakonoproekt 'O zashchite nravstvennosti'."

14 Michele Rivkin-Fish, "From 'Demographic Crisis' to 'Dying Nation': The Politics of Language and Reproduction in Russia," in *Gender and National Identity in Twentieth-Century Russian Culture*, eds Helena Goscilo and Andrea Lanoux (DeKalb: Northern Illinois University Press, 2006).

15 "Raikov, Gennady Ivanovich," in Colombo, ed., *Who's Who in Russia*, 606. He left the Duma in 2007, later joining United Russia, and serves as a member of the Central Electoral Commission of the Russian Federation; see https://lenta.ru/lib/14172377 (accessed March 21, 2016).

16 Aleksei Mitrofanov of the infamously national-populist Liberal Democratic Party of Russia proposed a law punishing consensual "lesbian relations" with five years' imprisonment. Victor Semenov, vice-chairman of the Agrarian Party of Russia suggested that masturbation be added as an offense to the Code of Administrative Infractions with a fine equivalent to twenty monthly average salaries. Chernyshev, "Zakonoproekt 'O zashchite nravstvennosti'."

17 Oleg Rashidov, "Zakonotvorchestvo G. I. Raikova. 'V kazhdoi derevne dolzhen byt' svoi durachok'," http://www.gay.ru/society/authorit/raikov/rashidov.htm (accessed January 5, 2005).

18 Ibid.

19 Reactions presented in the next two paragraphs: Aleksandr Ryklin, Dmitrii
    Khitarov, "Zhertva gennoi inzhenerii," *Ezhenedel'nyi zhurnal*, no. 18 (May 10,
    2002) http://ej.ru/018/life/profile/raikov/index.html (accessed January 6, 2005),
    also republished at http://www.gay.ru/society/phobia/rajkov/raikov.html
    (accessed March 21, 2016). Nemtsov response: "Boris Nemtsov ne khochet,
    chtoby vlast' vlezala v postel' k narodu," http://www.gay.ru/news/rainbow/
    2002/04/29.htm (accessed January 6, 2005).

20 Ryklin and Khitarov, "Zhertva gennoi inzhenerii."

21 "Boris Nemtsov ne khochet, chtoby vlast' vlezala v postel' k narodu."

22 Reznik remains a leading figure in the banking industry, and in United Russia,
    a party which grew out of Unity; he has been a Duma deputy up to the present;
    see http://www.duma.gov.ru/structure/deputies/131165 (accessed July 7, 2016).

23 Nikita Ivanov, "Zakonoproekt 'O zapreshchenii muzhelozhstva' osuzhdaiut
    deputaty i pravozashchitniki," April 22, 2002: http://www.gay.ru/news/
    rainbow/2002/04/24–1269.htm (accessed July 4, 2016). On the silence
    accompanying decriminalization in 1993, see Chapter 7.

24 In the same vein, and also on April 23, the deputy-speaker of the Duma,
    another Unity member, Lyubov Sliska, said "there was plenty to occupy the
    Duma" besides the antisodomy law. She commented to journalists that the
    Russian equivalent of the silly season had begun: Raikov's initiative must be
    the result of madness brought on by the arrival of "spring and magnetic
    storms" – "It's not the best way to draw attention to yourself," she tartly
    concluded (Ryklin and Khitarov, "Zhertva gennoi inzhenerii"). Similar
    arguments were voiced by the speaker of the Council of the Federation, the
    upper chamber of the Russian parliament. Responding on May 15 to a
    journalist's question about the draft law against homosexuality, Sergei
    Mironov said: "one always has to ask how much society needs such a law . . .
    Looking at proposals like this, you would think that in Russia every other
    issue was solved: salaries are being paid on time, the state budget is healthy,
    there's no crime . . ." ("Spiker Soveta Federatsii ne vidit smysla v novykh
    propravkakh, kasaiushchikhsia gomoseksualov," http://www.gay.ru/news/
    rainbow/2002/05/17a.htm (accessed January 6, 2005).

25 Elena Zdravomyslova and Anna Temkina, "Krizis maskulinnosti v
    pozdnesovetskom diskurse," in *O muzhe(n)stvennosti* ed. Sergei Ushakin
    (Moscow: Novoe literaturnoe obozrenie, 2002), 432–51.

26 For characterizations of the *muzhik* as powerful post-Soviet countertype, see
    Anna Rotkirkh, *Muzhskoi vopros: Liubov' i seks trekh pokolenii v
    avtobiografiiakh peterburzhtsev* (St. Petersburg: Izdatel'stvo Evropeiskogo
    Universiteta v Sankt-Peterburge, 2011), 230–67; Oleg Riabov and Tatiana
    Riabova, "The Remasculinization of Russia?" *Problems of Post-Communism*
    61, no. 2 (2014): 23–35.

27 Zdravomyslova and Temkina, "Krizis maskulinnosti v pozdnesovetskom
    diskurse," 451.

28 Elizabeth A. Wood, "Hypermasculinity as a Scenario of Power: Vladimir Putin's
    Iconic Rule, 1999–2008," *International Feminist Journal of Politics*, 18, no.
    3(2016): 329–50. I am grateful to the author for sharing an advance copy of this

article. See also Valerie Sperling, *Sex, Politics, and Putin: Political Legitimacy in Russia* (New York, Oxford: Oxford University Press, 2014), 29–33.

29 Marshall I. Goldman, "Putin and the Oligarchs," *Foreign Affairs* (November–December 2004), 41. On a trumped-up case raised by a fellow inmate against Khodorkovsky for supposed male sexual assault, see Chapter 1.

30 Wood, "Hypermasculinity as a Scenario of Power."

31 Bashkin, "Demograficheskii krizis: Potomstvu ob"iavlen boikot," 1, 4.

32 Ibid., 4.

33 An article appearing in the wake of the Legislation Committee hearing about Goriacheva's draft law offered unattributed estimates that up to four million abandoned children currently roamed the nation's streets, Inna Suprunova, "Maloletki dlia seksual'noi pokhoti. Zashchitit li ikh zakon?" *Parliamentskaia gazeta*, no. 53 (933), March 20, 2002, 1–2.

34 Natal'ia Dolgushina, "Tsvetki zhizhni rastut na asfal'te," *Parliamentskaia gazeta*, 63(942) April 1, 2002, 1–3.

35 Suprunova, "Maloletki dlia seksual'noi pokhoti," 1. Physician and "aesthete" Mikhail Sherstnev was tried for aggravated kidnapping and bodily harm after a string of affairs with teenage girls (which he wrote about in a locally published novel, *Etot zagadochnyi gorod*). Dr Sherstnev and an accomplice kidnapped and mutilated the young boyfriend of one victim.

36 Wood, "Hypermasculinity as a Scenario of Power"; Sperling, *Sex, Politics, and Putin.*

37 See Healey, "Defining Sexual Maturity as the Soviet Alternative to an Age of Consent."

38 Suprunova, "Maloletki dlia seksual'noi pokhoti," 2. Suprunova fails to mention the U.S. influence in this episode. For the "Planned Parenthood" curriculum and its fate, see Igor' Kon, *Podrostkovaia seksual'nost' na poroge XXI veka: Sotsial'no-pedagogicheskii analiz* (Dubna: "Feniks+," 2001), 131–2; and for a study of pilot projects of the early 1990s, Michele Rivkin-Fish, "Sexuality Education in Russia: Defining Pleasure and Danger for a Fledgling Democratic Society," *Social Science & Medicine* 49, no. 6 (1999): 801–14.

39 Suprunova, "Maloletki dlia seksual'noi pokhoti."

40 "Raikov pod ugrozoi: 'vliiatel'nye krugi' zhazhdut raspravy nad zakonotvortsem," http://www.gay.ru/news/rainbow/2002/05/29–1318.htm (accessed March 21, 2016). Raikov made the claims at a press conference on May 27, 2002.

41 Dilia Enikeeva, *Gei i lesbiianki* (Moscow: Astrel'/AST, 2003). Quotation from back cover. For a fuller analysis see Dan Healey, "*'Untraditional Sex' and the 'Simple Russian': Nostalgia for Soviet Innocence in the Polemics of Dilia Enikeeva," in *What is Soviet Now? Identities, Legacies, Memories*, eds Thomas Lahusen and Peter H. Solomon Jr. (Berlin: Lit Verlag, 2008).

42 Enikeeva, *Gei i lesbiianki*, 107–9. The sexopathologist explains the lure of homosex thus: "same-sex sex is more attractive than heterosexual sex. First the sexual technique and erotic pleasures are much more varied; second, two persons of the same sex know better each other's sexual desires; third, they are more open during love-making than reserved heterosexuals practicing 'vanilla

sex' and incapable of discussing erotic things; fourth, sex is the most significant aspect of two gays' (or two lesbians') relationship, and they pay a great deal of attention to it – not only the quantity, but the quality and the accompanying environment." (109).

43 Ibid., 106, 233–4, 236–7, 377–87.

44 Ibid., 397–8.

45 Ibid., 400–1.

46 She devoted a chapter to "Lesbian sex," 186–202, and there are brief references to lesbianism elsewhere: 110, 123–34, 240, 358. Enikeeva ignored the spring 2002 proposal to criminalize voluntary lesbian relations, but focuses entirely on Raikov's draft bill against gay male sex.

47 Recent Russian homophobic discourse has been extremely prolific, yet arguably until the Putin era diffuse and lacking political sophistication; see e.g. Elena Baraban, "Obyknovennaia gomofobiia," *Neprikovsnovennyi zapas*, no. 19 (2001): 85–93; for documentation of 1990s Russian homophobia, see Viktor Oboin, ed., *Gomofobiia v Sovremennoi Rossii 1993–2001 g.g. Dokumenty, Fakty* (Moscow: The author, 2001), deposited at Homodok, Amsterdam and the Canadian Lesbian and Gay Archives, Toronto.

48 Recent statistics are cited in E. A. Kashchenko, *Seksual'naia kul'tura voenno-sluzhashchikh* (Moscow: URSS, 2003), 166–7.

49 Dan Healey, *Homosexual Desire in Revolutionary Russia: The Regulation of Sexual and Gender Dissent* (Chicago: University of Chicago Press, 2001), 166–8, 187–8, 203, 239.

50 The "Decree on military-medical expertise," no. 123 of the Government of the Russian Federation was issued on February 25, 2003. (Enikeeva's book was authorized for printing on March 20, 2003.)

51 Nikolai Alekseev, Nikita Ivanov, D. V. Vorontsov, "Kommentarii k novomu polozheniiu o voenno-vrachebnoi ekspertize," http://www.gay.ru/society/authorit/army/123.htm (accessed April 2, 2003).

52 Ibid.

53 E.g. the website newsru.com reported the story with the headline "Now to beat the draft you have to be alcoholic, a drug addict, mental, or a homosexualist"; cited in Alekseev et al., "Kommentarii k novomu polozheniiu." BBC coverage mirrored this mistake: "Russian army to ban gays," March 13, 2003: http://news.bbc.co.uk/1/hi/world/europe/2848467.stm (accessed January 31, 2005).

54 "General-maior Kulikov: 'V meditsine net takogo diagnoza- gomoseksualizm'," http://www.gay.ru/news/rainbow/2003/11/27b.htm (accessed December 8, 2003). Kulikov made the statements at a press conference in Moscow on November 27, 2003.

55 Konstantin L. Bannikov, *Antropologiia ekstremal'nykh grupp: Dominantnye otnosheniia sredi voennosluzhashchikh srochnoi sluzhby Rossiiskoi Armii* (Moscow: RAN Institut etnologii i antropologii, 2002), 139–45. See also Kashchenko, *Seksual'naia kul'tura voenno-sluzhashchikh*, 151–64. Kashchenko does not associate rape with *dedovshchina* (a word he avoids) but notes the role of "moral humiliation" and punishment of "those of weak character"

in motivating military same-sex abuse. For an extended analysis of *dedovshchina* that evades systematic discussion of sexual abuse, see the articles in *The Journal of Power Institutions in Post-Soviet Societies*, no. 1 (2004): "Dedovshchina: From Military to Society," http://www.pipss.org/sommaire190.html (accessed September 5, 2005).

56 "V gosdumu vnesen zakonoproekt o zaprete 'propagandy gomoseksualizma'," http://www.gay.ru/news/rainbow/2003/09/23.htm (accessed September 23, 2003).

57 Tamara Shkel', "Duma nachala novyi pokhod za nravstvennost'," *Rossiiskaia gazeta*, no. 39 (3416), February 27, 2004, 3.

58 On "*Nashi*," summer camps for tens of thousands of Putin supporters, and the love and marriage campaigns, see Sperling, *Sex, Politics, and Putin*, 125–68.

Chapter 7: Stalinist Homophobia and the "Stunted Archive": Challenges to Writing the History of Gay Men's Persecution in the USSR

1 For an introduction on the Stalin era, see James R. Harris, *The Great Fear: Stalin's Terror of the 1930s* (Oxford: Oxford University Press, 2016); on the "special settlements," see Lynne Viola, *The Unknown Gulag: The Lost World of Stalin's Special Settlements* (New York and Oxford: Oxford University Press, 2007).

2 Viola, *The Unknown Gulag*, 73–113, discusses the planning and realities of the "special settlements" for de-kulakized peasants deported by collectivization drives; on ethnic cleansing in border regions see Terry Martin, "The Origins of Soviet Ethnic Cleansing," *The Journal of Modern History* 70, no. 4 (1998): 813–61; on rationales for terror against "enemies of the people" see J. Arch Getty and Oleg V. Naumov, *The Road to Terror: Stalin and the Self-Destruction of the Bolsheviks, 1932–1939* (New Haven and London: Yale University Press, 1999).

3 See e.g. Mark Iunge and Rol'f Binner, *Kak Terror stal "Bol'shim." Sekretnyi prikaz No. 00447 i tekhnologiia ego ispolzovaniia* (Moscow: AIRO-XX, 2003).

4 The nature of Stalin-era regular and secret police work against the population is only now being studied in detail; see David R. Shearer, *Policing Stalin's Socialism: Repression and Social Order in the Soviet Union, 1924–1953* (New Haven and London: Yale University Press, 2009); Paul Hagenloh, *Stalin's Police: Public Order and Mass Repression in the USSR, 1926–1941.* (Washington, D.C.: Woodrow Wilson Center Press; Baltimore: Johns Hopkins University Press, 2009).

5 See e.g. Shearer, *Policing Stalin's Socialism*, 181–218; Hagenloh, *Stalin's Police*, 89–146.

6 Shearer, *Policing Stalin's Socialism*, 405–36.

7   Dan Healey, *Homosexual Desire in Revolutionary Russia: The Regulation of Sexual and Gender Dissent* (Chicago: University of Chicago Press, 2001), 259–63.

8   I borrow this characterization of archives for queer history from Lisa Duggan, "The Discipline Problem: Queer Theory Meets Lesbian and Gay History," *GLQ: A Journal of Gay and Lesbian Studies* 2 (1995): 181.

9   As noted in Chapter 3, Kozin kept a diary over many years and it is not known how many volumes still exist, and whether the Magadan FSB archive, or other private persons, has them. Savchenko may possess further volumes too. In the late 1990s, Kozin's distant relatives contested Savchenko's possession of the 1955–6 diary, supposedly bequeathed to him by the singer, but were unsuccessful in launching an investigation; see Igor' Dorogoi, "K voprosu o sud'be dnevnikov Vadima Kozina," *Kolymskii trakt*, 11(311), March 16, 2005.

10   With some noteworthy exceptions; see Michael Makin, "Whose Kliuev, Who Is Kliuev? Polemics of Identity and Poetry," *The Slavonic and East European Review* 85, no. 2 (2007): 231–70, and my discussion in Chapter 8.

11   The volumes contain contextualizing essays by Anne Applebaum and Alexander Sidorov, but these fail to address the problem of the Gulag Queer. See Danzig Baldaev, *Russian Criminal Tattoo Encyclopaedia: Volumes I, II, III* (Gottingen and London: Steidl/Fuel, 2003, 2006, 2008), and my discussion in Chapter 1.

12   On these points see e.g. Dagmar Herzog, *Sexuality in Europe: A Twentieth-century History* (Cambridge and New York: Cambridge University Press, 2011), 122–9; Erik N. Jensen, "The Pink Triangle and Political Consciousness: Gays, Lesbians, and the Memory of Nazi Persecution," *Journal of the History of Sexuality* 11, no. 1/2 (2002): 319–49.

13   Lesbian sex was never criminalized in tsarist or Soviet law. Some women managed to live in lesbian relationships without problems, but others suffered for their non-conformity. I discuss examples in Chapter 4. See also, Healey, *Homosexual Desire in Revolutionary Russia*, 50–73; 196–202; 223–7; Francesca Stella, *Lesbian Lives in Soviet and Post-Soviet Russia: Post/socialism and Gendered Sexualities* (Basingstoke: Palgrave Macmillan, 2015).

14   Healey, *Homosexual Desire in Revolutionary Russia*, was based on field research conducted in 1995–6 in Moscow and St. Petersburg archives and libraries.

15   See the Preface for a discussion of Orthodoxy, the early Russian state, and same-sex regulation. On the tsarist regulation of same-sex love, see Healey, *Homosexual Desire in Revolutionary Russia*.

16   Marianna Muravyeva, "Personalising Homosexuality and Masculinity in Early Modern Russia," in *Gender in Late Medieval and Early Modern Europe*, eds Marianna Muravyeva and Raisa Maria Toivo (London: Routledge, 2012).

17   Discussed in Healey, *Homosexual Desire in Revolutionary Russia*, 100–25.

18   Ibid., 112–15. Early Soviet law allowed for prosecution of clerical same-sex offenses; and beyond Russia in southern and eastern republics of the USSR, the law against male homosexuality was significantly more repressive; see ibid., 153–62. Trotsky dismissed Kuzmin's literary work as part of the pre–1917

trend in Russian letters to "sexual individualism" and "anarchism of the flesh" in his 1923 survey, *Literature and Revolution*.

19 Almost all recent work on the "sexual revolution" examines Soviet public discussion about sex; for excellent examples see Eric Naiman, *Sex in Public: The Incarnation of Early Soviet Ideology* (Princeton: Princeton University Press, 1997); Gregory Carleton, *Sexual Revolution in Bolshevik Russia* (Pittsburgh: University of Pittsburgh Press, 2005). New work on "Soviet subjectivities" looks at self-fashioning and identity, but pays little attention to sexualities; see e.g. Jochen Hellbeck, *Revolution on my Mind: Writing a Diary under Stalin* (Cambridge and London: Harvard University Press, 2006). For a valuable critique of current work on queer subjectivities in early Bolshevik Russia, see A. Klesh, [Arthur Clech], "Istoriografiia russkoi gomoseksual'nosti do i posle Oktiabr'skoi revoliutsii: razlichnye podkhody i perspektivy," in *Kak my pishem istoriiu?* eds. Gregory Dufaud, Guillaume Garreta and L. A. Pimenova (Moscow: ROSSPEN, 2013).

20 For discussions based on published sources see Healey, *Homosexual Desire in Revolutionary Russia*, 44–6; 135, 146; Laura Engelstein, "Soviet Policy Toward Male Homosexuality: Its Origins and Historical Roots," in *Gay Men and the Sexual History of the Political Left*, eds G. Hekma, H. Oosterhuis and J. Steakley (Binghamton, NY: Harrington Park Press, 1995).

21 Khoroshilova has published a short article online based on an archival file discovered in the Central State Archive of the City of St. Petersburg (TsGA SPb f. 52, op. 2, d. 923): "Pervye travesty revoliutsionnogo Petrograda," http://arzamas.academy/mag/166-queer (accessed April 30, 2016). Roldugina's study is based on another file on the same case held in TsGA SPb, f. 52, op. 5, d. 52, l. 187; see Irina Roldugina, "Rannesovetskaia gomoseksual'naia subkul'tura: istoriia odnoi fotografii," *Teatr.*, no. 16 (2014), online at http://oteatre.info/rannesovetskaya-gomoseksualnaya-subkultura-istoriya-odnoj-fotografii (accessed April 30, 2016).

22 See http://arzamas.academy/mag/166-queer (accessed April 30, 2016).

23 Roldugina, "Rannesovetskaia gomoseksual'naia subkul'tura."

24 Censorship tightened during the 1920s and private publishers were eliminated by 1930. On Kuzmin and Kliuev, see Chapter 8; on Parnok, see Diana Lewis Burgin, *Sophia Parnok: The Life and Work of Russia's Sappho* (New York and London: New York University Press, 1994). For case histories, see e.g. Dan Healey, "Evgeniia/Evgenii: Queer Case Histories in the first years of Soviet power," *Gender & History* 9, no. 1 (1997): 83–106.

25 Robert Beachy, *Gay Berlin: Birthplace of a Modern Identity* (New York: Vintage, 2015); Laurie Marhoefer, *Sex and the Weimar Republic: German Homosexual Emancipation and the Rise of the Nazis* (Toronto and Buffalo: University of Toronto Press, 2015).

26 For documents offering a major research opportunity in this direction, see Irina Roldugina, "'Pochemu my takie liudi?' Rannesovetskie gomoseksualy ot pervogo litsa: novye istochniki po istorii gomoseksual'nykh identichnostei v Rossii," *Ab Imperio* no. 2 (2016): 183–216.

27 The meeting is described in Healey, *Homosexual Desire in Revolutionary Russia*, 162–71.

28 Dan Healey, *Bolshevik Sexual Forensics: Diagnosing Disorder in the Clinic and Courtroom, 1917–1939* (DeKalb: Northern Illinois University Press, 2009), 134–58.

29 See ibid., 3–16, 159–71.

30 Naiman, *Sex in Public*; Magali Delaloye, "Les bolcheviques se dessinent: l'expression de la virilité dans le cercle du Kremlin" *Clio: femmes, genre, histoire* 41, no. 1 (2015): 201–11.

31 "Iz Istorii Ugolovnogo Kodeksa: 'Primerno Nakazat' Etikh Merzavtsev'," *Istochnik: Dokumenty russkoi istorii: Prilozhenie k rossiiskomu istoriko-publitsisticheskomu zhurnalu "Rodina,"* no. 5–6 (1993): 164–5, citing documents from APRF, f. 3, op. 57, d. 37, ll. 24, 25–6.

32 APRF, f. 3, is devoted to the intelligence services, and has not been declassified (personal communication, David Brandenberger, June 20, 2016). Oleg Khlevniuk, an authority on archives of Stalin governance, describes thematic folders (*tematicheskie papki*) in the Presidential Archive as a feature of the information-organizing systems of the regime in the 1930s–50s; see O. V. Khlevniuk and Nora Seligman Favorov, *Stalin: New Biography of a Dictator* (New Haven: Yale University Press, 2015), 337. The same issue of the APRF journal also published further material from the same file, related to the anti-sodomy law, the letter of Harry Whyte to Stalin, discussed below.

33 "Iz Istorii Ugolovnogo Kodeksa: 'Primerno Nakazat' Etikh Merzavtsev'," 164.

34 I. A. Mazus, *Podpol'nye molodezhnye organizatsii, gruppy i kruzhki (1926–1953 gg.): spravochnik.* (Moscow: Vozvrashchenie; Gos. muzei GULAGa, 2014), 92–113, 113–17, 117–21.

35 GARF, f. 3316, op. 26, d. 146, l. 3. I am grateful to David Brandenberger for sharing this document with me. In 2001 I speculated that Justice Commissariat or Supreme Court jurists suggested the excision of these explicit passages from the law: I was wrong. See Healey, *Homosexual Desire in Revolutionary Russia*, 187–8.

36 The "Letter" states: "An assistant of the German military attaché, a friend and follower of the notorious Captain Roehm, managed to enter the homosexual circles in Moscow, and under cover of a homosexual 'organization' (homosexuality was still legal in Russia at that time), started a whole network of National-Socialist propaganda. Its threads extended into the provinces, to Leningrad, Kharkov, Kiev, etc. A number of persons in literary and artistic circles were involved: the private secretary of a very prominent actor, known for his homosexual inclinations, an important scientific collaborator of the Lenin Institute, etc. These connections were utilized by the Germans not only to procure military information, but also to sow dissent in government and Party circles. The aims of those directing this conspiracy were so far-reaching that the leaders of Soviet policy were compelled to intervene . . ." See Boris I. Nicolaevsky, *Power and the Soviet Elite: "Letter of an Old Bolshevik" and Other Essays* (London: Pall Mall, 1966), 31. To the best of my knowledge, the homosexual figures mentioned here have never been identified; on the provenance of the document, see Robert C. Tucker, "On the 'Letter of an Old Bolshevik' as an Historical Document," *Slavic Review* 51, no. 4 (1992): 782–5.

37 The other exception was Soviet Tajikistan; see Healey, *Homosexual Desire in Revolutionary Russia*, 185–6.

38 GARF, f. 3316, op. 2, d. 146, l. 3.

39 The corrective-labor colonies have been little studied, perhaps because most inmates were less educated "genuine" criminals; on the colonies see Steven Anthony Barnes, *Death and Redemption: the Gulag and the Shaping of Soviet Society* (Princeton: Princeton University Press, 2011), 25–7.

40 On the distinction between "socially alien" and "socially friendly" prisoners, see ibid., 87–8.

41 Healey, *Homosexual Desire in Revolutionary Russia*, 217–23.

42 E.g. there are no documents about these raids in N. Vert, S. V. Mironenko, and I. A. Ziuzina, eds, *Istoriia stalinskogo Gulaga. Konets 1920-kh – pervaia polovina 1950-kh godov: Sobranie dokumentov v 7-mi tomakh. Tom 1. Massovye repressii v SSSR* (Moscow: ROSSPEN, 2004); nor in V. N. Khaustov, V. P. Naumov, and N. S. Plotnikova, eds., *Lubianka: Stalin i VChK-GPU-OGPU-NKVD, ianvar' 1922-dekabr' 1936. Rossiia XX vek Dokumenty* (Moscow: Mezhdunarodnyi fond "Demokratiia," 2003).

43 Reich mentioned "politically motivated" arrests of homosexuals in January 1934 in Moscow, Leningrad, Kharkov, and Odessa in his essay "The Struggle for a 'New Life' in the Soviet Union" (1936); and in 1937 the Webbs also noted the "drastic" change in the law, ascribed to charges of conspiracy with "certain foreigners": Healey, *Homosexual Desire in Revolutionary Russia*, 336, n. 5.

44 V. A. Ivanov, "Kontrrevoliutsionnye organizatsii sredi gomoseksualistov Leningrada v nachale 1930-kh godov i ikh pogrom," *Noveishaia istoriia Rossiia*, no. 3 (2013): 126–43.

45 Irina Roldugina analyses the politics of Russia's archives for queer historians and argues for more sophisticated readings of available queer archives of the Soviet 1920s; she publishes documents from the FSB archive used by Ivanov, and others from the professional archive of Leningrad's leading psychiatrist, Vladimir M. Bekhterev. I am grateful to her for sharing an advance copy of the article: "'Pochemu my takie liudi?'"

46 Ivanov, "Kontrrevoliutsionnye organizatsii sredi gomoseksualistov Leningrada," 131.

47 Ivanov, "Kontrrevoliutsionnye organizatsii sredi gomoseksualistov Leningrada," 132, citing AU FSB RF po SPb i oblasti, d. P–9702, l. 28 (Pokazaniia L. K. Lisenko ot 14 avgusta 1933 g.).

48 Lisenko reportedly discussed the possible homosexuality of Jesus Christ, with other gay men whom he met in popular cruising spots (Ivanov, "Kontrrevoliutsionnye organizatsii sredi gomoseksualistov Leningrada," 139).

49 Roldugina, "'Pochemu my takie liudi?'"

50 Shearer, *Policing Stalin's Socialism*, 192–200; Hagenloh, *Stalin's Police*, 119–32.

51 For a meticulous description of the card-indexing system, see Shearer, *Policing Stalin's Socialism*, 161–9.

52 Shearer, *Policing Stalin's Socialism*, 196–8; 201; Vert et al., eds *Istoriia stalinskogo Gulaga*, 1: 149–51, 155–7.

53 For an official's complaint about discrepancies between published and oral instructions used by the secret police, and their effects on the passportization campaign, see Vert et al., eds *Istoriia stalinskogo Gulaga*, 1: 150–1.

54 "Iz Istorii Ugolovnogo Kodeksa: 'Primerno Nakazat' Etikh Merzavtsev'," 164. No archival citation for Yagoda's September 15, 1933 letter to Stalin is given.

55 Ivanov, "Kontrrevoliutsionnye organizatsii sredi gomoseksualistov Leningrada," 135. No archival reference for this figure is cited – perhaps indicating it came from "operational" documents in the file to which Roldugina was later denied access.

56 Ibid., 127. The letter first appeared in Viktor A. Ivanov, *Missiia ordena: mekhanizm massovoi repressii v Sovetskoi Rossii v kontse 20-kh – 40-kh gg. (na materialakh Severo-Zapada RSFSR)* (St. Petersburg: LISS, 1997), 59–61. In neither publication has Ivanov cited an archival reference for the letter.

57 Harry Oosterhuis, "The 'Jews' of the Antifascist Left: Homosexuality and Socialist Resistance to Nazism," in *Gay Men and the Sexual History of the Political Left*, eds G. Hekma, H. Oosterhuis and J. Steakley (Binghamton, NY: Harrington Park Press, 1995). Quotations from the Russian version of the "Brown Book," published ca. September 1933, *Korichnevaia kniga o podzhoge reikhstaga i gitlerovskom terrore* (Moscow: Izd-vo TsK MOPR SSSR, 1933), 59.

58 Praise for van der Lubbe's act could also be construed negatively by the secret police. A student in a group arrested in 1935 was accused, among other things, of praising "the act of van der Lubbe, calling him a hero, [saying] that he will go down in history and has become famous the world over and is talked about everywhere." He was shot on 3 April 1935 as a counterrevolutionary. See Mazus, *Podpol'nye molodezhnye organizatsii*, 128–30.

59 On Kliuev's local police file, see Makin, "Whose Kliuev, Who Is Kliuev?" 234 n8, 259, 261. On the retrieval of Kozin's diary from the Magadan archives of the FSB, see Kozin, *Prokliatoe iskusstvo*, 27–8.

60 Whyte's undated letter is located at APRF, f. 3, op. 57, d. 37, ll. 29–45. The letter is published in: G. Uait, "'Mozhet li gomoseksualist sostoiat' chlenom Kommunistichestkoi Partii?' Iumor iz Spetskhana [sic]," *Istochnik: Dokumenty russkoi istorii: Prilozhenie k rossiiskomu istoriko-publitsisticheskomu zhurnalu "Rodina,"* no. 5–6 (1993): 185–91. For my translation of the full letter, see Glennys Young. *The Communist Experience in the Twentieth Century: A Global History through Sources* (New York and Oxford: Oxford University Press, 2012), 88–98. On Whyte's life and career, see Jeffrey Meek, *Queer Voices in Post-war Scotland: Male Homosexuality, Religion and Society* (Basingstoke: Palgrave Macmillan, 2015), 83–8.

61 Meek, *Queer Voices in Post-war Scotland*, 86–8.

62 See Daniel Beer, *Renovating Russia: The Human Sciences and the Fate of Liberal Modernity, 1880–1930* (Ithaca and London: Cornell University Press, 2008); Kenneth M. Pinnow, *Lost to the Collective: Suicide and the Promise of Soviet Socialism, 1921–1929* (Ithaca and London: Cornell University Press, 2010), 2, 30, 52.

63 O. V. Khlevniuk, "Letters to Stalin: Practices of Selection and Reaction," *Cahiers du monde russe 56*, no. 2 (2015): 327–44.

64 Healey, *Homosexual Desire in Revolutionary Russia*, 189–90, 195–6.

65 GARF, f. R5441, op. 81a, d. 302, "Ob obvinenii v pederastii vracha Chufarovskogo i drugikh. 17.11.1939 – 14.03.1940." I am grateful to Irina Roldugina for telling me about this file, which she will describe in a forthcoming article. On Vyshinsky, see Arkadii Vaksberg, *Stalin's Prosecutor: The Life of Andrei Vyshinsky* (New York: Grove Weidenfeld, 1991).

66 Roldugina, "'Pochemu my takie liudi?'"

67 Makin, "Whose Kliuev, Who Is Kliuev?" 258; the inference that Kliuev had sex with minors is dismissed in Valerii Shubinskii, "Bitva mifov (Obzor knig o N. Kliueve i S. Esenine)," *Novoe literaturnoe obozrenie*, no. 89 (2008). My account in both the English and Russian versions of *Homosexual Desire in Revolutionary Russia* did not mention the charge of homosexuality brought against Kliuev in 1934.

68 RGASPI, f. 671, op. 1, dd. 249 and 254. (Ezhov's personal fond.) My thanks to Jon Waterlow for sharing these sources.

69 A purge of homosexuals in the People's Commissariat of Foreign Affairs began in April 1934 with the arrest of D. T. Florinsky, director of protocol. A sympathetic historian, Leonid Maksimenkov, implies that Florinsky was a protégé of the homosexual B. V. Chicherin, Commissar of Foreign Affairs until 1930. In a letter addressed to Stalin, Deputy Director of the OGPU Iakov S. Agranov described how Florinsky and many other homosexuals were removed from the commissariat in the spring and summer of 1934; see Leonid Maksimenkov, *Sumbur vmesto muzyki: Stalinskaia kul'turnaia revoliutsiia 1936–1938* (Moscow: Iuridicheskaia Kniga, 1997), 205–8, citing RGASPI, f. 17, op. 163, d. 1033, ll. 116–17. For the December 1934 expulsion of a Komsomol (Young Communist) member A. F. Grishin, an employee of the secret police, for being a "homosexualist" and "engaging in sodomy," see P. P. Aleksandrov-Derkachenko, *Russkoe i sovetskoe molodezhnoe dvizhenie v dokumentakh, 1905–1937 gg.* (Moscow: OMP-Press, 2002), 230. My thanks to Jon Waterlow for this source.

70 Healey, *Homosexual Desire in Revolutionary Russia*, 260–1.

71 On the catastrophic food-supply crisis in wartime, see Wendy Z. Goldman and Donald A. Filtzer, eds, *Hunger and War: Food Provisioning in the Soviet Union during World War II* (Bloomington: Indiana University Press, 2015); and more generally, John Barber and Mark Harrison, *The Soviet Home Front, 1941–1945: A Social and Economic History of the USSR in World War II* (London and New York: Longman, 1991).

72 See e.g. Allan Bérubé, *Coming Out under Fire: The History of Gay Men and Lesbians in World War Two* (New York: Macmillan, 1990); Matt Houlbrook, *Queer London: Perils and Pleasures in the Sexual Metropolis, 1918–1957* (Chicago: University of Chicago Press, 2005).

73 Arthur Clech, "The Great Patriotic War, a relative respite?" in *Being Homosexual in Europe during World War II*, ed. Régis Schlagdenhaufen

(Strasbourg: Editions du Conseil de l'Europe, forthcoming). I am grateful to Arthur Clech for an advance copy of his chapter.

74 Oleg Budnitskii, "Muzhchiny i zhenshchiny v Krasnoi Armii, 1941–1945," *Cahiers du monde russe* 52, no. 2–3 (2011): 405–22; Anna Krylova, *Soviet Women in Combat: A History of Violence on the Eastern Front* (Cambridge and New York: Cambridge University Press, 2010), 169 (for statistics); 283–8 (on heterosexual affairs).

75 Clech, "The Great Patriotic War, a relative respite?"

76 Krylova, *Soviet Women in Combat*, 283.

77 Ineta Lipša, "Homosexuals and Soviet Power: Suppression Mechanisms in the Latvian SSR, 1960s–1980s," paper presented at *European Social Science History Conference*, Valencia, Spain, 2016.

78 Teet Veispak, "Homosexuality in Estonia in the 20th Century: Ideological and Juridical Aspects," in *Sexual Minorities and Society: The Changing Attitudes toward Homosexuality in 20th Century Europe*, eds Udo Parikas and Teet Veispak (Tallinn: Institute of History, 1991), 108; Lipša, "Homosexuals and Soviet Power."

79 GARF, f. A353, op. 16s, d. 121, ll. 16–24. Strikingly, seven of Sverdlovsk's convictions fell in the second quarter, and five of Moscow's in the fourth quarter. Ivanovskaia oblast' and Chkalovskaia oblast' also reported clusters of five each in single quarters.

80 For Moscow see Dan Healey, "Moscow," in *Queer Sites: Gay Urban Histories since 1600*, ed. David Higgs (London: Routledge, 1999). For Leningrad Province, see Chapter 2.

81 Lipša, "Homosexuals and Soviet Power."

82 Uladzimir Valodzin, *Queer History of Belarus in the Second Half of the 20th Century: A Preliminary Study* (Minsk: http://belarusianqueerstory.noblogs.org, 2016), 20–1.

83 There is no definitive account of the first case against Paradzhanov but see James Steffen, *The Cinema of Sergei Parajanov* (Madison: University of Wisconsin Press, 2013), 29.

84 A. B. Bezborodov and V. M. Khrustalev, eds *Istoriia Stalinskogo Gulaga. Konets 1920-kh – pervaia polovina 1950-kh godov.* 7 vols. (Moscow: ROSSPEN, 2004), 4: 141 (document 55). Other examples for 1939 and 1948 are mentioned in Chapter 1.

85 LOGAV, f. 3820, op. 2, d. 3843 (a sixteen-year-old is raped and beaten by a seventeen-year-old recidivist; the pair knew each other from a children's colony they had previously lived in). Valodzin records the case of three prisoners in their twenties who were convicted of sodomy in Brest Province, early 1957; see *Queer History of Belarus*, 21.

86 Miriam Dobson, *Khrushchev's Cold Summer: Gulag Returnees, Crime, and the Fate of Reform after Stalin* (Ithaca and London: Cornell University Press, 2009), and see Chapter 1.

87 Healey, *Homosexual Desire in Revolutionary Russia*, 238.

88 Lipša, "Homosexuals and Soviet Power."

89   Healey, *Homosexual Desire in Revolutionary Russia*, 262.

90   Lipša, "Homosexuals and Soviet Power"; Veispak, "Homosexuality in Estonia in the 20th Century"; Valodzin, *Queer History of Belarus*, 23–6.

91   Healey, *Homosexual Desire in Revolutionary Russia*, 239–40; 245–6; on police entrapment, see Vladimir Kozlovskii, *Argo russkoi gomoseksual'noi subkul'tury: materialy k izucheniiu* (Benson, VT: Chalidze Publications, 1986), 196–9; and for Soviet Ukraine, A. Kravchuk and A. Gribanov, *Golubaia kniga. Polozhenie geev i lesbiianok v Ukraine* (Kiev: Tsentr "Nash Mir"; Nora-Print, 2000), 21.

92   Jaanus Samma and Eugenio Viola, *Not Suitable for Work. A Chairman's Tale* (Berlin and Tallinn: Sternberg Press & Centre for Contemporary Arts Estonia, 2015), 1–65.

93   Samma and Viola, *Not Suitable for Work*, 67–79. Veispak, "Homosexuality in Estonia in the 20th Century," 112, reports sporadic conviction rates for Estonia as a whole, with spikes in 1967 (seventeen) and 1970, 1972 (thirteen each year) but otherwise only 0–4 convictions per year in the 1960s-and early 1970s. Another peak at the end of the 1970s is noteworthy: 1978 (twelve); 1979 (ten); and 1980 (fifteen), perhaps related to the Olympics which brought sailing events to Tallinn. A total of 157 men were convicted for sodomy in Estonia between 1960 and 1989.

94   Lipša, "Homosexuals and Soviet Power."

95   Sergej Shcherbakov, "On the Relationship between the Leningrad Gay Community and Legal Authorities in the 1970s and 1980s," in *Sexual Minorities and Society: the Changing Attitudes toward Homosexuality in 20th Century Europe*, eds Udo Parikas and Teet Veispak (Tallinn: Institute of History, 1991).

96   Shcherbakov, "On the Relationship between the Leningrad Gay Community and Legal Authorities," 99; Kravchuk and Gribanov, *Golubaia kniga*, 20–1.

97   Sonia Franeta, *My Pink Road to Russia: Tales of Amazons, Peasants, and Queers* (Oakland: Dacha Books, 2015), 206, 214.

98   On Kozin's 1959 arrest see Boris Savchenko, "Vvedenie," in Kozin, *Prokliatoe iskusstvo*, 18.

99   See Savchenko, "Vvedenie," 16. On the culture ministry's attitude, see Boris Savchenko, *Vadim Kozin* (Smolensk: Rusich, 2001), 376–7.

100 Steffen, *The Cinema of Sergei Parajanov*, 197.

101 Vladimir Kirsanov, *69. Russkie gei, lesbiianki, biseksualy i transseksualy* (Tver': Ganimed, 2005), 353.

102 Ibid, 351–3; Steffen, *The Cinema of Sergei Parajanov*, 226–30.

103 Vladimir Kirsanov, *+31. Russkie gei, lesbiianki, biseksualy i transseksualy* (Moscow: Kvir, 2007), 84–7; Simon Karlinsky, "The Case of Gennady Trifonov," *New York Review of Books*, 33, 6 (10 April 1986).

104 L. S. Klein, *Trudno byt' Kleinom: Avtobiografiia v monologakh i dialogakh* (St. Petersburg: Nestor-Istoriia, 2009).

105 Kirsanov, *69. Russkie gei, lesbiianki, biseksualy i transseksualy*, 364–70. For translations of his work, see Yevgeny Kharitonov, *Under House Arrest* (London: Serpent's Tail, 1998).

106 See Kharitonov, "The Leaflet," and Trifonov, "Open Letter to Literaturnaya
     Gazeta," in Kevin Moss, ed., *Out of the Blue: Russia's Hidden Gay Literature*
     (San Francisco: Gay Sunshine Press, 1996), 224–5, 230–2; Kirsanov, *+31.
     Russkie gei, lesbiianki, biseksualy i transseksualy*, 88.

107 This focus on "celebrities" in LGBT history was highlighted with the recent
     pardon for British mathematician Alan Turing for his 1952 conviction for
     gross indecency (see Chapter 9). It was not followed by pardons for the
     estimated 49,000 other victims of this law. Benedict Cumberbatch launched
     a campaign to these ordinary victims; see http://www.bbc.co.uk/news/
     uk–31070115 (accessed January 31, 2015). "Turing's Law" of January 2017
     pardoned some ordinary victims.

Chapter 8: Shame, Pride, and "Non-traditional" Lives: The Dilemmas of Queering Russian Biography

1   Pervyi Kanal & Associated Press interview, September 4, 2013: http://ria.ru/
     politics/20130904/960605375.html (accessed January 6, 2014).

2   See "Net nikakikh dokazatel'stv gomoseksual'nosti Chaikovskogo," September
     17, 2013: http://www.interfax.ru/txt.asp?id=329409&sec=1483&sw=%EC%
     E5%E4%E8%ED%F1%EA%E8%E9&bd=18&bm=8&by=2013&ed=18&e
     m=9&ey=2013&secid=0&mp=2&p=1 (accessed March 18, 2015).

3   "Manuscripts don't burn" is of course the memorable phrase from Mikhail
     Bulgakov's *Master and Margarita*: Mikhail Bulgakov, *Izbrannoe: "Master i
     Margarita": Roman; Rasskazy* (Moscow: Khudozhestvennaia literatura,
     1983), 279. On the politics of archives and queer historical revisions of the
     "straight" past, see e.g. Charles E. Morris, "Archival Queer," *Rhetoric &
     Public Affairs* 9, no. 1 (2006): 145–51; Ann Cvetkovich, *An Archive of
     Feelings: Trauma, Sexuality, and Lesbian Public Cultures* (Durham and
     London: Duke University Press, 2003).

4   Adrienne Rich, "Compulsory Heterosexuality and Lesbian Existence," *Signs* 5,
     no. 4 (1980): 631–60.

5   Robert K. Martin, "Reclaiming our Lives," in *The Christopher Street Reader*,
     eds M. Denneny, C. Ortleb and T. Steele (New York: Perigee, 1983).

6   Brian James Baer, "Now You See It: Gay (In)Visibility and the Performance of
     Post-Soviet Identity," in *Queer Visibility in Post-socialist Cultures*, eds Narcisz
     Fejes and Andrea P. Balogh (Bristol: Intellect, 2013), 51.

7   See Chapter 6, "Reading Wilde in Moscow, or Le plus ça change: Translations
     of Western Gay Literature in Post-Soviet Russia" in Brian James Baer,
     Translation and the Making of Modern Russian Literature (New York and
     London: Bloomsbury Academic, 2016), 133–61.

8   Martin, "Reclaiming our Lives," 249.

9   For a critique of these assumptions in U.S. education, see William J. Letts and
     James T. Sears, eds. *Queering Elementary Education: Advancing the Dialogue
     about Sexualities and Schooling* (Lanham: Rowman & Littlefield, 1999).

10 For a sexologist's influential viewpoint, see Dan Healey, "'Untraditional Sex'
    and the 'Simple Russian': Nostalgia for Soviet Innocence in the Polemics of
    Dilia Enikeeva," in *What is Soviet Now? Identities, Legacies, Memories*, eds
    Thomas Lahusen and Peter H. Solomon Jr. (Berlin: Lit Verlag, 2008); and on
    homophobia in contemporary Russian psychiatric medicine, note Kevin Moss,
    "Straight Eye for the Queer Guy: Gay Male Visibility in Post-Soviet Russian
    Films," in *Queer Visibility in Post-Socialist Cultures*, eds Narcisz Fejes and
    Andrea P. Balogh (Bristol: Intellect, 2013), 204.

11 Eve K. Sedgwick, *Epistemology of the Closet* (Berkeley and Los Angeles:
    University of California Press, 1990).

12 David Smith, "Why Africa is the most homophobic continent on earth,"
    Observer, 23 February 2014: 32–3 (online at: http://www.theguardian.com/
    world/2014/feb/23/africa-homophobia-uganda-anti-gay-law, accessed March
    20, 2015). On Uganda see *Rule by Law: Discriminatory Legislation and
    Legitimized Abuses in Uganda* (London: Amnesty International, 2014), online
    at https://www.amnesty.org/en/documents/afr59/006/2014/en (accessed April
    13, 2016).

13 See e.g. Marianna Murav'eva, "'(Ne)traditsionnye seksual'nye otnosheniia'
    kak iuridicheskaia kategoriia: istoriko-pravovoi analiz," in *Na pereput'e:
    metodologiia, teoriia i praktika LGBT i kvir-issledovanii*, ed. Aleksandr
    Kondakov (St. Petersburg: Tsentr nezavisimykh sotsiologicheskikh issledovanii,
    2014).

14 See the essays in David M. Halperin and Valerie Traub, eds *Gay Shame*
    (Chicago: University of Chicago Press, 2009).

15 For Russian psychologists' perspectives on the impact of shame and
    homophobia, see Sergei Fadeev and Mariia Sabunaeva, "Samoskrytie
    kak kliuchevoi faktor stanovleniia gomoseksual'noi identitchnosti," and Dar'ia
    Kutuzova, "Narrativnaia praktika v rabote s kvir-obshchestvom," in *Vomozhen-
    li "kvir" po-russki? LGBT issledovaniia. Mezhditsiplinarnyi sbornik*, ed. Valerii
    Sozaev (St. Petersburg: LGBT organizatsiia Vykhod, 2010); see also Maksim
    Kasianchuk, "Internal'naia gomofobiia biseksual'nykh muzhchin," Aleksandr
    Kim and Elena Shumakova, "Dominiruiushchie povedencheskie patterny v
    strukture sotsial'noi adaptatsii u lits razlichnoi seksual'noi orientatsii," and
    Tat'iana Zborovskaia, "Spetsifika formirovaniia kartiny mira transgenderov v
    zavisimosti ot sotsiokul'turnykh realii: issledovanie assotsiativnykh norm na
    primere russkogo i anglisskogo iazykov," in *Na Pereput'e: metodologiia, teoriia i
    praktika LGBT i kvri-issledovanii*, ed. Aleksandr Kondakov (St. Petersburg:
    Tsentr nezaivisimykh sotsiologicheskikh issledovanii, 2014).

16 Eve Kosofsky Sedgwick, "Shame, Theatricality, and Queer Performativity:
    Henry James's *The Art of the Novel*," in *Gay Shame*, eds David Halperin and
    Valerie Traub (Chicago and London: University of Chicago Press, 2009), 59.
    See also Sebastien Chauvin, "Honte," in *Dictionnaire de l'Homophobie*, ed.
    Louis-Georges Tin (Paris: Presses Universitaires de France, 2003), 222–6.

17 On Goffman and the "sacred center of the common values of the society" in
    which the shamed person lives, see Deborah B. Gould, "The Shame of Gay
    Pride in Early AIDS Activism," in *Gay Shame*, eds David Halperin and Valerie
    Traub (Chicago and London: University of Chicago Press, 2009), 224.

18 Guy Hocquenghem, *Homosexual Desire* (Durham: Duke University Press, 1993), 143.

19 George Chauncey, "The Trouble with Shame," in *Gay Shame*, eds David Halperin and Valerie Traub (Chicago and London: University of Chicago Press, 2009), 280.

20 Vadim Kozin, *Prokliatoe iskusstvo* (Moscow: Vagrius, 2005), 209 (December 19, 1955). On this diary see Chapter 3.

21 Chauncey, "The Trouble with Shame," 279.

22 See e.g. Konstantin K. Rotikov, *Drugoi Peterburg* (St. Petersburg: Liga Plius, 1998); L. S. Klein, *Drugaia storona svetila: neobychnaia liubov' vydaiushchikhsia liudei: rossiskoe sozvezdie* (St. Petersburg: Folio-Press, 2002); Vladimir Kirsanov, *69. Russkie gei, lesbiianki, biseksualy i transseksualy* (Tver': Ganimed, 2005); idem., *+31. Russkie gei, lesbiianki, biseksualy i transseksualy* (Moscow: Kvir, 2007).

23 On homonationalism and critics of unthinking transnational imposition of a Western globalized LGBT rights agenda from the "West to the rest," see the Introduction to this volume.

24 On Kliuev's arrest and fate, see Michael Makin, "Whose Kliuev, Who Is Kliuev? Polemics of Identity and Poetry," *The Slavonic and East European Review* 85, no. 2 (2007): 231–70. On Kozin, see Boris Savchenko, "Vvedenie," in Kozin, *Prokliatoe iskusstvo*, 5–28. For Paradzhanov's arrests, see James Steffen, *The Cinema of Sergei Parajanov* (Madison: University of Wisconsin Press, 2013), 4–5, 29.

25 Kozin's 1955–6 diary is discussed in Chapter 3. Kliuev's letters from exile to his lover Anatoly Yar-Kravchenko, and documents from his police file in Tomsk, are published in T. Kravchenko and A. Mikhailov, eds *Nasledie komet. Neizvestnoe o Nikolae Kliueve i Anatolii Iare* (Moscow and Tomsk: Territoriia, 2006). Paradzhanov never described his 1948 prison experience; for comments on his 1970s imprisonment see Steffen, *The Cinema of Sergei Parajanov*, 193–4; and Kirsanov, Kirsanov, *69. Russkie gei, lesbiianki, biseksualy i transseksualy*, 349–50.

26 Martin, "Reclaiming our Lives," 249.

27 Ibid., 252–3.

28 Terry Castle, *The Apparitional Lesbian: Female Homosexuality and Modern Culture* (New York: Columbia University Press, 1993).

29 Andrew Hodges, *Alan Turing: The Enigma* (London: Burnett Books-Hutchinson, 1983).

30 See e.g. Bertram J. Cohler, *Writing Desire: Sixty Years of Gay Autobiography* (Madison: University of Wisconsin Press, 2007); Philip L. Hammack and Bertram J. Cohler, eds, *The Story of Sexual Identity: Narrative Perspectives on the Gay and Lesbian Life Course* (Oxford: Oxford University Press, 2009); Georgia Johnston, "Geographies of the Closet: The Lives of Paul Monette," *Biography* 25, no. 1 (2002): 171–9. A search of the academic journal *Biography* (March 30, 2014) turned up no analysis of biographies of LGBT figures *except* as autobiography.

31 There were exceptions to the dominant heteronormative voice in small-
    circulation "homophile" newsletters. Pre–1969 homophile organizations
    challenged homophobia in historical and biographical studies, but often
    these groups strove for recognition for the "respectable" homosexual, and the
    Stonewall generation accused them of being too ashamed of their sexual
    difference. This view of the homophile movement is undergoing revision. See
    e.g. Julian Jackson, *Living in Arcadia: Homosexuality, Politics, and Morality
    in France from the Liberation to AIDS* (Chicago: University of Chicago Press,
    2009); Hubert C. Kennedy, *The Ideal Gay Man: The Story of Der Kreis* (New
    York: Haworth Press, 1999).

32 See Alexander Poznansky, *Tchaikovsky: The Quest for the Inner Man* (New
    York: Schirmer Books, 1991). The myth of Tchaikovsky's suicide is forensically
    refuted in idem, *Tchaikovsky's Last Days: A Documentary Study* (Oxford:
    Clarendon Press, 1996).

33 For a sensitive analysis, see Michael Makin, *Nikolai Klyuev: Time and Text,
    Place and Poet* (Evanston: Northwestern University Press, 2010); idem.,
    "Whose Kliuev, Who Is Kliuev? Polemics of Identity and Poetry," *The Slavonic
    and East European Review* 85, no. 2 (2007): 231–70.

34 Makin, "Whose Kliuev, Who Is Kliuev?," 258–9.

35 Vitalii Shentalinskii, *Raby svobody: V literaturnykh arkhivakh KGB* (Moscow:
    Parus, 1995); Vitalii Shentalinskii and John Crowfoot *The KGB's Literary
    Archive* (London: Harvill Press, 1995).

36 Shentalinskii, *Raby svobody*, 265–74. The same erasure mars the English
    translation: ibid., *The KGB's Literary Archive*, 197–209.

37 On February 2, 1934, he was arrested under articles 58–10 and 151 (intercourse
    with someone not having achieved sexual maturity) with application of the
    "analogy" article 16, to signify the crime of sodomy, which was in the process of
    being added to the criminal code. Until March 7, 1934, there was no formal
    anti-sodomy statute, and the authorities used the much-criticized Soviet analogy
    principle (that allowed prosecution of an action "by analogy" to a stated crime)
    to convict homosexuals of consensual gay relations. The case is discussed in
    Chapter 7.

38 Makin, "Whose Kliuev, Who Is Kliuev?," 258.

39 Ibid., 258–5.

40 Konstantin Azadovskii, *Zhizn' Nikolaia Kliueva: dokumental'noe povestvovanie*
    (St. Petersburg: Zvezda, 2002); on this point see Valerii Shubinskii, "Bitva mifov
    (Obzor knig o N. Kliueve i S. Esenine)," *Novoe literaturnoe obozrenie*, no. 89
    (2008).

41 T. Kravchenko and A. Mikhailov, "V dalekie tridtsatye gody [introduction]," in
    Kravchenko and Mikhailov, eds. *Nasledie komet*, 3–11. This is a truly bizarre
    essay that veers between nearly naming the love that dare not speak its name
    and hiding behind various shields. Kliuev and Yar-Kravchenko's relations are
    compared to those Oscar Wilde and Alfred Douglas (down to the parallel of
    separation by the older "friend's" imprisonment in Tomsk and Reading prisons,
    respectively). Yar-Kravchenko's May 1933 marriage to the singer Zinaida
    Pavlovna Vorobeva is mentioned in the sketchiest of terms and her name and

the details of their courtship are simply ignored. Kliuev reacted to the marriage to the singer as a "betrayal"; see Azadovskii, *Zhizn' Nikolaia Kliueva*, 278.

42 Stanislav Iu. Kuniiaev and Sergei S. Kuniaev. *Sergei Esenin* (Moskva: Molodaia gvardiia, 2005), 78.

43 Ibid., 78–9. For a view that Esenin "discovered in himself a latent bisexuality" in these years in the Imperial capital, see Gordon McVay, *Esenin: A Life* (Ann Arbor: Ardis, 1976), 68. Both Kuniaevs and McVay rely on readings of the memoir of V. S. Cherniaevsky about Esenin for their opposing viewpoints. Shubinskii, "Bitva mifov," argues that Esenin's bisexuality "was not a literary fact" and "exaggerated attention to this question produces a comic effect."

44 For more on "simple Russian" attitudes toward homosexuals, see Healey, "'Untraditional Sex' and the 'Simple Russian'."

45 There are two English biographies (1977; 1999) and three Russian versions (1996; 1997; 2013). Here I focus on the principal versions in each language: N. A. Bogomolov and John E. Malmstad, *Mikhail Kuzmin: Iskusstvo, Zhizn', Epokha* (Moscow: Novoe literaturnoe obozrenie, 1996); John E. Malmstad and Nikolay Bogomolov, *Mikhail Kuzmin: A Life in Art* (Cambridge and London: Harvard University Press, 1999). The most recent version, with "a minimum of corrections and revisions, mostly to the bibliography," appeared in the popular "Lives of Remarkable People" series: Nikolai Bogomolov and Dzhon Malmstad, *Mikhail Kuzmin* (Moscow: Molodaia gvardiia, 2013).

46 For an excellent recent translation, see M. A. Kuzmin, *Wings*, trans. H. Aplin (London: Hesperus, 2007).

47 The diaries from 1905–15 have been published under the editorship of Bogomolov and S. V. Shumikhin: M. A. Kuzmin, *Dnevnik 1905–1907* (St. Petersburg: Ivan Limbakh, 2000); idem, *Dnevnik 1908–1915* (St. Petersburg: Ivan Limbakh, 2005). Extracts for 1921 were published in the journal *Minuvshee* in 1993. For 1934 see M. A. Kuzmin, *Dnevnik 1934 goda* (St. Petersburg: Ivan Limbakh, 1998). I had the good fortune to read the unpublished diaries of the 1920s in the Russian State Archives of Literature and Art in 1996: their queer observations of Soviet life merit further study, and should be at the heart of any attempt to trace the intellectual and transnational sources of Russian queer self-fashioning.

48 Malmstad and Bogomolov, *Mikhail Kuzmin*, 10.

49 Bogomolov and Malmstad, *Mikhail Kuzmin*, 12.

50 Compare page 139 in English with page 136 in Russian.

51 Compare page 229 in English with page 181 in Russian.

52 Baer, *Translation and the Making of Modern Russian Literature*, 142. The 2013 Russian version deploys estheticization (another technique of "packaging" described by Baer) to domesticate Kuzmin's homosexuality as a literary and artistic, rather than an experiential, fact of the poet's life; see Bogomolov and Malmstad, *Mikhail Kuzmin* (2013), 18–19.

53 Malmstad wrote his first Kuzmin biography in the 1970s using rare Soviet archival material (obtained at some risk, since for this interest he was later barred from receiving a Soviet visa) and perhaps the language of that treatment

was imported into the later English version without sufficient consideration of the language and approach used. See John Malmstad, "Mixail Kuzmin: A Chronicle of His Life and Times," in *Mixail A. Kuzmin: Sobranie stikhov*, ed. John Malmsted (Munich: W. Fink, 1977).

54 On Kozin see Chapters 3 and 9 in this volume.

55 Savchenko quotes the last line of Famusov in the 1825 Aleksandr Griboedov play "Woe from Wit," a Russian catchphrase encapsulating conformist concern for conventional morality.

56 Boris Savchenko, "Predislovie" in Vadim Kozin, *Prokliatoe iskusstvo* (Moscow: Vagrius, 2005), 6–7.

57 The diary is peppered with Savchenko's footnotes archly speculating on Kozin's possible sexual adventures with men and youths mentioned by the diarist: Kozin, *Prokliatoe iskusstvo*, 103, 161, 171, 200, etc.

58 The classic statement of this thesis is Michel Foucault, *The History of Sexuality: Vol 1, an Introduction*, trans. Robert Hurley (London: Penguin, 1978); see also Jeffrey Weeks, *Against Nature: Essays on History, Sexuality and Identity* (London: Rivers Oram Press, 1991); Edward Stein, ed., *Forms of Desire: Sexual Orientation and the Social Constructionist Controversy* (New York: Routledge, 1990); Annamarie Jagose, *Queer Theory: An Introduction* (New York: New York University Press, 1996).

59 See e.g. Regina Kunzel, *Criminal Intimacy: Prison and the Uneven History of Modern American Sexuality* (Chicago: University of Chicago Press, 2008); on complex "identity careers" that belie a simple hetero-homo paradigm for the USA and UK, see Francesca Stella, *Lesbian Lives in Soviet and Post-Soviet Russia: Post/socialism and Gendered Sexualities* (Basingstoke: Palgrave Macmillan, 2015), 18–19.

60 For a critique of these tendencies, see David M. Halperin, *How to Do the History of Homosexuality* (Chicago: University of Chicago Press, 2002).

61 Of course, the destruction of Turing's writing related to his sex life is part of the puzzle. I am indebted for these reflections on Turing to Laura Doan, "On the Entanglements of Queer Memory and History – the Case of Alan Turing," 2014 Stonewall Lecture, University of Southampton; this essay is now published: Laura Doan, "Queer History/Queer Memory: The Case of Alan Turing," *GLQ: A Journal of Gay and Lesbian Studies* 23, no. 1 (2017): 113–36. Another deconstruction of the Turing cult is Chris Waters, "Making the Past Visible: Alan Turing, the Gay Left, and Queer Stories of 1950s Britain," paper delivered at the European Social Science History Conference, Valencia, Spain, April 1, 2016.

62 Another important critique of "the quest for a bounded queer subject" is Matt Houlbrook, "Thinking Queer: The Social and the Sexual in Interwar Britain," in *British Queer History: New Approaches and Perspectives*, ed. Brian Lewis (Manchester: Manchester University Press, 2013). The quotation about the "gaze" is from ibid., 141.

63 For a discussion of these issues see Chapter 9.

64 Kravchenko, and Mikhailov, eds *Nasledie komet*, 43 (Kliuev to Anatolii, December 21, 1929).

65 On the "spiritual homosexual" in Russian culture, see Brian James Baer, *Other Russias: Homosexuality and the Crisis of Post-Soviet Identity* (New York: Palgrave Macmillan, 2009).

66 Makin, *Nikolai Klyuev*, 226. The "autobiographical" account is "Gagar'ia sud'bina," in N. A. Kliuev, *Slovesnoe drevo* (St. Petersburg: Rostok, 2003), 31–42.

67 Stella, *Lesbian Lives in Soviet and Post-Soviet Russia.*

68 For Clech's problematization of Russian/Soviet gay identities, and his call for more sophisticated conceptualization of same-sex subjectivities, see A. Klesh [Arthur Clech], "Istoriografiia russkoi gomoseksual'nosti do i posle Oktiabr'skoi revoliutsii: razlichnye podkhody i perspektivy," in *Kak my pishem istoriiu?* eds Gregory Dufaud, Guillaume Garreta and L. A. Pimenova (Moscow: ROSSPEN, 2013).

69 Roskomnadzor published in December 2013 "Criteria of Internet Content Harmful for Children's Health and Development" written by a team of child psychologists. It recommends "on LGBT community sites lists of famous personages of the present and of the past, who engage in or engaged in non-traditional sexual relations" should be removed (83): http://rkn.gov.ru/docs/Razdel_6.pdf (accessed April 13, 2016).

70 Heather K. Love, "Emotional Rescue," in *Gay Shame*, eds David Halperin and Valerie Traub (Chicago: University of Chicago Press, 2009), 258.

71 Makin, *Nikolai Klyuev*, 69.

72 Quoted in Baer, *Translation and the Making of Modern Russian Literature*, 138; and see Moss, "Straight Eye for the Queer Guy."

73 M. Zolotonosov, "Kniga o 'golubom peterburge' kak fenomen sovremennoi kul'tury," *Novyi mir*, 5 (1999): 185–91, quotation at 197, quoted in Baer, "Now You See It," 45; referring to Konstantin K. Rotikov, *Drugoi Peterburg* (St. Petersburg: Liga Plius, 1998).

Chapter 9: On the Boulevards of Magadan: Historical Time, Geopolitics, and Queer Memory in Homophobic Russia

1 Magadan as a municipality dates from 1939, but the secret police established it by decree in 1931 and the town grew from penal origins; see Pavel Grebeniuk, *Kolymskii led: Sistema upravleniia na Severo-Vostoke Rossii 1953–1964* (Moscow: ROSSPEN, 2007), 17–44, statistics at 23.

2 Kseniya Melnik, *Snow in May: Stories* (New York: Henry Holt and Company, 2014).

3 See http://alkrylov.livejournal.com/273439.html (accessed April 14, 2016).

4 See: RIA Novosti, April 3, 2013, http://ria.ru/spravka/20130403/930433749.html; Vadim Kozin "Unofficial" fan site: http://vadimkozin.ru. Both accessed January 11, 2014.

5 See http://alkrylov.livejournal.com/273439.html (accessed April 14, 2016).

6 See http://www.gayrussia.eu/russia/6081 (accessed April 14, 2016). One aspect overlooked by LGBT activists was the ambivalent attitude of Krylov to the local gay propaganda law. He led the Magadan Youth Chamber's discussion group on adoption of the law, apparently, supporting it (see http://www.magoblduma.ru/mop/news/2012/03/article3006 [accessed April, 2016]). Despite this, his photo blog of the unveiling of the Kozin sculpture was widely used on LGBT websites. Krylov may have had a change of heart, as in 2015 he also blogged positively, if clumsily, in support of same-sex partnerships and parental rights; see http://alkrylov.livejournal.com/534462.html and http://alkrylov.livejournal.com/531312.html (accessed April 14, 2016).

7 I borrow the concept of "remembering collectives" from Alexander Etkind, "Post-Soviet Hauntology: Cultural Memory of the Soviet Terror," *Constellations* 16, no. 1 (2009): 182–200. My analysis of Turing commemoration is heavily indebted to the work of Laura Doan and Chris Waters.

8 Andrew Hodges, *Alan Turing: The Enigma* (London: Vintage, 1992, 1983).

9 Lucy Noakes and Juliette Pattinson, *British Cultural Memory and the Second World War* (London: Bloomsbury Academic, 2014).

10 In July 2009 I visited the Kozin Museum; its director told me that Kozin's failure to marry was "the greatest tragedy of his life. The only love of his life was his music." Curatorial purging also tidies the Kozin legacy; heaps of papers and magazines the collector-singer used to pile up on his upright piano, floors, and shelves are all gone. Books line the walls in tidy order and the bed suggests monastic celibacy.

11 Erik N. Jensen, "The Pink Triangle and Political Consciousness: Gays, Lesbians, and the Memory of Nazi Persecution," *Journal of the History of Sexuality* 11, no. 1/2 (2002): 319–49.

12 See the introduction to: Dipesh Chakrabarty, *Provincializing Europe: Postcolonial Thought and Historical Difference* (Princeton and Oxford: Princeton University Press, 2008), 4.

13 Ibid., 4, 6–9.

14 Of course one could do the same for Turkey, Ukraine, Georgia, and numerous other nations positioned on "margins" or "crossroads" in historical hierarchies. On the construction of Eastern Europe as intermediary between Occident and Orient, see Larry Wolff, *Inventing Eastern Europe: The Map of Civilization on the Mind of the Enlightenment* (Stanford: Stanford University Press, 1994).

15 On the acceleration of time in the Soviet imagination, see Stephen E. Hanson, *Time and Revolution: Marxism and the Design of Soviet Institutions* (Chapel Hill: University of North Carolina Press, 1997).

16 The literature on the end of "transitology" – the study of transitions to liberal democracy in the late twentieth century – is large, but see Thomas Carothers, "The End of the Transition Paradigm," *Journal of Democracy* 13, no. 1 (2002): 5–21.

17 See e.g. Cai Wilkinson, "Putting 'Traditional Values' Into Practice: The Rise and Contestation of Anti-Homopropaganda Laws in Russia," *Journal of Human Rights* 13, no. 3 (2014): 363–79; Emil Persson, "Banning 'Homosexual

Propaganda': Belonging and Visibility in Contemporary Russian Media," *Sexuality & Culture* 19, no. 2 (2015): 256–74.

18 Expressed e.g. at the Valdai Conference in 2013 just after the adoption of the "gay propaganda" law: see http://en.kremlin.ru/events/president/news/19243 (accessed August 20, 2015).

19 See Joseph S. Nye, *Soft Power: The Means to Success in World Politics* (New York: Public Affairs, 2004); the details in this paragraph are drawn from Human Rights Watch, "The Spread of Russian-Style Propaganda Laws": http://www.humanrightsfirst.org/resource/spread-russian-style-propaganda-laws (accessed April 16, 2016).

20 Of course, LGBT rights remain controversial within the EU, and conflicts in Poland and other new accession states emerge not primarily from Russian "soft power" influence but from internal social sources; see Conor O'Dwyer, "Gay Rights and Political Homophobia in Postcommunist Europe: Is there an 'EU Effect'?" in *Global Homophobia: States, Movements, and the Politics of Oppression*, eds Meredith L. Weiss and Michael J. Bosia (Urbana, Chicago and Springfield: University of Illinois Press, 2013).

21 Russian LGBT Network, a national umbrella group of activists, declared 2008 its first "year of commemoration of gay and lesbian victims of political repression," and declared December 17 a day of commemoration since then. See e.g. http://xn--80ank2a.xn--p1ai/new/archive/view/76186 and http://www.lgbtnet.ru/ru/content/17-dekabrya-den-pamyati-geev-i-lesbiyanok-zhertv-politicheskih-repressiy (both accessed March 23, 2014). Similar dilemmas bedeviled homosexuals in Communist East Germany as they sought to come to terms with Nazi persecution; see Josie McLellan, *Love in the Time of Communism: Intimacy and Sexuality in the GDR* (Cambridge: Cambridge University Press, 2011), 115–18.

22 For some treatments of this process see Polly Jones, *Myth, Memory, Trauma: Rethinking the Stalinist Past in the Soviet Union, 1953–70* (New Haven and London: Yale University Press, 2013); Denis Kozlov, *The Readers of Novyi Mir: Coming to Terms with the Stalinist Past* (Cambridge: Harvard University Press, 2013); Graeme J. Gill, *Symbols and Legitimacy in Soviet Politics* (Cambridge: Cambridge University Press, 2011); and idem, *Symbolism and Regime Change in Russia* (Cambridge: Cambridge University Press, 2013).

23 Etkind, "Post-Soviet Hauntology," points to some important differences between the two regimes and the possibilities for "mature understanding" of a violent past; but even he measures Russia against the German yardstick. For similar assumptions that Russian "coming to terms" with the violent past should follow German models, see e.g. Catherine Merridale, *Night of Stone: Death and Memory in Twentieth-Century Russia* (New York: Viking, 2000); Anne Applebaum, *Gulag: A History of the Soviet Camps* (London: Allen Lane, 2003); Orlando Figes, *The Whisperers: Private Life in Stalin's Russia* (London: Allen Lane, 2007).

24 See Etkind, "Post-Soviet Hauntology"; Irina Paperno, "Exhuming the Bodies of Soviet Terror," *Representations* 75, no. 1 (2001): 89–118; Lynne Viola, "The Question of the Perpetrator in Soviet History," *Slavic Review* 72, no. 1 (2013): 1–23.

25 Etkind, "Post-Soviet Hauntology," 188.

26 Here I am invoking terms found in: Elena Baraban, "Obyknovennaia gomofobiia," *Neprikovsnovennyi zapas*, no. 19 (2001): 85–93; and Adi Kuntsman, "'With a Shade of Disgust': Affective Politics of Sexuality and Class in Memoirs of the Stalinist Gulag," *Slavic Review* 68, no. 2 (2009): 308–28.

27 For a 2009 seminar in St. Petersburg, see http://www.svoboda.org/content/transcript/478910.html (accessed January 17, 2014); for a seminar on human rights including feminist historians Plungian and Roldugina, at the Moscow Book Fair's Memorial tent, see http://www.memo.ru/d/199170.html (accessed April 20, 2016); for the latest Roldugina seminar presenting her archival work, see http://www.memo.ru/d/258284.html (accessed April 20, 2016).

28 See the influential Pierre Nora, "Between Memory and History: Les Lieux de Mémoire," *Representations*, no. 26 (1989): 7–24; and for deeper contextualization, Jeffrey K. Olick, Vered Vinitzky-Seroussi, and Daniel Levy, eds, *The Collective Memory Reader* (Oxford: Oxford University Press, 2011).

29 Lisa Duggan, "The Discipline Problem: Queer Theory Meets Lesbian and Gay History," *GLQ: A Journal of Gay and Lesbian Studies* 2 (1995): 179–91.

30 Yet activists and scholars did sense an affective relationship with the recovery of a previously concealed heritage; see "In defense of historicism" in David M. Halperin, *How to Do the History of Homosexuality* (Chicago: University of Chicago Press, 2002), 1–23.

31 Duggan, "The Discipline Problem," 181; and see the analysis of Thomas R. Dunn, "'The Quare in the Square': Queer Memory, Sensibilities, and Oscar Wilde," *Quarterly Journal of Speech* 100, no. 2 (2014): 216–20.

32 Halperin, *How to Do the History of Homosexuality*, 15; See also e.g. Valerie Rohy, "Ahistorical," *GLQ: A Journal of Gay and Lesbian Studies* 12, no. 1 (2006): 61–83.

33 Rohy, "Ahistorical," 65–71.

34 Ann Cvetkovich, *An Archive of Feelings: Trauma, Sexuality, and Lesbian Public Cultures* (Durham: Duke University Press, 2003); Charles E. Morris, "The Mourning After," in *Remembering the AIDS Quilt*, ed. Charles E. Morris (East Lansing: Michigan State University Press, 2011).

35 Charles E. Morris, "My Old Kentucky Homo: Lincoln and the Politics of Queer Public Memory," in *Rhetoric, Culture, and Social Critique: Framing Public Memory*, eds Kendall R. Phillips, Stephen Browne and Barbara Biesecker (Tuscaloosa: University of Alabama Press, 2004).

36 Vladimir Kirsanov, *69. Russkie gei, lesbiianki, biseksualy i transseksualy* (Tver': Ganimed, 2005), 398.

37 Oboin transferred significant parts of the collection he assembled to IHLIA-Homodok in Amsterdam in 2000; he left Russia in 2001.

38 *Ostrov* appeared between 1999 and 2004 and published at least nineteen issues; E. Gusiatinskaia and Iu. Smirnova, eds *Antologiia lesbiiskoi prozy* (Tver': Kolonna Publications, 2006).

39 There is as yet no catalog of these publications. For a guide to lesbian and gay organizations in Russia in the 1990s, see Paul Legendre, *V poiskakh sebia: Polozhenie geev i lesbiianok v sovremennoi Rossii* (Moscow: Charities Aid Foundation, 1997).

40 Irina Roldugina and Nadia Plungian, *Kvirfest 2013: 20 let otmeny st. 121 UK RSFSR* (St. Petersburg: Vykhod, 2013); an English version, entitled *Queerfest 2013: Twenty Years since the Repeal of Article 121 of the Soviet Criminal Code*, is available at: https://issuu.com/coming_out_spb/docs/queerfest2013_eng_b0eb8bb2b8ec23?e=10986299%2F6870278 (accessed April 19, 2016).

41 Roldugina and Plungian, *Kvirfest 2013*, 2, 39.

42 For example, the Moscow Archive of Lesbians and Gays is collaborating with anti-HIV activist Evgeny Pisemsky to produce an online LGBT History website. On "*Deti–404*" (Children–404) see http://www.deti–404.com/ru/video (accessed April 19, 2016). Of course, its pages of letters from young bloggers describing queer life for teenagers in Russia constitutes a particular archive of trauma; see Wilkinson, "Putting 'Traditional Values' Into Practice," 372.

43 Dar'ia Traiden, "Drugie golosa," exhibition catalog-poster, *My est'*, May 16–20, 2015, Studio 67, Minsk.

44 See https://makeout.by (accessed April 20, 2016).

45 See e.g. https://makeout.by/2015/07/27/kogdato-eto-mesto-nazyvali-balkonom.html (accessed April 20, 2016).

46 http://rt.com/politics/moscow-city-court-gay–247 (accessed August 16, 2012).

SELECTED FURTHER READING

Baer, Brian James, "Now You See It: Gay (In)Visibility and the Performance of Post-Soviet Identity." In *Queer Visibility in Post-socialist Cultures*, edited by Narcisz Fejes and Andrea P. Balogh (Bristol: Intellect, 2013).

Baer, Brian James, *Translation and the Making of Modern Russian Literature* (New York & London: Bloomsbury Academic, 2016).

Gessen, Masha, Joseph Huff-Hannon, Bela Shaevich, Andrei Borodin, Dmitri Karelsky, and Svetlana Solodovnik, *Gay Propaganda: Russian Love Stories* (New York: OR Books, 2014).

Healey, Dan, *Homosexual Desire in Revolutionary Russia: The Regulation of Sexual and Gender Dissent* (Chicago: University of Chicago Press, 2001).

Healey, Dan, "The Disappearance of the Russian Queen, or How the Soviet Closet Was Born." In *Russian Masculinities in History and Culture*, edited by Barbara Evans Clements, Rebecca Friedman and Dan Healey (Basingstoke, England and New York: Palgrave, 2002).

Healey, Dan, "Homosexual Existence and Existing Socialism: New Light on the Repression of Male Homosexuality in Stalin's Russia." *GLQ: A Journal of Lesbian and Gay Studies* 8, no. 3 (2002): 349–78.

Healey, Dan, "'Untraditional Sex' and the 'Simple Russian': Nostalgia for Soviet Innocence in the Polemics of Dilia Enikeeva." In *What is Soviet Now? Identities, Legacies, Memories*, edited by Thomas Lahusen and Peter H. Solomon Jr. (Berlin: Lit Verlag, 2008).

Healey, Dan, "The Sexual Revolution in the USSR: Dynamic Change beneath the Ice," in *Sexual Revolutions*, edited by Gert Hekma and Alain Giami (Basingstoke: Palgrave Macmillan, 2014).

Jensen, Erik N., "The Pink Triangle and Political Consciousness: Gays, Lesbians, and the Memory of Nazi Persecution." *Journal of the History of Sexuality* 11, no. 1/2 (2002): 319–49.

Lenskyj, Helen Jefferson, *Sexual Diversity and the Sochi 2014 Olympics: No More Rainbows* (Basingstoke: Palgrave Pivot, 2014).

Moss, Kevin, "Straight Eye for the Queer Guy: Gay Male Visibility in Post-Soviet Russian Films." In *Queer Visibility in Post-Socialist Cultures*, edited by Narcisz Fejes and Andrea P. Balogh (Bristol: Intellect, 2013).

Murav'eva, Marianna, "Traditional Values and Modern Families: Legal Understanding of Tradition and Modernity in Contemporary Russia." *Journal of Social Policy Studies* 12, no. 4 (2014): 625–38.

Riabov, Oleg and Tatiana Riabova, "The Remasculinization of Russia?" *Problems of Post-Communism* 61, no. 2 (2014): 23–35.

Sperling, Valerie, *Sex, Politics, and Putin: Political Legitimacy in Russia* (New York, Oxford: Oxford University Press, 2014).

Stella, Francesca, "Queer Space, Pride, and Shame in Moscow." *Slavic Review* 72, no. 3 (2013): 458–80.

Stella, Francesca, *Lesbian Lives in Soviet and Post-Soviet Russia: Post/socialism and Gendered Sexualities* (Basingstoke: Palgrave Macmillan, 2015).

Thoreson, Ryan, "From Child Protection to Children's Rights: Rethinking Homosexual Propaganda Bans in Human Rights Law." *Yale Law Review* 124, no. 4 (2015): 1327–44.

Wilkinson, Cai, "Putting 'Traditional Values' Into Practice: The Rise and Contestation of Anti-Homopropaganda Laws in Russia." *Journal of Human Rights* 13, no. 3 (2014): 363–79.

Yusupova, Marina, "Masculinity, Criminality and Russian Men." *Sextures: E-journal for Sexualities, Cultures, and Politics* 3, no. 3 (2015): 46–61.

INDEX

Page numbers in *italics* refer to illustrations.